SOUTHERN IRISH LOYALISM, 1912–1949

SOUTHERN IRISH LOYALISM, 1912–1949

BRIAN HUGHES AND CONOR MORRISSEY

LIVERPOOL UNIVERSITY PRESS

First published 2020 by
Liverpool University Press
4 Cambridge Street
Liverpool
L69 7ZU

This paperback edition published 2022

British Library Cataloguing-in-Publication data
A British Library CIP record is available

ISBN 978-1-78962-184-6 cased
ISBN 978-1-80085-479-6 paperback

Typeset by Carnegie Book Production, Lancaster
Printed and bound by CPI Group (UK) Ltd, Croydon CR0 4YY

Contents

IV Lost Counties? Loyalism at the Border

Dedicated to Professor David Patrick Brian Fitzpatrick,
SFTCD, MRIA (1948–2019)

Acknowledgements

The editors would like to offer our thanks to the contributors for sharing their research with us, and for their unfailingly efficient responses to our very many requests and queries. We are grateful to Liverpool University Press for taking on the project, and to Alison Welsby and Christabel Scaife in particular for their support and guidance. Additional thanks are due to the team at Carnegie Book Production for their diligence in preparing the manuscript for production.

The idea for an edited collection on this topic arose from a seminar funded by a generous award from the Irish Research Council, without which this book would not have been possible. All of the speakers and attendees at that event have made a valuable contribution to the contents that follow. Dr Brian Hughes would also like to thank colleagues at what was then An Foras Feasa, Maynooth University, for their support and assistance in organising the seminar.

This book is dedicated to the late Professor David Fitzpatrick, one of Ireland's finest historians and sorely missed by family, friends, and colleagues. David was a supervisor and mentor to the editors and to several of the contributors. The imprint of his work – especially, but not limited to, the seminal *Politics and Irish life* (1977) and *Descendancy* (2014) – is apparent throughout. We are grateful to Jane Leonard and Hannah and Julia Fitzpatrick for allowing us dedicate this volume to his memory.

Figures

Tables

Abbreviations

(Abbreviations specific to individual chapters are spelled out on first use in that chapter)

BMH WS	Bureau of Military History Witness Statement (Military Archives of Ireland)
DL	Deputy Lieutenant
HC	House of Commons (UK)
HL	House of Lords (UK)
IDL	Irish Dominion League
IGC	Irish Grants Committee
IPP	Irish Parliamentary Party
IRA	Irish Republican Army
IUA	Irish Unionist Alliance
IWM	Imperial War Museum, London
KC	King's Counsel
MAI	Military Archives of Ireland
MP	Member of Parliament (UK)
NAI	National Archives of Ireland
NLI	National Library of Ireland
PRONI	Public Record Office of Northern Ireland
RIC	Royal Irish Constabulary
TCD	Trinity College Dublin
TD	Teachta Dála (Member of the Irish Parliament)
TNA	The National Archives, Kew

UAPL	Unionist Anti-Partition League
UUC	Ulster Unionist Council
UVF	Ulster Volunteer Force
UWUC	Ulster Women's Unionist Council

Contributors

Frank Barry is Professor of International Business and Economic Development at Trinity Business School, Trinity College Dublin. Much of his research in recent years has been on Irish economic, business, and industrial history.

Elaine Callinan completed her PhD studies with Trinity College Dublin in 2018 and currently lectures in Modern Irish History at Carlow College, St Patrick's. She has written chapters, a number of journal articles, and peer reviewed material for publication, and her book *Electioneering and Propaganda in Ireland, 1917–1921: Votes, Violence and Victory* will be published later this year.

Jonathan Cherry is a lecturer in Geography at the School of History and Geography, Dublin City University. A historical geographer, his research interests lie in the evolution and transformation of the Irish landscape over the past four centuries. He has a long-standing interest in the history of the Maxwell family of Farnham, the focus of his postgraduate research.

Seamus Cullen holds a PhD in history from Dublin City University. His main research focus has been the local history of County Kildare and, in particular, military history between 1798 and 1923. He has published several works on the period, and is the author of *Kildare: The Irish Revolution, 1912–23* (Dublin, 2020).

Ian d'Alton is a historian of southern Irish Protestantism, unionism, and loyalism from the eighteenth to the twentieth centuries. He has been a Visiting Fellow at Sidney Sussex College, Cambridge and is a Visiting Research Fellow, Centre for Contemporary Irish History, Trinity College Dublin. He is co-editor, with Dr Ida Milne, of *Protestant* and *Irish: The Minority's Search for Place in Independent Ireland* (2019).

Seán William Gannon is an independent researcher, focusing on modern Ireland, the British Empire, and their intersections. His *The Irish Imperial Service: Policing Palestine and Administering the Empire, 1922–1966* was published in 2019.

Brian Hughes is a lecturer in the Department of History at Mary Immaculate College, University of Limerick. He is the author of *Defying the IRA? Intimidation, Coercion, and Communities during the Irish Revolution* (Liverpool University Press, 2016; paperback 2019) and is currently working on a book on Dublin in the Four Courts Press *Irish Revolution, 1912–23* series.

Alan McCarthy was conferred with a PhD by University College Cork in 2019. His research has appeared in publications such as the *Holly Bough* and *Éire-Ireland*, while he has also contributed to radio and television documentaries. He is the author of *Newspapers and Journalism in Cork, 1910–1923: Press, Politics and Revolution*, published in 2020.

Pat McCarthy holds a PhD and MBA from University College Dublin and worked for many years in the pharmaceutical manufacturing sector. He is the author of *The Irish Revolution 1912–23, Waterford* (2015); *Waterford and the 1916 Rising* (2016); *The Redmonds and Waterford: A Political Dynasty, 1891–1952* (2018) and has published extensively in a range of journals. He is currently a Research Associate in the School of History and Geography, Dublin City University and is working on a history of the pharmaceutical manufacturing industry in Ireland.

Katherine Magee holds an MA from Maynooth University, which she obtained after completing a BA in History from the University of Ulster. Her research focuses on East Donegal unionists during the time of the Boundary Commission.

Conor Morrissey is Lecturer in Irish/British History at King's College London. His first book, *Protestant Nationalists in Ireland, 1900–1923*, was published in 2019.

Daniel Purcell completed his PhD in 2018 supervised by Dr Anne Dolan and Professor David Fitzpatrick. His research focuses on Irish border Protestantism, 1916–23. He has recently published a chapter in S. Bayó Belenguer and Nicola Brady's *Pulling Together or Pulling Apart? Perspectives on Nationhood, Identity, and Belonging in Europe* (2019) and is currently working on the Fermanagh volume of the Four Courts Press *Irish Revolution, 1912–23* series.

Joseph Quinn is Second World War Research Associate at the National Archives, Kew. He completed his doctorate at the Centre for Contemporary Irish History in Trinity College Dublin in 2016. His thesis is entitled 'Volunteering and Recruitment in Ireland during the Second World War' and he is currently preparing a monograph on this topic.

Brian M. Walker is Professor Emeritus of Irish Studies at Queen's University Belfast. He was formerly a member of the politics school and a director of the Institute of Irish Studies at Queen's. Recent books include *A Political History of the Two Irelands: From Partition to Peace* (2012) and *Irish History Matters: Politics, Identities and Commemoration* (2019).

Fionnuala Walsh is Lecturer in Modern Irish History at University College Dublin with particular research interests in First World War studies and gender history. She completed her PhD and Irish Research Council Postdoctoral Fellowship at Trinity College Dublin. Her monograph *Irish Women and the Great War* was published in 2020.

Donald Wood grew up in a Protestant farming community in West Cork in the 1950s. Following emigration to England, he pursued a career in the IT industry. Now retired, an interest in family history has extended to the local history of West Cork and the period of the Irish War of Independence.

Note on Terminology

The focus of this book is the 26 counties that became the Irish Free State in 1922. The use of the phrase 'southern Ireland' or 'southern Irish' to describe this territory is not unproblematic. For one, it obscures the fact that County Donegal contains the most northerly point on the island. It is also potentially politically or culturally loaded. Notwithstanding these issues, the term 'southern' is used in this book primarily for the ease with which it allows us to separate the loyalism we are interested in from what is usually described as 'Ulster Loyalism' or 'Ulster Unionism'. It is also a term used regularly by contemporaries.

In 1937, *Bunreacht na hÉireann*, or the Constitution of Ireland, officially replaced the Irish Free State with Éire, or Ireland, as the official title of the state (the constitution also claimed the whole island as the 'national territory' until the 1990s). After the Republic of Ireland Act came into effect in 1949, the state was to be known as the Republic of Ireland, usually shortened in practice to Ireland. Where appropriate, the state is referred to by its contemporary usage in this book. When referring to periods that transcend these chronological markers, 'southern Ireland' or '26 counties' are used – again, purely for the sake of simplicity.

Unionism (upper case) is understood in this book to refer to political parties or members of those parties; unionism (lower case) is used to describe political support or preference for the maintenance of Ireland within the United Kingdom of Great Britain and Ireland ('the Union'). Loyalism has a much broader definition and, here, refers to any manifestation of attachment or allegiance to one or a combination of Britain, the Union, or the Empire. Contributors have generally followed this approach but have also been given some flexibility in their application of labels, particularly when referring to the period post-1922, when the Act of Union ceased to exist.

For consistency, place names are applied as per contemporary usage in the period in which they are mentioned, thus: Queen's County before 1922 and Laois afterwards. County Londonderry and Derry city are also used for consistency, and not to imply any particular agenda. Where place names are reproduced in quotes, usage is maintained as in the original. Quotations are reproduced as in the original throughout, including punctuation, spelling, and grammatical errors.

Southern Irish Loyalism from Home Rule Crisis to Republic: An Introduction

Brian Hughes and Conor Morrissey

This volume concerns the nature of Irish loyalism where it existed among a minority: in the 26 counties that were granted independence from British rule in 1922. Over 14 chapters, it will highlight the experiences of southern Irish men and women whose loyalties, either on the basis of their ideology or their employment, were to the British Crown or Empire between the introduction of the third Home Rule bill in 1912 and the creation of the Republic of Ireland in 1949. This is the first scholarly study solely dedicated to the topic since R.B. McDowell's 1997 *Crisis and Decline*.[1] Each of the essays is drawn from contributions to a two-day conference, 'Southern Irish Loyalism in Context', hosted at Maynooth University in July 2017 and generously funded by an Irish Research Council New Foundations award. The essays collected here represent recent research on aspects of southern Irish loyalism, with perspectives from history, politics, economics, and geography and with authors ranging from talented postgraduate students and early career scholars to established academics. While each of the individual essays sets out and operates within its own parameters, this essay-length introduction aims to provide a chrono-logical, historiographical, and thematic framework for the volume as a whole.

Why pursue southern Irish loyalists, or loyalism, at all? For most historians, the ethno-religious character of the central conflict in Irish history is self-evident. F.S.L. Lyons, for example, identified four groups who collided within Irish society: the native (Catholic) Irish, the English, the Ulster Protestants, and the Anglo-Irish.[2] More recently, the Northern Ireland Troubles demonstrates that much of the history of the island can be understood as a conflict between Catholics, generally nationalists, and Protestants, who were generally unionists. While Protestants perhaps inevitably dominate, we pursue a slightly different line of enquiry. We focus less on a religious identity

---

[1] R.B. McDowell, *Crisis and Decline: The Fate of the Southern Unionists* (Dublin, 1997).

[2] F.S.L. Lyons, *Culture and Anarchy in Ireland, 1890–1939* (Oxford, 1979).

(Protestantism), or a firm political programme (unionism), and more on the outlook, perspective, or economic choice that characterised southern Irish loyalism. It must first be stated that the southern loyalists discussed in this volume have little in common with its current, Northern Irish incarnation. There is little to link Ulster loyalism, a largely working-class movement that carries connotations with paramilitarism, and which, at certain periods, adopted an ambivalent attitude to the Union with Britain, with the southern loyalists found here.[3] In fact, the reader seeking contemporary parallels may find more resonances with modern middle-class Ulster unionism, whose politics is rooted in a sense of British citizenship.[4]

We define unionism as support for an unreformed union with Britain and the constitutional settlement of 1801. The term loyalist, then, applies in a much broader sense: allegiance to, or service to, Britain, the Crown, or the Empire. This volume essentially discusses two groups. First, there were those individuals, mostly although not exclusively Protestant, who were ideologically committed to the continued connection with the British Crown or Empire. Some were 'diehards' and opposed Irish self-government until the Anglo-Irish Treaty, or beyond. Others had a strong preference for the Union, but by 1918 or before understood that some form of home rule was inevitable. Catholic loyalists, a long-neglected group, are also assessed in this volume. Not all loyalists were *unionists*, however. Some Home Rulers, in seeking a self-governing Ireland within the Empire, were engaged in a project which sought to preserve the connection with Britain. (It must be noted that pro-Empire sentiment could be found even at the summit of the Nationalist Party. John Redmond, a notable example, sought a self-governing Ireland within the Empire, but that is beyond the scope of this volume.)[5]

It is more challenging, or even impossible, to categorise the second group ideologically. These are the servants of the Crown: soldiers, civil

---

[3] For some comparison of Ulster and southern unionism, see Alvin Jackson, 'Irish Unionism, 1870–1922', in D. George Boyce and Alan O'Day (eds), *Defenders of the Union: A Survey of British and Irish Unionism since 1801* (Abingdon, 2001), pp. 115–36. For contemporary loyalism, see, for example, Steve Bruce, *The Edge of the Union: The Ulster Loyalist Political Vision* (Oxford, 1994); Peter Shirlow and Mark McGovern (eds), *Who are 'The People'? Unionism, Protestantism and Loyalism in Northern Ireland* (London, 1997); Jennifer Todd, 'Two Traditions in Unionist Political Culture', *Irish Political Studies*, 2/1 (1987), pp. 1–26; Arthur Aughey, 'Between Exclusion and Recognition: The Politics of the Ulster Defence Association', *Conflict Quarterly* (1985), pp. 40–52.

[4] The 'Ulster British' concept, discussed in Todd, 'Two Traditions in Unionist Political Culture'.

[5] James McConnel, 'John Redmond and Irish Catholic Loyalism', *English Historical Review*, 125/512 (2010), pp. 83–111; Alvin Jackson, *Judging Redmond & Carson* (Dublin, 2018), pp. 136–45.

servants, policemen, and others, who acted in the interests of Britain, both in Ireland and abroad. Religion is even less pertinent here: Catholics served alongside Protestants in the Dublin Castle administration, the RIC, the armed forces, and in imperial service.[6] Even if taking the 'Queen's shilling' did not 'automatically induce loyalism', the 'economic imperative', as James McConnel has put it, should not immediately invalidate Catholic claims to loyalty.[7] As several chapters show, many of these individuals were motivated by feelings of allegiance to the Crown or Empire. Other Irish-born servicemen and policemen would have rejected the designation outright: plenty had nationalist, or even republican, leanings.[8] Alvin Jackson has suggested that recruitment to the British army in Ireland 'largely hinged on a variety of social and economic circumstances, rather than any overt political consideration'.[9] Similarly, the reasons Irishmen joined the RIC or served in policing or administration across the Empire were varied, with ideology rarely, if ever, the sole determinant.[10] By placing servants of the Crown alongside ideologically committed loyalists, a range of parallel experiences and insightful contrasts will emerge.

Paul Bew, writing in 1998, argued against a 'partitionist history' where historians neglect the administrative unity of Ireland prior to partition, which can result in an artificial narrative that views Ireland as two distinct blocks before such a division actually emerged.[11] While we agree with this sentiment, we hope an exception can be made for this volume. The experience of loyalists in Ulster was markedly different from their brethren in the southern three provinces. This was the case even during the 1918 General Election campaign, the last all-island election, as shown by Elaine Callinan in Chapter 2. In the south, the political and demographic basis simply did not exist for the sort of stage-managed displays of unanimity

---

[6] See Chapter 8.

[7] McConnel, 'Redmond and Irish Catholic Loyalism', p. 86. For more on this, see the Afterword.

[8] See, for example, Paul Taylor, *Heroes or Traitors? Experiences of Southern Irish Soldiers Returning from the Great War, 1919–1939* (Liverpool, 2015), pp. 13–15.

[9] Alvin Jackson, 'Ireland, the Union, and the Empire, 1800–1960', in Kevin Kenny (ed.), *Ireland and the British Empire* (Oxford, 2004), p. 142.

[10] For discussion of this for the British army, see David Fitzpatrick, 'The Logic of Collective Sacrifice: Ireland and the British Army, 1914–1918, *Historical Journal*, 38/4 (1985), pp. 1017–30; Peter Karsten, 'Irish Soldiers in the British Army, 1792–1922: Suborned or Subordinate', *Journal of Social History*, 17/1 (1983), pp. 31–64. For the RIC, see Elizabeth Malcolm, *The Irish Policeman, 1822–1922: A Life* (Dublin, 2006), pp. 58–67; for colonial administration, see David Fitzpatrick, 'Ireland and the Empire', in Andrew Porter (ed.), *The Oxford History of the British Empire*, vol. 3: *The Nineteenth Century* (Oxford, 1999), pp. 509–15 and Chapter 8.

[11] Paul Bew, *Ideology and the Irish Question: Ulster Unionism and Irish Nationalism 1912–1916* (Oxford, 1998), pp. ix–xix.

that characterised Ulster Day in 1912, nor, by any means, could they hope
to force the sort of constitutional arrangements that came to pass in the
north from 1920. Furthermore, the period 1916 to 1920 was a difficult one for
border unionists and loyalists, who would never have considered themselves
to be 'southerners' and suddenly bore the unwanted 'southern' label. This
volume will follow contemporaries by describing these unfortunates as
'southern loyalists' after partition. Those who served the Crown through
the armed services or administration also had a different experience. The
nature of policing in large parts of the six counties that became Northern
Ireland, for instance, was very different from that experienced by colleagues
elsewhere, while – in the right places – Ulster could be a safe haven for
disbanded policemen. Over 1,300 (including over 500 Catholics) joined the
Royal Ulster Constabulary up to February 1923.[12]

   Who were the southern loyalists? In 1914, there were 327,000 Protestants in
the 26-county area, out of a total Protestant population of about 1,100,000.[13]
But not all Protestants were unionists. Protestant republicans, a small but
highly influential group, have received significant attention.[14] Larger, but
less researched, are Protestant Home Rulers.[15] In contrast to many, or most,
Catholic Home Rulers, Protestant Home Rulers were usually what Alan O'Day
termed 'material Home Rulers', viewing the attainment of self-government
as a means of reconciling Irish classes and creeds, which would allow for
the peaceful development of the country.[16] The endorsement of Home Rule

[12] Brian Hughes, *Defying the IRA? Intimidation, Coercion, and Communities during
     the Irish Revolution* (Liverpool, 2016), pp. 21–39, 192–200.
[13] McDowell, *Crisis and Decline*, p. 4.
[14] See, recently, Conor Morrissey, *Protestant Nationalists in Ireland, 1900–1923*
     (Cambridge, 2019); R.F. Foster, *Vivid Faces: The Revolutionary Generation in
     Ireland, 1890–1923* (London, 2014); Valerie Jones, *Rebel Prods: The Forgotten Story
     of Protestant Radical Nationalists and the 1916 Rising* (Dublin, 2016); Martin
     Maguire, 'Protestant Republicans in the Revolution and After', in Ian d'Alton
     and Ida Milne (eds), *Protestant and Irish: The Minority's Search for a Place in
     Independent Ireland* (Cork, 2019).
[15] For studies that discuss the careers of Protestants within the Irish Parliamentary
     Party, see James McConnel, *The Irish Parliamentary Party and the Third Home
     Rule Crisis* (Dublin, 2013); Patrick Maume, *The Long Gestation: Irish Nationalist
     Life, 1891–1918* (Dublin, 1999); Bew, *Ideology and the Irish Question*. For recent,
     useful lives of Protestant Home Rulers, see Jennifer Regan-Lefebvre, *Cosmopolitan
     Nationalism in the Victorian Empire: Ireland, India and the Politics of Alfred
     Webb* (Basingstoke, 2009); Colin Reid, *The Lost Ireland of Stephen Gwynn: Irish
     Constitutional Nationalism and Cultural Politics, 1864–1950* (Manchester, 2011).
     See also Conor Morrissey, '"Rotten Protestants": Protestant Home Rulers and the
     Ulster Liberal Association, 1906–1918', *Historical Journal*, 61/3 (2018), pp. 743–65.
[16] Alan O'Day, *Irish Home Rule, 1867–1921* (Manchester, 1998).

for many of these Protestants did not dilute in any way their loyalty to the Crown, which remained of paramount importance. Pat McCarthy (Chapter 10) highlights the career of Sir John Keane of County Waterford, who combined a belief in Home Rule with strong loyalty to the Crown and Empire.[17] It was not only prominent figures who held such views. Agnes Martin, a housewife from Dublin, supported Dominion Home Rule, she said, as the best way to avoid succumbing to the 'forces of anarchy and disorder which are threatening the stability and almost the civilisation of the country'. Fidelity to the Crown was central to her politics: it was, she said, 'in the foreground'.[18] Throughout this volume we will hear of loyalists such as Agnes Martin, whose political beliefs would be tested in the period 1912 to 1949.

Home Rule, 1912–1918

It remains one of the mysteries of Irish history why southern unionists, who between 1886 and 1918 were never able to return more than two members of parliament for geographic constituencies (the two Dublin University seats were solidly unionist), believed they could prevent the passing of Home Rule in perpetuity. Had they been willing, they could have struck a fine bargain; Redmond stated, 'I have publicly declared my willingness to give practically any safeguard asked for by the Protestants of the country'.[19] But with the introduction of the Home Rule bill, southern unionists, acting through their vehicle, the Irish Unionist Alliance, organised an energetic propaganda campaign in Britain, and a series of provincial meetings in the south of Ireland. At one meeting in Cork city, Lord Bandon, a prominent landowner, denied that the southern unionist opposition to Home Rule was softening: 'If possible we are more opposed than ever'.[20] This may have been true, but with little room for manoeuvre, the approach they adopted would lead them to ruin. First, southern unionists could rely on an extensive and well-connected parliamentary and aristocratic network of supporters, who sought, until it became impossible, to protect their interests. More significant was the reliance on Edward Carson's campaign to prevent the imposition of Home Rule in Ulster, believing that this would wreck the entire bill. Carson, a southerner and member for Dublin University, was aiming at this, stating, 'if Ulster succeeds, Home Rule is dead. Home Rule is impossible for Ireland

---

[17] See Chapter 10.
[18] *Irish Statesman*, 17 Jan. 1920.
[19] John Redmond to Edward Culverwell, 19 Nov. 1912 (NLI, MS 15,254).
[20] *Cork Constitution*, 22 Apr. 1912.

without Belfast and the surrounding parts'.[21] However, by 1914, partition had taken on great momentum. In March 1914, under pressure from the British government, Redmond was forced to acquiesce to the 'temporary' exclusion of Ulster from Home Rule.[22] The separation of southern unionists and loyalists from their brethren in the north now seemed inevitable.

As Fionnuala Walsh describes in Chapter 6, southern loyalists viewed the outbreak of the Great War as providential – a chance to demonstrate continued loyalty to the British connection. By this period there was substantial discord in loyalist ranks, with prominent unionists such as Lord Monteagle, Lord Fingall, and Bryan Cooper (briefly member for South Dublin) suggesting that Home Rule with safeguards was better than partition. A sense of wartime détente with constitutional nationalism even saw the influx of a substantial number of country gentlemen into Redmond's National Volunteers.[23] But there would be no salvation for southern unionism. The Easter Rising of 1916 produced a course of events which would lead to the destruction of constitutional nationalism and the replacement of their demand, Home Rule, for a republic. In the aftermath of the Rising, southern unionists enjoyed their final major success. Following negotiations with Lloyd George, Carson accepted the principle of Home Rule for 26 counties. A large delegation of southern unionists went to London, where they were received by the prime minister and the Unionist members of cabinet.[24] The outcome of this was that the principal Unionist cabinet ministers, Walter Long and Lord Lansdowne, schemed against and ultimately destroyed the proposal.[25] However, the southern unionist delegation also suffered a setback; their leader, Lord Midleton, reported that 'we were repeatedly reminded that the Home Rule Act was on the Statute Book' and 'we were invited to make suggestions as to safeguards'.[26]

During the Irish Convention, 1917–18, Lord Midleton led a group of realistic-minded southern unionists, known as 'Midletonites', to rapprochement with Redmond's nationalists. Nothing came of Midleton's proposal, an all-Ireland parliament with authority over internal taxation but control of customs reserved to Westminster, due to resistance from both Ulster unionists and

---

[21] Edward Carson, Oct. 1911, quoted in Brendan O'Leary, *A Treatise on Northern Ireland*, vol. 1: *Colonialism* (Oxford, 2019), p. 300.

[22] O'Day, *Irish Home Rule*, pp. 258–9.

[23] See, for example, *Irish Times*, 6, 7, 8, 10, 13 Aug. 1914.

[24] Memorandum from Lord Midleton and others to members of the Irish Unionist Alliance, 15 Apr. 1918 (TNA, PRO 30/67/38).

[25] Patrick Buckland, *Irish Unionism I: The Anglo-Irish and the New Ireland, 1885–1922* (Dublin, 1972), chap. 3.

[26] Memorandum from Lord Midleton and others to members of the Irish Unionist Alliance, 15 Apr. 1918 (TNA, PRO 30/67/38).

rebels from within Redmond's party.[27] The emergence of the Midletonites, however, demonstrated that a substantial group of southern unionists were now willing to jettison support for an unreformed union in order to prevent partition and retain a connection with Britain. Loyalism, ultimately, would trump unionism. Southern loyalists and constitutional nationalists may have been finding they had much in common, but the political winds were blowing in a different direction. In the general election of December 1918, Ulster unionists prevailed in the north, and Sinn Féin, demanding a republic, dominated in the south. As shown by Elaine Callinan (Chapter 2), southern unionists put up a brave fight in a small number of constituencies, but their programme had no popular appeal. Southern loyalists, from this period on, would find themselves bereft of leadership, and at the mercy of much larger political forces.[28]

Revolution, 1919–1923

As the Sinn Féin members elected in 1918 founded Dáil Éireann, and created their own counter-state from January 1919, the IRA carried out a campaign of guerrilla warfare. As several chapters in this volume demonstrate, unionists and loyalists were outnumbered and outgunned in their communities, usually relying on the Crown forces for protection but frequently left without any. Where resistance was offered to the republican campaign, it was low-level, subtle, and often ineffective.[29] Southern loyalists were, instead, the victims of intimidation and violence that ranged from petty annoyance to arson and shooting. The nature and motivation for republican violence against loyalists, and most particularly against Protestants, as discussed below, has perhaps drawn more recent attention than any other aspect of Irish revolutionary history. But the diversity – and inconsistency – of threat and violence from county to county and district to district is highlighted here in chapters by Pat McCarthy on Waterford (Chapter 10), Seamus Cullen on Kildare (Chapter 11), in Seán William Gannon's study of Irish colonial servants (Chapter 7), and in Alan McCarthy's examination of the life of Henry Lawrence Tivy in Cork

---

[27] For the Convention, see R.B. McDowell, *The Irish Convention, 1917–18* (London and Toronto, 1970).

[28] For the ineffective and unrealistic reactions of some southern unionists to the triumph of Sinn Féin, see Buckland, *Irish Unionism I*, pp. 143ff.

[29] Peter Hart, *The I.R.A. at War 1916–1923* (Oxford, 2003), pp. 228–32. See also Brian Hughes, '"The Entire Population of This God-forsaken Island is Terrorised by a Small Band of Gun-men": Guerrillas and Civilians during the Irish Revolution', in Brian Hughes and Fergus Robson (eds), *Unconventional Warfare from Antiquity to the Present Day* (Basingstoke, 2017).

(Chapter 9). What is clear is that there was no single loyalist experience of revolution.

The Government of Ireland Act was passed into law in November 1920; it would create two Irish parliaments with limited control over domestic matters, one for the 26-county southern Ireland and another for the six north-eastern counties. As the bill, introduced in early 1920 by David Lloyd George's coalition government, was debated in parliament, the three Unionists elected to southern seats in 1918, and their colleagues in the Lords, opposed it. Their argument that the Union was the only way to protect the southern minority went unheeded and ultimately achieved nothing more than the addition of a couple of minor safeguards.[30] At the same time, the act was being rendered obsolete in the south where the proposed Dublin parliament was permanently adjourned having only met once (its northern equivalent met for the first time in July 1921).

The result of the republican conflict against the British, the (disputed) 1921 Anglo-Irish Treaty and the creation of the Irish Free State in 1922, meant that the Union was 'gone beyond recall' for even the most diehard. Considering oneself a unionist after 1922 was, as R.B. McDowell described it, 'an attitude of mind rather than membership of a political party'.[31] Any notion of what it meant to be a 'southern unionist' had been fundamentally changed by 1920 anyway. As Colin Reid has put it, this was 'when "Ulster" firmly replaced "Irish" before the "unionist" designation'.[32] The Ulster Unionist Council's acceptance of a six-county border in March 1920 formalised the abandonment of Cavan, Donegal, and Monaghan. This was a betrayal (as those on the wrong side of the decision saw it) that had been in the making since at least 1916.[33] Of course, as David Fitzpatrick has observed, in committing to sign the Ulster Solemn League and Covenant and the Women's Declaration in 1912, loyalist men and women in the three counties had themselves 'prepared through that very Covenant to abandon the far more vulnerable loyalist minority in Leinster, Munster and Connaught'.[34] If, as Patrick Buckland suggested, anger in the borderlands of Ulster was directed more towards the British government in 1916, resentment towards their six-county brethren was made clear in 1920. Lord Farnham, a leading organiser in Cavan, and subject of Chapter 13, for example, immediately complained to Hugh de Fellenberg Montgomery in

---

[30] McDowell, *Crisis and Decline*, pp. 72–7.
[31] McDowell, *Crisis and Decline*, p. 163.
[32] Colin Reid, 'Democracy, Sovereignty and Unionist Political Thought during the Revolutionary Period in Ireland, c.1912–1922', *Transactions of the Royal Historical Society*, 27 (2017), pp. 212–13.
[33] Buckland, *Irish Unionism I*, pp. 58–9.
[34] David Fitzpatrick, *Descendancy: Irish Protestant Histories since 1795* (Cambridge, 2014), pp. 40–1.

Tyrone that 'what we feel more than anything is that we can no longer call ourselves Ulstermen. We in Cavan were prouder of being Ulstermen than anyone in the whole province'.[35] The grand master of the Orange Order in Ireland, Sir James Stronge, protested to Montgomery that 'the three counties have been thrown to the wolves with very little compunction'.[36] Still, as a whole, the Order's leadership refused to countenance the protests of Cavan and Monaghan delegates that it should reject a six-county settlement and instead demand a nine-county Ulster.[37] Tim Wilson has noted the 'profound sense of disorientation' that characterised the Twelfth speeches that followed in Monaghan in July.[38] At the commemoration of the Relief of Derry in Ballybay later that year, attended by Monaghan and Cavan members of the Royal Black Preceptory, the rector of Drum, Reverend Robert Burns, proclaimed that he 'could not talk about the Union – the Union is dead'.[39]

As Fitzpatrick notes, the Order had 'no practical strategy for defending loyalists outside the six counties' while violence intensified from 1920.[40] With their brethren in the rest of southern Ireland already lost, border loyalists' attention eventually turned to making their case for inclusion in the 'northern territory' to the Boundary Commission, which was finally convened in 1924 under Article 12 of the Anglo-Irish Treaty.[41] Many southern loyalists in border regions held out hope of having the border redrawn to take them out of the Irish Free State. Edward Saunderson, for one, petitioned to have the 'whole demesne of Castle Saunderson … transferred into Northern Ireland'.[42] Colonel John George Vaughan Hart, of wealthy landowning stock in Kilderry, County Donegal, and the subject of Chapter 14, was a prominent member of the Donegal Protestant Registration Association (DPRA) that campaigned to have parts of East Donegal placed under the Belfast parliament. Tellingly, the DPRA had been preceded by the Donegal Unionist Association, which was renamed in 1922 as the term 'no longer has the same meaning as it had before'.[43] As

---

[35] Buckland, *Irish Unionism I*, p. 59; Farnham to Montgomery, 13 Mar. 1920 (PRONI, D627/435/10).

[36] Quoted in Fitzpatrick, *Descendancy*, pp. 43–4. See also Chapter 12.

[37] Fitzpatrick, *Descendancy*, p. 44.

[38] Tim Wilson, 'The Strange Death of Loyalist Monaghan, 1912–1921', in Senia Pašeta (ed.), *Uncertain Futures: Essays about the Irish Past for Roy Foster* (Oxford, 2016), p. 179.

[39] *Northern Standard*, 14 Aug. 1920.

[40] Fitzpatrick, *Descendancy*, p. 45.

[41] Terence Dooley, *The Plight of Monaghan Protestants, 1912–1926* (Dublin, 2000), pp. 50–7; Peter Leary, *Unapproved Routes: Histories of the Irish Border, 1922–72* (Oxford, 2016), pp. 31–59.

[42] Edward Saunderson to Secretary, Boundary Commission, 30 Apr. 1925 (PRONI, CAB/61/131).

[43] Leary, *Unapproved Routes*, p. 52.

noted in Chapter 11, a similar name change took place in County Kildare. All, however, was made futile by the ultimate collapse of the commission and the tripartite agreement in December 1925 that finalised six county partition.

The seminal work on this topic has been Michael Laffan's *The Partition of Ireland* (1983).[44] More recently, Paul Murray has produced a definitive exploration of the origins and consequences of the Boundary Commission, while Peter Leary's *Unapproved Routes* (2016) offers a series of sophisticated case studies highlighting the impact of the border on everyday lives.[45] As Brexit has thrown the Irish border back into public consciousness, a number of new historical studies of partition have followed.[46] But the fate of those Tim Wilson has described as 'partition's loyalist discontents' in border regions is still often only peripheral to the more traditional focus on nationalism versus Ulster unionism.[47] This book offers three chapters on loyalists from the 'lost' counties of Ulster. Daniel Purcell (Chapter 12) examines the impact of revolution on loyalists in Cavan and Monaghan, while Jonathan Cherry's biographical study of Lord Farnham highlights how he was forced to adapt first to political defeat, then to exile, and finally to a return to Cavan. Loyalist lives also crossed county – later state – boundaries. This was especially the case in a place like Pettigo, most of which was in Donegal but where a local rector claimed that the people 'have always been loyal to the King and desire to live under the Union Jack ... We are really geographically and economically part of County Fermanagh'.[48] The experiences of Colonel Hart at the Donegal border with County Londonderry are again illustrative. Hart's cross-border existence offers a valuable case study of the political and practical implications of border making, as well as the attempts of residents to overcome or carry on in spite of them.

It was not, of course, only the Protestants of the 26 counties who could feel disorientation and disillusionment at the collapse of the Union. Nevertheless, given the close association between Protestantism and loyalism, one of the issues at stake in this volume is the pronounced numerical decline in the Protestant population of the 26 counties between

---

[44] Michael Laffan, *The Partition of Ireland, 1911–1925* (Dublin, 1983).

[45] Paul Murray, *The Irish Boundary Commission and its Origins, 1886–1925* (Dublin, 2011); Leary, *Unapproved Routes*.

[46] See, for example, Diarmaid Ferriter, *The Border: The Legacy of a Century of Anglo-Irish Politics* (London, 2019); Donnacha Ó Beacháin, *From Partition to Brexit: The Irish Government and Northern Ireland* (Manchester, 2019); Robert Lynch, *The Partition of Ireland, 1918–1925* (Oxford, 2019); Cormac Moore, *The Birth of the Border: The Impact of Partition on Ireland* (Kildare, 2019).

[47] Wilson, 'Strange Death', p. 174.

[48] Petition by Rev. William Ivers Stewart to the Boundary Commission, Dec. 1924 (PRONI, CAB/61/125).

1911 and 1926. The figure in real terms – a drop of about one-third – is not in doubt.[49] Explaining it has proven more challenging, not least the part played by 'forced' migration. In 1973, Robert E. Kennedy attributed the decline to 'extraordinarily high rates of emigration' but as 'the Irish government was careful to protect the rights of the Protestant minority, it seems reasonable to conclude that the Protestants left voluntarily'.[50] A decade later, Kurt Bowen suggested that 'intimidation and violence ... played a part in prompting the exodus' and went 'a long way to explain the unprecedented flight of the minority during these transitional years'. ('With their ostentatious loyalism, their ascendancy backgrounds, and their isolated residences in the countryside [the Anglo-Irish gentry] stood out as helpless symbols and as convenient targets for anti-British sentiment'.)[51] Enda Delaney's judicious study, published in 2000, placed the decline within broader demographic trends and, while noting that minority emigration was 'substantial', highlighted the difficulty of assigning 'a direct causal link between sectarian intimidation or harassment and migration'.[52] Much more provocative was Peter Hart's tentative use of the term 'ethnic cleansing' in a chapter first published in 1996 and later as part of *The I.R.A. at War* (2003). While playing down comparisons with other ethnic conflicts elsewhere in the same chapter, Hart also argued that it was ultimately the shock of the violence of 1920 to 1923 that precipitated the 'Protestant exodus'.[53]

Hart's conclusions have been challenged by a number of recent studies. Andy Bielenberg calculated that when other factors are taken into account there is a residual of between 2,000 and 16,000 Protestants who could have left Ireland owing to revolutionary terror.[54] This was followed by David Fitzpatrick's forensic analysis of the Methodist population of West Cork. For Fitzpatrick, the impact of violence was 'fairly minor' and 'the inexorable

---

[49] *Saorstát Éireann: Census of Population, 1926*, vol. 3 (1929), p. 1.

[50] Robert E. Kennedy Jr, *The Irish: Emigration, Marriage, and Fertility* (Berkeley, CA, 1973), pp. 119, 138.

[51] Kurt Bowen, *Protestants in a Catholic State: Ireland's Privileged Minority* (Kingston and Montreal, 1983), pp. 21–5.

[52] Enda Delaney, *Demography, State and Society: Irish Migration to Britain, 1921–1971* (Liverpool, 2000), pp. 69–83.

[53] Hart, *The I.R.A. at War*, pp. 225–8, 239. The chapter was first published as 'The Protestant Experience of Revolution in Southern Ireland', in Richard English and Graham Walker (eds), *Unionism in Modern Ireland: New Perspectives on Politics and Culture* (Basingstoke, 1996).

[54] Andy Bielenberg, 'Exodus: The Emigration of Southern Irish Protestants during the Irish War of Independence and the Civil War', *Past & Present*, 218 (2013), pp. 199–233. See also Barry Keane, 'Ethnic Cleansing? Protestant Decline in West Cork between 1911 and 1926', *History Ireland*, 20/2 (2012).

decline of southern Protestantism was mainly self-inflicted'.[55] Donald Wood makes an original contribution to this debate in Chapter 1, where, based on new statistical and demographic analysis, he places stronger emphasis on the impact of revolution as a contributor to Protestant population decline than Bielenberg or Fitzpatrick.[56] The intricacies of one of the most important demographic shifts in Irish history will, no doubt, continue to prompt disagreement. Definitive conclusions about Catholic loyalist migration may remain even more elusive.

During the debate on the Anglo-Irish Treaty on 3 January 1922, Constance Markievicz spoke of 'Southern Unionists' as

> the English garrison against Ireland and the rights of Ireland ... that class of capitalists who have been more crushing, cruel and grinding on the people of the nation than any class of capitalists of whom I ever read in any other country, while the people were dying on the roadsides.

Markievicz's depiction of 'anti-Irish Irishmen', a 'small minority of traitors and oppressors', was a pointed reference to members of the old ascendancy, particularly (though not exclusively) the occupants of Ireland's 'Big Houses'.[57] Terence Dooley has estimated that 76 country houses were burned in the 26 counties between January 1920 and July 1921; 26 in Cork alone. Burning escalated significantly during the Civil War, with 199 recorded cases in 1922 and 1923 (though occupants were usually left physically unharmed and often treated with courtesy).[58] This act could be symbolic, as Gemma Clark has pointed out, with arson having the power to undermine the place of a building, and by extension its owner, in a community.[59] The motivation for attacks on individual properties, however, usually featured some combination of political, military, agrarian, and communal factors. Personal relationships and reputations were also important – or at least perceived to be – in dictating

---

[55] Fitzpatrick, *Descendancy*, pp. 159–80. This research was first published as 'Protestant Depopulation and the Irish Revolution', *Irish Historical Studies*, 38/152 (2013), pp. 643–70.

[56] For additional discussion of this issue, see contributions to this volume by Brian Walker (Chapter 3) and Ian d'Alton (Chapter 5).

[57] Dáil Debates, 3 Jan. 1922.

[58] Terence Dooley, *The Decline of the Big House in Ireland: A Study of Irish Landed Families, 1860–1960* (Dublin, 2001), pp. 181–97. James S. Donnelly Jr has claimed that 50 'Big Houses and suburban villas' were burned in Cork from 1919 to 1921: 'Big House Burnings in Cork during the Irish Revolution, 1920–21', *Éire-Ireland*, 47/3&4 (2012), pp. 141–97.

[59] Gemma Clark, *Everyday Violence in the Irish Civil War* (Cambridge, 2014), pp. 54–97.

which houses were attacked and also those that were left. Some family stories have survived whereby a house was spared owing to local popularity or good communal relations.[60] The estate houses of two figures featured in this volume, Lord Farnham and Colonel John Hart, remained relatively unscathed.

Independence, 1922–1949

The fate of unionists and loyalists who remained at home after independence – the majority – has drawn considerable attention. There was, by international comparison at least, a reasonably quick restoration of order after May 1923 and the end of the Civil War prompted by the Anglo-Irish Treaty. Nevertheless, the formation of an Irish Free State in 1922 meant a potentially uncertain future for many who resided there.

The ex-servicemen who survived a world war abroad and then revolution at home have been one source of particular interest. In the 1990s, Jane Leonard was the first historian to examine seriously the impact of revolution on veterans of the Great War.[61] More recently, Paul Taylor has suggested that Leonard, and others, overstated the extent to which ex-servicemen were deliberate targets for intimidation and violence solely on the basis of their army service. Taylor's heavy focus on retrospective accounts in the Bureau of Military History means that he potentially underplays the relevance of past service to the Crown in dictating communal relations. Otherwise rigorous research in the files of the Irish Grants Committee (IGC) also neglects the fathers, mothers, and wives who referred to a former British army husband or son in their own claims for compensation. Taylor does, however (as Leonard did before him), convincingly argue that Irish ex-servicemen were no worse off than others of their class in terms of employment and housing.[62] Michael Robinson, Eoin Kinsella, and Paul Huddie have similarly examined the efforts of the British Ministry of Pensions and private charity to provide for physically and mentally disabled ex-servicemen in the Irish Free State.[63] This work suggests that there was little

---

[60] See, for example, Jane O'Hea O'Keeffe, *Voices from the Great Houses: Cork and Kerry* (Cork, 2013), pp. 21, 46, 60–1. See also the example of Coolcarrigan House in County Kildare in Chapter 11.

[61] Jane Leonard, 'Getting Them at Last: The IRA and Ex-Servicemen', in David Fitzpatrick (ed.), *Revolution? Ireland, 1917–1923* (Dublin, 1990); 'Facing "the Finger of Scorn": Veterans' Memories of Ireland after the Great War', in Martin Evans and Ken Lunn (eds), *War and Memory in the Twentieth Century* (Oxford, 1997).

[62] Taylor, *Heroes or Traitors?*, chaps 5 and 6.

[63] Michael Robinson, '"Nobody's Children?" The Ministry of Pensions and the Treatment of Disabled Great War Veterans in the Irish Free State, 1921–1939', *Irish Studies Review*, 25/3 (2017), pp. 316–35; Eoin Kinsella, *Leopardstown Park*

widespread or malicious discrimination at an institutional level, and Irish ex-servicemen were in some ways better off than their peers in Britain. Still, the cold official attitudes and sometimes violent public opposition to Great War commemoration in the interwar years identified by Jane Leonard and Mandy Link remain part of the story.[64] The cumulative impact of more subtle slights, insults, and prejudices requires further analysis.

The (by now former) policemen of the RIC have also received some attention.[65] Disbanding the force took most of the first eight months of 1922, with the last members leaving Dublin Castle in August.[66] As men gradually filtered home, governments on both sides of the border were 'confronted with the problem of the release into civil life of some 13,000 men', many without suitable qualifications, unable to support themselves or their families indefi-nitely, and with few prospects; a problem exacerbated by a general economic depression and what the RIC Tribunal, founded to administer grants and allowances, coyly termed the 'political situation in Ireland'.[67] There were some fears expressed for what might happen to these former Crown servants, and while none of the worst predictions came to pass, many suffered from violence and intimidation of varying degrees. Some were forced to leave Ireland for their personal safety or to seek work. The majority stayed and settled into life in the Irish Free State.[68]

Rather than old policemen or soldiers, it was owners of the 'Big Houses' who were perceived by one TD to be, 'generally speaking, the remnants of England's loyal garrison in this country'. Country mansions were also, by

---

Hospital 1917–2017: A Home for Wounded Soldiers (Dublin, 2017); Paul Huddie, 'Legacies of a Broken United Kingdom: British Military Charities, the State and the Courts in Ireland, 1923–29', *Irish Economic and Social History*, 45/1 (2018), pp. 3–22.

[64] Leonard, 'Twinge of Memory', pp. 103–5; Mandy Link, *Remembrance of the Great War in the Irish Free State, 1914–1937* (Cham, 2019), pp. 152–75.

[65] Kurt Fedorowich, 'The Problems of Disbandment: The Royal Irish Constabulary and Imperial Migration, 1919–29', *Irish Historical Studies*, 30/117 (1996), pp. 88–110; Kent Fedorowich, 'Reconstruction and Resettlement: The Politicization of Irish Migration to Australia and Canada, 1919–29', *English Historical Review*, 114/459 (1999), pp. 1143–78; Seán William Gannon, *The Irish Imperial Service: Policing Palestine and Administering the Empire, 1922–1966* (Cham, 2019), pp. 23–104; Hughes, *Defying the IRA?*, pp. 192–200.

[66] Donal J. O'Sullivan, *The Irish Constabularies 1822–1922: A Century of Policing in Ireland* (Dingle, 1990), p. 369.

[67] 'Brief summary of the work of the Royal Irish Constabulary Tribunal', Apr. 1928 (TNA, HO 45/13029).

[68] Hughes, *Defying the IRA?*, pp. 192–200. For the experiences of ex-army officers, see Loughlin Sweeney, *Irish Military Elites, Nation and Empire, 1870–1925* (Cham, 2019), pp. 213–30.

1922, prohibitively expensive to keep, unfit for purpose, and thus hardly worth rebuilding even if an owner wished to remain in Ireland (which many did not).[69] The 1923 Damage to Property (Compensation) Act could be restrictive, with compensation inadequate and slow to arrive when granted, as experienced by newspaper proprietors the Tivy family (see Chapter 9).[70] But, as Emer Crooke has recently demonstrated, while Fianna Fáil in power was 'less conciliatory towards the British government and any remains of their authority or representatives in Ireland' than Cumann na nGaedheal had been, policy towards country houses was more concerned with the public purse and financial viability than vindictiveness towards former enemies.[71]

By the mid-1920s, persistent lobbying, particularly from the 'diehard' faction within the Conservative Party, convinced the British government that southern Irish loyalists had not been adequately compensated for losses suffered after the July 1921 Truce and that this should be rectified (or, at least, that it was politically expedient to do so). In 1926, a committee was set up under Lord Dunedin to investigate and report on remaining British government obligations to southern loyalists, and whether any further action might be taken. Dunedin's report forced the British government to acknowledge, for the first time, their 'debt to southern Irish loyalists'. A second Irish Grants Committee, which followed an earlier scheme founded in 1922, duly met for the first time in October 1926. Eventually, it would deal with over 4,000 applications and recommend 2,237 awards. As several of the chapters in this volume make clear, IGC records are an invaluable source of near-contemporary first-hand testimony on the personal impact of the Irish Revolution.[72] They also offer revealing insights into what it meant to be a southern Irish loyalist in the first decade or so after partition. 'Southern' was rigidly defined and applied solely to the 26 counties that became the Irish Free State in 1922. That an applicant suffering loss in north Donegal was considered 'southern' while another in south Fermanagh was not is just one of the many anomalies of Irish partition and a border that was, in many senses, arbitrarily applied. All the same, this remains the common means of dividing 'north' from 'south', preferable more for its simplicity than its accuracy – and applied in this volume with that caveat in mind.

The IGC's criteria for what constituted a 'loyalist' were more flexible. Applicants were simply asked to account for their loss and how it related to

---

[69] Emer Crooke, *White Elephants: The Country House and the State in Independent Ireland, 1922–73* (Dublin, 2018), pp. 1–16.

[70] Dooley, *Decline of the Big House*, pp. 197–207.

[71] Crooke, *White Elephants*, pp. 16–70.

[72] The files are used extensively in this volume in Chapter 6 (Fionnuala Walsh), Chapter 9 (Alan McCarthy), Chapter 10 (Pat McCarthy), and Chapter 11 (Seamus Cullen).

their 'allegiance to the government of the United Kingdom'. Bank passbooks, valuations, medical certificates, and other documentation were necessary to prove financial loss but applicants were left relatively free to decide on the particulars that would best demonstrate their allegiance to the British government and its consequences.[73] A significant proportion of applicants were women and, as shown in Fionnuala Walsh's chapter, their claims offer unique access to the voices of 'ordinary' loyalist women. An interpretive sense of a loyalism that could range from political activism, to armed service in the uniform of the Crown, to much more mundane or vague expressions of 'support', 'preference', or 'liking' remains useful for the purposes of this book.

The material in the IGC files also raises questions about the impact of sectarianism before and after southern independence. R.B. McDowell was certain that 'there was no declared hostility to protestants on religious grounds. But the protestant was often a unionist where a unionist was a *rara avis*'.[74] Peter Hart went much further than this in his explanation of the killing of 13 Protestants over three nights in the Bandon Valley area of West Cork in April 1922: 'In the end, the fact of the victims' religion is inescapable. These men were shot because they were Protestant. ... The sectarian antagonism which drove this massacre was interwoven with political hysteria and local vendettas, but it was sectarian none the less'. For Hart, this was not an 'isolated event' but rather an eruption of latent but deeply held feelings of distrust and paranoia.[75] Hart's book was widely praised on its publication in 1998, winning the Christopher Ewart-Biggs Memorial Prize, but also drew a number of fierce critics, most notably Brian P. Murphy, Niall Meehan, and the Aubane Historical Society.[76]

In 2012, John M. Regan argued that Hart had elided important evidence and hypotheses that did not suit his sectarian interpretation of the massacre; an example of what Regan sees as a broader problem of agenda-driven writing in Irish history.[77] This prompted a robust defence from Hart's doctoral supervisor David Fitzpatrick, who suggested that 'in his rush to be interesting, original and provocative, his sins were those of a creator rather than a denier'.[78] Hart

---

[73] See Irish Grants Committee, Report of Committee, 1930 (TNA, CO 762/212).

[74] R.B. McDowell, *The Church of Ireland, 1869–1969* (London, 1975), p. 109.

[75] Peter Hart, *The I.R.A. and its Enemies: Violence and Community in County Cork, 1916–1923* (Oxford, 1998), pp. 288–92.

[76] See Brian P. Murphy and Niall Meehan, *Troubled History: A 10th Anniversary Critique of Peter Hart's* The IRA and its Enemies (Aubane, 2008).

[77] John M. Regan, 'The "Bandon Valley Massacre" as an Historiographical Problem', *History*, 97 (2012), pp. 70–98. See also John M. Regan, *Myth and the Irish State* (Dublin, 2013).

[78] David Fitzpatrick, 'Ethnic Cleansing, Ethical Smearing and Irish Historians', *History*, 98/239 (2013), p. 143.

may indeed have been let down by some of his more provocative sound bites, and at times pushed his thesis further than the evidence might allow. Equally, it is naïve to rule out religion as a means of understanding the nature of revolutionary violence in Ireland. The loyalism of the victims and their allegiance to Britain (in whatever forms that may have come) was surely relevant to the choices made on those nights, though unlikely to have been a single, defining motivator. This was not least the case in small, rural parishes where everyone knew everyone else, where they prayed, went to school, and often socialised along denominational lines; and where the label 'Protestant' was applied with notable regularity in newspapers, police records, witness testimony, and compensation claims and could be readily associated by republicans with loyalty to the 'enemy'.[79]

Even if there was no systematic, co-ordinated campaign of violence, arson, or intimidation targeted directly against Protestants with the aim of removing them from their communities, it was surely possible for some Protestants to believe – even incorrectly – that there was.[80] Those on the ground relied on what they saw, heard, or read, whether or not it was accurate. Brian Walker outlines the reaction of Church of Ireland bishops to the killings in the Bandon Valley. His chapter (Chapter 3) also demonstrates the wide range of attitudes, perceptions, and motivations that can be found in their public pronouncements. A decision to return to Ireland after leaving was also potentially informed in the same way. The *Cork Examiner*'s report of the 'exodus' that followed the April 1922 killings very quickly – and perhaps with a local audience in mind – framed it as a 'temporary' withdrawal until peaceful conditions had resumed.[81] And, as David Fitzpatrick found in his study of West Cork Methodists, most 'either resisted the pressure to leave home or subsequently returned', including the wife of one of the victims.[82]

The end result of those nights in April 1922 is not in dispute, but speculation about the motivations for the killings is, as Regan acknowledges, somewhat futile when perpetrators have yet to be identified.[83] The rounds of argument and counterargument that have filled this vacuum have often been counter-productive, generating more heat than light.[84] There is, too, a danger that

[79] Hughes, *Defying the IRA?*, p. 132.
[80] In 1975, Jack White suggested that 'Protestants tended to think that they were specially singled out for these attentions'; see his *Minority Report: The Anatomy of the Southern Irish Protestant* (Dublin, 1975), p. 84.
[81] *Cork Examiner*, 1 May 1922.
[82] Fitzpatrick, *Descendancy*, p. 240.
[83] Regan, 'The "Bandon Valley Massacre"', pp. 74–5.
[84] For more on this and the 'Peter Hart affair', see Ian McBride, 'The Peter Hart Affair in Perspective: History, Ideology, and the Irish Revolution', *Historical Journal*, 61/1 (2018), pp. 249–71.

testy debates about the Bandon Valley killings will cloud or obscure other aspects of the loyalist experience of revolution, many of which are explored in this book. While there may be some shared characteristics, Pat McCarthy's Waterford (Chapter 10) and Seamus Cullen's Kildare (Chapter 11) are in many respects strikingly different from Peter Hart's Cork. R.B. McDowell suggested that 'compared to the thorough methods for dealing with unpopular minorities developed during the twentieth century in eastern and central Europe and elsewhere, the harassment of loyalists was not notably severe'.[85] Broadly speaking, this remains sensible. While there has been much focus on the violence that did happen, there has been less interest in explaining its absence – why did loyalists, a small and vulnerable minority in southern Ireland, not suffer more?[86]

A similar question might be asked of the treatment of the Protestant minority after 1922, something that has recently divided historians. Robin Bury's *Buried Lives* (2017) offers a rather bleak picture. At best he sees 'low-intensity unhappiness' and at worst – such as during the Fethard-on-Sea boycott in the late 1950s – 'cultural and constitutional discrimination', a state that was 'institutionally and emotionally anti-Protestant', and a form of 'social and cultural apartheid'.[87] Others have approached the disconnect Protestants felt from Catholic nationalist Ireland with more nuance.[88] While acknowledging the very real difficulties faced by a minority population in such a homogeneous society, Daithí Ó Corráin has suggested that historians and commentators have tended to overemphasise events like the 1950 Tilson case and the Fethard-on-Sea boycott and that these are most adequately viewed as exceptions rather than the rule. For Ó Corráin, Hubert Butler's description of the Protestant community as a 'confident minority' captures the Church of Ireland's 'self-assurance in the practice of its religion and place in Irish society'.[89] And while the experience of the Church of Ireland is not always applicable to other, smaller Protestant denominations, a similar impression emanates from a recent collection of essays (to which the editors

---

[85] McDowell, *Crisis and Decline*, p. 135.

[86] Hart did pose a similar question, something often ignored by his critics. See *The I.R.A. at War*, pp. 244–5.

[87] Robin Bury, *Buried Lives: The Protestants of Southern Ireland* (Dublin, 2017). For alternative interpretations, see reviews of the book by Ian d'Alton, *Irish Times*, 4 Mar. 2017 and Kim Bielenberg, *Irish Independent*, 19 Mar. 2017.

[88] See, for example, Heather Crawford, *Outside the Glow: Protestants and Irishness in Independent Ireland* (Dublin, 2010) and Marianne Elliott, *When God Took Sides: Religion and Identity in Ireland: Unfinished History* (Oxford, 2009), pp. 216–35.

[89] Daithí Ó Corráin, *Rendering to God and Caesar: The Churches and the Two States in Ireland, 1949–73* (Manchester, 2008), pp. 70–105.

are contributors).[90] It is also the case that some Protestant isolation was self-imposed, and not always a bad thing.[91] While some kept themselves to themselves, Protestants who had formerly been aligned with unionist politics continued to seek, and sometimes gain, election in independent Ireland on a range of different platforms.[92] Nor did the worst predictions of the unionist business community come to pass, as shown in Chapter 4 by Frank Barry.

In 1936, a British Ministry of Pensions report referred to 'long-standing, reputable firms who were pro-British' in southern Ireland.[93] But to what extent were surviving residues of loyalty to the old order expressed, and tolerated, in the new order? Even if they felt themselves an isolated or persecuted minority, those that McDowell termed 'ex-unionists' continued to demonstrate their 'Britishness' after 1922. In this context a term like 'ex-loyalist' does not seem to apply in the way that 'ex-unionist' might. Ian d'Alton's suggestion that after 1922 'political unionism rebranded itself as cultural royalism' has much to recommend it.[94] Epithets could also be applied by others without the subject's approval. Michael d'Alton, for instance, considered himself 'pro-British', and even from a 'West British background', but rejected the term 'West Briton' (which usually came with derogatory connotations).[95]

The remnants of loyalism in independent Ireland, both the readily visible and the more understated, have long been established in 'royalist' memoirs. Brian Inglis recalled that in the Malahide of his youth, 'in everyday matters, the fact than an Irish Free State did exist was hardly noticeable'.[96] Many associations, clubs, and professional bodies still carried the 'Royal' prefix, Dublin still had more streets named after Queen Victoria than London, and, though now painted green instead of red, the postboxes still contained the royal cipher.[97] It was also still possible to spend time in independent Ireland with 'like-minded people' and 'ignore repugnant elements of the new

---

90 d'Alton and Milne, *Protestant* and *Irish*. See also Caleb Wood Richardson, *Smyllie's Ireland: Protestants, Independence, and the Man Who Ran the* Irish *Times* (Bloomington, IN, 2019), where the author aims to explore that group's successes rather than its failures.

91 See Chapter 5.

92 Bowen, *Protestants in a Catholic State*, pp. 48–65; McDowell, *Crisis and Decline*, p. 55; David Fitzpatrick, *The Two Irelands, 1912–1939* (Oxford, 1998), p. 203.

93 Taylor, *Heroes or Traitors?*, p. 228.

94 Ian d'Alton, 'Protestant "Belongings" in Independent Ireland, 1922–49', in d'Alton and Milne, *Protestant* and *Irish*, p. 28.

95 See Chapter 5. For 'West British' as an insult, see Nora Robertson, *Crowned Harp: Memories of the Last Years of the Crown in Ireland* (Dublin, 1960). Brian Inglis used the term ironically for his memoir: *West Briton* (London, 1962).

96 Inglis, *West Briton*, p. 15.

97 Ian d'Alton, '"A Vestigial Population"? Perspectives on Southern Irish Protestants in the Twentieth Century', *Éire-Ireland*, 44/3&4, p. 39.

regime'. Sending children to school in Britain or Northern Ireland avoided the perceived impositions of a Catholic/nationalist educational environment, and compulsory teaching of the Irish language.[98] Leaving the theatre before 'The Soldier's Song' was played, listening to British radio stations, eschewing Gaelic football and hurling in favour of soccer, rugby, or cricket, or insisting that Dún Laoghaire was still Kingstown, Portlaoise was still Maryborough, and Cobh was still Queenstown were more subtle forms of resistance.[99] In the privacy of one's own home one could still listen to the Queen's Christmas broadcasts.[100]

Once again, displays of loyalism were not the preserve of Protestants or the former ascendancy class. In 1924, for instance, 20,000 veterans were joined by an estimated crowd of 50,000 in observing the two-minute silence at College Green in Dublin. While not all were there for the same reasons, or partook in the same way, 'God Save the King' was sung and Union flags were flown while a Celtic cross was unveiled in honour of the 10th Irish Division.[101] That same year, the first official state commemoration of the Easter Rising was, by necessity of the bitter divides of the Civil War, a small, sombre affair.[102] Large crowds continued to wave the Union flag and sing 'God Save the King' at armistice ceremonies as late as the 1950s, first at the Phoenix Park (until 1939) and then at Islandbridge.[103] Over 250,000 poppies were sold in Dublin in 1925 alone (100,000 were sold in Belfast) and high sales continued into the 1930s.[104] None of this happened, of course, without opposition, and republicans protested against such shows of 'imperialism'.[105] Whether all of the veterans themselves were choosing to see it that way is a different matter.

In late 1931 and early 1932, 'Bee', the cartoonist for the Fianna Fáil-supporting *Irish Press*, regularly pilloried Cumann na nGaedheal as a party that was in the pocket of 'ex-unionists' who 'hold the purse strings'.[106] In one cartoon published shortly before the Fianna Fáil victory in the 1932 General Election,

---

[98] McDowell, *Crisis and Decline*, pp. 167, 180.

[99] McDowell, *Crisis and Decline*, p. 167; d'Alton, 'Protestant "Belongings"', p. 29; Elliott, *When God Took Sides*, pp. 225–6.

[100] d'Alton, '"A Vestigial Population"?', p. 38. Alternatively, as d'Alton suggests, doing so in private can be read as an example of the ways in which loyalty was kept 'in-house and in-church'.

[101] Jane Leonard, 'The Twinge of Memory: Armistice Day and Remembrance Sunday in Dublin Since 1919', in English and Walker, *Unionism in Modern Ireland*, p. 102.

[102] *Irish Times*, 5 May 1924.

[103] Leonard, 'Twinge of Memory', pp. 102–3.

[104] Taylor, *Heroes or Traitors?*, p. 213.

[105] Leonard, 'Twinge of Memory', pp. 103–5; Taylor, *Heroes or Traitors?*, p. 241.

[106] Quote in *Irish Press*, 5 Dec. 1931. See also 12, 25 Dec. 1931; 2, 7, 14, 27 Jan., 6 Feb. 1932.

the leader of a group of 'ex-unionist' gentlemen declared satisfaction that even if W.T. Cosgrave was not returned to power their money had been well spent by Cumann na nGaedheal, whose anti-Fianna Fáil propaganda had served to 'defame the natives far better than we used to do it'.[107] As late as 1937, a placard displayed in Waterford warned that:

> Ex-Unionists
> Freemasons
> Are helping England again
> Irish people vote
> Fianna Fáil.[108]

While this did not represent an official party message, and it is difficult to judge the impact on potential voters, the existence of this kind of rhetoric at all is evidence of the paranoia that continued to lurk in independent Ireland. In reality, there was little to suggest that southern loyalists would or could serve as a surreptitious fifth column. As noted in Seán William Gannon's chapter, and elsewhere in the volume, many of those with the strongest aversion to the arrival of Irish independence simply chose to leave. Those who remained had demonstrated a commitment, if sometimes reluctant or begrudging, 'to recognise the legitimacy of the new administration'.[109] Nora Robertson described opponents of the Treaty as the 'back-woodsmen among the Irish Unionists'.[110] Nevertheless, Lionel Fleming suggested that the majority of his co-religionists 'remained unconverted to the new way of life' and 'did not regard the Irish nation as having anything to do with them':

> It had to be accepted, of course, as a system to which one must now pay one's income tax, but never, until the end of their lives, would they speak of the government as 'our government'. In spite of the supposed treachery of Britain, their flag remained the Union Jack and their anthem 'God Save the King'.[111]

There was no newfound devotion to nationalist Ireland here, but nor was there an explicit challenge to its authority.

[107] *Irish Press*, 15 Feb. 1932. The cartoon was published before the election but was pre-empting the result and the gentlemen's response 'after the election'.
[108] Photograph entitled 'Canvassing for Fianna Fáil during the 1930s, Cappoquin', *c.*1937 (Waterford County Museum).
[109] *Church of Ireland Gazette*, 13 Jan. 1922; *Irish Times*, 16 Jan. 1922; McDowell, *Crisis and Decline*, pp. 177–96; White, *Minority Report*, pp. 86–8.
[110] Robertson, *Crowned Harp*, p. 144.
[111] Lionel Fleming, *Head or Harp* (London, 1965), p. 93.

Loyalty to Britain, moreover, did not necessarily have to mean disloyalty to, or rejection of, the Irish Free State. TCD could fly the tricolour *and* the Union flag in the 1930s. And, as Nora Robertson put it in 1960, 'In respecting new loyalties it had not seemed incumbent upon us to throw our old ones overboard'.[112] Generational shifts are important too. While Fleming described standing defiantly on College Green with fellow TCD students on Armistice Day – 'the morning, and the British Empire as well, were ours' – he soon fell out of the habit and belatedly discovered along with his peers that 'Irish Protestantism was not necessarily the same as Irish "loyalism"'.[113] By the time Michael Viney went to Malahide in the 1960s in search of 'West Brits', he was told that for a younger generation, educated in Irish rather than British public schools, 'The Union Jack doesn't mean much to them'.[114]

Whatever the meaning of the Union flag, younger men and women from the 26 counties continued to seek service under the Crown throughout the interwar years. As Seán William Gannon shows in Chapter 7, a strong tradition of employment in the British Colonial Service (primarily among the gentry and middles classes) did not cease in 1922, and southern Irish-born recruits continued to join in significant numbers into the 1960s when the Colonial Office closed. The proportion of southern Irish-born soldiers and NCOs in the British army remained steady at 5 per cent to 6 per cent of the total between 1922 and 1939.[115] Steven O'Connor has argued that protests against recruitment had a narrow appeal among the public in the Free State and a 'marginal effect on politics'. As recruitment increased in the 1930s, the Irish government was unwilling to interfere, recognising the benefit of another 'safety valve' for a generation unable to find work at home. And while there was some resentment about serving members wearing their British uniforms in public, this was, for the most part, tolerated; it was even celebrated in the *Irish Times*, which occasionally printed photographs of newly married officers in uniform.[116] Ian d'Alton's uncle, Michael d'Alton, remembered in Chapter 5, was just one of the tens of thousands of southern Irish recruits who served in the Second World War. Both d'Alton and Joseph Quinn (Chapter 8) highlight the complexity of southern Protestant volunteering during the war: a broadly defined allegiance to Britain only

---

[112] d'Alton, 'Protestant "Belongings"', p. 31.

[113] Fleming, *Head or Harp*, pp. 96–107.

[114] *Irish Times*, 26 Mar. 1965.

[115] See Keith Jeffery, 'Ireland and the British Army since 1922', in Thomas Bartlett and Keith Jeffery (eds), *A Military History of Ireland* (Cambridge, 1996) and Steven O'Connor, *Irish Officers in the British Forces, 1922–45* (Basingstoke, 2014), pp. 16–22.

[116] O'Connor, *Irish Officers*, pp. 153–73.

one motivation among many.[117] It seems too, as Quinn points out, that most of those same volunteers remained favourably disposed to the Irish state's policy of neutrality. As did those at home whom the British high commissioner in Dublin, Sir John Maffey, described as 'loyalists in the old sense of the word'.[118]

The terminal date for this book is 1949. After 1922, membership of the Commonwealth had allowed loyalists in the Irish Free State to 'continue to manifest their deep-rooted convictions – loyalty to the Crown, enthusiasm for the British connection, pride in the Irish contribution to the Empire – in time honoured ways'. They could even argue that flying the Union flag, toasting the monarch, or singing 'God Save the King' was a demonstration of 'strict respect for constitutional forms'.[119] Taoiseach John A. Costello's announcement in September 1948 that his government would be repealing the External Relations Act and declaring a republic can, then, be seen as another crucial moment – perhaps a final moment – of rupture for southern Irish loyalism. Even though Ireland was the only Commonwealth state to remain neutral in the Second World War, and, as Deirdre McMahon has noted, 'by the end of the war the Irish relationship with the Commonwealth was almost invisible', the break could still be perceived as 'an attack on the symbolism that had sustained the royalists'.[120] This was especially the case for those who had accepted the Anglo-Irish Treaty on the basis of the continued ties to Britain afforded by Commonwealth membership. They could, however, expect little sympathy from the overwhelming majority who supported the government's intentions. In December 1948, the Republic of Ireland Act was passed in the Dáil with little difficulty.

Ultimately, those who had supported Irish membership of the Commonwealth were once again forced to adapt to a new dispensation. It did not come easily or with universal agreement, but the Church of Ireland adjusted quickly enough to praying for 'our Rulers' rather than the king.[121] The grand lodge of the Orange Order, and its 'Eire Subcommittee', founded in 1939, failed to come to any agreement on changes to the printed laws and rituals of the association. But in Donegal, and perhaps elsewhere, 'the printed

---

[117] For more work on Irish volunteering during the Second World War see the notes to Chapter 8.

[118] White, *Minority Report*, pp. 109–10.

[119] McDowell, *Crisis and Decline*, p. 170.

[120] Deirdre McMahon, 'Ireland, the Empire and the Commonwealth', in Kevin Kenny (ed.), *Ireland and the British Empire* (Oxford, 2004), pp. 212–13; d'Alton, 'Protestant "Belongings"', p. 32.

[121] d'Alton, 'Protestant "Belongings"', p. 32; Miriam Moffit, 'This "Rotten Little Republic": Protestant Identity and the "State Prayers" Controversy, 1948', in d'Alton and Milne, *Protestant and Irish*.

ritual would be varied in practice to accommodate the Republic'.[122] On 20 April 1949, two days after the Easter Monday on which Éire officially became a Republic, the *Irish Times* lamented withdrawal from the Commonwealth but also recognised that 'the milk has been spilled now, and we must accept things not as we might like them to be, but rather as they are'. It was, readers were reminded, 'the duty of every citizen, whatever his or her personal views may be, to give unconditional loyalty to the new State'.[123] In 1960, Nora Robertson reflected that 'even this rupture was more in *posse* than in *esse* ... Like the curse on the Rheims jackdaw, nobody seemed a penny the worse'.[124]

The chapters that follow present a broad range of loyalism and a diverse collection of loyalists in southern Ireland. They are evidence of the flexibility and adaptability of the loyalties and allegiances of individuals and collectives. There is not necessarily a consensus among authors on what it meant to be a loyalist, or their experiences from Union to Republic, nor is it the editors' intention for it to be so. The aim here is, rather, to present a series of challenges – some gentle, some more provocative – to easy narratives.

---

[122] Fitzpatrick, *Descendancy*, pp. 48–9.
[123] *Irish Times*, 20 Apr. 1949.
[124] Robertson, *Crowned Harp*, p. 181.

1

Crisis and Decline? Protestants and Unionists in Revolution

CHAPTER I

Protestant Population Decline in Southern Ireland, 1911–1926

Donald Wood

Much has been written about the substantial decline during the 1911–26 intercensal period of the Protestant population of the 26 counties that formed the Irish Free State in 1922.[1] During that period, the Protestant population declined from 327,179 to 220,723, a reduction of 32.5 per cent, whereas overall population decline was just 5.34 per cent.[2] As historians mull over the causes of this steep decline and the possible influences of revolutionary violence, the debate on the subject has sometimes become bitter, with a variety of conflicting conclusions being hotly contested.

While the departure of the British administration in 1922 made a significant contribution to Protestant decline, early studies of population change during this period argued emigration of civilian Protestants was the principal cause of decline. This was the conclusion of the census statisticians of 1926 who pointed to the wide geographical spread of the decline and estimated that the British military withdrawal contributed about a quarter of it.[3] Later studies also argued that emigration was the major reason for Protestant decline. Robert E. Kennedy, in his 1973 study, dealt at length with Protestant decline during the revolutionary period. He concluded, amongst other things, that the 1911–26 decline was primarily caused by the outmigration of native Protestants rather than natural decline or the departure of non-native Protestants.[4] He argued that, with the Free State government adopting a benign attitude to

---

[1] In this chapter 'Protestant' is taken to include all non-Catholics. While Episcopalians constituted the majority of the non-Catholics in 1911, there were also smaller Methodist, Presbyterian, Baptist, and Jewish communities as well as some 10,000 classified as 'others'.

[2] *Saorstát Éireann: Census of Population, 1926*, vol. 3 (1929), Table 1B and vol. 1 Table 4.

[3] *Saorstát Éireann: Census of Population, 1926*, vol. 10 (1934), Chapter 4, 'Birthplaces and Religions', p. 47.

[4] Robert E. Kennedy Jr, *The Irish, Emigration, Marriage, and Fertility* (Berkeley, CA, 1973), pp. 137–8.

minorities, emigration was voluntary, but he also thought fear of harm played a part. Enda Delaney addressed the high level of Protestant emigration both during and after the revolutionary period. While concluding that violence did influence some Protestant emigration, Delaney thought there was insufficient evidence to estimate how much was terror-driven.[5] Andrew Bielenberg in 2013 also argued that outward migration was the main cause of decline. Bielenberg suggests that the majority of the native Protestant exodus was voluntary, the result of economic and other factors, with revolutionary violence playing a relatively minor part.[6] David Fitzpatrick came to quite different conclusions in his analysis of Methodist membership records for the period 1911–26. He concluded that the main source of Protestant decline was 'a failure to recruit new members because of low fertility and nuptiality, exacerbated by losses through mixed marriage and conversion'. Fitzpatrick's analysis has the merit of looking at Methodist population movements in short three-year periods and charting the various components of change by period, a significant advantage over the two snapshots of population at either end of the long and eventful intercensal period of 1911 to 1926. Methodist records show a high level of gross Methodist outward migration in the three years 1911–14, numerically more than during the revolutionary period. This, Fitzpatrick argues, indicates that revolutionary violence had a limited effect on Methodist migration patterns.[7] There would, then, appear to be very different views about the principal reasons for Protestant decline during this period.

Drawing on information from a variety of census reports, the online census data of 1901 and 1911, and the Registrar General's annual reports, this study concludes, first, that the sharp decline in the civilian Protestant population that occurred between the censuses of 1911 and 1926 was primarily due to emigration. Depletion analysis of the 1911 civilian Episcopalian population clearly shows population loss primarily amongst younger age groups. Secondly, a dramatic decline in Protestant marriage numbers indicates much of that exodus occurred during the turbulent years between 1920 and 1924. Finally, analysis of population trends in the decades before 1911 shows little evidence of a long-term relative Protestant decline that might have presaged a demographic collapse between 1911 and 1926.

[5] Enda Delaney, *Demography, State and Society: Irish Migration to Britain, 1921–1971* (Liverpool, 2000), pp. 76–8.
[6] Andy Bielenberg, 'Exodus: The Emigration of Southern Irish Protestants during the Irish War of Independence and the Civil War', *Past & Present*, 218 (2013), pp. 199–233.
[7] David Fitzpatrick, 'Protestant Depopulation and the Irish Revolution', *Irish Historical Studies*, 38/152 (2013), pp. 643–70.

Demographics, 1881–1946

The population of the 26 counties that became the Irish Free State had been in consistent decline since the Famine of the 1840s. It has been argued that Protestant decline had long been much higher than Catholic decline. Garret Fitzgerald stated Protestant decline between 1861 and 1911 was almost 45 per cent, compared with a Catholic decline of 30 per cent.[8] But Fitzgerald was wrong. While his Catholic figure was approximately right, Protestant decline during this period was is in fact 30 per cent, much the same as Catholic decline (see Table 1.1 below).

In 1881, civilian Protestants, numbering some 378,000, made up 9.82 per cent of the overall 26-county civilian population.[9] By 1911, when their civilian numbers had reduced to approximately 300,000, Protestants still accounted for 9.71 per cent of the civilian population. Arguments about relatively high Protestant decline in the decades before 1911 are not supported by these figures. While Table 1.1 shows continuous population decline between 1881 and 1911, both nationally and for Protestants, the percentage of the Protestant civilian population in the 26 counties barely changed during that period. National intercensal decline was as high as 10.9 per cent between 1881 and 1891 and as low as 2.6 per cent between 1901 and 1911. Protestant decline was more even, varying between 9.7 per cent between 1881 and 1891 and 5.6 per cent between 1891 and 1901. Kennedy argued that an increased Protestant decline between 1901 and 1911 (7.1 per cent) might have signalled the flood that was to follow. The end of the privileged economic and political status for Protestants was already beginning. Apprehension at actual and impending change may have contributed to increased Protestant emigration during this decade.[10] But Protestant decline between 1901 and 1911 was minor compared with what followed. While overall Protestant numbers declined by 16,373 between 1901 and 1911, the 1911–26 decline was 106,456. After allowing for the departure of British military and their dependants, the annual rate of Protestant decline during the period 1911–26, measured at 21.2 per thousand per annum, was almost three times that of the preceding decade. The decline from 1911 to 1926 was something much more than just the continuation of any long-term trend.

---

8 Garret FitzGerald, *Reflections on the Irish State* (Dublin, 2003), p. 147.
9 Calculated as Protestant census figure less number of Protestant military and dependants.
10 Kennedy, *The Irish*, p. 135.

Table 1.1 Twenty-Six County population change, 1881–1946

Intercensal Period	National Annual Rate of Decline (per thousand)	National Annual Rate of Migration (per thousand)	Civilian Protestant Annual Rate of Decline (per thousand)	Civilian Protestant Percentage of Population at Start of Period
1881–91	-10.9	-16.3	-9.7	9.82%
1891–1901	-7.4	-11.9	-5.6	9.97%
1901–11	-2.6	-8.2	-7.1	10.13%
1911–26	-3.7	-8.8	-21.2	9.71%
1926–36	-0.1	-5.6	-12.7	7.39%
1936–46	-0.4	-6.3	-13.3	6.53%

Estimated 1911–26 decline and emigration rates allow for extraordinary items like Great War deaths and British withdrawal.

Sources: Census of Population of Ireland, 1946, vol. 3 (1952), Table 1A. Numbers of Protestant British military in 26 counties in each census up to 1911 accumulated from census reports 1881–1911, Area Houses and Population, vols 1–4, Occupations of the People, 1881–1911. Number of British treaty port military in 1926 and 1936 estimated from number of Protestants in the relevant District Electoral Divisions of Cork and Donegal in Irish Free State census reports 1926 and 1936, vol. 3, pt 1, Table 12.

An Ageing Population?

Table 1.2 Percentages of population aged over 45, 1901–1946

Census	National Percentage of over 45s	Percentage of Church of Ireland/Episcopalians (over 45s)	Excess of Church of Ireland/Episcopalians (over 45s)
1901	23.58%	26.15% (Church of Ireland)	2.57%
1911	25.81%	29.28% (Church of Ireland)	3.47%
1926	28.04%	35.58% (Episcopalians)	7.54%
1936	29.30%	38.31% (Episcopalians)	9.01%
1946	29.74%	41.46% (Episcopalians)	11.72%

Sources: Percentages for 1901 and 1911 obtained from the online census database: http://census.nationalarchives.ie/ (accessed 3 Oct. 2016). Percentages for 1926–46 obtained from census reports for 1926, vol. 3, pt 1, Table 13A; 1936, vol. 3, pt 1, Table 13A; and 1946, vol. 3, pt 1, Table 11A.

One possible indication of an infertility-led decline is an ageing population and this has been proposed in the past.[11] A higher incidence of older Protestants has been a feature of all 26-county census returns during the twentieth century. An analysis of age profiles in the censuses of 1901 to 1946 shows that most of the growing age gap between Protestants and Catholics occurred after 1911. Table 1.2 shows the percentage of people, both nationally and by denomination, who were aged over 45 in the period 1901–46. Church of Ireland numbers are not tabulated separately from other Episcopalians in census reports from 1926 onwards, but to avoid any distorting effect of the British military presence, Church of Ireland numbers only are measured in 1901 and 1911. With the British military mostly comprising young Church of England men, using Episcopalian numbers for the period up to 1911 would give a biased result. The gap between the Church of Ireland and national percentages of over 45s in 1911 (3.47 per cent) had more than doubled (to 7.54 per cent) in 1926 and the gap between Episcopalians and Catholics increased further as the twentieth century progressed. As Sexton and O'Leary pointed out, the changes that so distorted twentieth-century Protestant demographics did not occur until after 1911.[12]

Nuptiality

An unwillingness to marry has been cited as a contributor to greater levels of Protestant decline.[13] The marriage rates for both Catholics and Protestants were published annually in the reports of the Registrar General. The relevant Catholic and Protestant marriage rates per thousand of population in the 26 counties for each of the census years 1881 to 1911 are shown in Table 1.3. The figures indicate that in 1911 Protestant marriage rates had declined by 12 per cent since 1881. Most of that decline occurred between 1881 and 1891, a period that would have little direct impact on 1911–26 fertility. During the two decades prior to 1911, there was very little decline in Protestant marriage rates (just 4 per cent, from 5.14 to 4.92 per thousand of population). Catholic marriage rates, on the other hand, had improved by some 34 per cent between 1881 and 1911. The extraordinary statistic is the extremely low Catholic marriage rate of the 1880s. The 1891–1911 period was one of marked

---

[11] Barry Keane, 'Ethnic Cleansing? Protestant Decline in West Cork between 1911 and 1926', *History Ireland*, 20/2 (2012).

[12] J.J. Sexton and Richard O'Leary, 'Factors Affecting Population Decline in Minority Religious Communities in the Republic of Ireland', in *Building Trust in Ireland Studies Commissioned by the Forum for Peace and Reconciliation* (Belfast, 1996), n. 22.

[13] Fitzpatrick, 'Protestant Depopulation', pp. 650, 663 (Table 7).

Table 1.3 Catholic and Protestant marriage rates, 1881–1911

Census Year	Catholic Marriages	Catholic Marriage Rate (per thousand)	Protestant Marriages	Protestant Marriage Rate (per thousand)
1881	13086	3.78	2265	5.60
1891	12461	4.02	1900	5.14
1901	13368	4.64	1783	5.19
1911	14272	5.07	1611	4.92

Sources: Annual Report of the Registrar-General on Marriages, Births and Deaths in Ireland, 1881, 1891, 1901, and 1911: www.cso.ie/en/statistics/birthsdeathsandmar-riages/archive/annualreportsonmarriagesbirthsanddeathsinirelandfrom1864to2000/ (accessed 23 May 2019); Catholic and Protestant populations in each census year 1881–1911 from *Saorstát Éireann: Census of Population, 1926*, vol. 3 (1929), Table 1A.

Catholic nuptiality improvement but little change in Protestant nuptiality. By 1911, the rates of marriage of the two communities were similar. The Catholic rate was 5.07 per thousand while the Protestant rate was 4.92.

The annual Registrar General's report also allows a detailed analysis of nuptiality trends during the period 1911–26. The numbers of Catholic and Protestant marriages registered in each year are reported, giving a view of how things changed during the period (Figure 1.1). The figures reveal that marriage numbers among all denominations fell from their 1911 levels during the Great War but had recovered fully by 1920. Following the establishment of the Irish Free State, Catholic numbers declined a little throughout the 1920s, but had recovered to 1911 levels by 1940. Protestant marriage numbers, by contrast, declined dramatically during the period 1921–4. From 1,621 marriages in 1920, there were just 987 in 1924. This was a spectacular collapse. From then on, Protestant marriage numbers steadied but did not recover. As the 1926 census returns revealed, Protestant marriage rates per thousand of population had only declined by 10 per cent since 1911 while marriage numbers had declined by 40 per cent.[14] The pool of potential

---

[14] *Annual Report of the Registrar-General on Marriages, Births and Deaths in Ireland, 1911*, abstracts for totals of marriages by religion in 26 counties. *Saorstát Éireann: Census of Population, 1926*, vol. 3 (1929), Table 1A. Marriage rates for 1926 from *Annual Report of the Registrar-General on Marriages, Births and Deaths in Ireland*, 1927, p. ix (Table II). Protestant marriage rates had declined from 4.92 (per thousand of population) in 1911 to 4.41 in 1926. Corresponding Catholic marriage rates were 5.07 (1911) and 4.58 (1926) – a very similar decline.

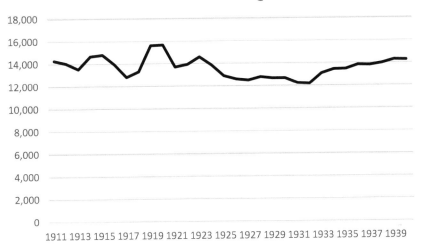

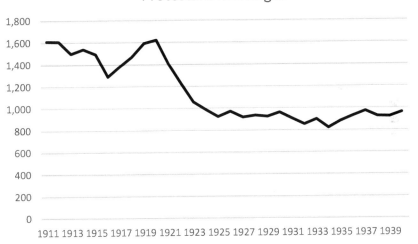

1.1 Numbers of Catholic and Protestant marriages in the 26 counties, 1911–1940

Sources: *Annual Report of the Registrar-General on Marriages, Births and Deaths in Ireland, 1911–1940*, abstracts for totals of marriages by religion in 26 counties, available at (www.cso.ie/en/statistics/birthsdeathsandmarriages/ archive/annualreportsonmarriagesbirthsanddeathsinirelandfrom1864to2000/) (accessed 23 May 2019).

Protestant marriage partners had been diminished significantly since 1911. The Protestant marriage numbers reported in the annual reports of the Registrar General indicates that the decline in numbers occurred mainly between 1920 and 1924.

Comparative Fertility

Promoters of the idea of long-term infertility as a cause of Protestant decline tend to compare Protestant fertility unfavourably with that of Catholics. Robert E. Kennedy proposed, amongst other things, a thesis about fertility in Ireland which broadly stated that the higher one went up the socio-economic scale the smaller the family size. Using census evidence, he showed that family sizes were significantly larger amongst the unskilled than amongst those in professional occupations.[15] One other standout feature of Irish fertility rates in 1911 was how much lower Dublin fertility rates for all religions were compared with corresponding rural rates.[16] Dublin Catholic fertility rates in 1911 languished 13 per cent below overall 26-county Catholic rates. There was a distinct urban–rural divide. In 1911, some 30 per cent of native Protestants lived in Dublin county compared with just 13 per cent of Catholics.[17] The same difference between urban and rural fertility rates was evident in the census of England and Wales in 1911 when the child–woman ratio (CWR) in rural areas was 14.6 per cent above that of urban areas.[18] Protestants were also over-represented in managerial, professional, and skilled occupations and very under-represented in unskilled occupations. A lower fertility rate for Protestants is to be expected.

CWR in England and Wales in 1931 is calculated at 30 children per hundred women of childbearing age,[19] the same as the southern Irish Episcopalian rate of 1926.[20] In England and Wales, the CWR in 1921 was 35.1. Despite that

---

[15] Kennedy, *The Irish*, pp. 188–9.

[16] Dublin Catholic child–woman ratio (CWR) in 1911 is calculated at 39.4 compared with a national Catholic rate of 45.4. CWR measured as the ratio of number of children under 5 per 100 women aged 15 to 44: http://census.nationalarchives.ie/ (accessed 16 Oct. 2016).

[17] See 1911 census returns: http://census.nationalarchives.ie/ (accessed 16 Oct. 2016).

[18] *Census of England and Wales 1911*, Ages and Condition as to Marriage, pp. 7–8 and 11–12 (Tables 4 and 6): www.histpop.org (accessed 10 Nov. 2016).

[19] General Tables, England and Wales, 1921 (p. 127) and 1931 (p. 125): www.histpop. org (accessed 16 Oct. 2016).

[20] Barry Keane, 'Church of Ireland Fertility as an Agent of Decline, 1901–1961': www.academia.edu/18208742/Church_of_Ireland_fertility_as_an_agent_of_ decline_1901-1961 (accessed 17 Oct. 2016).

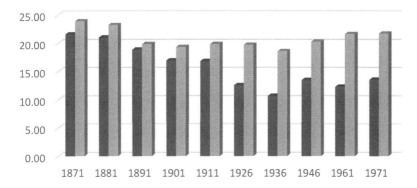

Annual Episcopalian birth rates from no. of children in censuses
Annual Catholic birth rates from no. of children in censuses

1.2 Episcopalian and Catholic birth rates in the 26 counties, 1866–1971
Sources: Estimated from number of children counted in censuses 1871–1971.
Saorstát Éireann: Census of Population, 1926, vol. 1 (1928), Table 1 and *Census of Population of Ireland, 1971*, vol. 1 (1972), Table 1; *Census of Ireland, 1871, 1881, 1891*, and *1901*, 'Religious Professions and Education of the People', Tables 32 and 33; and *Census of Ireland 1911. General Report, with Tables and Appendix* [Cd. 6663], HC 1913, 'Education of the People', Tables 29a and 30. Religious populations 1871–1971 from *Saorstát Éireann: Census of Population, 1926*, vol. 3 (1929), pt 1, Table 9; *Ireland. Census of Population, 1926*, vol. 3, (1939) pt 1, Table 13A; *Census of Population of Ireland, 1946*, vol. 3 (1952), pt 1, Table 13A; *Census of Population of Ireland, 1961*, vol. 7 (1965), Table 10; *Census of Population of Ireland, 1971*, vol. 9 (1977), Table 8.

significant drop in fertility, the population of England and Wales had increased between 1921 and 1931. Yet the southern Irish Episcopalian population was in steep decline. Fertility is not necessarily the defining determinant of population change.

With full Irish civil registration commencing in 1864, the census reports from 1871 onwards show birth and death registration figures for the whole population, but without any religious breakdown. Most studies that estimate Irish natural change by religion only start with 1926. Estimates of natural change by religion for periods before this are more difficult to come by. A basis for estimating comparative birth rates for different religions prior to 1911 is found in census reports of the 1871 to 1911 period.[21] Census statisticians

[21] Drawn from Census of Ireland reports, 1871, 1881, 1891 and 1901, 'Religious Professions and Education of the People', Tables 32 and 33 and *Census of Ireland,*

from 1871 onwards measured literacy rates amongst those old enough to have
gone to school. From 1871, they produced a report, by religion, of all those
over the age of five and the percentages that were illiterate (in 1911, the cut-off
age was increased to nine). Since total numbers in each religion are also
available, the number of under-fives by religion (under-nines in 1911) in each
census is therefore known. It is thus possible to infer an approximate birth
rate for each religious group for the years preceding each census, beginning
in 1871. These figures for numbers of children in each census up to 1911[22] and
equivalent figures for the numbers of children of each religious group from the
census reports of 1926 onwards[23] allow a comparison of inferred birth rates
for different religious groups from 1871 to 1971. The inferred birth rates shown
in Figure 1.2 are likely to be an underestimate of actual birth rates because
infant mortality is not considered. Contrary to the idea that Protestant and
Catholic birth rates had been diverging significantly for some decades before
1911, birth rates for both Catholics and Protestants were changing at much the
same rate from 1871 until 1911, and birth rate decline for both communities
was levelling off around the turn of the century.

Natural population growth for the 26 counties from 1901 to 1911 is
estimated at 5.64 per thousand per annum of the average intercensal
population.[24] However, with inferred Protestant birth rates for the period
up to 1911 just 2.94 per thousand per annum below inferred Catholic rates,
and assuming similar mortality rates for both communities,[25] it is likely that
Protestant natural change too was positive until 1911, with Protestant decline
up to this point entirely due to emigration. But 1926 figures show a dramatic
change had occurred. The number of Episcopalian children recorded in 1926
infers a birth rate of under 12 per thousand per annum during the previous
five years. By 1926, inferred Catholic birth rates remained much as they were
from 1901 to 1911, opening a yawning 'fertility gap' between the two religious
groups. While the rate of Catholic natural change remained positive in 1926,
Protestant natural change was suddenly deeply negative. The discrepancy
between inferred birth rates of Protestants before and after 1911 is very clear.

   1911. General Report, with Tables and Appendix [Cd. 6663], HC 1913, 'Education
   of the People', Tables 29a and 30.
[22] Census of Ireland reports, 1871, 1881, 1891 and 1901, 'Religious Professions and
   Education of the People', Tables 32 and 33 and *Census of Ireland, 1911. General
   Report,* 'Education of the People', Tables 29a and 30.
[23] *Saorstát Éireann: Census of Population, 1926,* vol. 1 (1928), Table 1 and *Census of
   Population of Ireland, 1971,* vol. 1 (1972), Table 1.
[24] *Saorstát Éireann: Census of Population, 1926,* vol. 1 (1928), Table 1.
[25] Table 1.2 indicates that, up to 1911, there was little difference between the
   percentage of older people amongst Church of Ireland membership and the
   population at large. Mortality rates would then be expected to be similar.

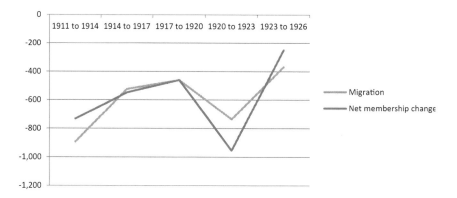

1.3 Methodist gross emigration and decline
Source: David Fitzpatrick, *Descendancy: Irish Protestant Histories since 1795*
(Cambridge, 2014), Table 8.12 (p. 256).

This was a seismic change rather than the continuation of any established pattern. With apparent fertility rates dropping by 10 per cent during this period and the Protestant population declining by over 30 per cent, most of the decline resulted from causes other than infertility. In 1926, there were some 36,000 Episcopalian women of childbearing age in the Free State.[26] The corresponding 1911 figure had been 55,000.[27] The decline in the number of children per thousand of population was the result of this catastrophic decline in the number of potential mothers that might have produced them rather than a major failure in the fertility of those remaining.

Fitzpatrick, however, argued that Protestant decline was largely 'self-inflicted'.[28] Using a multiplier of 20, he estimated from Methodist decline figures that, in the three years from 1920 to 1923, Protestant numbers would have declined by roughly 19,000 because of new membership failing to keep pace with losses through cessation, death, emigration, and conversions. 'The long-term decline in the South's Protestant community had accelerated significantly', he concluded, and an inability to recruit because of infertility he deemed the major cause.[29]

---

[26] *Saorstát Éireann: Census of Population, 1926*, vol. 3 (1929), Table 1, Table 13A.

[27] Counting the number of Episcopalian women aged 15 to 44 in the 26 counties that formed the Irish Free State: http://census.nationalarchives.ie/ (accessed 24 Oct. 2016).

[28] David Fitzpatrick, *Descendancy: Irish Protestant Histories since 1795* (Cambridge, 2014), p. 180.

[29] Fitzpatrick, *Descendancy*, p. 180.

Figure 1.3 compares how Methodist gross emigration and membership change varied in each three-year period between 1911 and 1926. Methodist membership decline in each three-year period tracks gross emigration extremely closely. If net transfers to the North are added to the migration losses, the two lines of the graph move even closer together. Emigration would appear to be an extremely important agent of decline throughout the period. Young Methodists who became full members between 1911 and 1926 at the age of 16 were born between 1895 and 1910. The age profile of Methodist children counted in the 1911 census should give an indication of any major fertility problems that might have precipitated a fertility-led 31 per cent drop in Methodist membership numbers between 1911 and 1926. However, an analysis of online census data for 1911 shows little sign that Methodist child numbers were in serious decline before 1911. The numbers for each year of age from 1 to 15 were remarkably stable in 1911.[30] Figures from the 1901 and 1911 censuses also indicate that fertility rates for the much larger Church of Ireland community barely changed during that period. Church of Ireland CWRs have been calculated at 34 in 1901 and 35 in 1911.[31]

British Military and Their Dependants

The departure of almost all British military personnel and their dependants in 1922 certainly contributed significantly to the 1911–26 Protestant decline. A small Treaty Ports force of 1,456 was all that remained in 1926 of the 26,445 army and navy personnel from 1911 (of whom 19,957 were Protestant).[32] The 1911 census statisticians had determined that, in Dublin city and county, the military dependency ratio (number of dependent wives and children per soldier) was 37 per hundred.[33] An analysis of 1911 census data for garrison districts outside of Dublin found a much lower military dependency ratio

---

[30] Using the online search facility, it is found that 763 children aged 1 to 3 in the 26 counties were returned as Methodists in the 1911 census, while there were 743 Methodists aged 13 to 15: http://census.nationalarchives.ie/ (accessed 30 Oct. 2016).

[31] Keane, 'Church of Ireland Fertility as an Agent of Decline'.

[32] Occupation of the people for 26 counties drawn from *Census of Ireland, 1911. General Report*, 'Occupations of the People'. Residual 1926 forces based on number of British born engaged in defence: *Saorstát Éireann: Census of Population, 1926*, vol. 3 (1929), Part 2, Table 15.

[33] *Census of Ireland, 1911. General Report*, 'Area, Houses, and Population', Tables 71 and 72.

of about 23 dependants per hundred soldiers.[34] Whereas in the cities the ratio of wives to military husbands was about 1 to 7, in places like Fermoy, Kilworth, Buttevant, and the Curragh it was nearer 1 to 12 and the dependency ratio in these places was 20 to 24 per hundred soldiers. Since over 74 per cent of military were stationed outside the two main urban areas of Dublin and Cork, the 1911 dependency ratio for Dublin is not an accurate basis for a national statistic. A national military dependency ratio of 28 per hundred is estimated to be more appropriate than the Dublin rate. Such a ratio would give, allowing for a residual Treaty Port presence in 1926, an estimated contribution of 24,265 departing British military and dependants to Protestant decline.

Depletion of the 1911 Protestant Population, 1911–1926

The online census data for 1911 and the census reports of 1926 allow an analysis of how the 1911 populations of different religions had declined by 1926. This study has compared the numbers aged 15 and over in 1926 with the entire population of 1911. Thus, the influence of factors such as migration and mortality on population change can be estimated. Factors other than migration and mortality had only a minor effect on depletion of the 1911 population (Table 1.4). This analysis points to civilian emigration being the major cause of Protestant decline. The estimated Protestant emigration rate of 17.44 for 1911–26 is extraordinarily high, compared with both the Catholic rate for the same period (7.0) and the Episcopalian emigration rate of 8.0 during the period 1926–36.[35] If civilian Protestants had emigrated during the period from 1911 to 1926 at the same rate as Catholics, Protestant emigration would have amounted to about 27,100. Since Protestant emigration is estimated at 67,517, this suggests excessive Protestant migration of about 40,400 during this period.

A more detailed depletion analysis by age group can also be performed on a representative sample of Protestants utilising 1911 census data. The Episcopalian population of the 26 counties, numbering 249,935 in 1911 and 164,215 in 1926, was analysed.[36] Using the online search facility, an age profile of the civilian Episcopalian population of 1911 was prepared. Comparing the 1911 numbers with the numbers in the corresponding age groups of 1926 that

---

[34] Counting the numbers of Church of England men, women, and children in garrison areas outside Dublin in 1911: http://census.nationalarchives.ie/ (accessed 12 Dec. 2016).

[35] Bowen, *Protestants in a Catholic State*, p. 29.

[36] *Saorstát Éireann: Census of Population, 1926*, vol. 3 (1929), Table 1A.

Table 1.4 Free State Counties civilian population depletion, 1911–1926

	Catholics	Protestants	Notes
1911 Population	2,812,509	327,179	
Less Great War dead	2,797,009	322,179	
Less 1911 British military and dependants	2,788,561	296,634	(Civilian population)
Civilian populations aged 15 and over in 1926	1,932,949	169,664	
1911–26 depletion of 1911 civilian population	855,676	126,970	
Assumed mortality rates, 1911-26 (per 1,000 per annum of average population)	16.00	17.00	
Estimated 1911–26 mortality of 1911 civilian populations	566,589	59,453	
Estimated 1911–26 emigration of 1911 civilian populations	289,087	67,517	
Estimated 1911–26 emigration rates (per 1,000 per annum of average population)	7.00	17.44	

Sources: Population numbers from *Saorstát Éireann: Census of Population, 1926*, vol. 3 (1929), Table 1. Protestant Great War dead estimated at 5,000, after J.J. Sexton and Richard O'Leary, 'Factors Affecting Population Decline in Minority Religious Communities in the Republic of Ireland', in *Building Trust in Ireland Studies Commissioned by the Forum for Peace and Reconciliation* (Belfast, 1996), p. 14. British military numbers from *Census of Ireland*, 1911. *General Report, with Tables and Appendix* [Cd. 6663], HC 1913, 'Area, Houses and Population' and 'Occupation of the People' (calculated for 26 IFS counties). Military dependants estimated at 28 per 100 servicemen. Civilian populations of 1926 from *Saorstát Éireann: Census of Population, 1926*, vol. 3 (1929), Table 13A. Allowances made for estimated British treaty port forces of 993. Catholic mortality rates assumed similar to national rate (*Saorstát Éireann: Census of Population, 1926*, vol. 1 (1928), Table 3). Protestant mortality rate assumed to be the 17 per thousand per annum estimated for Episcopalians 1926–36 (Kurt Bowen, *Protestants in a Catholic State: Ireland's Privileged Minority* (Kingston, 1983), p. 29).

were by then 15 years older, a depletion chart for each 1911 age group was developed (Table 1.5).

Table 1.5 Civilian Episcopalian age group cohort depletion, 1911–1926

Ages in 1911 Census	1911 Estimated Civilians	Ages in 1926 Census	1926 Estimated Civilians	Estimated 1911–26 Depletion
0–9	37,975	15–24	25,793	12,182
10–19	37,945	25–34	21,224	16,721
20–29	33,941	35–44	21,054	12,887
30–39	33,402	45–54	21,968	11,435
40–49	28,004	55–64	17,277	10,727
50–59	21,595	65–74	12,541	9,054
60–69	16,939	75–84	5,498	11,441
70–79	10,993	85–94	1,045	9,948
80 plus	3,071	95 plus	63	3,008

Table 1.5 indicates two distinct reasons for depletion of the 1911 civilian Episcopalian population. There is the effect of increasing mortality in the older age groups but far more significant is the higher loss of Episcopalian numbers among younger age groups of 1911, as indicated in Figure 1.4. The losses of the 1911 Episcopalian population then aged under 40 represents 55 per cent of all depletion of the 1911 civilian Episcopalian population in that period. Episcopalian Great War deaths made a minor contribution.[37] Rather than most losses occurring in older age groups, depletion occurred mainly amongst younger adults, a phenomenon that can only be explained by heavy net outward migration. It is worth contrasting the 1911–26 Episcopalian depletion profile with depletion during the period 1971–81, when emigration rates were low and the Episcopalian population decreased by just 3 per cent.[38]

The difference between the two depletion profiles is striking (Figures 1.4 and 1.5). During the period 1911–26, the main losses were in the younger age groups. Between 1971 and 1981, there was little or no depletion amongst these younger age groups. Over 97 per cent of depletion of the 1971 Episcopalian population occurred in those already aged over 40 in 1971. Mortality of the old had replaced emigration of the young as the principal agent of population depletion.

[37] Sexton and O'Leary estimated southern Irish Episcopalian war deaths at 5,000 (73 per cent of all Protestant deaths).
[38] *Census of Population of Ireland, 1981*, vol. 5 (1985), Table 1B.

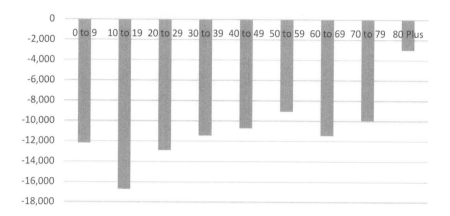

1.4 Episcopalian depletion, 1911–1926 (by 1911 age group)
Sources: Search of 1911 online census data, counting those returned as
members of the Churches of Ireland and England in each age group,
excluding military and their dependents, to establish 1911 age demographics
of civilian Episcopalians (http://census.nationalarchives.ie/) (accessed 14
Nov. 2016). *Saorstát Éireann: Census of Population, 1926*, vol. 3 (1929), Table
13A for corresponding figures of 1926 Episcopalian age demographics.

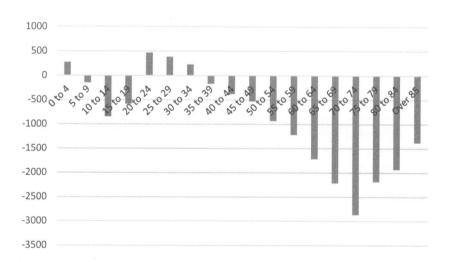

1.5 Episcopalian depletion, 1971–1981 (by 1971 age group)
Sources: Census of Population of Ireland, 1971, vol. 9 (1986), Table 8 and
Census of Population of Ireland, 1981, vol. 5 (1985), Table 7.

Departing British or Emigrating Irish?

The British military establishment of 1911 was very concentrated in a limited number of large garrisons, with almost 75 per cent stationed in just three counties. By contrast, only 610 army and navy personnel were stationed in the whole province of Connacht. Almost half the civil service was in Dublin and most of them were Catholic. Out of 8,041 civil service officers and clerks in the 26 counties in 1911, 3,915 were in Dublin city and county and 5,595 of them were Catholic.[39] Yet, some of the highest levels of Protestant decline are to be found in counties with little or no British administrative presence.[40] Robert E. Kennedy calculated native Protestant decline, making three assumptions about the number of foreign-born counted in Ireland in 1911. The assumptions were that none, half, or all foreigners were Protestants. All three assumptions resulted in a calculation of the same rate of native decline, which was also the same as total Protestant decline. From this Kennedy concluded that foreign-born Protestants declined at the same rate as native Protestants.[41]

Since a significant proportion of foreign-born Protestants in 1911 were British military and their dependants (about 25 per cent), almost all of whom left in 1922, it follows that the rate of decline in foreign-born civilian Protestants was lower than that of native Protestants. The occupational profile of British-born civilians, particularly those born in England and Wales, was primarily that of skilled and managerial groups.[42] In the census reports of both 1911 and 1926 there is a distinct sense of foreign-born, mostly British, workers filling skills gaps in parts of the Irish workforce. In 1911, 70 per cent of the civilian British-born population were Protestant.[43] With the British-born civilian community of 1926 showing very similar skills and job profiles to their 1911 compatriots,[44] it would be surprising if their religious profile were very different.

While the census reports of 1926 do not break down nationality by religion, the statisticians implicitly assumed that all foreign-born counted in every

[39] For numbers of civil servants and military in various counties and provinces, see *Census of Ireland, 1911. General Report*, 'Education of the People', Tables 29a and 30 and 'Occupations of the People'.

[40] *Saorstát Éireann: Census of Population, 1926*, vol. 3 (1929), Table 8B.

[41] Kennedy, *The Irish*, p. 120.

[42] *Saorstát Éireann: Census of Population, 1926*, vol. 10 (1934), chap. 4, pp. 49–57 and *Census of Ireland, 1911. General Report*, 'Occupations of the People'.

[43] Interrogation of census database: http://census.nationalarchives.ie/ (accessed 20 Oct. 2016).

[44] *Saorstát Éireann: Census of Population, 1926*, vol. 3 (1929), Table 15.

census since 1861 were Protestants.[45] Although they were certainly not correct in making this assumption, the percentage they came up with for native Protestant decline during the period 1911–26 was just about the same as for all Protestants. In doing so, they may have somewhat erratically predicted Robert E. Kennedy's observation that Protestant decline was principally native. Certainly, most of the British military who left were Protestants, but there is little sign of a matching outflow of foreign Protestant civilians. It is likely that the civilian outflow of Protestants was mainly Irish-born.

The Economy and Emigration

In the early 1920s, the Irish labour market was undoubtedly unbalanced. Large numbers of demobilised military had returned after the Great War. The loss of the spending power of the departing British administration was felt keenly in areas where they were stationed. The turmoil of revolution and civil war left the emergent Free State economy in a fragile condition. These factors might well have combined to stimulate heavy outmigration for economic reasons. Yet, the period 1911–26 was characterised by the lowest national rates of emigration since the Famine. Bielenberg supported his argument that the economy was a major reason for Protestant emigration with a table of Protestant decline in various occupations, examples of industrial decline, and some individual records of Protestants departing for economic reasons.[46] A comparison of employment changes between 1911 and 1926 in various occupations that includes both major religious groupings shows a very different picture (Table 1.6). In all these occupations, Protestant losses were consistently high, while Catholic numbers in the same professions mostly increased. It was an unlikely sort of economic downturn that affected an economically advantaged minority group like Protestants so severely but left the Catholic majority unscathed.

Emigration, Revolutionary Violence, and Regime Change

Historians also disagree about the pattern of Protestant emigration during this period. Bielenberg states that most Protestant emigration happened after 1920. Fitzpatrick emphasised that more Methodists left in the three years 1911–14 than between 1920 and 1923. However, the migration figures published in

---

[45] *Saorstát Éireann: Census of Population, 1926*, vol. 10 (1934), chap. 4, p. 46. They estimated the number of native Protestants in each census by subtracting *all* foreign-born from the total number of Protestants counted.

[46] Bielenberg, 'Exodus', p. 233.

Table 1.6 Occupational changes of Protestants and Catholics in Ireland, 1911–1926

Occupations	Protestants			Catholics		
	1911	1926	Change	1911	1926	Change
Barristers/Solicitors	807	516	-36.0%	895	840	-6.2%
Doctors	619	447	-27.8%	1,032	1,604	+55.4%
Dentists	239	176	-26.2%	261	360	+37.8%
Veterinary Surgeons	100	73	-26.8%	172	221	+28.4%
Civil Engineers/ Surveyors	566	352	-37.8%	615	626	+1.8%
Authors, Editors, Journalists	139	95	-31.5%	406	472	+16.2%
Teachers	2,786	2,095	-24.8%	12,588	14,107	+12.1%
Civil Service Officials/ Clerks	2,544 1,733		-31.9%	5,597	10,241	+83.0%

Sources: *Census of Ireland, 1911. General Report, with Tables and Appendix* [Cd. 6663], HC 1913, 'Area, Houses, and Population', Table 29 and 'Occupations of the People' (calculated for 26 counties); *Saorstát Éireann: Census of Population, 1926*, vol. 3 (1929), Table 17.

his Methodist study are gross rather than net, reflecting only those leaving rather than all migration traffic. Since migration is usually measured as the difference between those emigrating and those immigrating, the timing and volume of inward migration are also needed to formulate overall migration patterns of the period. Methodist records of transfers between southern and northern districts, which do reflect traffic in both directions, indicate a very different pattern of migration between north and south from that of the outward movement of Methodists to places overseas. Whereas gross migration overseas during the period 1911–14 (894) was greater than from 1920 to 1923 (793), net movement to the North of 202 from 1920 to 1923 was over six times higher than the 31 of the period from 1911 to 1914.[47]

Bielenberg suggests that Protestants dissatisfied with the new regime or escaping a depressed economy would have left at a higher rate before 1926 than after 1926. The economic argument is questionable, but the dissatisfaction argument undoubtedly has some validity. He concluded that, of 61,000 estimated civilian Protestant emigrants, between 2,000 and 16,000 left

[47] Fitzpatrick, *Descendancy*, p. 256 (Table 8.12).

'involuntarily'.[48] He had first estimated voluntary Protestant emigrants to be between 11.2 per cent and 14.5 per cent of total emigration between 1911 and 1926, with overall migration between 1911 and 1926 estimated at 405,029.[49] He thus arrived at a range of 45,000 to 59,000 for voluntary Protestant migration, leaving a residual range of between 2,000 and 16,000 involuntary migrants. In doing so he erroneously included in his 'voluntary' Protestant migrants a percentage of all departing British military and their dependants, and a percentage of Irish Great War dead of all religions. Calculating voluntary Protestant migration more correctly at between 11.2 per cent and 14.5 per cent of 'normal' migration[50] yields a range of total voluntary Protestant migration between 38,600 and 50,000. It follows that Bielenberg's algorithm should yield a range of involuntary Protestant emigration of 11,000 to 22,400. Bielenberg's use of 1926–36 comparative emigration rates as a model for the period 1911–26 is also questionable. Pre-independence Ireland was a very different place from that of the 1930s. Emigration declined significantly during the Great War.

Table 1.4 estimates civilian Protestant emigration from 1911 to 1926 at 67,500, of which some 40,000 might be deemed excessive. This represents the number who migrated for reasons ranging from dissatisfaction with regime change through to fear of violence and to actual violence against their person or property. Quite how many fell into the 'dissatisfaction' and how many fell into the 'fear' categories are questions that may never be accurately established, as most emigrants did not leave a record of why they left.

Conclusions

Some accounts of long-term Protestant decline paint a picture of a minority that had been a shrinking proportion of the overall population for generations, with decline during the period 1911–26 just a continuation of this long-term trend. This ignores the very similar rate of decline of Catholics in the decades before 1911. And nobody has ever suggested a problem with Catholic fertility. Fitzpatrick concluded from Methodist records that infertility rather than emigration was the principal reason for southern Protestant decline. An alternative view of Methodist records is that recruitment matched or bettered the combined effects of defection and mortality, while Methodist decline

---

[48] Bielenberg, 'Exodus', p. 233.
[49] *Saorstát Éireann: Census of Population, 1926*, vol. 1 (1928), Table 1.
[50] Kennedy, *The Irish*, p. 79. He estimated 'normal' or civilian emigration for all religions from the 26 counties for 1911 to 1926 at about 345,000, by subtracting Great War dead of all religions and British military and dependants from overall migration figures.

followed the pattern of Methodist emigration throughout the 15-year period with uncanny precision.

Before 1911, Protestant birth rates would appear to have kept pace with or exceeded mortality rates. The relatively 'aged Protestant population' that might have signified high natural decline was not a feature of southern Irish demographics until after 1911.[51] Long-term demographic collapse was not a primary cause of 1911–26 Protestant decline. Bielenberg rightly highlights the complexity of motives for native Protestant emigration during this period. He draws attention to particularly high levels of Protestant decline in the western counties. His arguments that it was an exodus primarily fuelled by harsh economic conditions are less convincing, as the economic downturn he describes appears to have affected Protestants far more seriously than Catholics. But, when he comes to estimating the impact of revolutionary violence and what he termed 'involuntary migration', his calculation is mathematically wrong, resulting in a significant underestimate. Delaney states that, while Protestants may not have been discriminated against as a religious group, there were some aspects of early Free State policy, particularly those relating to the promotion of Gaelic language and culture, which discriminated against them as a cultural group.[52] According to Eugenio Biagini, the European experience is that discrimination against minorities, whether ethnic, cultural, or religious, has tended to occur at a local rather than a national and official level.[53] The collapse of Protestant marriage numbers in 1922 to 1923 coincided with a time when there was limited government control and less law and order. Annual returns of Protestant marriage numbers from 1911 onwards point to most Protestant decline of the intercensal period occurring after 1920. Methodist population movements between south and north display a similar characteristic. Both imply a relationship between Protestant emigration levels and the upheavals of warfare and political change. The events of the turbulent period contributed to a profound disruption of the civilian Protestant community of Ireland. Decline through emigration was over double what might be expected for purely economic reasons. What remained was a relatively aged Protestant population with high mortality rates and low birth rates. Declining numbers were the norm in succeeding decades. A long shadow had been cast on the Protestant community of independent Ireland.

[51] See Table 1.2.
[52] Delaney, *Demography*, p. 82.
[53] *Irish Times*, 7 Feb. 2015.

CHAPTER II

Voting to Maintain the Union in 1918: 'One of the strongest pillars upon which they stood'

Elaine Callinan

The Great War ended on 11 November 1918 and Lloyd George's 'war party' took advantage of Britain's victory by setting a general election date for 14 December before the disruption of demobilisation could be felt. Parliament was dissolved on 25 November, allowing for an intensive three-week propaganda campaign in Ireland for 80 seats (including universities). The 1918 election was the first modern election in the British Isles, with mass media-style propaganda campaigns, systemisation of electoral practice, and democratisation of the electorate. Running contemporaneously to war and revolution in this era were political struggles that were equally crucial to the transformation of politics in Ireland. As 1918 was the last all-island election, this chapter aims to assess the political propagandising of unionism across Ireland.

Unionists were galvanised to defend the Union and demonstrate their loyalty to the Crown, and they organised to secure electoral majorities in their strongholds. The vastly expanded electorate in 1918 necessitated more sophisticated propaganda campaigns to inspire and motivate heretofore electorally dormant voices.[1] Southern Unionists too, like their Nationalist counterparts, sought to persuade and at times manipulate opinion to draw support for their policies.

Electioneering

By 1918, Unionists had devolved candidate selection to Unionist Associations, but in Ulster the process was rigorously monitored from the centre. The Ulster Unionist Council (UUC) provided a permanent supervisory and active electoral machine and the Irish Unionist Alliance (IUA) – founded in 1891 out of the Irish Loyal and Patriotic Union – aimed to unite unionists to represent

---

[1] The Representation of the People Act 1918 tripled the electorate in Ireland from 700,000 to nearly 2,000,000.

unionism on an all-Ireland basis. However, the formation of the UUC in 1905, which was technically part of the IUA, saw the beginning of a division between north and south within Irish Unionism. The IUA remained an organisation for the southern provinces with the UUC concentrating on Ulster.[2] For the 1918 general election candidates were nominated by Unionist Associations in almost every Ulster constituency, but in the southern provinces there were many areas with no Unionist representatives.[3] Across Leinster, Munster, and Connaught candidate selection and electoral support was mainly drawn from the Protestant population. Unionist Associations in these provinces followed a geographic pattern of Protestant population density, and many supporters were farmers, small business owners, or Church of Ireland clergymen. Unionists in the three southern provinces were never able to attain mass party status because local branches varied in strength. Unionist support was limited to certain sections of the population, described by Alan O'Day as being usually 'Protestant, anglicised, propertied and aristocratic'.[4] Speaking of the unionist population in the House of Commons in 1919, Maurice Dockrell (elected for Rathmines in 1918) remarked that:

> this House seems to have been constantly reminded that ... outside Ulster there did not exist such a thing as a Unionist – in fact ... Unionists were almost as extinct as the Dodo ... they are so few in number. Perhaps some Honourable Members will be surprised to hear that I am the sole representative in this House of about 350,000 Unionists.[5]

In Dublin, the Unionist Association met in their offices at 10 Leinster Street in late November 1918 to select candidates for a number of constituencies. John Good, a building contractor, was unanimously selected for the Pembroke Division; Simon Maddock, member of the Executive Committee of the IUA, honorary secretary of the South County Dublin Unionist Association, and a Justice of the Peace, was selected for the St Patrick's Division (although he

---

[2] In 1919, the IUA finally split apart with the founding of the breakaway Unionist Anti-Partition League. The Ulster Unionist Party (UUP) continued to operate in Northern Ireland.

[3] Unionists did not contest in the following Ulster constituencies: Armagh South, Belfast (Falls, St Anne's, Shankill, Victoria – although a Unionist Labour candidate often contested), Cavan, Donegal, and Monaghan South. In the three southern provinces unionists only contested in Cork, Dublin, and East Wicklow.

[4] Alan O'Day, *Reactions to Irish Nationalism, 1865–1914* (London, 1987), pp. 369–71.

[5] Hansard, HC, vol. 114, cols 126–7 (24 Mar. 1919). Dockrell's figures are his own and obviously include all unionists/Protestants in Ireland regardless of voting age. His number is about 50,000 higher than calculations based on the southern Protestant population in the 1911 census.

withdrew before the election); and Henry Hanna, a commercial and labour lawyer, was unanimously chosen for the St Stephen's Green Division.[6] A meeting of the South Dublin Unionist Association, held in the Shelbourne Hotel on 22 November, approved Maurice Dockrell and Sir Thomas Robinson as candidates after their selection by the Executive Council for the Rathmines and South Dublin Divisions respectively. Unionists in Cork city selected two candidates, Daniel Williams and Thomas Farrington, and Alexander Keane came forward as a Unionist candidate for East Wicklow. Candidate selection afforded an opportunity for press propaganda as the nomination and selection processes received editorial attention (even if the candidate later withdrew). For instance, the *Irish Times* on 3 December 1918 published an extensive article on the selection of Dockrell, referring to him as 'an able business man, a generous and fair employer, and a hard worker and organiser in many good causes'.[7]

In 1918, the devolution of control to local organisations worked for Unionists; however, the UUC's political focus was primarily on Ulster. The adroit supervision of candidate selection from a centralised system brought success for Unionists in Ulster. In the south many decisions were taken by local associations, though they did adhere to the overall Unionist directive to support the Union. As will be discussed later, southern unionists challenged the focus on Ulster. Candidate selection was only one aspect of electioneering in the drive to capture votes. Raising funds and incorporating a variety of propaganda methods and themes also proved necessary for a party's potential electoral success.

During the third Home Rule crisis, unionists had risen to the challenge of protecting the Union against the threat of Home Rule to mount an aggressive propaganda campaign by escalating appeals for funds. The anti-Home Rule income had been expended in the two-year battle from 1912 to 1914 by generating propaganda in newspapers and books, and creating postcards, posters, pamphlets, banners, film, badges, and a host of ephemeral items.[8] The mastermind behind the anti-Home Rule propaganda campaigns was Sir James Craig MP, who had gleaned expert marketing techniques and business acumen from his family's Dunville whiskey business. These fundraising skills and marketing abilities were rekindled for elections and managed by the UUC Standing Committee. This was the organisation which directed the path and policy of unionism until 1920.[9] Professional, university educated candidates

---

[6] *Irish Times*, 23 and 25 Nov. 1918.

[7] *Irish Times*, 3 and 9 Dec. 1918.

[8] A.T.Q. Stewart, *The Ulster Crisis: Resistance to Home Rule, 1912–14* (London, 1967); John Killen, *John Bull's Famous Circus: Ulster History through the Postcard, 1905–1985* (Dublin, 1985); Ewan Morris, *Our Own Devices: National Symbols and Political Conflict in Twentieth-Century Ireland* (Dublin, 2005).

[9] John F. Harbinson, *The Ulster Unionist Party 1882–1973* (Belfast, 1973), pp. 40–1.

within unionism rallied the political and business elite of Ulster who donated large sums to ensure votes favoured Unionist candidates. Unlike nationalists – advanced and moderate – who petitioned for funds piecemeal, unionists were financed by a small number of wealthy individuals and commercial interests that rallied fellow elites to donate to the cause.

To supplement larger donations, unionists, like other parties, relied on local clubs to provide revenue and disseminate specific local propaganda. By 1915, there were 369 clubs on the register and 133 clubs had sent in returns of officers for 1915. A further three clubs later joined bringing the total to 372.[10] A UUC meeting of 30 April 1919 stated there was a total of 372 clubs still in existence (although in the interim of 1917 and 1919 four were stated to have been wound up and two were described as virtually non-existent).[11] While some of these funds were possibly allocated to southern electoral propaganda that held universal unionist messages, southern candidates undoubtedly made contributions from their own finances. Many were involved in business. Maurice Dockrell, for instance, ran the Dockrell family builders' providers, John Good ran J. & P. Good, a large and successful firm, which for many years held the contract for maintaining the government's public buildings, and Simon Maddock was a director of public companies.

Appeals for funds by southern Unionist candidates were made in the *Irish Times*, such as that by the Cork city candidates who set up a fund to 'assist in defraying the expenses of the election'.[12] Funds were also received from the Unionist Central Office in London who claimed that they had made provision for certain contests in Ireland to the value of £2,143, which was the remainder of a full donation of £4,000. This assistance was provided for the expenses of contests in Dublin and was issued through Arthur Samuels, MP for Dublin University. There were, however, occasional challenges to the allocation of these funds. For instance, the Central Office disputed having to reimburse the election expenses of Alexander Parker Keane in East Wicklow who had been defeated by Sinn Féin's Seán Etchingham by 3,316 votes. Unionist voters in the constituencies of Bray and Greystones had polled well up to 2 o'clock on election day, but nationalist voters had come out in force after working hours in Enniskerry, Newtown, and other rural districts leading to the defeat of Parker Keane.[13] The Central Office complaint was that they had not been consulted on the contest in East Wicklow.[14]

---

[10] UUC Minutes, 23 Feb. 1914 (PRONI, D1327/1/2).
[11] Minutes of Meeting of the Executive Committee of the Unionist Clubs Council, 25 Feb. 1914, 26 Mar. 1915, and 30 Apr. 1919 (PRONI, D1327/1/2).
[12] *Irish Times*, 27 Nov. 1918.
[13] *Freeman's Journal*, 16 Dec. 1918.
[14] Unionist Central Office, London to Edward Carson, 9 Apr. 1919 (PRONI, D1507/A/29/26).

Unionists were determined to secure victory mainly in Ulster constituencies, particularly where Protestants were in the majority. In the three southern provinces, as noted above, Unionists entered contests only in Cork (2 candidates), East Wicklow (1 candidate), the Pembroke, Rathmines, St Patrick's, and St Stephen's Green constituencies of Dublin, Dublin South, and Dublin University (2 candidates).[15] Therefore, finances collected only needed to be expended among 26 Ulster constituencies and eight southern constituencies.[16] Electioneering and propaganda campaigns required considerable financial outlay and the fundraising success of unionists afforded the opportunity to fund more extravagant campaigns. The Central Council absorbed the cost of creating and disseminating universal unionist propaganda, such as rules or decrees, to local constituencies and candidates during elections and provided advice on propaganda methods, but local associations also raised funds to disseminate propaganda for their candidates.

Speeches were a key method of propaganda and a crucial factor was personality and delivery to ensure positive audience perceptions. Edward Carson was the key spokesperson for unionism in Ireland, and according to William O'Brien his angular and austere appearance was 'as inexpressive as a jagged hatchet'. Yet his sombre and sober countenance assumed charismatic proportions for unionists.[17] He had assertively piloted unionists through the Home Rule crisis of 1912 to 1914 and, according to his contemporary George Peel, 'the power which he exercised in that quarter was scarcely otherwise than royal and the allegiance according to him might have been envied by kings'.[18] Cartoonists in this era satirised the monarchical tendencies alleged by Carson's political opponents, who sometimes disdainfully referred to him as 'King Carson'.[19] Nonetheless, his indomitable personality created an authority that continued to bear down on opponents in election campaigns in 1918, and drew crowds of supporters to public meetings. Ulster's opposition to the Home Rule bill had activated the threat of force in the face of dissent by the British government. Carson responded to these reproaches by promoting defiance to

---

[15] *Weekly Irish Times*, 30 Nov. 1918.

[16] This figure includes Queen's University in Belfast, but does not include independent or labour unionists.

[17] In Conor Cruise O'Brien (ed.), *The Shaping of Modern Ireland* (London, 1960), p. 87. On charismatic authority, see Steve Bruce, *God Save Ulster* (Oxford, 1986), pp. 199–200; Ann Ruth Willner, *The Spellbinders: Charismatic Political Leadership* (London, 1984).

[18] Bruce, *God Save Ulster*, pp. 211–13; James H. Allister and Peter Robinson, *Edward Carson: Man of Action* (Belfast, 1985), p. 15; George Peel, *The Reign of Sir Edward Carson* (London, 1914), pp. 3, 9.

[19] Joseph P. Finnan, 'Punch's Portrayal of Redmond, Carson and the Irish Question, 1910–1918', *Irish Historical Studies*, 33/132 (2003), pp. 424–51.

the existing Westminster government while unionists kept the province 'in trust for the Empire and under the king'.[20]

Carson's speeches reduced complexities to a series of points that culminated with the key issue upon which action was needed. The plight of the Protestant community in Ulster in the face of the Home Rule threat formed the opening or backdrop, which was regularly followed by the claim that there should be 'no coercion of Ulster'. Arguments were made in the form of a question, with a one-word answer that inspired an audience to react. For instance, in his address to the annual meeting of the UUC in November 1918, Carson theatrically unpicked the idea of 'self-determination' by asking should there be 'self-determination by the South and West of Ireland of the destinies of Ulster?' and answering 'Never!', to which there was an instantaneous response in 'cheers' by the audience.[21] Carson closed this speech, as he did others, by championing the advantages of the Union, claiming that 'the people of this country were the spoiled children of the United Kingdom' and that they (unionists) had made the mistake of not taking their share in government. He did not need to use the words 'vote unionist', they were already there in the closing argument.[22]

Unionists tirelessly argued that the government was attempting to pass an unconstitutional act and that the response had to be 'no Home Rule'. For Carson, unionism represented the values he held in esteem: honour, decency, integrity in public life, justice, and the civilising force of the Empire.[23] He maintained that there were fundamental differences between Protestants and Catholics that were 'deep rooted, historical questions, traditions, ideas and race too which you cannot get rid of'.[24] These differences were too severe to coalesce under one Irish parliament and for a British government to impose its existence was a 'nefarious conspiracy'.[25] His rhetoric often comprised urgent directness of action, but he was rarely patronising. Unionists were persuaded into collusion in his planned schemes both against Home Rule and in attaining votes through his regular use of the first person plural 'we' or 'ourselves'. This provided logic and collective motivation, but the disadvantage was that alternative perspectives and perceptions were limited. In his speech

[20] *The Times*, 15 Sep. 1913.
[21] *Anglo-Celt*, 23 Nov. 1918.
[22] *Irish Times*, 16 Nov. 1918; *Anglo-Celt*, 23 Nov. 1918. See also H. Montgomery Hyde, *Carson* (London, 1987), p. 23.
[23] Andrew Gailey, 'King Carson: An Essay on the Invention of Leadership', *Irish Historical Studies*, 30/117 (1996), p. 70.
[24] Ian Colvin, *The Life of Lord Carson*, vol. 2 (London, 1934), pp. 116–17, 121.
[25] Carson was referring to Herbert Asquith's government in this instance: Montgomery Hyde, *Carson*, pp. 290–1, 315; Colvin, *Life of Edward Carson*, vol. 2, p. 85.

to the annual UUC meeting in Belfast, Carson told his audience that 'we cannot afford to wait in a great community like this' for government answers, and stated: 'let us ... have the legislation that is suited to us'.[26] There was no need to change opinion amongst the supporters of unionism, but this form of rhetoric to swing borderline votes was weak and entirely impracticable for those outside the collective 'we'. Carson, however, appealed mainly to those who adhered to unionist beliefs and sense of identity, so by drawing on the collective he attempted to orchestrate feelings of inclusivity and devotedness to a common cause across the entire island.

However, Carson's speeches occasionally caused concern for southern unionists. The letters to the editor section of the *Irish Times* in 1918 divulge the variances in southern unionist opinion. One example came on the issue of partition and criticised the 'entire policy' of the speech delivered by Carson to the UUC in 1918 because it was 'limited to Ulster' with 'no thought of the southern unionists'. Trepidation was voiced on whether 'Ulster, on the question of Home Rule, has definitely adopted the policy of "ourselves alone" or whether in the future ... Ulster unionists will stand shoulder to shoulder with their unionist brethren in the South'.[27] A week or so later another writer ('A Woman Voter') disagreed that Carson had 'abandoned us'. The difficulty within southern unionism, it was claimed, was that they 'were scattered and unable to affect any real stand or return any member to represent them in parliament'. Carson's maxim, it was argued, was to 'concentrate on Ulster, knowing that practical work for the Union' would be achieved and therefore 'Home Rule Ireland would never accept a division of the island'. Carson was likened to a bridge player holding an immensely strong hand, whereas southern unionists held weak and scattered cards. With the Sinn Féin opponent on one side and home rulers on the other, a strong hand was necessary to gain a 'grand slam' to culminate in 'closer connection with Great Britain and her colonies'.[28]

Speeches and addresses by southern unionist candidates regularly appeared in the *Irish Times*. This was the forum through which southern unionists could appeal to supporters for votes. Unionists regularly contributed to and received editorial comment in the Dublin *Daily Express*, *Morning Mail*, the *Daily Irish Telegraph*, the *Belfast Telegraph* (published in Londonderry to cover the western counties of Ulster until 1951), *The Irish Post* (which catered for a largely Protestant readership in and around Cavan), *Carlow Sentinel*, *Kilkenny Moderator*, and the *Waterford Standard*, to name a few. Classified advertisements were regularly used to deliver a short, pertinent, and effective message, and many candidates used their local newspaper.

---

[26] *Anglo-Celt*, 23 Nov. 1918.

[27] *Irish Times*, 16 Nov. 1918 (letter to the editor from J.H. Nunn, Dublin).

[28] *Irish Times*, 29 Nov. 1918.

These advertisements usually contained a simple message that could be conveyed using the least amount of words and space. For instance, the Unionist candidate John Good purchased a one column × one inch classified advertisement that appealed to voters in Dublin's Pembroke Division, which simply said: 'Voters! Our Empire Needs Your Help. Do Your Duty. Support Law and Order. And vote for Good'. Classified advertisements also appeared within the interior of newspapers, and political candidates favoured these over the front page because the paid-for space appeared more like editorial.

The advertising theories that emerged in the early 1900s and Great War propaganda also led to an understanding of how to control the behaviour of consumers, and how to elicit emotions such as fear, rage, and love to activate purchase.[29] Posters in 1918 frequently adopted the parlance of personal interaction by using the second person singular or plural and employed familiar colloquial idiom. In addressing audiences directly there was an invitation to become active, and this created a more intimate atmosphere, similar to a two-way conversation. Taking a brief example from election propaganda in 1918, we see Unionists attempt to elicit an emotional response by issuing a poster entitled *The Two Irelands. Facts. Not Fiction*, where the question posed was: 'will the British Public stand by Ulster, whose sons stood by them, or will they support Sinn Féin Ireland, which stabbed Britain in the back, and has such a ghastly record of disloyalty and crime?'[30] War sentiments were still raw and the intent behind this appeal was to stir those feelings and elicit a sense of conscience towards those who supported or died in the war effort to garner support for the unionist cause.

Posters were supplemented by handbills, postcards, and the personal canvass. The door-to-door canvass was an essential component for checking the register of electors, for face-to-face contact by a candidate or a candidate's representative, and to ascertain whether a voter could be relied upon to attend the poll. Unionists believed that an early, effective canvass 'by means of earnest and intelligent voluntary workers is by far the most powerful aid to success'. The IUA in southern Ireland applied for canvassers in the *Irish Times* for divisions where they ran candidates and urged that 'no time be lost in offering and undertaking this valuable voluntary service'. They also appealed to the 'large number of women electors' whose assistance 'can help in canvassing

[29] R.E. Fancher, *Pioneers of Psychology*, 2nd edn (New York, 1990); D.P. Schultz and S.E. Schultz, *A History of Modern Psychology*, 9th edn (Belmont, CA, 2008). The relevance of these studies to consumer advertising is evident in the fact that the J. Walter Thompson advertising agency in New York City hired Watson in 1920. Pavlov's experiments conducted research on how animals learned to respond to a conditioned stimulus.

[30] *Sinn Féin 'Guarantees' 'Safeguards' for Ulster*, c.1918 (PRONI, D1327/20/4/142, UC 114); *The Two Irelands, Facts Not Fiction*, c.1918 (PRONI, D1327/20/4/142, UC 132).

and on the polling day'.[31] Lock and Harris argue that many voters vote for the same party as they have in the past because a voter's views on what parties stand for remain remarkably stable.[32] Therefore the personal canvass offered opportunities to suggest a viable alternative to fixed opinions.

Symbols also worked well and were a cheap propaganda exercise, although their creation was time-consuming and required manpower. Unionist identity and convictions were frequently embodied in the Union flag. For instance, during Dockrell's nomination to represent unionists in Rathmines, Dublin, one of his supporters reminded the audience that 'the Union Jack was the flag for which Sir Maurice Dockrell sent three sons to fight [in the Great War], and it was for that flag that Mr Samuels sacrificed his only son'.[33] Union colours were represented on pin badges, such as one styled like a rosette with the words 'Union is Strength'. The reverse side marked this as a series of 'no surrender' badges that could be obtained from 'all newsagents or direct, post free' from the printers.[34] Southern unionists were more limited than Ulster unionists in their displays of public decorative bunting during the general election, but the pin badge was worn by candidates and their supporters. The clever location or shrewd placement of symbols and flags carried an electoral message to wider audiences. Automobiles and other vehicles were used creatively by all during election campaigns, being adorned with flags and party colours, and the IUA appealed for 'horse-drawn vehicles or motors' to be donated to the southern Unionists' campaign to transport the candidates, and ferry voters to polling booths on election day.[35]

Nationalist election speakers laid claim to the heroes of earlier Irish nationalism: Wolfe Tone, Emmet, Parnell, Davitt, and O'Connell, as well as to the memory of the 1798 rebellion and Grattan's parliament. During his campaign in Waterford, John Redmond maintained that with the advent of Home Rule 'they now had an opportunity Parnell or O'Connell never had – that no one had since the days of Grattan'.[36] Unionists, on the other hand, to demonstrate the current programme of inclusivity within their agenda and

[31] *Irish Times*, 6 Dec. 1918. In a later election manual they also appealed for women's support and votes: *Unionist Central Office Parliamentary Election Manual* (1921), p. 67 (PRONI, D1327/20/4/148).

[32] Phil Harris and Andrew Lock, 'Machiavellian Network Marketing: Corporate Political Lobby and Industrial Marketing in the UK', *Journal of Marketing Management*, 12/4 (1996), pp. 313–28.

[33] *Irish Times*, 3 Dec. 1918.

[34] No Surrender Badge by Wm. Strain & Sons Ltd, Belfast, 'Union is Strength'. Wording on reverse also states that 'special wording supplied for unionist demonstrations at moderate prices' (Elaine Callinan, private collection).

[35] *Irish Times*, 6 Dec. 1918.

[36] *Waterford News*, 22 Mar. 1918.

to dispute IPP claims for a reconstitution of Grattan's parliament, maintained that Grattan's parliament was a 'so-called Irish Parliament [that] was a gathering of representatives of the aristocracy and the Anglican ascendancy' where 'the Irish people were not represented at all'. They argued that this parliament passed 32 coercion acts which ultimately led to the 1798 rebellion, and what saved Ireland was the Act of Union.[37] Unionists even refuted the existence of an Irish nation prior to the English conquest. Even during the Druidic or the Christian periods, their pamphlets alleged, the country had never been whole or undivided. Ireland 'has had many kings and rulers at one time' and that it was only under British rule that 'Ireland ever approached unity'.[38]

Imperial rhetoric was a feature of unionist propaganda during the Great War and continued throughout the general election campaign. Arguments insisted that the British Empire embodied civilisation and therefore 'in all future legislation the democracy of Ulster is to march on hand in hand with the democracy of Great Britain'. During the 1918 general election, unionist voters were reminded that 'they took up arms to retain their citizenship in a United Kingdom and an Empire which had proved itself in the war the greatest asset of civilization and freedom that the world had ever seen', and that when war broke out 'their duty was to march their men into the camp of the empire'.[39] The moral justification for winning at the polls was to remember the 'work and sacrifice' of the 'brave men' and 'those at home who mourned because they would never again look upon the faces of the brave men who had done so much for us'.[40] The rhetoric of empire was merged with that of war sacrifice and upheld by southern Unionist candidates in the general election campaign. Dockrell stated that he was the candidate 'who represented the people who shed their blood for the Empire, the people who, during the war, had fought for all they were worth'. He was a 'strong advocate for the maintenance of the Union' because 'it was one of the strongest pillars upon which they stood'.[41] In Dublin's Pembroke Division John Good stated that 'peace' could only be attained in this post-war election by ensuring that the 'commerce of our Empire', which had 'been sacrificed in order to win the war', had to be 'restored and remodelled' so that 'our Empire may be able to hold its own in competition in the various markets of the world'. The Empire, according to Good, was the only model to rebuild Ireland's

---

[37] *Some Facts about the Union and the Irish Parliament*, c.1918 (PRONI, D1327/20/4/142, UC 101).

[38] *America and Ireland, What American Protestants say*, c.1918 (PRONI, D1327/20/4/142, UC 121).

[39] *Anglo-Celt*, 23 Nov. 1918.

[40] *Irish Times*, 15 Nov. 1918.

[41] *Irish Times*, 23 Nov. 1918.

industry as 'these important matters would require a large sum of money'.[42] Sir Thomas Robinson held that unionists 'should be more confirmed than ever that their one and only policy was to stand together under the flag of the British Empire'.[43]

The armistice in November 1918 ended the threat of conscription, but the after-effects continued into the general election, and through to the 1920 local elections, albeit with reduced import and mention. In complete contrast to nationalist media, unionist publications and leaders had upheld unconditional support for conscription. The *Irish Times* stated that 'the whole unionist population of Ireland will accept conscription'. The Church of Ireland archbishops stated that 'Ireland's sons' had been 'omitted from the call' when conscription had been applied to England and Scotland, and that this 'would have been readily obeyed two years ago'. They called for prayer 'with special urgency that God will bless our arms and save our country in this grave hour of national danger'.[44] Carson had maintained that conscription shared the war burden evenly, and that it was the only way to make every man take his fair share in the duties and privileges of British citizenship. He professed to being 'ashamed' about the much reduced Irish divisions that needed replacements because of those who had been slaughtered by the enemies of Britain.[45] In a general election speech he referred to his efforts to include Ireland in conscription in 1916, but that Ulster was 'besmirched because they had allowed themselves to be dragged at the heels of the Nationalist Party in the South and West'.[46] The *Church of Ireland Gazette* and the *Ulster Guardian* believed conscription should not be a religious issue 'as between Protestants and Roman Catholics', but rather it was an issue of political standing as to whether people are nationalist or unionist.[47]

During by-elections and the general election campaign, the IPP and unionists continuously vilified Sinn Féin's post-Easter Rising rhetoric. Ulster unionists, according to Buckland, viewed the Rising with some complacency. Others found humour in the rebellion. Adam Duffin, the old liberal unionist, likened the Rising to a 'comic opera founded on the Wolf Tone fiasco a hundred years ago' and acerbically hoped that the rebels had captured Birrell, the chief secretary.[48] Many saw the Rising as an act of predictable treachery and proof that nationalists were disloyal at heart, regardless of war-time enlistment. A

---

[42] *Irish Times*, 11 Dec. 1918 [speech by John Good].
[43] *Irish Times*, 23 Nov. 1918.
[44] *Irish Times*, 18 Apr. 1918 [letter from archbishops of Armagh and Dublin].
[45] Geoffrey Lewis, *Carson: The Man Who Divided Ireland* (London, 2005), pp. 80, 180–2.
[46] *Anglo-Celt*, 23 Nov. 1918.
[47] *Church of Ireland Gazette*, 26 Apr. 1918 and *Ulster Guardian*, 29 Apr. 1917.
[48] Adam Duffin to D. Duffin, 25 Apr. 1916 (PRONI, MIC 127/17); Patrick Buckland,

unionist handbill demanded to know whether loyalists should trust to 'the "common sense" of those guilty of the madness of Easter Week 1916'.[49] A letter to the editor of the *Irish Times* from T.S. Lindsay of Malahide, County Dublin, who claimed to be a true Irishman 'proud of Ireland, loving Ireland, intensely anxious to promote her prosperity in every way', stated that the military had not 'yielded to the superior strength of the attackers' of the Union. The author, who claimed not to be 'the mouthpiece of any party or organisation' and who wished only to express the views he believed were 'shared by very many', asserted that the Rising proved that a Dublin parliament would mean 'absolute ruin to our unfortunate country'.[50]

Unionists sought to gain votes by highlighting the material benefits of the Union. Augustine Birrell, chief secretary during the Home Rule crisis, had pointed out that Irishmen received over £1 million more in benefits, mainly for old age pensions and land purchase, than they paid in taxes. Unionists repeatedly promoted this argument. Housing concerns instigated debate and passion during the 1920 local elections. A letter to the *Limerick Leader* condemned 'the wretched housing of the working classes, and the "scourge of profiteering"'. High rates were killing the building trade and paralysing the investor. The solution proffered was to 'be our own landlords by purchasing our own houses' to have 'a direct interest in keeping down the rates'.[51] In the South Dublin Parliamentary Division, the Unionist Sir Thomas Robinson highlighted that 'there were other questions of great importance' and those were the 'housing of the working classes and of the poor'. Dockrell promised to ensure the 'betterment of the working classes'.[52]

Unionists, however, denied claims that the country was over-taxed, and denied that a separate legislature would benefit the Irish economy. According to a 1918 handbill they claimed that Ireland under the Union had been permitted to have a separate Exchequer until 1817 and during this time the national debt rose from £28 million to £147 million. An end to this insolvency only arrived when the exchequers were united and Great Britain accepted responsibility for the debt. They argued that the theory of over-taxation in Ireland had only been invented to justify financial proposals for Home Rule, starting with Gladstone's bill in 1886.[53] Other unionists highlighted that the great problem facing industry was reconstructing and reorganising due to

Irish Unionism II: Ulster Unionism and the Origins of Northern Ireland, 1886–1922 (Dublin, 1973), p. 105.

[49] *Sinn Féin 'Guarantees' 'Safeguards' for Ulster.*

[50] *Irish Times*, 18 Mar. 1918.

[51] *Limerick Leader*, 16 Jan. 1920.

[52] *Irish Times*, 23 Nov. 1918.

[53] *Has Ireland Been Robbed by England?* c.1918 (PRONI, D1327/20/4/142, UC 111).

the war.[54] The priority, they claimed, should be the development of Irish industries, reform of primary education, and the extension of technical and university education.[55] The completion of land purchase through the Land Acts was a paramount concern to sustain prices to ensure a proper return to farmers. Unionists warned that if Ireland separated from the British Empire and obtained a republic then there would be 'no markets for cattle and produce'. In Cork City, Daniel Williams argued that a vote for Sinn Féin would disenfranchise Cork's important commercial and industrial centre, so the 'strong protecting arm of Great Britain' was necessary.[56]

In 1912, the formation of a Home Rule parliament in Dublin seemed almost tangible, but by 1918 all had changed. Unionists, with their belief that the Union was 'the constitutional form best designed to protect Irish Protestants from subjugation to a Catholic minority', refused to accept a Dublin parliament.[57] Unionism, particularly in Ulster, swelled into aggressive repudiation of any form of Home Rule. Unionist propaganda created the impression that Ulster was firmly Protestant and unionist. As Buckland states, this was not the case as only the county borough of Belfast and the counties Antrim, Armagh, Down, and Londonderry (including the city) had Protestant majorities.[58] Furthermore, unionism was not a homogeneous entity across the island because the position and concerns of southern unionists differed. As leading IPP MP T.P. O'Connor remarked in a letter to John Dillon in 1916, there was a 'strong protest of the southern unionists against any form of partition', which made the solution of temporary exclusion 'more difficult than ever'.[59]

Population counts and tax contribution comparisons between Ulster and the other three provinces were published to highlight that Ulster paid more and that Ulster was 35 per cent more valuable than Munster and Connaught combined. Ulster unionists, mainly through the voice of Carson, demanded that partition would be permanent because of the commercial, industrial, and social position of Belfast and Ulster compared with the rest of Ireland.[60] He regularly maintained that 'we in Ulster will never give up our freedom and our liberty for any man'. This point was restated by southern Unionists who proclaimed (often in their *Irish Independent* advertisements) that the 'true interests of this country are best served by a steadfast maintenance for the whole of Ireland of the Legislative Union'. Henry Hanna voiced opposition to partition, which 'would be disastrous to the interests of Southern Unionists'.

---

[54] *Irish Times*, 29 Nov. 1918.
[55] *Irish Times*, 29 Nov. 1918.
[56] *Irish Times*, 10 Dec. 1918.
[57] David Fitzpatrick, *The Two Irelands, 1912–1939* (Oxford, 1998), p. 24.
[58] Buckland, *Ulster Unionism II*, p. 93.
[59] T.P. O'Connor to John Dillon, 31 Oct. 1916 (TCD, MS 6741/355).
[60] *Ulster and Ireland*, c.1918 (PRONI, D1327/20/4/142, UC 120).

Dockrell bound Ireland's interests with those of Great Britain and would 'oppose any measure involving the partition of Ireland'.[61]

Initially, all sides had held the opinion that Ireland must remain undivided, but as the expected short world war dragged on constitutional nationalists inclined towards a temporary compromise. Sinn Féin believed abstention from Westminster was the 'only logical and long-called-for protest against the Union'. The IPP utterly rejected Sinn Féin policy and attempted to mollify both unionists and nationalists in Ulster by insisting on a policy of consent.

Results

Did unionists convince voters in the counties they hoped to hold after partition, and were they successful in any other areas of Ireland? Did they appeal to those voters newly enfranchised because of the Representation of the People Act 1918? The election returned 73 seats for Sinn Féin, 35 for Unionists, one independent Unionist, and six IPP MPs (seven if T.P. O'Connor's Liverpool seat is taken into account). The total electorate in contested constituencies in 1918 was 1,462,895.[62] The total valid poll for the 80 seats (including universities) in county and borough constituencies across the provinces was 1,045,539, taking spoiled and absent voters into account.[63]

There were 21 triangular contests in the general election: seven in Leinster and 14 in Ulster, where the battle was usually between Sinn Féin, IPP, and Unionist candidates. These contests provided 69 candidates in total. A triangular contest in three of the four Dublin constituencies saw Unionists contend against Nationalists. Sinn Féin's victory was comprehensive in Dublin and in Dublin South George Gavan Duffy won by a margin of 779 votes over the unionist candidate, Sir Thomas Robinson, and by 1,314 over the IPP's Thomas Clarke. In all other constituencies, Sinn Féin's margin was in excess of 2,000 votes, with, for example, Constance Markievicz in the St Patrick's Division attaining 4,083 more votes than her nearest rival, the Nationalist William Field.[64] In Dublin County, Sinn Féin made a clean sweep, except

---

[61] *Irish Independent*, 30 Nov. 1918 [two columns × five inch advertisements by Henry Hanna and Maurice Dockrell].

[62] Brian Walker, *Parliamentary Election Results in Ireland, 1918–92* (Dublin, 1992), pp. 4–9.

[63] Walker, *Parliamentary Election Results in Ireland, 1918–92*, pp. 4–9. The total number of electors on the register for the county and boroughs including uncontested seats and excluding universities was 1,921,601: *Irish Independent*, 30 Dec. 1918.

[64] Except for the Rathmines constituency, where the unionist Maurice Dockrell won.

in Rathmines, where Dockrell recaptured the constituency by beating the combined vote of Sinn Féin and the IPP by 54.

In Dublin's Pembroke and South Dublin Divisions, the results were surprising victories for Sinn Féin in both constituencies. Good was defeated by Desmond FitzGerald in Pembroke by a strong 1,976 majority, with the IPP candidate Charles O'Neill attaining only 2,629 votes out of a total poll of 12,881.[65] Dublin South and Pembroke had previously been held by unionists.[66] Cork City and County were previous strongholds of the All-For-Ireland League, who withdrew to make way for Sinn Féin, even though in the December 1910 elections they had won eight seats.[67] In Cork City, two seats polled over 20,500 votes each for Sinn Féin, crushing the IPP candidates who mustered a mere 7,500 votes between them. Serious violent disturbances erupted in Cork during the campaign. Two unionist canvassers, Major J.H. Phillips and Andrew Williams (brother of the candidate Daniel Williams), encountered stone-throwing and verbal abuse as they motored through the Cork suburb of Blackpool, but 'miraculously' they escaped injury.[68] Overall, only a few constituencies witnessed this level of violence. The rest were like East Wicklow, which, according to the *Irish Times*, 'was fought in a spirit of friendly rivalry, and no incident occurred throughout the day that would mar the harmonious relations'.[69]

A second Unionist candidate, Thomas Farrington, also contested in Cork City, but lost out to both constitutional and separatist Nationalists. The combined votes of the two Unionist candidates did not even come near the lowest Nationalist vote.[70] The story in Ulster was different, although Unionists had hoped to win 30 seats in total and did not do as well as expected; 26 seats were secured which still exceeded their previous parliamentary representation by 8.[71]

---

65 Prior to the 1918 general election, Pembroke formed part of the central part of the South Dublin constituency, which extended into a small area of North Dublin.

66 Dublin South wins had alternated between unionist and IPP candidates. In January 1910, the unionist Bryan Cooper had narrowly defeated the IPP's William Cotton, but an about-turn in December 1910 gave the victory to Cooper. In 1906, the unionist Walter Long won the constituency, and in 1900 the IPP candidate John Joseph Mooney defeated the Irish unionist candidate Horace Plunkett (by 1912 Plunkett had become a convinced Home Ruler).

67 Joseph V. O'Brien, *William O'Brien and the Course of Irish Politics, 1881–1918* (London, 1976), pp. 201–2.

68 *Irish Times*, 23 Dec. 1918.

69 *Irish Times*, 17 Dec. 1918.

70 Daniel Williams attained 2,519 votes and Farrington 2,254 votes, with Richard L. O'Sullivan, Nationalist, coming in at 7,162. Walker, *Parliamentary Election Results in Ireland, 1918–92*, p. 5.

71 This number includes Labour unionists and universities.

Spoiled votes, either through ignorance or on purpose, were uncounted across the elections. Some ballot sheets had 'God Save the King' written across them, indicating that they were unionist in a constituency with no representative candidate, and others wrote 'unionist' or 'nationalist' according to their bias. The new Representation of the People Act allowed for servicemen over 19 to vote and to do so *in absentia* if in France or Belgium; all others could appoint proxies, but there were problems with these votes.[72] Servicemen may have been too distant to have received their voting papers in a timely manner for the three-week election lead in, they may have been missing-in-action, or the registers may have been incorrect. Their absence no doubt affected overall results. Sir Thomas Robinson lamented that it was 'most discreditable that the Act passed for the purpose of enabling absent voters to record their votes should have so failed its aim'. He further asserted that 'many thousands' were 'deprived of the opportunity of voting at this election'.[73] An absence of long-term emigration opportunities due to the war also affected voter numbers, as did the influenza pandemic in 1918 and 1919, which infected an estimated 800,000 people and killed at least 20,057 on the island.[74] Some may also have stayed away from the polls in hostile constituencies where Irish Volunteer and Hibernian aggression offered an intimidating presence.

The franchise had been granted to women over the age of 30 years to vote and run as candidates in by-elections and general elections, but there were still some property restrictions.[75] Unionists, like Sinn Féin, created propaganda directly aimed at women. By 1912, with at least 100,000 members in the Ulster Women's Unionist Council (UWUC), the female voice stirred, particularly during the Home Rule crisis.[76] Unionists were prodded from within to take steps in every constituency to 'provide for close co-operation of men and

---

[72] Hansard, HC, vol. 110, cols 1780–3 (4 Nov. 1918).

[73] *Irish Times*, 29 and 30 Nov. 1918.

[74] For further information on the influenza pandemic, see Ida Milne, *Stacking the Coffins, Influenza, War and Revolution in Ireland, 1918–19* (Manchester, 2018).

[75] Representation of the People Act 1918 (UK Parliamentary Archives, HL/PO/PU/1/1918/7&8G5c64). According to the Act, 'A woman shall be entitled to be registered as a parliamentary elector for a constituency (other than a university constituency) if she … is entitled to be registered as a local government elector in respect of the occupation in that constituency of land or premises (not being a dwelling-house) of a yearly value of not less than five pounds or of a dwelling-house, or is the wife of a husband entitled to be so registered'. See also Eric J. Evans, *Parliamentary Reform in Britain, c.1770–1918* (London, 2013), p. 135.

[76] During the Home Rule crisis, 228,991 Ulster unionist women signed the Declaration associating themselves with the men of Ulster 'in their uncompromising opposition to Home Rule'. Another 5,055 women had signed elsewhere: Stewart, *The Ulster Crisis*, p. 66.

women in the unionist organisations'.[77] In 1918, and in later elections, women were encouraged 'to endeavour to interest other women ... to see that their votes are registered in the constituency in which they live'.[78] Failure to cast a vote was warned against because 'a very great responsibility will soon be placed upon us in the exercising of our vote'. Unionist women were warned to be wary of IPP and Sinn Féin candidates who were posing as unionists, because they 'are prepared to promise anything to catch our vote, and to support many schemes that are quite impracticable of fulfilment'.[79]

Diane Urquhart maintains that a communication network had been formed among unionist women during wartime fundraising initiatives and that this had important political implications in strengthening unionist solidarity.[80] Nancy Kinghan points out that female Orange Lodges became a useful networking arena, particularly when they were given representation on the UWUC in 1920.[81] Meetings to petition unionist women collectively were enabled by the formation of these organisations, and it was advised that when addressing female unionists meetings that 'they should be addressed by the candidate and women speakers whenever possible'.[82] Unionists, like Sinn Féin, encouraged women to become active politically as canvassers, lobbyists, and supervisors of electoral registers. Propaganda was specifically targeted at women, outlining their role and responsibilities not only as wives and mothers but also in relation to church, home, country, and empire. Henry Hanna and Maurice Dockrell placed small advertisements in the *Irish Independent* that addressed 'Ladies and Gentlemen'. The *Freeman's Journal* highlighted that 'the women's vote is a new factor in the election campaign, and as it roughly represents from forty to fifty per cent of the electorate, it will exercise an enormous influence on the result of the elections'.[83] According to the *Irish Independent*, 'in Belfast alone there were 85,000, in one of the Tipperary divisions women were half the total electorate'.[84] While no Unionist women

[77] President of the Ulster Women's Unionists Council to members of the council, 1918 (PRONI, D1507/A/27/3).
[78] Poster, *Women Electors – Consider!* undated, c.1918–29 (PRONI, D1327/20/4/142, UC 155).
[79] Poster, *Women Electors – Consider!* undated, c.1918–29 (PRONI, D1327/20/4/142, UC 155).
[80] Diane Urquhart, *Women in Ulster Politics, 1890–1940: A History Not Yet Told* (Dublin, 2000), pp. 65–6.
[81] Nancy Kinghan, *United We Stood: The Official History of the Ulster Women's Unionist Council, 1911–1974* (Belfast, 1975), p. 41.
[82] Unionist Central Office Parliamentary Election Manual, 5th edn, Aug. 1921 (PRONI, D1327/20/4/148).
[83] *Freeman's Journal*, 26 Nov. 1918
[84] *Irish Independent*, 18 Nov. 1918.

candidates were fielded, by targeting propaganda at women voters, Ulster Unionists gained advantage on polling day.

Conclusion

Unionists remained consistent in their opposition to Home Rule and in 1918 the same messages were reassigned to electoral campaigns that became reinvigorated and energised by Great War rhetoric. Unionists funded and managed numerous propaganda methods to persuade voters, convincing the electorate to support their brand of politics. In 1918, the devolution of control to local organisations worked for Unionists, but with a focus on Ulster the control over decisions was more straightforward, and monitoring candidate selection procedures was easier. A small number of contests in the south also facilitated this process but made it difficult to make an impact. There is no doubt that the adroit supervision of candidate selection from a centralised system brought success for unionists (and Sinn Féin, whereas abdication to local control by the IPP and Labour yielded limited outcomes).

In speeches and in print, Unionists excelled in propaganda that used consistency in message, slogan, theme, and image, such as 'keep Ulster in the Empire by Voting Unionist'. Speeches were supplemented with newspaper editorial and advertisements (to reach wider audiences and those distanced from speakers at open air meetings) and canvassing, and clever displays of symbols and colour created presence. Novel approaches to propaganda furthered electoral success, as did using vehicles decorated with party colours.[85] For instance, Edward and Lady Carson had toured their constituency on polling day in a vehicle decorated with Union flags and bunting.[86] Unionist skills lay in adapting and regenerating their sharp anti-Home Rule message to persuade political adherence to their philosophy, and they held fast to a time-honoured fidelity to the union. Ideological disparities between separatists and unionists were propagated across electoral propaganda efforts, highlighting the divergent views on the governance of Ireland. Unionist propagandistic strength was homogeneity of message and an array of propaganda techniques conveyed their doctrine. Unionist voters adhered to the call for collective balloting, which brought victory in Ulster and in a pocket of Dublin in 1918.

As Ulster unionists inched closer to partition, southern adherents grew frustrated and anxious, and began to vacillate between embracing and impairing Home Rule negotiations, evident in their letters to newspaper editors. Carson privately complained that southern unionists had not been

---

[85] *Irish Independent*, 1 May 1917.
[86] *Irish Times*, 23 Dec. 1918.

'prepared to run any risks ... it is very difficult to ascertain what the South and West want us to do as they only talk in generalities'.[87] The gradual popularisation and localisation of the movement in the northern counties pulled apart a tentative all-Ireland unionism, and ultimately left southern unionists stranded in a nationalist-dominated Free State.[88]

[87] Alvin Jackson, *Sir Edward Carson* (Dublin, 1993), p. 32.
[88] Alvin Jackson, *Ireland 1798–1998: War, Peace and Beyond* (Oxford, 1999), p. 227.

CHAPTER III

Southern Protestant Voices during the Irish War of Independence and Civil War: Reports from Church of Ireland Synods

Brian M. Walker

The experiences of southern Protestants from 1919 to 1923 have recently attracted increased attention from historians. In the past, most books on the Irish War of Independence and Civil War avoided mention of the position of southern Protestants. When we turn to histories of the Church of Ireland, we find only the briefest account of the impact of this period. For example, in Walter Alison Phillips's edited three-volume *History of the Church of Ireland*, published in the 1930s, there are whole chapters devoted to the early Patrician period, but events of a decade previously are covered in one page, where the author writes: 'it could give no pleasure to the present writer to recall for others the dark and terrible deeds done in Ireland during one of the darkest periods in her history'.[1] More recently, the subject has attracted greater attention. In particular, the work of the late Peter Hart included an examination of the position of southern Protestants in these years.[2] The murder of ten Protestants in the Dunmanway area of West Cork in April 1922 has become an issue of considerable interest and controversy.[3] In the last few years, a number of important articles have studied the fate of Protestants in the revolutionary period.[4] What is agreed is that during these years Protestants in the 26 counties which became the Irish Free State experienced a drastic fall

---

[1] Walter Alison Phillips (ed.), *History of the Church of Ireland: From the Earliest Times to the Present Day*, vol. 3 (Oxford, 1933), pp. 412–13.

[2] Peter Hart, *The I.R.A. at War 1916–1923* (Oxford, 2003).

[3] Barry Keane, *Massacre in West Cork: The Dunmanway and Ballygroman Killings* (Cork, 2013). See review by B.M. Walker in *Irish Independent*, 31 May 2014. Also, Stephen Howe, 'Killings in Cork and the Historians', *History Workshop Journal*, 77 (2014), pp. 160–86.

[4] Andy Bielenberg, 'Exodus: The Emigration of Southern Irish Protestants during the Irish War of Independence and the Civil War', *Past & Present*, 218 (2013), pp. 199–233; David Fitzpatrick, 'Protestant Depopulation and the Irish Revolution', *Irish Historical Studies*, 38/152 (2013), pp. 642–70.

in numbers. What is not agreed is why this happened, and explanations for the decline have ranged widely from ethnic cleansing to voluntary emigration and demographic factors.

In this chapter the experiences of southern Protestants during the period 1919–23 will be charted through eyewitness accounts in the form of speeches from annual synods of the Church of Ireland, a source which hitherto has been largely ignored. Throughout these turbulent years, a general synod of church members continued to meet in Dublin each May, after which local diocesan synods were held in various locations, covering the whole country. Members of the Church of Ireland comprised the largest section of the Protestant population in the 26 counties which became the Irish Free State. In 1911, members of the Church of Ireland numbered just under 250,000, slightly over three-quarters of the Protestant population, and nearly 8 per cent of the total population.[5] In the 26 counties, there were 29 dioceses, but only ten bishops and two archbishops, each of whom, apart from the archbishop of Armagh, the bishop of Meath, and the bishop of Clogher, was responsible for a number of dioceses. In some cases joint synods were held while in others there were separate synods (to assist in identifying the geographical location of the dioceses, the places where the synods took place have been recorded in this text). Consisting of elected lay and clerical members, the synods were concerned primarily with general church matters, but during this time contemporary political issues intruded. These events began with a speech by the bishop, who acted as president, and it is their speeches which were reported in the press, especially the *Irish Times*.[6] As both leaders and observers of their dioceses, the bishops in these speeches reflected many of the concerns and anxieties of their community. Through these contemporary statements we can gain a valuable insight into the experiences of southern Protestants during the revolutionary period. Sometimes they are outspoken in their comments, while at other times they are restrained, perhaps reflecting the dangerous times they lived in, or a desire not to concern or cause panic.

A brief commentary can be made about the bishops, who numbered 14 during these years. All were born and educated in the south, except for the northerner A.E. Ross, bishop of Tuam and Killala, J.A.F. Gregg, bishop of Ferns, Ossory and Leighlin, later archbishop of Dublin, and finally archbishop of Armagh, born and brought up in England, but with strong Cork clerical antecedents and connections. Ross also served as a chaplain in the Great War from 1916 to 1918 and was the recipient of a Military Cross for bravery. All except two were graduates of Trinity College Dublin and the Divinity School at

---

[5] *Saorstát Éireann: Census of Population, 1926*, Religion and Birthplaces, vol. 3 (1929), p. 1.

[6] Easy access to this source is provided via the *Irish Times* Digital Archive.

Trinity. In the cases of the archbishop of Armagh, the bishop of Clogher, and the bishop of Derry and Raphoe, their dioceses were cross-border after 1920. All had extensive parochial experience, except for J.H. Bernard, archbishop of Dublin, who resigned in June 1919 to become provost of Trinity. After Bernard's resignation, C.F. D'Arcy became archbishop of Dublin. Following the death in April 1920 of J.B. Crozier, the primate and archbishop of Armagh, D'Arcy was elected to succeed him in June 1920, after which Gregg became archbishop of Dublin in September 1920. In 1919 their average age was 58 years.

Before 1921, all were unionist in their politics. In May 1917, however, while remaining unionist, J.A.F. Gregg, then bishop of Ossory, B.J. Plunket, bishop of Tuam and Killala, and later bishop of Meath, and Thomas Sterling Berry, bishop of Killaloe and Clonfert, had broken ranks with their fellow bishops to sign a declaration against partition, along with 17 Catholic bishops.[7] This led to a counter declaration from the archbishop of Armagh, J.B. Crozier, and the four Ulster bishops, but caused no long-term schism among the bishops. Bishops Plunket and Sterling Berry joined the general committee of the Irish White Cross Association, set up in 1921 to distribute funds raised by the American Committee for Relief in Ireland, which caused criticism in the press from Lord Ashtown on the grounds that the committee members included Michael Collins and 'other notorious republicans'.[8] C.R. Dowse, bishop of Cork, Cloyne and Ross, was one of four patrons of the Tomas MacCurtain memorial fund and one of two patrons, along with the Catholic bishop of Cork, Daniel Cohalan, of the Cork Distress Committee, set up to deal with distress and unemployment following the burning of the city.[9]

The First Synods after the War, 1919

The first general synod of the Church of Ireland after the Great War opened in Dublin on 12 May 1919. In his speech, the primate, Dr J.B. Crozier, began by saying that 'the awful cloud of war, as far as the Central Powers are concerned, has passed away'. He concluded with 'an eloquent reference' to the debt everyone owed to the 'Contemptible Little Army', under Lord French, which 'so nobly and bravely resisted the German onslaught in 1914'.[10] At this general synod and subsequent diocesan synods the main subject of concern was reform of the parochial structures and the deployment and stipends of clergy in light of population changes in Ireland since disestablishment. In early

[7] R.B. McDowell, *The Church of Ireland, 1869–1969* (London, 1975), p. 108.
[8] *Irish Times*, 16 Mar. 1921.
[9] *Cork Examiner*, 10 Apr. 1920; *Freeman's Journal*, 7 Jan. 1921.
[10] *Irish Times*, 17 May 1919.

June, at the Kilmore synod in Cavan, Bishop W.R. Moore pointed out that
the Church of Ireland had experienced a fall in numbers over the previous
40 years which necessitated a reorganisation of parishes. He noted that
their decrease countrywide was less in proportion than the decrease among
Catholics over this period, and in the decade 1901 to 1911 was only some 5,000,
but 'on account of the fewness of their numbers they felt it more'.[11] Church
of Ireland members were widely dispersed and in many parts of the country
were in small numbers, which created special problems.

The bishops' speeches at synods in June and July contained little or no
reference to current political problems. At the very end of July 1919, however, at
the Killaloe synod, held at Nenagh, County Tipperary, Bishop Thomas Sterling
Berry declared: 'the policy adopted by the British government in its treatment
of Ireland in recent years has been disastrous to the peace of the country. The
policy has been a combination of vacillation and irritation'. He continued: 'But
no policy, however misguided, could justify crimes which make all true lovers
of Ireland hang their heads in sorrow and shame'. He denounced the murder
of policemen.[12] At the synod of the united dioceses of Cork, Cloyne and Ross
on 22 October 1919 in Cork, Bishop C.B. Dowse stated: 'Murder, robbery and
crime stain our native land, and call forth our sternest and most uncompromising condemnation'. He expressed strong sympathy and admiration for the
police 'who are serving their country with such splendid loyalty, and who, in
the discharge of their duties and in their efforts to maintain law and order,
are brutally attacked, and often foully murdered. We owe them a deep sense
of gratitude, far beyond anything words can convey'.[13] Between 1919 and 1921,
a total of 90 members of the Royal Irish Constabulary lost their lives in Cork
county and city.[14]

Reforms and Concerns at Synods, 1920

Reports from synods in 1920 reveal concern about a deteriorating situation
in Ireland. At the general synod in May 1920, the new archbishop of Dublin,
C.F. D'Arcy, in place of the recently deceased primate, gave the president's
address. He described how 'the issues were so confused, the outlook so obscure'
and how they had been horrified by 'the deeds of bloodshed which had in the

---

[11] *Irish Times*, 7 Jun. 1919. For confirmation of these figures, see W.E. Vaughan and
A.J. Fitzpatrick (eds), *Irish Historical Statistics: Population 1821–1971* (Dublin,
1978), p. 49.

[12] *Irish Times*, 1 Aug. 1919.

[13] *Irish Times*, 23 Oct. 1919.

[14] W.J. Lowe, 'The War against the R.I.C., 1919–21', *Éire-Ireland*, 37/3&4 (2002), p. 94.

past few months stained the records of their country'.[15] The question of reform of the church in the face of falling numbers in parts of Ireland and growth in others, in particular Belfast, was the main issue of discussion at the synod. In November 1920, a special general synod of the church was convened in Dublin to deal with the question of parish amalgamations and revised stipends for clergy.[16] In the speeches of the bishops at diocesan synods during 1920 there was often mention, usually brief, of the troubled times they lived in. At the Elphin synod at Boyle, County Roscommon, on 9 June, sympathy was expressed by Bishop W.R. Moore with 'the men of that splendid force, the Royal Irish Constabulary' and with 'the many, both of their own communion and others, who had been the victims of outrage either against their person or their property'.[17]

Similar views were expressed at other June synods. At the Tuam synod at Tuam, County Galway, Bishop A.E. Ross referred to the murder of the land agent Frank Shawe-Taylor, apparently over a land dispute, and stated: 'Disorder and lawlessness have gone very far. We feel very impotent'.[18] Bishop R.D'A. Orpen, who presided at the Limerick synod in Limerick city, declared that 'the country must suffer intensely while strife between brethren, which was the saddest of all strife, continued'.[19] Addressing the Cashel synod at Cashel, County Tipperary, Bishop Robert Millar talked of 'events which are taking place all around us, so full of callous cruelty, of extreme inhumanity, of utter indifference to the laws of God'. The meeting of the Dublin diocesan synod in July was mainly concerned with electing a new archbishop, and the only comment about the situation by the acting president, C.B. Dowse, bishop of Cork, apart from stressing the importance of choosing 'a fit and proper person to serve his church in this great crisis', was that: 'the land they loved so well was rent asunder and stained with terrible crime'.[20]

In October 1920, a number of synods were held. At the synod for Cork and Ross, in Cork city, Bishop C.B. Dowse noted briefly that 'the past year had been marked by some unpleasant events, both within their united diocese and also within its bounds', but stated that 'amid the various disturbances and disorders which had taken place amongst them, the ordinary ministrations of their church had been uninterrupted'.[21] A second synod of Dublin diocese heard their new archbishop, Dr J.A.F. Gregg, briefly deplore the violence

[15] *Irish Times*, 19 May 1920.
[16] H.E. Patton, *Fifty Years of Disestablishment: A Sketch* (Dublin, 1922), pp. 303–5.
[17] *Irish Times*, 10 Jun. 1920.
[18] *Irish Times*, 25 Jun., 26 Oct. 1920.
[19] *Irish Times*, 26 Jun. 1920.
[20] *Irish Times*, 31 Jul. 1920.
[21] *Irish Times*, 29 Oct. 1920.

and call for reconciliation.[22] The longest comments on the political situation came from Bishop Thomas Sterling Berry at the Clonfert and Kilmacduagh synod in Ballinasloe, County Galway. He remarked: 'Things have drifted into a state of anarchy and strife'. He then declared: 'Ireland can never work out her salvation through murder and bloodshed. But, on the other hand, England cannot maintain her hold on Ireland by bringing the weapon of coercive legislation and coercive actions upon the attenuated population of this little island'. He urged 'better understanding between Great Britain and Ireland'.[23] Sterling Berry also talked about the need to reorganise parishes with small numbers, a subject raised by the archdeacon of Dublin, Reverend T.S. Lindsay, in an article in the *Irish Times* at the end of December 1920. He pointed to diminishing membership of the church over a long time, a process 'shared with all the other religious denominations'. However, he stated that this was now advancing at a more rapid rate for their church, 'as large numbers of her members are leaving the country and settling in England due to the terrible condition of things that prevails here'. He claimed that 'in hundreds of country parishes the congregations are reduced'.[24] Nonetheless, A.F. Maude, secretary of the Representative Church Body, the central financial trustee body of the church, in his annual report for 1920 (produced in May 1921) remained positive. He wrote of 'much unrest' and 'times of adversity', but he also reported 'increased financial stability' for the church nationally during the year in spite of the political difficulties.[25]

Gloom and Hope at Synods, 1921

Reports from synods in 1921 painted a much gloomier picture, although some also carried messages of hope. In his address to the general synod in May 1921, the new primate, Archbishop C.F. D'Arcy, spoke at length about the violent state of the country: 'The things that had happened in their country during the past year had been so terrible, so disastrous, so fateful, in relation to the social and moral life of the whole country as to be paralysing'. He referred to several members of the synod who had been murdered. He then declared: 'Members of our church, and others, in several parts of the country – quiet, defenceless farmers for the most part – have been most cruelly killed. We do not know for what reasons, and can but conjecture that it was because

[22] *Irish Times*, 19 Oct. 1920
[23] *Irish Times*, 28 Oct. 1920.
[24] *Irish Times*, 29 Dec. 1920.
[25] *Fifty-first Report of the Proceedings of the Representative Body of the Church of Ireland*, pp. 34–5.

their political views were not acceptable'.[26] In early July 1921, at the Limerick diocesan synod, in place of the bishop who had resigned, Dean T.A.P. Hackett spoke of how 'murder and destruction of property went unchecked'. He hoped that 'religious strife might not aggravate the present troubles' and stated his opinion that: 'where their people had suffered it was not because of their religious opinions, and, as the present representative of the city and county clergy, he was glad to say that never in their experience had the relations between all religions been more harmonious'.[27]

At a number of synods reference was made to church members and others who had been murdered by republicans. In his address to the Ardagh synod in Longford in late July, Bishop W.R. Moore referred to 'the death of Mr William Latimer, who was so cruelly murdered, which reminded them of the dreadful times through which they had been passing. One of their most highly esteemed clergymen had had to leave the country simply because he acted as a loyal citizen'. He thought that 'it would serve no good purpose to dwell at length on the awful state of their country, which had been especially bad in parts of their diocese – Ballinalea and Ballina – except to express his deep sympathy with those who had had so much to endure'.[28] A few days later, at the Kilmore synod at Cavan, Bishop Moore expressed great shock at the murder of the elderly Reverend John Finlay, former dean of Leighlin, who had been killed in June outside his burned-out home in County Cavan. Both the Belfast and Dublin press carried a letter from four local Catholic parish priests, expressing their 'horror and indignation at the crime'.[29] Bishop Moore observed that their numbers were becoming fewer: 'Very large numbers of their church people had left the south and west during the last two years, and they knew not what the future had in store for them'.[30]

At the Tuam synod in Tuam, County Galway, and the Killala synod in Ballina, County Mayo, Bishop A.E. Ross was both brief and guarded in his addresses. He spoke of 'this time of lawlessness and strife and hatred' but hoped that 'a spirit of conciliation may save us from still worse things'.[31] At the Waterford synod in August, Bishop Robert Miller referred to the killing of the 60-year-old Mary Lindsay, 'a personal friend of my own', from

[26] *Irish Times*, 11 May 1921. For another reference to the killing of these farmers, see Dennis Kennedy, *The Widening Gulf: Northern Attitudes to the Independent Irish State, 1919–49* (Belfast, 1988), p. 51.

[27] *Irish Times*, 2 Jul. 1921.

[28] *Irish Times*, 20 Jul. 1921. For more on Latimer, see Brian Hughes, *Defying the IRA? Intimidation, Coercion, and Communities during the Irish Revolution* (Liverpool, 2016), pp. 125–6.

[29] *Belfast Telegraph*, 15 Jun. 1921; *Irish Times*, 16 Jun. 1921.

[30] *Irish Times*, 23 Jul. 1921.

[31] *Irish Times*, 7 and 23 Jul. 1921.

Coachford, County Cork, who had alerted the authorities to a planned IRA ambush.[32] Subsequently, she and her driver were kidnapped, held prisoners for over four months, and then executed.[33] Besides such fatalities, the period from early 1920 to mid-1921 included sectarian attacks against members of the Protestant community, such as the burning of three Church of Ireland churches in County Clare in 1920, and threats and outrages against Protestant farmers in various parts of the country.[34]

The truce of mid-July 1921 created hope. At the Killaloe synod at Nenagh, County Tipperary, in August 1921, Bishop Thomas Sterling Berry commented: 'We have been living through dark days – days of trouble, days of mourning – here in our land. Now there comes the dawn of a new hope'.[35] In October, at the Ferns synod, Bishop J.G.F. Day spoke of 'an intense longing for peace'. He described how: 'A real spirit of tolerance prevailed since the treaty. Protestant and Roman Catholic farmers were living side by side in perfect friendliness … such a thing as religious bitterness or intolerance, was almost unknown in that part of Ireland'.[36] Later that month, at the Ossory synod at Kilkenny, Bishop Day recorded his concern that the rights of the minority in the new political arrangements in southern Ireland would be protected: 'they are real Irishmen, with just as strong and patriotic a love for their country as any other portion of the country'.[37]

At the united synod of Cork and Ross in Cork at the end of October, Bishop C.R. Dowse spoke briefly and cautiously about how 'for their country, especially for their own diocese, the year had been one of fearful happenings and tragic events'.[38] At the 1910 December general election, the two Cork City seats and six out of seven County seats had been won by the All-for-Ireland League led by William O'Brien and his policies of reconciliation between former landlords and tenants, and between north and south.[39] In contrast to such moderation, however, an estimated 50 'big houses' or suburban villas

---

[32] *Irish Times*, 23 Jul. 1921.

[33] Robin Bury, *Buried Lives: The Protestants of Southern Ireland* (Dublin, 2017), pp. 35–6.

[34] For these and other examples of intimidation of Protestants 1920–1, see Kennedy, *The Widening Gulf*, pp. 49–54; Bielenberg, *Exodus*, pp. 206–9; Terence Dooley, *The Plight of Monaghan Protestants, 1912–1926* (Dublin, 2000), pp. 42–5; Bury, *Buried Lives*, chaps 2 and 3.

[35] *Irish Times*, 5 Aug. 1921

[36] *Irish Times*, 13 Oct. 1921.

[37] *Irish Times*, 26 Oct. 1921

[38] *Irish Times*, 26 Oct. 1921.

[39] Sally Warwick-Haller, 'Seeking Conciliation: William O'Brien and the Ulster Crisis, 1911–14', in D. George Boyce and Alan O'Day (eds), *The Ulster Crisis: 1885–1921* (Basingstoke, 2006), pp. 146–64.

in Cork city and county, most owned by members of the Church of Ireland, were destroyed by the IRA during the War of Independence.[40] Later, an IRA commander in West Cork, Tom Barry, described targeting the homes of 'loyalists' in reprisal for the activities of the British army: 'our only fear was that, as time went on, there would be no more loyalist homes to destroy'.[41] After referring to the deaths of Major George O'Connor, Tom Bradfield, and Mary Lindsay, Bishop Dowse declared: 'We must hope on. ... We thankfully recognise that throughout our diocese so many churchmen and Roman Catholics live side by side in terms of friendship and goodwill'.[42]

In 18 October 1921, J.A.F. Gregg, the new archbishop of Dublin, spoke at the Dublin diocesan synod. He expressed thanks that there was 'a truce from bloodshed', but voiced worries about the safeguarding of their rights in any new settlement. Gregg declared that, as a minority, 'we differ from the majority in religion, in politics, in *ethos* generally', and referred to their aloofness from 'the political movement directed against the British connection, in so far as the methods adopted by its supporters seem to us to be wrong'. He said: 'Although we are as truly Irish as are many in the other camp, the differences are so marked as to cause us to seem alien in sympathy from the more extreme of our countrymen'. He insisted: 'Whatever our religious or political outlook may be, here is our home, and we have every right to be here'. Gregg then stated that it would be a very bad day if large numbers left, but if they were to stay, they needed to have confidence for the future. He asked not for 'preferential treatment' but that they be 'assured of a fair chance'. He observed: 'A good many people have already left Ireland, just because they can choose where they live, and they refuse to remain in so disturbed an atmosphere'.[43]

In October, at the Ferns synod in Enniscorthy, referring to political talks, Bishop J.G.F. Day expressed hope that 'in spite of difficulties, an honourable compromise might be arrived at'. He also observed that 'A real spirit of tolerance prevailed since the truce. Protestant and Roman Catholic farmers were living side by side in perfect friendliness ... such a thing as bitterness or intolerance, was almost unknown in that part of Ireland'.[44] At the Clonfert synod at Ballinasloe, County Galway, in late October 1921, Bishop Thomas Sterling Berry warned: 'Do not share the action of those who in timid apprehension are already quitting the homes of their forefathers and the land

---

[40] See James S. Donnelly Jr, 'Big House Burnings in County Cork during the Irish Revolution, 1920–21', *Éire-Ireland*, 47/3&4 (2012), pp. 141–97.

[41] Tom Barry, *Guerilla Days in Ireland* (Cork, 1955), p. 115.

[42] For information on O'Connor, Bradfield, and Lindsay, see Gerard Murphy, *The Year of Disappearances: Political Killings in Cork* (Dublin, 2010), pp. 64, 73, 89–90.

[43] *Irish Times*, 18 Oct. 1921.

[44] *Irish Times*, 27 Oct. 1921.

of their birth'.[45] A week later, probably in response to these comments, at the synod of Ardfert and Aghadoe, at Tralee, County Kerry, Bishop H.V. White stated: 'If hundreds of my fellow countrymen are leaving the country, they are doing so for no light cause, and are certainly not urged by unmanly panic. They know why they go, and they go to the great and permanent loss of Ireland'.[46] He also pleaded for toleration, arguing that in the past there had been toleration between Christians, but now it was implied that the minority should be grateful 'that we are allowed to share any of the rights and liberties of ordinary citizens'. He declared that he 'refused to be grateful to anyone but the Almighty for permission to breathe the air of my native land'. On Sunday, 11 December 1921, at the conclusion of a sermon in Dublin, Archbishop J.A.F. Gregg spoke of the prospects for peace, following negotiations in London between Sinn Féin representatives and the British government: 'We may not all like the facts: many of us had no desire for a change of our constitution. But it will be our wisdom to acknowledge them and reckon with them ... it concerns us all to offer to the Irish Free State, as shortly to be constituted, our loyalty and good-will'.[47]

A Deteriorating Situation and the General Synod, May 1922

When the next general synod was held in May 1922, however, these hopes for a peaceful future had not materialised. In early 1922, the RIC was disbanded and members of the British army were withdrawn, with the result that much of the countryside was subject to considerable lawlessness. Enlistment for a new police force began in February, but the Garda Síochána was not established until 1923. In addition, the situation in Northern Ireland in early 1922 had deteriorated, with attacks by the IRA and tough government counter measures. Sectarian conflict in Belfast included the murder on 23 March of five members of the Catholic McMahon family, and large numbers of Belfast Catholics fled south.[48] In March and early April, a series of meetings of southern Protestants in Cork, Limerick, and elsewhere condemned the outrages in Belfast, often stressing good church relations in the south.[49] One such meeting at Nenagh, County Tipperary, heard Bishop Thomas Sterling Berry of Killaloe declare: 'We have come together, not from any sense of forebodings – not because

---

[45] *Irish Times*, 26 Oct. 1921.

[46] *Irish Times*, 4 Nov. 1921.

[47] *Irish Times*, 12 Dec. 1921.

[48] For the McMahon murders, see Tim Wilson, '"The Most Terrible Assassination That Has Yet Stained the Name of Belfast": The McMahon Murders in Context', *Irish Historical Studies*, 37/145 (2010), pp. 83–106.

[49] *Irish Times*, 5 Apr. 1922

we wish to ward off disaster from ourselves. We come together as Irishmen, deeply aggrieved at occurrences which bring reproach and dishonour upon our country'.[50]

At the end of April 1922, however, republicans were responsible for the killing in the Dunmanway district of County Cork of ten Protestants, of whom all but one were members of the Church of Ireland.[51] These murders, which were viewed by many as reprisals or revenge for what had happened in the north, were strongly condemned by Catholic and government spokesmen.[52] The attacks raised great concerns among the Protestant community. In a sermon shortly afterwards, the bishop of Limerick, Dr H.V. White, who described himself as a personal friend of one of the victims, declared: 'We scattered, disarmed members of the Church in the south of Ireland have had in the murders of last week a grim reminder of our helplessness'.[53] What made the situation worse was that such events were not seen in isolation but as part of a much wider picture of intimidation experienced by many members of the Church of Ireland at this time. During the early months of 1922, the press reported many other examples of intimidation of Protestant families and businesses (often viewed as reprisals for violence in the north), which forced large numbers to leave.[54] Agrarian outrages affected the property of many Protestant landowners and farmers, while Protestant businesses were also seized or destroyed.[55] Although the War of Independence was over, those seen as loyalists, including not just Protestants but also Catholic ex-members of the RIC, were subject to widespread intimidation. In early May 1922, the archbishop of Dublin, J.A.F. Gregg, recorded in his diary: 'A week of v.great

---

[50] *Irish Times*, 10 Apr. 1922

[51] Keane, *Massacre in West Cork* and Walker's *Irish Independent* review. These murders at Dunmanway were preceded by the murder of three other Protestants at Ballygroman, Co. Cork and the 'disappearance' of their bodies after the shooting of a member of the IRA who had entered their home.

[52] In their condemnation of these murders, Michael Collins, Dr Daniel Colohan, Catholic bishop of Cork, and Éamon de Valera all saw them as reprisals for northern murders: *Irish Times*, 13 May 1922; *Cork Examiner*, 1, 13 May.

[53] *Church of Ireland Gazette*, 5 May 1922.

[54] See Kennedy, *The Widening Gulf*, pp. 114–29; Bielenberg, 'Exodus', pp. 207–13. By spring 1922, perhaps as many as 20,000 arrived in Britain as refugees from Ireland, although not all were members of the Church of Ireland: Niamh Brennan, 'A Political Minefield: Southern Loyalists, the Irish Grants Committee and the British Government, 1922–31', *Irish Historical Studies*, 30/119 (1997), p. 406. See T.A.M. Dooley, 'Protestant Migration from the Free State to Northern Ireland, 1920–25: A Private Census for Co. Fermanagh', *Clogher Record*, 15/3 (1996), pp. 87–132.

[55] Bielenberg, *Exodus*, pp. 207–9; S.J. Watson, *A Dinner of Herbs: The History of Old St Mary's Church, Clonmel* (Clonmel, 1988), pp. 190–2.

anxiety as to the church's future. News of evictions, ejections and intimi-
dations everywhere. Where is it all to lead to? Is it beginning of end, or short
term? Prol.Govt so far seems powerless to intervene'.[56]

On 9 May 1922, the general synod of the Church of Ireland met for its usual
annual meeting. In his speech, the primate, Archbishop C.F. D'Arcy, began by
saying that it was impossible to meet there that day 'without some reflection
upon the present condition of the country'. He confessed that, personally, he
'remained, after all that had happened, and in spite of the disastrous blunders
of a succession of British governments, a firm believer in the principles which
they had been accustomed to describe as unionism'. 'However', he declared,
'we must face things as they are, we have to prepare to meet a new order in
this country'. He then went on to state that the clergy and laity of the church,
in southern Ireland and in Northern Ireland, were prepared to do their duty
as Irishmen, 'to obey the law of the state to which they belong', and were
'most anxious to live in terms of goodwill with all classes and creeds among
our fellow countrymen'. He talked of the 'veritable nightmare of violence and
bloodshed, which has been in existence for some time in parts of our country,
north and south', and their deep sorrow over 'the shocking deaths recently
afflicted on some members of our church and the expulsion of many others'.
D'Arcy referred to Dunmanway, noting all the victims were Protestant, and
warned: 'Nothing more awful could happen than that the political strife in
the country should become a war of religion'.[57]

That evening, after a special meeting of all southern synod members, a
deputation, consisting of the archbishop of Dublin, the bishop of Cashel,
and Sir William Goulding, a prominent businessman, was chosen to meet
the government 'to lay before them the dangers to which protestants in the
twenty-six counties are daily exposed'.[58] Two days later, the members of this
deputation met Michael Collins and W.T. Cosgrave. They told Collins that
they were willing and anxious to remain 'as loyal citizens of the government
of Ireland', brought to his attention 'many cases in which their co-religionists
had suffered persecution in various parts of the country', and asked for
assurances that the government desired to retain them. Collins assured them
that 'the government would protect its citizens, and would ensure civil and
religious freedom in Ireland, and that spoliation and confiscation would not
be countenanced by the Irish government'.[59]

On the same day that the Church of Ireland deputation met Collins, a
well-attended convention of southern Protestants, mostly members of the

---

[56] George Seaver, *John Allen Fitzgerald Gregg, Archbishop* (Dublin, 1963), p. 121.
[57] *Irish Times*, 10 May 1922.
[58] *Irish Times*, 10 May 1922.
[59] *Irish Times*, 13 May 1922.

Church of Ireland, from the south and west of the country, was held at the Mansion House in Dublin. Speeches denounced attacks on both Catholics in Belfast and Protestants in Cork and elsewhere. Speakers sought to demonstrate southern Protestant sympathy for the plight of northern Catholics and to emphasise good relations between Protestants and Catholics in the past and present. Many saw attacks on Protestants in the south primarily as a result of general lawlessness and a response to northern outrages.[60] These efforts brought little or no improvement to the situation. On 23 June 1922, the *Church of Ireland Gazette* reported that 'in certain districts in southern Ireland inoffensive Protestants of all classes are being driven from their homes, their shops and their farms in such numbers that many of our little communities are in danger of being entirely wiped out'. Whatever the concerns of the government about the Protestant minority, it faced other major political issues, leading to civil war in June 1922. The next nine months in the country saw more deaths, destruction, and lawlessness than in the previous three years.

Diocesan Synods during the Civil War

There continued to be annual meetings of Church of Ireland synods, although some were cancelled, postponed, or not reported on, thanks to dangers and destruction caused by the Civil War. At the end of May 1922 at the Dublin diocesan synod, the archbishop of Dublin, J.A.F. Gregg, talked of losses in their ranks: 'The changing circumstances of our country have led some of our synodsmen to leave Ireland, while others have been transferred officially to the service of the northern government'. He expressed hope that 'the movements which have taken place against the members of our church, and which have, undoubtedly, tended to assume a complexion of a sectarian kind' would not continue. He believed these actions against church members occurred 'partly because they possess what other people covet, partly because they are weak and have few friends, and partly because they do not profess the same political or religious views as the majority'. He was certain that public opinion in Ireland would be shocked if it was made 'fully aware of all the sufferings which have been inflicted on innocent protestants living quietly in various parts of the twenty-six counties'. The archbishop expressed his belief in the good intentions of the government and appealed for its support: 'In the name of my co-religionists, I ask for fair play from our fellow countrymen'.[61] A few days later, at the Kildare synod, at Kildare, Archbishop Gregg referred to the demographic impact on Kildare parish and cathedral of the withdrawal of

[60] *Irish Times*, 13 May 1922.
[61] *Irish Times*, 30 May 1922.

British troops from the Curragh, and also mentioned the need to appoint chaplains to the new Irish army, as 'already members of our church are entering the service of the Free State'.[62]

At the Limerick diocesan synod in Limerick on 5 July 1922, Bishop H.V. White spoke of how their numbers had fallen over the last half century, and then went on to say: 'It is far from satisfactory to have to face the fact that Ireland is losing many of her best, most patriotic and progressive citizens, who are forced to leave their native land by economic causes or by political and religious intolerance'.[63] The press reported that 'owing to the disturbed condition of the country' Bishop White could not attend the synod of Ardfert and Aghadoe at Tralee, County Kerry, in September.[64] At the end of summer 1922, Bishop W.R. Moore spoke at the Elphin synod at Boyle, County Roscommon, where he declared that 'many of their people had suffered, and were suffering, cruel wrongs both in person and property, and some of their parishes had been thereby sadly depleted, notably the parish of Mount Talbot'. Shortly afterwards, at the Kilmore synod at Cavan, he stated that the church had suffered severely: 'Even in their own diocese a considerable number of people had left the country, and in the more southern and western dioceses the exodus of their people had been calamitous. Many had suffered and were suffering the most cruel wrongs in person and property'. He expressed regret at the deaths of Michael Collins and Arthur Griffith.[65]

In October 1922, Bishop J.G.F. Day addressed the Leighlin synod at Carlow. He referred to the lawless conditions: 'Many of our people have suffered severely under these conditions. Some of them have been driven from their homes and lands. I suppose there are few, if any, of our people who entirely escaped molestation'.[66] He still continued to hope for the best: 'The vast majority of the people are quiet and law-abiding, and the members of different religious denominations are living side by side on the best of terms, and doing all they can to help one another'. That same month at the Ferns synod in Enniscorthy, County Wexford, Bishop Day spoke of great uncertainty and anxiety: 'Their hearts were heavy as they thought of the sufferings of their people of all classes'. He paid special tribute to the clergy, who he said had stuck to their posts 'living in loneliness and in an atmosphere of open or veiled hostility. They had discharged their duty in danger and distress. Many had seen their flocks dwindle to almost vanishing point'.[67] At the Meath October synod

---

[62] *Irish Times*, 2 Jun. 1922.
[63] *Church of Ireland Gazette*, 28 Jul. 1922. See also *Irish Times*, 13 Jun. 1922.
[64] *Irish Times*, 7 Sep. 1922.
[65] *Irish Times*, 7, 11 Sep. 1922.
[66] *Irish Times*, 14 Oct. 1922.
[67] *Irish Times*, 2 Oct. 1922.

in Dublin, Bishop B.J. Plunket referred to the suffering of church members: 'some having lost their homes have left our shores; others, with no security for life or property, or with no prospect of employment, are, for the moment at any rate, exiled from their native land'.[68]

Twice postponed, the synod of Killaloe, Kilfenora, Clonfert and Kilmacduagh was held at Nenagh, County Tipperary, on 14 October 1922, where 'the business was expeditiously despatched'. Bishop Thomas Sterling Berry delivered a brief address in which 'sympathetic reference was made to the misfortunes recently sustained by members of the diocese', but the only detail mentioned in the press report was a short reference to the burning of a church at Ahascragh in July (which led to a protest of Catholic people in the area against the destruction).[69] These brief comments undoubtedly reflect caution on the part of the bishop, or concern not to cause alarm. In the archives of the Department of Justice in Dublin, however, is a letter dated 10 June 1922, written by Sterling Berry to draw attention to the state of affairs in north Tipperary. He wrote:

> There is scarcely a Protestant family in the district which has escaped molestation. One of my clergy has had his motor car and a portion of his house burned ... Some other houses have been burned. Cattle have been driven off farms. Protestant families have been warned to leave the neighbourhood. Altogether a state of terrorism exists.

About such conditions, he added: 'Happily they stand in glaring contrast to the state of things here and elsewhere in the diocese of which I have charge'.[70]

In spite of this positive remark about 'elsewhere', other clergy and members of his dioceses were subjected to serious violence of person and property that were not – whether through pragmatism or lack of information – mentioned at the synods.[71] The most shocking of such incidents is revealed in another record in the Department of Justice papers. On 16 June, a gang of armed republicans broke into the Biggs family home at Hazelpoint, Dromineer, Nenagh, County Tipperary. They consumed a quantity of alcohol, and Mrs Eileen Biggs was raped. The couple fled to Dublin where Eileen Biggs entered hospital. The police document reported: 'In view of the serious condition of Mrs Biggs, it is not inconceivable that the guilty party may be charged with manslaughter'.[72] She survived and later in August two men were charged in

---

[68] *Irish Times*, 13 Oct. 1922.
[69] *Church of Ireland Gazette*, 28 Jul. 1922; *Tuam Herald*, 29 Jul. 1922.
[70] Letter from T. Sterling Berry, 10 Jun. 1922 (NAI, JUS/H5/372).
[71] See Gemma Clark, *Everyday Violence in the Irish Civil War* (Cambridge, 2014), p. 90.
[72] Correspondence relating to the Biggs family, Jun. 1922 (NAI, JUS/H5/386). See also Clark, *Everyday Violence*, p. 187.

a local court with the crime and released on bail. It seems that in the end no action was taken against them.

Attempts to hold synods for the dioceses of Tuam and Killala during 1922 were unsuccessful, due to prevailing lawless conditions. Incidents in these dioceses included the burning in late June of Ballycronree orphanage, Clifden, County Galway, run by the Irish Church Mission, and the destruction and looting in November of the Church of Ireland church at Moyrus, County Galway.[73] On 25 October 1922, Bishop C.R. Dowse spoke to the united Cork synod in Cork city. He asked: 'Who can adequately describe the times through which our people have passed during the last few months? The memories of those ghastly massacres in West Cork can never pass away'. He acknowledged the messages of support his community had received, from organisations such as the Cork Corporation and Cork Catholic Young Men's Association. He insisted that they were entitled to full rights of citizenship, not as favours but as fundamental rights.[74]

Synods for the border dioceses were held in September–October 1922. At the Clogher synod at Enniskillen, County Fermanagh, referring to the south, Bishop Maurice Day described 'families broken up, their residences burned over their heads, they themselves, or those of them who were allowed to survive, fugitives from their native land, or trying to remain, living in daily terror of further outrage and death'.[75] Addressing the annual synod of Derry and Raphoe, in Derry city, Bishop C.I. Peacocke stated that he 'need not dwell on the awful crimes that defiled their land during the last twelve months', especially against those who were members of his church, 'namely, in the south and west, but to some extent at least in parts of his own diocese in County Donegal'.[76] At the diocesan synod of Armagh, in Armagh, Archbishop C.F. D'Arcy referred to the terror and misery experienced by populations elsewhere at the time, such as in Eastern Europe. He then declared: 'Of our own land it is difficult to speak. Anarchy and outrage have left terrible scars. Many of the very best of our people have been driven from our shores. The sufferings which have been endured can never be told'. He expressed hope that in the south 'the forces of order will succeed in overcoming the forces of anarchy. The anarchy which has prevailed over great tracts of this country has placed members of our church in these parts in a position of the utmost difficulty'.[77]

---

[73] See condemnation of Moyrus attack by Archbishop Gilmartin of Tuam: *Irish Times*, Dec. 1922.
[74] *Irish Times*, 26 Oct. 1922.
[75] *Irish Times*, 30 Sep. 1922.
[76] *Irish Times*, 17 Oct. 1922.
[77] *Irish Times*, 27 Oct. 1922.

The last synods of the year were addressed in early November by Bishop Robert Miller. Earlier, on 8 October 1922, at Christ Church, Leeson Park, Dublin, Bishop Miller had preached on behalf of poorer parishes in the south and west. He spoke of how 'during the past few years the whole church has passed through experiences which caused grave apprehension regarding our future in this country. Many of our people were driven from their homes, many others left through fear of violence, with the result that many of our parishes, especially where the numbers are small, are unable to meet their financial responsibilities'. Nonetheless, he said that they had been encouraged by the 'broad spirit of toleration' which was shown by the members of parliament. His advice to church members was: 'live in the land of your birth and work for its highest good'.[78] In early November, Bishop Miller addressed synods at Cashel, County Tipperary, for Cashel and Emly, and at Waterford city for Waterford and Lismore. At both he declared that, besides interference with property, 'dreadful and unspeakable crimes have been committed'. He went on: 'Honest, brave men will face physical violence, the destruction of their property, but such deeds as we are now speaking of chill the hearts of strong men and fill them with an overwhelming desire to get away from a country where, in their opinion, civilisation is losing its hold'.[79] He acknowledged the good intentions of the government, but he urged them to take greater steps to protect its citizens.

The following months witnessed further deterioration in the situation. The new Irish Free State constitution did not provide specific safeguards for the Protestant minority, but in December 1922 a large number of Protestants and former unionists, over 20, mostly members of the Church of Ireland, were nominated by the government or elected to the new Irish Senate in an effort to acknowledge the role of the minority in the new state. This was an important gesture of reconciliation and tolerance by the new Irish government, which was acknowledged as such by Church of Ireland sources.[80] Unfortunately, it proved to be a double-edged sword. Whereas during the War of Independence and earlier in 1922 homes of loyalists had been deliberately targeted by republicans because their owners were seen as supporters or former supporters of the British government, now the homes of Protestant senators were targeted by anti-treaty forces because their owners were viewed as supporters of the Free State government, while other country houses continued to be destroyed in an effort to create chaos to undermine the state.[81]

[78] *Irish Times*, 9 Oct. 1922.
[79] *Irish Times*, 6, 8 Nov. 1922.
[80] *Church of Ireland Gazette*, 22 Dec. 1922.
[81] Terence Dooley, *The Decline of the Big House in Ireland: A Study of Irish Landed Families, 1860–1960* (Dublin, 2001).

In late 1923, W. Alison Phillips estimated that 50 country houses were burned between January and November 1922, while another 89 were torched between the beginning of November 1922 and the ceasefire of early spring 1923, which he described as 'the worst and most ruinous period of destruction'.[82] More recently, Terence Dooley has put the total figure at 199.[83] A majority were owned by members of the Church of Ireland. Intimidation of church members during the Civil War extended well beyond owners of country houses.[84] An editorial in the *Irish Times* on 3 October 1922 described 'losses which have fallen with peculiar severity upon the ex-unionists of the south and west – upon farmers and shopkeepers as well as upon the owners of great estates and lordly mansions', and stated that 'the exodus from Southern Ireland will continue so long as the campaign of destruction flourishes'. It rejected the idea that there was any 'well organised system' in this campaign of destruction and violence but also claimed that the southern minority were the 'foremost sufferers' in the current disorders and called for support from government.[85]

Most fatalities during the civil war involved combatants from the two sides.[86] However, members of the Protestant community endured widespread violence for a mixture of political, economic, and sectarian reasons, as we know from evidence later given by many of them to the Irish Grants Committee, which offered compensation to loyalists for the loss suffered in the period after the Truce.[87] People were intimidated because they were seen as ex-unionists or loyalists. R.B. McDowell has noted that Catholic loyalists were attacked as well as Protestants, but, as McDowell suggested, 'Protestants were singled out for harassment because religion was the easiest way of identifying a person's politics'.[88] Land agitation, including boycott and seizure of property, affected many Protestant farmers and landowners. In her study of violence during the Civil War in Waterford, Limerick, and Tipperary, Gemma Clark has concluded that for members of the Protestant community, 'no one, and nowhere, was completely safe'. Protestant-owned shops and businesses were boycotted. 'Threatening letters, many issued on behalf of the anti-Treaty IRA, made specific threats against the Protestant community. The compensation evidence suggests that the victim's denomination was important to the

[82] W.A. Phillips, *The Revolution in Ireland, 1906–1923* (London, 1923), p. 291.
[83] Dooley, *Decline of the Big House*, pp. 286–7.
[84] *Irish Times*, 3 Oct. 1922.
[85] *Irish Times*, 3 Oct. 1922.
[86] *Irish Times*, 18 May 1923.
[87] See Bury, *Buried Lives*, chaps 2 and 3.
[88] R.B. McDowell, *Crisis and Decline: The Fate of the Southern Unionists* (Dublin, 1997), p. 129.

perpetrator. Attacks on Protestant institutions and religious personnel leave even less room for doubt about the attacker's sectarian agenda'.[89]

Comments by two Catholic bishops at the time confirm the harsh treatment of Protestants and also their strong condemnation of these events. In February 1923, the Catholic bishop of Cork, Daniel Cohalan, described how 'Protestants have suffered severely during the period of the civil war in the south' and urged that 'charity knows no exclusion of creed'.[90] Speaking at Nenagh in North Tipperary in May 1923, the Catholic bishop of Killaloe, Michael Fogarty, appealed to a higher sense of patriotism, noting that 'their Protestant fellow countrymen – he regretted to have to say it – were persecuted and dealt with in a cruel and coarse manner'.[91] In the last week of May 1923, a ceasefire was declared in the Civil War, which brought an end to most if not all the violence against members of the Protestant community.

In the conclusion to his report for the Representative Church Body for 1922, A.F. Maude, the secretary, painted a very different picture to that for 1920. On the earlier occasion he could remain positive 'in the midst of much unrest' and draw attention to evidence in the report of increased financial stability in the church generally. In the conclusion for 1922, however, he stated: 'The Church of Ireland cannot escape its part in the fortunes of the whole country; and our people have borne perhaps even more than their fair share of the losses and disappointments of the past year'. He continued:

> The serious drop in the payments of parochial assessments ... is an indication of a diminished church population in large districts, and of inability on the part of those who remain to make up the sums needed for the maintenance of public worship in many parishes. Numbers of the most generous friends of the church have left Ireland.[92]

Synods in the Aftermath, 1923

On 16 May 1923, the general synod of the Church of Ireland met in Dublin. The previous evening, the bishop of Derry and Raphoe, J.I. Peacocke, in a sermon at St Patrick's Cathedral, Dublin, spoke of the ordeal that people had endured for several years: 'For whatever reason – some because of their religion, often for political or social causes – the members of their church

[89] Clark, *Everyday Violence*, p. 199.
[90] *Irish Times*, 17 Feb. 1923.
[91] *Irish Times*, 8 May 1923.
[92] *Fifty-third Report of the Representative Body of the Church of Ireland* (1923), p. 31.

had been much the worst sufferers in this time of disturbance'. He continued: 'Very many of them, who would have been good and loyal subjects of the Free State, and who only asked to be allowed to live quietly in their homes, had been driven from home and everything, out of the country. The country was the poorer for their loss, no less than the church'.[93] The next day, the primate, Archbishop D'Arcy, took a more cautious and broader approach. He declared that it was not an easy task to address the synod at present, 'when silence and quiet, steady work were better than speech'. He spoke briefly about a 'very anxious and terrible year of suspense and trouble. Tens of thousands of all classes and creeds had fled from the land; many of the very best were gone'. 'Their church', he declared, 'had suffered especially, although all churches had been impoverished. The restraints of religion and morality had been relaxed in the general confusion'.[94] He was now hopeful that order and peace would be restored. The following day, 18 May 1923, an editorial in the *Irish Times* declared that members of the Church of Ireland had 'suffered more than the members of any other community in Ireland from the recent disorders because, for a variety of reasons, they were exposed peculiarly to the greed and violence of lawless men'. Nonetheless, the paper believed that, for the church, 'there had been no slackening of her spiritual efforts' and she was 'calmly confident of her capacity for service to the new Ireland'.[95]

Two other synods were held in Dublin in late May 1923. At the Dublin diocesan synod, the archbishop of Dublin, J.A.F. Gregg, talked of events in the diocese over the previous year: burnings, shootings, and various forms of intimidation had produced their effect, he suggested, and had caused people to leave. He stated that not all who had moved elsewhere were forced to do so, but they left in many cases because they wanted 'security and tranquillity'. Others, 'in various walks of life', and 'their number was not small', were forced to go. At the same time, he pointed out that 'there were very large numbers of them still there, and that very large numbers of them went about their affairs just as they used to'.[96] The following week the archbishop addressed the Glendalough and Kildare diocesan synod in Dublin. He talked of grievous havoc in the two dioceses in the last year, and he mentioned a number of stately homes which had been destroyed. One parish had lost three such homes.[97]

The united Cork diocesan synod occurred in Cork on 13 June 1923. In his address, Bishop C.R. Dowse referred to the decrease of the Church of Ireland population in Cork. 'During the last two and a half years', he said,

[93] *Irish Times*, 15 May 1923.
[94] *Irish Times*, 16 May 1923.
[95] *Irish Times*, 18 May 1923.
[96] *Irish Times*, 29 May 1923.
[97] *Irish Times*, 1 Jun. 1923.

'Our church population has decreased by 8 per cent. It is serious but does not call for despair. Many of our people have gone. Neither we nor our country could afford to lose them. Their houses have been burned. Destruction has marched through the land. The ruins of Ireland may well make all who really love her weep'.[98] In fact, the 1926 census report showed a considerably higher figure of Church of Ireland decrease, after excluding army and navy figures, of around 30 per cent for the whole period, 1911 to 1926. Dowse's underestimate may be an effort on his part not to be too pessimistic, simple lack of knowledge of the full picture, or partly reflecting decline in the three years after his speech.[99] 'But, notwithstanding all our losses', he continued, 'we are not going to be chilled into inactivity, or to give way to depression. That way lies disaster'. He referred to the clergy and their wives: 'In loneliness and danger, in trial and distress, they have remained steadfast and have stood by their people, helping them, and being helped by them'. He also acknowledged that 'during these trying days they have acted as good citizens. They have lived in friendliness and good-fellowship with their Roman Catholic neighbours, and Roman Catholic and Churchmen have proved mutually helpful to each other all over the diocese'.[100]

Also in mid-June 1923, Bishop H.V. White, at the Limerick synod, asked: 'Why have hundreds of industrious protestant Irishmen and women left their native land?' To this he answered: 'Because they felt that they were not welcome here, and that satisfactory careers could not be secured for their boys and girls in their own country'. Nonetheless, he stated: 'I believe that anything like a protestant exodus from the Irish Free State would be deplored by our present rulers'. He urged harmonious relations between the clergy of the two churches.[101] A month later, Bishop White at Tralee, County Kerry, addressed the annual synod of the dioceses of Ardfert and Aghadoe. He referred to positive changes in conditions since last year and also changes

---

[98] *Irish Times*, 14 Jun. 1923. See also Murphy, *Year of Disappearances*.

[99] Between 1911 and 1926, the total Church of Ireland population fell by 40 per cent in Cork County and 52.8 per cent in Cork City: *Census of Population for Ireland, 1926*, p. 10. In 1911, the census recorded 4,390 members of the British army and navy in Cork city and county as Episcopalian (Church of Ireland). We can add another 28 per cent (1,229) to allow for dependants, giving a total of 5,619. Between 1911 and 1926, the Church of Ireland population fell by 12,675 (43 per cent) from 29,568. After excluding army and navy figures, the fall in the Church of Ireland population was 7,056, which represents 29.5 per cent of the original 1911 civilian population. *Census of Ireland, 1911. Area, Houses, and Population: Also the Ages, Civil or Conjugal Condition, Occupations, Birthplaces, Religion, and Education of the People. Province of Munster* [Cd. 6050], HC 1912–13, pp. 184–203.

[100] *Irish Times*, 18 May 1923.

[101] *Irish Times*, 14 Jun. 1923.

in the clergy. He mentioned how 'Canon Wade and his wife bravely stood months of persecution, camping, rather than living in a house stripped of its furniture'. They had now moved, as had Reverend Jumeux of Ardfert, 'due to the exodus of his people from Ardfert'. He mentioned other parishes whose numbers had been greatly reduced: 'the parish of Sneem, by a series of outrages and burnings had lost many of its chief supporters'.[102]

On 3 July 1923, Bishop Robert Miller spoke in Waterford at the Waterford diocesan synod: 'We have had many losses through removals from the diocese, but yet those of our people who remain have shown their love for the church to a remarkable degree'. He pointed out how there had recently been 'a campaign against the constituted authorities, resulting in terrible outrages upon the properties of supporters of the Free State Government'.[103] A resolution was passed expressing horror at the murder of farmer Henry Colclough, Clougheen, Cahir, County Tipperary, on 30 May. Speaking two days later to the Cashel diocesan synod at Cashel, Bishop Miller noted how since the last synod the diocese had passed through a time of great anxiety, 'but we are here today with hopeful hearts'.[104] On 5 July 1923, Bishop W.R. Moore addressed Elphin synod at Boyle, County Roscommon. He talked of the 'very dreadful condition of things' since they last met but acknowledged improvements of the last few months due to the success of the Free State army. He stated: 'One of the saddest features of the situation is that so many of our communion have been driven from the country. By their expulsion such citizens ... are now much fewer than they were'. 'Not a few in our diocese have suffered most grievous wrongs, both in person and property, and the numbers that have suffered in other parts of the country are even much greater'. He continued, 'many parishes in the south and west are almost derelict, because of the numbers which have been driven from their homes ... Yet we see signs on all sides of the loyalty of our people to their church'.[105]

At the very end of July, Bishop Thomas Sterling Berry spoke to the Killaloe diocesan synod at Nenagh, County Tipperary. Referring to the last two years in the diocese, he said that there had been much suffering and loss and expressed deep sympathy with all who had personally suffered: 'we miss today many who were always present at our synod'. Nonetheless, he stated that he was convinced that 'it is better to think of the present and of the future than of the past ... To forget the things that are behind is one great help towards reaching forth into the things that are before'. He warned: 'one of the worst results of civil strife is the risk that it may leave behind it antagonisms which will

---

[102] *Irish Times*, 29 Jun. 1923.
[103] *Irish Times*, 4 Jul. 1923.
[104] *Irish Times*, 6 Jul. 1923.
[105] *Irish Times*, 6 Jul. 1923.

endure for many generations'. He praised the 'ideal of a generous forgiveness and forgetfulness of the past'.[106] Clearly, for the sake of the future, Sterling Berry chose not to dwell on what had happened. He resigned in March 1924 and the subsequent joint synod for Killaloe and Clonfert, held in April in Limerick, was presided over by Gregg, archbishop of Dublin. Gregg was not so reticent. He paid tribute to Sterling Berry, 'the last years of whose episcopacy had been saddened ones for Ireland'. 'In the unsettled conditions of Europe during these years Ireland had not escaped, and there was perhaps no part of the country more unsettled than within the boundaries of the united dioceses'. Gregg then stated: 'Dreadful deeds had been committed, and the destruction of life and property was widespread and happy homes were broken up through violence. Some people in comfortable circumstances had been reduced to poverty, and the population of the dioceses, as far as the Church of Ireland was concerned, had suffered very considerably'.[107]

The synods of the three cross-border dioceses in October 1923 have little comment on southern conditions, apart from educational matters. At the synod for the diocese of Meath, held in Dublin on 12 October, Bishop B.J. Plunket referred to those 'who cannot be with us today, because they have been exiled from their native land. Driven from their homes, they have been forced to seek safety and shelter across the channel'. He recorded that among the synodsmen, 'no less than seven, have had their homes destroyed – burnt and desecrated at the hands of their fellow countrymen'.[108] During October 1923, Bishop J.D.F. Day spoke at three synods for the south-eastern dioceses of Ossory, Ferns and Leighlin. At each, he mentioned the names of families whose homes had been destroyed. He expressed concern that many men and women had left because of these attacks and he feared they would not return. At the same time he warned against pessimism.[109]

Also in October, Bishop John Orr, who replaced the deceased Bishop Ross, addressed the Tuam diocesan synod at Tuam, County Galway.

> We of the Church of Ireland love our country. We would not be true members of the Church of Ireland if we did not. Our very name, of which we are justly proud, betokens our lineage. We are the church of the whole, and not of a part of Ireland, and no power on earth will ever, please God, partition our church, whatever it may do with our country.[110]

[106] *Irish Times*, 1 Aug. 1923.
[107] *Freeman's Journal*, 6 Apr. 1924.
[108] *Irish Times*, 12 Oct. 1923.
[109] *Irish Times*, 3, 13, 27 Oct. 1923
[110] *Irish Times*, 12 Oct. 1923.

At the Killala and Achonry synod two weeks later, at Killala, County Mayo, Bishop Orr stated: 'Many of our people have left our shores to seek new homes elsewhere. We hope they will be happy in the lands of their adoption, and we ask them not to forget us who remain, and who are endeavouring, amidst many discouragements to keep afloat the banner of the church'.[111]

Final Observations

In this chapter we have heard the voices of some of those who lived during this troubled period. The subject and tenor of the bishops' speeches varied greatly – from descriptions of violence and expulsions to more cautious and guarded comments, and to efforts to find hope for the future. We have learnt something about the trials endured by many members of the Church of Ireland during the revolutionary years. During the War of Independence, members suffered intimidation and loss, but speeches at the synods reveal that the worst experience for most of those affected came afterwards, during the first half of 1922 and throughout the Civil War from June 1922 until the end of May 1923. The church had experienced what many described at the time as the 'exodus' of large numbers of its members, a term with strong Old Testament connotations. A full analysis of the decline in church numbers is provided elsewhere by this author and also by Don Wood in this volume.[112] In summary, Great War dead, departing army personnel and their dependants after 1921, and 'voluntary' economic emigrants account for slightly over half the fall of 85,000 in the Church of Ireland population in the period 1911–26. This leaves a figure of around 40,000. Some of these left because they did not like the new regime but most, it is reasonable to say, were 'non-voluntary' emigrants who were forced to leave because of contemporary conditions, as these synod speeches recorded.

The term 'ethnic cleansing' is inappropriate to describe what happened because it does not compare fairly with events elsewhere in this era when ethnic and religious minorities were attacked and expelled in very large numbers, such as the Greeks in Asia Minor. At the same time, these revolutionary years saw the exodus of substantial numbers of members of the Church of Ireland, due in considerable measure to the widespread violence or threat of violence that many in their community suffered. In this same period, thousands of Belfast Catholics were also forced to leave their homes and many came south, but it seems that most returned to the north: between 1911 and

---

[111] *Irish Times*, 29 Oct. 1923.
[112] See B.M. Walker, *Irish History Matters: Commemoration, Identity and Politics* (Dublin, 2019).

1926, the number of Catholics in Belfast went up, although their proportion of the population fell slightly.[113] The marked fall in the number of members of the Church of Ireland indicates that relatively few who left returned.

Through contemporary eyewitness accounts, we have heard the story of the many southern members of the Church of Ireland who were forced to leave Ireland at this time. Of course, it is also the narrative of the greater number of members of the church who stayed, in spite of the extremely severe pressures on their community. While speakers at the synods told of violence against members, they spoke as well of efforts to maintain good relations between denominations and they urged their own people to stay. They acknowledged that during these turbulent years others also endured violence and destruction. Members of the government and Catholic clergy and laity had denounced such attacks on the Protestant community. The majority of members of the Church of Ireland did not join this exodus. Many who suffered attack and loss, or fear of attack and loss, chose to stay – in part, no doubt, because they would not give up their only means of livelihood but also, in part, out of a sense of patriotism and a desire to contribute to the new state and society.[114] In the professions and business they continued to take a major role. Members of the Church of Ireland played a prominent part in both Dáil Éireann and the Irish Senate, at least over the next decade.[115]

For most of the survivors, however, who determined to continue to make Ireland their home, the approach they adopted, as Bishop Thomas Sterling Berry urged in 1923, was to forgive and to forget. In his 1930s *History of the Church of Ireland*, Walter Alison Phillips chose not to recall 'the dark and terrible deeds done in Ireland' at this time.[116] A 1953 *History of the Church of Ireland* covered these events and losses in one line.[117] Probably, in the circumstances of the times and for the sake of those who remained, this was the best approach. Today, however, in the twenty-first century, we can look at these matters again and investigate them fully. As we do, we can recall once more the words of Archbishop C.F. D'Arcy at the general synod of May 1923, when he praised the 'quiet courage and persistence' of church members, along

---

[113] Vaughan and Fitzpatrick, *Irish Historical Statistics: Population 1821–1971*, pp. 67–9; McDowell, *Crisis and Decline*, p. 131.

[114] *Irish Times*, 3 Oct. 1922.

[115] Out of a total of 153 TDs, Protestants (mostly members of the Church of Ireland) numbered 9 in 1922, 14 in June 1927, 12 in 1932, but 7 in 1937 and 3 in 1948. See B.M. Walker, *A Political History of the Two Irelands: From Partition to Peace* (Basingstoke, 2012), p. 59.

[116] Phillips, *Church of Ireland*, pp. 412–13.

[117] T.J. Johnston, J.L. Robinson, and R.W. Jackson, *A History of the Church of Ireland* (Dublin, 1953), p. 269.

with their 'Christian fortitude and true patriotism', which he believed gave hope for the future.[118]

[118] *Irish Times*, 16 May 1923.

CHAPTER IV

The Southern Unionist Business Community and the Economics of Home Rule and Secession

Frank Barry

The decline of Irish industry in the nineteenth century had a lasting effect on nationalist economic thinking. Other regions – including some in Britain and many across the peripheries of Europe and beyond – were similarly affected by the massive price declines and transport cost reductions of the industrial revolution era.[1] That these developments followed the passage of the Act of Union made all strands of Irish nationalism wary of the processes of free trade and economic integration.[2] Protectionism was a fundamental element of Arthur Griffith's *Sinn Féin Policy* of 1907 and an equivalent desire for greater self-sufficiency was evident in all of the new states to emerge in Europe in the aftermath of the Great War.[3]

It was widely assumed then that a new Irish state would be protectionist from the outset.[4] Analysis of the economic dimension to unionist attitudes has focused on the export orientation of Ulster's industries, for which free trade was vital. Most of the substantial exporting businesses elsewhere in the country were also in unionist hands, however, and the interests of these southern businesses would be similarly threatened by impediments to international trade. The southern unionist business elite was also fearful of the increased taxation which it saw as an inevitable consequence of exiting the UK fiscal union. 'Loyalism' was not just a matter of historical, political, and religious fellow-feeling or fear of ethno-religious domination. It was also a

---

[1] Cormac Ó Gráda, *Ireland: A New Economic History, 1780–1939* (Oxford, 1994), pp. 307, 348; Sidney Pollard, 'Industrialization and the European Economy', *Economic History Review*, 26/4 (1973), pp. 636–48.

[2] Mary E. Daly, *Industrial Development and Irish National Identity, 1922–1939* (Syracuse, NY, 1992), pp. 4–5.

[3] Arthur Griffith, *The Sinn Féin Policy* (Dublin, 1907), p. 14; Ivan Berend, 'The Failure of Economic Nationalism: Central and Eastern Europe Before World War II', *Revue Économique*, 51/2 (2000), pp. 315–22.

[4] David Johnson, *The Interwar Economy in Ireland* (Dundalk, 1989), p. 21.

reflection of economic self-interest. Some substantial Catholic business owners were among the supporters of the status quo.

Though the 'leavers' and 'remainers' of a hundred years ago were largely divided along ethno-religious lines, there are some beguiling parallels with the Brexit debates of recent times. Both sides, then as now, differed in their interpretations of the historical consequences of political and economic union and in their expectations of the consequences of secession. The southern business elite was highly sceptical of what it saw as the utopian assumptions (or 'magical thinking', as European Commission President Jean-Claude Juncker termed it in 2017) of economic nationalists who posited that exiting the union would yield windfall gains in ways that were difficult not only to quantify but to identify. There are social parallels too. Leavers, then as now, were decried by their critics as parochial, the 'Big Houses' being described by one opponent as 'oases of culture, of uprightness and of fair dealing, in what will otherwise be a desert of dead uniformity [where] lofty ideals, whether of social or imperial interest, will be smothered in an atmosphere of superstition, greed and chicanery'.[5] In the language of today, the leavers – those rooted in the local – were 'from somewhere', while the remainers – the self-perceived metropolitan elite – were 'from anywhere'.[6]

Nor is the political 'echo chamber' of today without its parallels. Nora Robertson, in her memoir of life in an Irish ascendancy family, recalled that the southern unionists were led by those 'who had never in their lives mixed with educated nationalists'.[7] One reported, upon meeting IPP delegates at the Irish Convention in 1917, that 'we liked the nationalists a great deal better than we expected'.[8] Though Protestant and Catholic businessmen interacted with each other in the various chambers of commerce, they 'moved in separate social circles'.[9] The divergent interpretations of the historical consequences of union were not, of course, solely due to a lack of communication: people adhere to the narratives that support their political and economic interests.[10]

---

[5] J.M. Wilson, cited in Patrick Buckland, *Irish Unionism I: The Anglo Irish and the New Ireland, 1885–1922* (Dublin, 1972), p. xxi.

[6] David Goodhart, *The Road to Somewhere: The Populist Revolt and the Future of Politics* (London, 2017).

[7] Nora Robertson, *Crowned Harp: Memories of the Last Years of the Crown in Ireland* (Dublin, 1960), p. 104.

[8] Buckland, *Irish Unionism I*, p. 99.

[9] Fergus Campbell, *The Irish Establishment, 1879–1914* (Oxford, 2009), p. 223.

[10] For an analysis of the roots of these narratives, see Liam Kennedy, 'Nationalism and Unionism in Ireland', chap. 3 in *Unhappy the Land: The Most Oppressed People Ever, the Irish?* (Sallins, 2016).

Nationalist historiography had focused on the decline of Irish manufacturing under the union. It played down the fact that, as James Meenan wrote in 1943,

> Free Trade encouraged new industries while it destroyed the old. The new industries owed their rise and prosperity to exactly the same circumstances of free import and free competition that had proved fatal to their predecessors. The same decade that saw the Famine witnessed the rise of the linen and ship-building industries. The second half of that seemingly most un-industrial century saw the reorganisation of the brewing and distilling trades and a growth in the export of biscuits and jute. [It] is a curious misreading of Irish history between the Famine and the Treaty that ignores the achievements of these trades.[11]

That these and other successful southern export industries were ignored by nationalist writers may be related to the fact that they were almost exclusively under unionist ownership.

Unionist Dominance of Southern Irish Business

By the end of the nineteenth century, the great landowners had been overtaken by the business elite as the richest sector of Irish society.[12] That this new elite was also predominantly Protestant and unionist is not solely a consequence of the concentration of industry in Ulster.[13] A submission by the Dublin Chamber of Commerce to the Unionist Convention of 1892 stated that 'As a corporate body we have no politics, yet we are essentially a unionist chamber ... solely and simply because in defending the union we are defending the commercial interests with which we are identified'.[14] Similarly, a history of the Limerick Chamber notes that its ethos was fundamentally unionist until the 1920s. Though Catholic merchants had played an important role in the

---

[11] James Meenan, 'Irish Industry and Industrial Policy 1921–1943', *Studies*, 32/126 (1943), pp. 209–18 (at p. 211).

[12] Campbell, *Irish Establishment*, p. 200.

[13] Though the non-Catholic share of the population of the Irish Free State area declined from 10.4 per cent in 1911 to 7.4 per cent in 1926, Protestants made up 30 per cent to 40 per cent of employers and managers in most industrial sectors in the new state (Census of Population, 1926). The census provides no details of the size categories of the firms involved, which is the focus of particular attention here.

[14] Cited in Enda MacMahon, *A Most Respectable Meeting of Merchants: Dublin Chamber of Commerce. A History* (Dublin, 2014), p. 140.

organisation since its foundation, 'few nationalists held the presidency until after independence, with the notable exception of Protestant Home Ruler, [bacon producer] Alexander Shaw'.[15]

In none of the southern export sectors mentioned by Meenan – brewing, distilling, biscuits, and jute – 'was Irish consumption above a quarter, at the best, of the annual production'.[16] The leading firms in each of these sectors were under unionist ownership. Guinness was by far the most substantial firm in brewing, and the largest manufacturing firm outside of Ulster. At a time when no more than 20 or so southern manufacturers had a workforce in excess of 500, the brewery at St James's Gate employed around 4,000.[17] Lords Ardilaun and Iveagh, the leading representatives of the Guinness family, were conservative unionists, and two of Iveagh's sons sat on the Tory benches at Westminster. Other unionist-owned southern breweries included Beamish & Crawford in Cork, Findlater's Mountjoy Brewery in Dublin, and the Castlebellingham and Drogheda breweries of the Cairnes family in County Louth.[18]

Biscuit company W. & R. Jacob was another major southern employer, with a workforce of around 3,000. The chairman and managing director, George Newson Jacob, was a member of the Dublin Unionist Association and one of a group of businessmen who submitted a 13-point critique of the economics of Home Rule in 1913.[19] The jute firm alluded to by Meenan was Goodbody's of Clara, King's County (County Offaly). The Goodbodys, like the Jacobs, were Quakers. Goodbody family members served on most of the unionist committees of the era. Though the whiskey trade was in the doldrums at the time, the proprietors of Jameson's and Power's were among the wealthy elite. Andrew Jameson was one of the most prominent southern unionists and was a governor and director of the Bank of Ireland as well as chairman of the distilling company.[20] Power's was owned by a Catholic unionist family. Besides

---

[15] Matthew Potter, *Limerick's Merchants: Traders and Shakers* (Limerick, 2015), p. 76. The presidency of the Cork Incorporated Chamber of Commerce and Shipping alternated between Catholics and Protestants, as may be gleaned from the list of past presidents provided in *Cork: Its Trade and Commerce* (Cork, 1919), p. 27.

[16] Meenan, 'Irish Industry', p. 211.

[17] The employment numbers quoted in the chapter come from a database compiled by the author and described in Frank Barry, 'The Leading Manufacturing Firms in the Irish Free State in 1929', *Irish Historical Studies*, 42/162 (2018), pp. 293–316.

[18] Evidence of the unionist affiliation of the business owners referred to in the chapter is provided in the Appendix to this chapter.

[19] *Irish Independent*, 11 Nov. 1913.

[20] Buckland, *Irish Unionism I*, p. xix; Pauric J. Dempsey, 'Jameson, Andrew', in James McGuire and James Quinn (eds), *Dictionary of Irish Biography* (Cambridge, 2010): http://dib.cambridge.org/viewReadPage.do?articleId=a4253.

the ailing Dublin Distillers, which would collapse in the 1920s, the other large whiskey company, Cork Distilleries, was under nationalist ownership. In comparison with Jameson and Power's however, its sales were oriented more towards the home market.

Large exporting firms in sectors other than those mentioned by Meenan included the Condensed Milk Company of Ireland, British chemicals firm Kynoch's, bacon company Henry Denny & Sons, and fertiliser producer Goulding's. Most of the private creameries had been crowded out by the rapid expansion of the co-operatives since their emergence in the closing decades of the nineteenth century. The Condensed Milk Company was by far the largest of the private creameries to remain in operation. It employed around 3,000 in its network across Munster in the period prior to its collapse in the early 1920s. Along with firms such as Henry Denny, Goodbody jute and Carroll's tobacco, it prospered in the Great War era. The value of condensed milk exports from Ireland came to fully half that of brewery exports in 1920. The company was controlled from its Lansdowne base on the banks of the Shannon in Limerick city by the 'strongly unionist' Church of Ireland businessman Sir Thomas Henry Cleeve.[21]

The leading foreign-owned manufacturing company before Henry Ford commenced tractor production in Cork city in 1919 was Birmingham firm Kynoch's, owned by Arthur Chamberlain, brother of the leading British Liberal Unionist MP. The closure of its cordite, explosives, and chemicals plant at Arklow in 1918 led to the loss of 3,000 jobs.[22] Though there had been persistent claims since the establishment of the Arklow plant in 1895 that the British government had looked with disfavour on the decision to establish an Irish operation, its closure was apparently related to the UK-wide restructuring of the industry at the end of the Great War.[23]

Waterford-based Henry Denny & Sons was the largest of the Irish bacon producers. It operated a number of plants across Munster, including a substantial one in Limerick, which had become the centre of the bacon trade. Several of Henry Denny's sons had taken over the running of the firm's London agency in the mid-nineteenth century and a member of this English branch of the family was responsible for the Great War provisioning of bacon supplies for the British army. Charles Edmond Denny, head of the Irish branch, was a member of the General Council of the Irish Unionist Alliance in 1919.

---

[21] Shaun Boylan, 'Cleeve, Sir Thomas Henry', in James McGuire and James Quinn (eds), *Dictionary of Irish Biography* (Cambridge, 2010): http://dib.cambridge.org/viewReadPage.do?articleId=a1729.

[22] *Irish Times*, 25 Jan. 1905; 20 Feb. 1912; 16 and 19 Feb. 1918.

[23] Anthony Cannon, 'Arklow's Explosive History: Kynoch, 1895–1918', *History Ireland*, 14/1 (2006).

Goulding's, by far the largest Irish fertiliser producer, employed around 900 in its six plants in what would soon be the Free State area and a further 300 or so in its plants north of the future border. Sir William Goulding was a leading southern unionist and his brother, Lord Wargrave, sat as a Unionist member of the House of Commons until raised to a peerage in 1922.[24] The Gouldings and Dennys were members of the Church of Ireland.

Most of the substantial export-oriented textile and clothing companies were also under Protestant and unionist control. Limerick Clothing, established by Scottish expatriate Peter Tait in the 1800s, had developed an international reputation as a producer of military uniforms. Tait went bankrupt when a consignment of Alabama cotton bartered for Confederate uniforms was seized by Union forces, and the company was taken over in the 1890s by a group of Limerick businessmen, the most prominent of whom was the unionist milling magnate J.F.G. Bannatyne. The sole Catholic among the new owners, notably, was Stephen O'Mara, proprietor of the second largest Irish bacon company.[25] O'Mara, who appears to have shared a friendship with Bannatyne, had served briefly as a Home Rule MP and his family would come to play a significant role in the independence movement.[26] Another firm which had developed a substantial international reputation in the nineteenth century was Balbriggan hosiery manufacturer Smyth & Co., which had come into the ownership of local unionist and Church of Ireland family the Whytes towards the end of the century. Balbriggan also hosted the 'Sea Banks' hosiery facility of English firm Deeds, Templar & Co., which was destroyed when the town was ransacked by the 'Black and Tans' in 1920.[27] Each of the hosiery firms had a workforce of around 500. Though many of the employees were 'outworkers' – employees who worked off-site – they enjoyed relatively steady employment compared to other outworkers across the country.

The largest of the southern linen firms of the time was Cork Spinning & Weaving. Established by the Presbyterian Ogilvie family in 1889, it employed around 1,000 in the 1920s. Greenmount Spinning & Weaving of Harold's Cross in Dublin employed around 600 and was controlled by the Pims, a

---

[24] *Weekly Irish Times*, 18 Jul. 1925.

[25] Sharon Slater, *A Stitch in Time: A History of Limerick Clothing Factory* (Limerick, 2017), p. 48.

[26] Stephen O'Mara Snr. would later take the pro-Treaty side and serve briefly as a Free State senator. Two of his sons, James and Stephen, would act as Dáil Éireann envoys to the USA but take opposing positions on the Treaty, one becoming a pro-Treaty TD, the other a mayor of Limerick and lifelong supporter of Fianna Fáil. Shaun Boylan, 'O'Mara, Stephen', in James McGuire and James Quinn (eds), *Dictionary of Irish Biography* (Cambridge, 2009): http://dib.cambridge.org/viewReadPage.do?articleId=a6892.

[27] *Irish Times*, 1 Feb. 1921.

well-known unionist family of Quaker extraction. Another Protestant-owned firm, Boyne Weaving of Drogheda, employed around the same number. The operations would be integrated to form Greenmount & Boyne in 1925. Smaller firms in the sector included Charles Gallen & Co. of Balbriggan and Dundalk Linen, owned by the Achesons of Tyrone. The Gallens were a Catholic family of Ulster origin. Fearful of the disruption of the linen supply chain that partition would entail, they viewed the establishment of the Free State with disquiet.[28]

Internationally trading firms are of particular significance since they would have had most to fear from the disruption to trade that independence was presumed to entail. Among export-oriented firms, the sole large employer in nationalist hands was Martin Mahony's Blarney Woollen Mills. There were a greater number of large Catholic and nationalist-owned firms in domestically oriented manufacturing sectors.[29] Though the reasons for this are yet to be identified, historical differences in access to capital may have been a contributory factor given the capital outlay involved in developing an export network. Even in domestically oriented categories, however, most of the large firms were also under unionist ownership.[30] Flour milling was dominated by the Limerick-based Bannatyne conglomerate, which included a number of other firms as subsidiaries and came under the control of the Goodbody family in the 1890s. Other unionist flour millers included the Church of Ireland families the Odlums and the Pollexfens. Cantrell & Cochrane was the largest mineral water producer. Its proprietor, Sir Henry Cochrane, was a member of the Irish Unionist Alliance, as was Sir John Nutting, proprietor of E. & J. Burke, the largest bottling company. Johnston, Mooney & O'Brien, one the largest bakeries in the country, was controlled by prominent unionist John Mooney. The largest firms in paper, printing, and publishing were Hely's and Alexander Thom & Co. Though Charles Wisdom Hely maintained a low profile politically, there is evidence of his family's support of conservative unionist

---

[28] Private communication with Gallen family.

[29] Among such firms were clothing and footwear company Dwyer's of Cork, agricultural machinery producer Philip Pierce & Co. of Wexford, and Boland's and Kennedy's bakeries in Dublin. William Martin Murphy's main business ventures – the *Irish Independent*, Clery's, and the Dublin United Tramway Company – were also home market oriented.

[30] Bielenberg refers to the over-representation of Protestants in the ownership and management of the southern industrial sector as 'almost as striking as the dominance of Protestants in land ownership prior to the Land Acts': Andy Bielenberg, 'The Industrial Elite in Ireland from the Industrial Revolution to the First World War', in Fintan Lane (ed.), *Politics, Society and the Middle Class in Modern Ireland* (Basingstoke, 2010), p. 169.

causes.[31] Thom's was chaired by a member of the Pim family and successive managing directors took an active part in unionist politics.

Of the seven major department stores in Dublin in the decades to independence, only Clery's – part of the business empire of William Martin Murphy – was under Catholic nationalist control.[32] Hardware and builders' provisioning was another traditionally Protestant sector. Sir Maurice Dockrell, principal of one of the leading Dublin hardware firms, was elected as an Irish Unionist Alliance MP for Dublin Rathmines in the 1918 general election. J. & P. Good was one of the largest building contractors. Its proprietor, John Good, was unionist, as were the proprietors of the largest coal-distribution businesses, William Hewat of Heitons and Robert Tedcastle of Tedcastle McCormick. The owners of T. & C. Martin, the major Dublin timber business, were among a group of Catholic unionist businessmen.[33]

Most of the banks operating in the Free State at independence were also unionist in ethos. These included the Bank of Ireland, the Provincial, the Royal, and the three Belfast-headquartered institutions: Ulster Bank, the Northern, and the Belfast Bank.[34] Bank of Ireland was the most significant: Oliver MacDonagh points out that the members of its court of directors in the immediate pre-independence era 'were unionists to a man, and the great majority of staff would have regarded themselves as "loyalists"'.[35] This was true across much of the rest of the financial sector also. By far the largest accountancy firms of the era were Craig Gardner and Stokes Brothers & Pim.[36] Robert Stokes and Sir Robert Gardner were among the 150 southern business leaders to criticise the Home Rule bill in 1913.[37]

Dwarfing even Guinness as the largest private-sector employer in the 26 counties was the Great Southern & Western Railway Co., which had a workforce of over 8,000 in 1907. The second largest rail company, the Great Northern, employed almost 3,000 in the Free State alone in 1925. Sir William Goulding, chairman of the Great Southern, and Fane Vernon, chairman of the

[31] For example, he and his wife hosted a meeting of the Conservative Women's Franchise Association at their home in 1910: *Freeman's Journal*, 26 Nov. 1910.
[32] Frank Barry, 'The Life and Death of Protestant Businesses in Independent Ireland', in Ian d'Alton and Ida Milne (eds), *Protestant and Irish: The Minority's Search for Place in Independent Ireland* (Cork, 2019).
[33] 'The Roman Catholic Petition', *Irish Times*, 24 Mar. 1893.
[34] The National, the Hibernian, and the Munster & Leinster Bank, by contrast, were broadly nationalist in orientation: Campbell, *Irish Establishment*, p. 202.
[35] Oliver MacDonagh, 'The Victorian Bank, 1824–1914', in F.S.L. Lyons (ed.), *Bank of Ireland 1783–1983: Bicentenary Essays* (Dublin, 1983), p. 44.
[36] Tony Farmar, *The Versatile Profession: A History of Accountancy in Ireland since 1850* (Dublin, 2013), p. 65.
[37] 'Home Rule Finance: A Tory Business View', *Irish Independent*, 27 Nov. 1913.

Great Northern, were leading unionists, and the boards of both companies remained strongly unionist-dominated in the decades to independence.[38]

Not all significant Protestant business owners were unionist, however. The Dublin Dockyard Co., which had a workforce of around 1,000 at the end of the Great War, was controlled by an exclusively Protestant board of British-born engineers led by Scottish Presbyterian John Smellie. Smellie attended a meeting of Protestant Home Rulers that was addressed by Douglas Hyde and W.B. Yeats in 1913. Also in attendance were various members of the Quaker flour-milling family the Shackletons, the Unitarian proprietors of brush-maker I.S. Varian & Co., and Robert Woods, proprietor of the large Dublin jam and confectionery manufacturer Williams & Woods.[39] Some families were divided in their political loyalties. Though the Kilkenny Catholic brewers and bottlers the Smithwicks were well-known nationalists – one had been a leading Repealer, another a Home Rule MP – John Smithwick was a signatory to the 1893 Catholic petition against Home Rule.[40] Similarly, while most of the Shackletons followed in the footsteps of their predecessor Abraham (d.1912), a member of the Protestant Home Rule Association, the proprietor of the Anna Liffey mill in Lucan, George Shackleton, was a committee member of the Irish Unionist Alliance in the lead-up to independence.

The boundaries between unionism and moderate nationalism had been less sharply delineated in earlier times. Many moderate nationalists, including Limerick bacon producer and Protestant Home Ruler Alexander Shaw, had welcomed Queen Victoria on her visit to Ireland in 1900.[41] Colonel John Eustace Jameson, a director of the William Jameson distillery on Marrowbone Lane (one of the several that made up the Dublin Distillers Co.) and a Home Rule MP in the 1890s, had 'clear imperialist sympathies'.[42] He was labelled by one local party member as 'a Tory in disguise and a trader whose main aim in Parliament was to sell his whiskey'.[43] He later switched allegiance to the Tories.

---

[38] *Irish Times*, 1 Mar. 1917 [GSW]; 24 Feb. 1916 [GNR].
[39] *Irish Times*, 25 Jan. 1913.
[40] *Irish Times*, 24 Mar. 1893. The petition held that 'the intended legislation would not only mean ruin to business and the general prosperity, but would damage the interests of their religion' (*Irish Times*, 28 Mar. 1893). Daniel O'Connell's younger son, owner of the Phoenix Brewery in Dublin, also signed the petition, stating that he was sure that if his father were alive, he would not consent 'to hand over Ireland to the tender mercies of the so-called Nationalist leaders': *Irish Times*, 31 Mar. 1893.
[41] Tadhg Moloney, *Limerick Constitutional Nationalism, 1898–1918: Change and Continuity* (Newcastle upon Tyne, 2010), p. 58.
[42] Patrick Maume, *The Long Gestation: Irish Nationalist Life, 1891–1918* (Dublin, 1999), p. 33.
[43] Bielenberg, 'Industrial Elite', p. 166.

Though the religious ethos of many business firms remained identifiable up to the 1960s, as Tony Farmar notes, their political ethos could shift with changes in ownership and management.[44] Maurice Brooks of the leading Dublin builders' providers, Brooks Thomas, had been a Liberal MP for Dublin 'in the days before the question of Home Rule became the all-important issue which it has been in latter years'.[45] On his death in 1905 the chairmanship of the company passed to his son-in-law Richard Gamble, a member of the City of Dublin Unionist Association.[46] Sir John Arnott Snr, who died in 1898, had been a leading unionist industrialist with business interests across a broad range of sectors.[47] The Arnott family retained ownership of the *Irish Times* until 1946, but control of the Dublin department store which bears the family name passed in 1909 to the Presbyterian family of Alexander Nesbitt, a Redmondite Home Ruler.[48] And though the Limerick firm of J.P. Evans & Co., dairy engineers and agricultural machinery suppliers, was part of the business empire of Sir Thomas Henry Cleeve, the manager of the company in 1900 was a member of the United Irish League who went on to serve several terms as mayor of Limerick.[49]

The Threat of Home Rule

Unionists differed from much of the nationalist population in their international outlook and commitment to the imperial project. Their 1917 proposal that customs revenue be retained by Westminster as an Irish contribution to war debt and common defence would, however, also preclude the possibility of a trade war and ensure continued Irish representation in the imperial parliament.[50] In an apparent conciliatory response to nationalist demands they suggested that control of excise be separated from customs and delegated to the prospective new Irish parliament. By a happy coincidence, this would have the consequence of protecting the Irish brewing and

---

[44] Tony Farmar, *Heitons – A Managed Transition: Heitons in the Irish Coal, Iron and Building Markets, 1818–1996* (Dublin, 1996), p. 34.

[45] *Irish Independent*, 7 Dec. 1905.

[46] Enda MacMahon, *Brief Biographies of the Past Presidents of Dublin Chamber of Commerce, 1783–2011* (Dublin, 2012), p. 92.

[47] *Irish Times*, 21 Dec. 1983.

[48] *Irish Times*, 21 Dec. 1983; Ronald Nesbitt, *At Arnott's of Dublin, 1843–1993* (Dublin, 1993), pp. 59–64.

[49] Moloney, *Limerick Constitutional Nationalism*, p. 58.

[50] 'Memorandum by Southern Unionists on Fiscal Autonomy', *Report of the Proceedings of the Irish Convention* (Dublin, 1918), appendix vii, p. 83.

distilling industries from the temperance-oriented British parliamentarians of the era.[51]

Southern unionists had a range of concerns other than those pertaining to trade, security, and international affairs. A 1913 statement by 150 'Tory business leaders' warned that Home Rule would raise the cost of finance and drive capital and industry from the country.[52] They used their influence in the House of Lords to have the Government of Ireland Act amended to protect private property from expropriation and secured the abolition of the provision that allowed an Irish parliament to impose additional income tax or surtax.[53] Unionists were not just fearful of being targeted by a Home Rule parliament: they were highly sceptical of nationalist competence on fiscal matters, of which Lord Midleton, their principal spokesman at the time, complained to Churchill in terms that bordered on the racist. 'The Irish are morally cowards [and] exceedingly ignorant', he wrote. 'Greatest extravagances will probably be proposed and the proceedings in the Dail Eireann show you how the government are likely to have their hands forced'.[54] A Dublin Chamber of Commerce report warned that the lack of economic expertise would be exacerbated by partition, which would deprive the prospective southern parliament 'of the steadying influence and business training of the men of Ulster'.[55]

As the wealthier segment of the population, unionists particularly feared the enactment of 'hasty legislative proposals at the expense of the 350,000 loyalists who will be practically unrepresented but who pay most of the taxes'.[56] Expectations around the future tax burden were a major point of divergence between the two sides. That Ireland was overtaxed had been an article of nationalist faith since O'Connell and had been supported by the findings of the Financial Relations Committee of 1896.[57] Government spending on Ireland had grown substantially since then, however, and the Primrose Committee, established in advance of the Home Rule Act of 1914, reported that the Irish surplus had since turned to deficit.[58] The old age pension was the subject of

---

[51] Buckland, *Irish Unionism I*, pp. 109–18. Buckland reports that unionists at the Convention took advice on fiscal matters from the Guinnesses.

[52] *Irish Independent*, 27 Nov. 1913.

[53] Buckland, *Irish Unionism I*, p. 231.

[54] Buckland, *Irish Unionism I*, p. 267.

[55] *Irish Times*, 1 Jun. 1920.

[56] Buckland, *Irish Unionism I*, p. 266.

[57] William Hynes, 'To What Extent Were Economic Factors Important in the Separation of the South of Ireland from the United Kingdom and What Was the Economic Impact?', *Cambridge Journal of Economics*, 38/2 (2014), pp. 369–7; *Irish Times*, 20 Apr. 1912.

[58] *Irish Times*, 20 Apr. 1912.

particular comment. The Pensions Act of 1908 had been designed with the industrial population of Great Britain in mind, though the same rates were payable in Ireland under the unified system of administration. The Primrose Committee regarded it as 'absolutely certain' that an act designed by an Irish Parliament 'would not have been of such a costly character as to absorb at one stroke nearly one-third of the total revenue of the country'.[59]

There were clear divisions even within the Irish Parliamentary Party on most of the major economic issues of the day.[60] The presumption that independence would bring prosperity, however, clouded the vision of most on the nationalist side. Tom Kettle, one-time Irish Party MP and first professor of national economics at UCD, argued that much of the fiscal burden was the result of past misgovernment, which, he assumed, would be rectified by Home Rule.[61] Arthur Griffith saw no reason why the island could not provide a living for a population of 15 million.[62] Erskine Childers, though he too was convinced that independence would unleash prosperity, was almost alone among nationalists in recognising the financial difficulties that might have to be faced in the near term:

> If there were no alternative between financial independence without a farthing of temporary aid, and permanent financial dependence ... it would pay Ireland a thousandfold in the future to choose the former scheme, remodel taxation promptly to meet the initial deficit, and with equal promptitude set on foot such a drastic reduction of expenditure as would ensure the rapid attainment of a proper financial equilibrium. When once the Irish realized the issue, they would accept the responsibility with all its attendant sacrifices, which would no doubt be severe.[63]

---

[59] *Irish Times*, 20 Apr. 1912.

[60] 'Imagining Home Rule', chap. 10 in James McConnell, *The Irish Parliamentary Party and the Third Home Rule Crisis* (Dublin, 2013). William Martin Murphy, the leading Catholic nationalist businessman of the era, is credited, however, with winning moderate nationalist opinion to the view that the power of taxation, including Customs and Excise, was the very essence of self-government and that any parliament without these powers would not be worth having: Andy Bielenberg, 'Entrepreneurship, Power and Public Opinion in Ireland: The Career of William Martin Murphy', *Irish Economic and Social History*, 27 (2000), pp. 25–43.

[61] Thomas Kettle, *Home Rule Finance: An Experiment in Justice* (Dublin, 1911), pp. 33–5, cited in Cormac Ó Gráda, '"The Greatest Blessing of All': The Old Age Pension in Ireland', *Past & Present*, 175/1 (2002), pp. 124–61.

[62] Arthur Griffith, *The Resurrection of Hungary* (Dublin, 1918), p. 166.

[63] Erskine Childers, *The Framework of Home Rule* (London, 1911), p. 283, cited in Graham Brownlow, 'The Political Economy of the Ulster Crisis: Historiography, Social Capability and Globalisation', in D. George Boyce and Alan O'Day (eds), *The Ulster Crisis: 1885–1921* (Basingstoke, 2006), pp. 27–46 (at pp. 31–2).

The Free State

The Unionist Alliance split in 1919 with the more pragmatic elements within southern unionism breaking away to form the Unionist Anti-Partition League.[64] Midleton informed the British cabinet a few years later that 'almost all the most influential businessmen and the largest landowners in the south' were now 'willing to concede their financial interest to an Irish parliament rather than face the continuance of the chaos of the last 15 years'.[65] Complete fiscal autonomy was ceded by the British at a late stage in the Anglo-Irish Treaty negotiations, and Walter Guinness pronounced in parliament that the only alternative to the Treaty was chaos: 'In accepting it they might be embarking on a slippery slope, but a slippery slope was preferable to a precipice'.[66]

Independence was to prove much less traumatic for the unionist business community than had been feared. Only very modest trade barriers were imposed in the 1920s. The Fiscal Inquiry Committee, which issued its advice in 1923, deemed few of the industries seeking protection worthy of 'the indulgence which is, perhaps, rightly extended to extreme youth'.[67] The main factor behind the government's rejection of the Griffith policy, however, was the impact it would have on agriculture, which, in the committee's view, 'must be considered as of paramount importance'.[68] Farmers could be prosperous only if they were able to export, and to export meant competing on the British market which offered tariff-free access to agricultural products from across the world.[69] This required that Irish costs be kept to a minimum, while tariffs, whether levied on producer or consumer goods, would inevitably drive up prices. Cumann na nGaedheal was careful, for this reason, to reduce and later abolish duties on tea to offset the impact on the cost of living of the experimental tariffs introduced in the 1920s.[70] The hostility of agricultural interests to protection diminished with the onset of the Great Depression. Falling commodity prices eroded belief in free trade in agricultural economies across the globe. Kevin O'Rourke judges it inevitable that Ireland would have followed suit, even in the

---

[64] R.B. McDowell, *Crisis and Decline: The Fate of the Southern Unionists* (Dublin, 1997), p. 65.

[65] Buckland, *Irish Unionism I*, p. 218.

[66] McDowell, *Crisis and Decline*, p. 112.

[67] Fiscal Inquiry Committee, *Final Report*, 1923, para. 96.

[68] Fiscal Inquiry Committee, *Final Report*, 1923, para. 87.

[69] James Meenan, 'From Free Trade to Self Sufficiency', in F. MacManus (ed.), *The Years of the Great Test, 1926–39* (Cork, 1967), p. 71.

[70] Anna Devlin and Frank Barry, 'Protection versus Free Trade in the Free State Era: The Finance Attitude', *Irish Economic and Social History*, 46/1 (2019), pp. 3–21.

absence of the Economic War.[71] Mary Daly concurs, questioning whether the 1932 self-sufficiency experiment could even have been attempted 'if difficult conditions had not created sufficient agricultural support for protection to remove the implicit farming veto over industrial tariffs that had existed throughout the twenties'.[72]

The Great Depression would also impact on the stance of other export sectors. Goodbody Jute welcomed the protection it received from the encroachment of cheap imports from Calcutta, and expansion of the domestic sugar industry provided a new source of demand for its output of sacks, bags, and twine. Dundalk Linen, which had been threatened by the erection of a customs frontier with Northern Ireland in 1923, lobbied for the imposition of a tariff on linen imports, as did Greenmount & Boyne.[73] The department stores expanded their manufacturing businesses behind the tariff wall: Arnott's 'thanked God and the government's economic nationalism of the 1930s for the development of new knitting and making-up industries which became vital during the period of the Emergency and were very useful for years afterwards'.[74] Timber firm T. & C. Martin and other builders' providers benefited from the expansion in public construction under Fianna Fáil. Guinness and Jacob's insured themselves by building or extending factories in England.

There had been fears on the part of internationally trading businesses and financial interests that independence might lead to a severing of the currency link with sterling. By the time a decision on currency matters came to be made in 1927, hyperinflation had led to the collapse of a number of continental currencies and 'hostility toward inflation [had become] the *leitmotif* of economic policy across Europe'.[75] Meenan quotes former unionist Major Bryan Cooper, whom he describes as 'one of the most enlightened members of the Dáil', to the effect that 'once you begin to tamper with currency you begin to operate an inflation that leads to national disaster'.[76] The one-to-one link with sterling was retained and would survive until 1979, when the European project was under way.

Southern unionist concerns that the new state might prove financially irresponsible were definitively laid to rest. The state was born into fiscal crisis.

---

[71] Kevin O'Rourke, 'Ireland and the Bigger Picture', in David Dickson and Cormac Ó Gráda (eds), *Refiguring Ireland: Essays in Honour of L.M. Cullen* (Dublin, 2003).

[72] Daly, *Industrial Development*, p. 174.

[73] Donal Hall, 'Partition and County Louth', *Journal of the County Louth Archaeological and Historical Society*, 27/2 (2010), pp. 243–82; *Irish Times*, 7 Dec. 1931.

[74] Nesbitt, *Arnott's of Dublin*, 112.

[75] Patricia Clavin, *The Great Depression in Europe, 1929–1939* (New York, 2000), pp. 31–3.

[76] James Meenan, *The Irish Economy since 1922* (Liverpool, 1970), p. 217.

Compensation for property losses and expenditure on the army absorbed almost three-quarters of government revenue in 1924.[77] Had the share of the UK national debt for which the country was liable under the Anglo-Irish Treaty been called in, it would have left the new state close to bankruptcy.[78] The pensions burden accounted for the bulk of social welfare spending and was an obvious target for adjustment.[79] The rate inherited from British rule would have had to be cut by between one-third and one-half were a relationship to national income equal to Britain's to be established. The Department of Finance recommended a cut of one-fifth. Finance Minister Ernest Blythe's cut of one shilling amounted to a reduction of one-tenth and is widely agreed to have been a factor in the party's loss of power in 1932. It was undertaken in preparation for the launch of the first national loan when establishing the creditworthiness of the state was a priority.[80] There was a danger already, as T.K. Whitaker would write of a later 'dark night of the soul', that 'the achievement of independence would prove to have been a futility'.[81]

As for the alternative of raising income tax, here too the government was constrained. It was believed that if economics lay at the core of the north–south divide then low taxation might make a united Ireland more attractive to northern unionists.[82] A further constraint was the danger of capital flight. 'Some of those who paid large amounts in income tax were out of sympathy with the new regime and transferred their domicile to Great Britain'.[83] It was not that higher taxation would trigger large-scale migration but that: 'A small difference in the burden of taxation in the two countries may be sufficient to cause a diversion of taxable income that would seriously perturb the exchequer

---

[77] John FitzGerald and Seán Kenny, '"Till Debt Do Us Part": Financial Implications of the Divorce of the Irish Free State from the UK, 1922–6', Lund Papers in Economic History, No. 166, Lund University, 2017.

[78] Fitzgerald and Kenny, 'Financial Implications'; John FitzGerald and Seán Kenny, 'Managing a Century of Debt', *Journal of the Statistical and Social Inquiry Society of Ireland*, 48 (2018–19), pp. 1–40.

[79] Ó Gráda, 'Old Age Pension in Ireland'. Though Ó Gráda is critical of the regressive direction of Cumann na nGaedheal fiscal policy, he accepts Blythe's assertion that a commitment to economy which did not include a cut in the old age pension would have lacked credibility.

[80] Mel Farrell, '"Few Supporters and No Organisation"? Cumann na nGaedheal Organisation and Policy, 1923–33', PhD thesis, NUI Maynooth, 2011, pp. 228–35.

[81] T.K. Whitaker, *Protection or Free Trade: The Final Battle* (Dublin, 2006), p. 8.

[82] John Regan, *The Irish Counter Revolution, 1921–1936: Treatyite Politics and Settlement in Independent Ireland* (Dublin, 2001), p. 254; Kevin O'Higgins to Frank MacDermott, 17 Jun. 1927 (NAI, MS 1065/1/2), cited in Mel Farrell, '"Few Supporters and No Organisation"?', p. 103.

[83] Meenan, *Irish Economy*, p. 246.

authorities'.[84] The double taxation agreement signed with the UK in 1926 (based on a model advocated by the League of Nations) necessitated responding even more closely to developments in British taxation. It was for this reason that it became customary to delay the Irish budget for several weeks until after the British budget had been announced.[85] By 1928, the Irish tax rate had been reduced below that of the UK, and would remain lower under subsequent Fianna Fáil administrations.[86]

The business elite did not have everything its own way, however. The Free State did not follow the UK in abolishing corporation profits tax in 1924. Parliamentary criticism was led by former unionist John Good, now an independent TD.[87] Dáil criticism of the Shannon scheme was led by another former unionist, William Hewat, Business Party TD for Dublin North and proprietor of the coal distribution company Heitons. Sir John Keane – described by Manning and McDowell as 'if not representative of' then 'very close to the major banking and financial interests in the state' – declared himself 'appalled by the government's "nationalisation" of land'. He now saw the electricity sector as being subjected to this same 'poisonous virus of nationalisation'.[88] Hewat and Good were among the principal opponents of the state-led amalgamation of the railways in the first decade of independence.[89]

Though the Provisional Government had appointed the Bank of Ireland as its financial agent in 1922, Fanning refers to the 'strained relations' that prevailed between state and bank in 1923 and 1924.[90] The bank proved unwilling to advance the sums sought by government without a guarantee from the British authorities, but Andrew Jameson, acting on behalf of the

---

[84] Simon Kepple, 'A Survey of Taxation and Government Expenditure in the Irish Free State, 1922–1936', MA thesis, University College Cork, 1938. That lower income taxation was a factor in Anglo-Irish calculations is suggested by Nora Robertson, *Crowned Harp*, p. 145.

[85] Kepple, 'Survey of Taxation and Government Expenditure in the Irish Free State', pp. 11–12, 75–7.

[86] Meenan, *Irish Economy*, p. 246.

[87] Dominic de Cogan, 'The Wartime Origins of the Irish Corporation Tax', *Irish Journal of Legal Studies*, 3/2 (2013), pp. 15–32.

[88] Maurice Manning and Moore McDowell, *Electricity Supply in Ireland: The History of the ESB* (Dublin, 1984), p. 37. Keane and others also made clear their preference that the project be conducted by a British rather than a German firm: Lothar Schoen, 'The Irish Free State and the Electricity Industry', in Andy Bielenberg (ed.), *The Shannon Scheme and the Electrification of the Irish Free State* (Dublin, 2002), p. 41.

[89] *Weekly Irish Times*, 17 May 1924.

[90] Ronan Fanning, *The Irish Department of Finance, 1922–58* (Dublin, 1978), pp. 88, 91.

bank, was rebuffed when he travelled to London to seek the latter's support.[91] Even after the Civil War had ended and the government was returned in the election of August 1923 the banks refused to underwrite the proposed national loan without a substantial commission. Their stance particularly incensed the Department of Finance, since it meant 'that [they] declined to make any subscription whatever to the Loan on the terms on which it will be issued to the general public'.[92] In the event, the loan was oversubscribed and tensions began to ease from that point. The banks' practice of depositing their excess liquidity in London had long been the target of nationalist criticism. Though the claim that this deprived the Irish economy of investment finance was largely rejected by the Banking Commissions of the 1920s and 1930s, the Agricultural Credit Corporation (ACC) and the Industrial Credit Corporation (ICC) were established in 1927 and 1933 respectively as alternative sources of finance.[93] Only in the late 1960s, when the stability of sterling had come increasingly into question, were the 'external assets' of the Associated Banks transferred to the Central Bank.[94]

The unionist accounting monopoly was more aggressively tackled. As Tony Farmar records: 'The flow of business in the 1920s and 1930s from official sources to both Craig Gardner and Stokes Brothers & Pim, which between them audited the majority of companies quoted on the Stock Exchange, was disproportionately small'.[95] The auditing contracts for both the ACC and the Electricity Supply Board went to emerging Catholic firms and the plethora of new semi-state companies established by Fianna Fáil – and the auditing contracts for companies sponsored by the ICC – served to further address the inherited imbalances.[96] Most of the old unionist firms nevertheless remained on the list of the 'fifty largest Irish industrial companies' published for the first time in 1966.[97] These included Goulding's, Hely's, Switzer's, Jacob's, Arnott's, Goodbody's, Brooks Thomas, Heiton, Greenmount & Boyne, E. & J. Burke, and T. & C. Martin. Also included were the Irish subsidiary of Ranks, which had bought out the Bannatyne/Goodbody flour-milling conglomerate in 1930,

[91] Fanning, *Irish Department of Finance*, pp. 91–2.
[92] Fanning, *Irish Department of Finance*, p. 97, citing Joseph Brennan, secretary of the department.
[93] Cormac Ó Gráda, *A Rocky Road: The Irish Economy Since the 1920s* (Manchester, 1997), p. 66.
[94] T.K. Whitaker, 'Ireland's External Reserves', in T.K. Whitaker, *Interests* (Dublin, 1983).
[95] Farmar, *Versatile Profession*, p. 70.
[96] Farmar, *Versatile Profession*, p. 70.
[97] *Irish Times*, 8 Nov. 1966. Guinness, Denny, and Williams & Woods do not appear on the list, which included only companies traded on the Dublin Stock Exchange (Williams & Woods had been bought out by UK firm Crosse & Blackwell in 1928).

and United Distillers, into which Jameson and Power had merged with Cork Distilleries.[98]

Conclusion

Unionists dominated the 'commanding heights' of southern as well as northern Irish business prior to independence. Continued access to the external market was of paramount importance to export interests in both future jurisdictions. That agriculture was the predominant industry in the Free State area meant that anything beyond the experimental tariffs instituted by Cumann na nGaedheal would not have been politically feasible until circumstances changed with the onset of the Great Depression. The Free State was far from alone in its protectionist response to the new global environment of the 1930s.[99] Potentially more threatening to the southern unionist business elite was the prospect that independence would lead to substantial increases in taxation. The fear that nationalist governments would prove fiscally irresponsible was not realised. The Cumann na nGaedheal governments of the 1920s were constrained by the need to establish the creditworthiness of the state, by concerns that high taxation would further alienate northern unionism, and by the very real threat of capital flight.

[98] The opening up of the economy hastened the pace of change dramatically, such that by 1973 the era of tightly controlled family businesses was at an end and many formerly unionist and nationalist firms had merged (with the formation of the major banking groups a notable example). Barry, 'Life and Death of Protestant Businesses in Independent Ireland'.

[99] O'Rourke, 'Ireland and the Bigger Picture', pp. 342–55.

Appendix: Selected Sources on Unionist Affiliations

Source	Business Leaders
Great Unionist Demonstration, 1887.[100]	Lord Ardilaun, James Talbot Power, John Jameson, Sir John Arnott, T.P. Cairnes, Maurice Dockrell, Robert Tedcastle, Pim (various), Goodbody (various).
Unionist Convention Dublin, 1892.[101]	J.F.G. Bannatyne, Pim (various), T.P. Cairnes, Maurice E Dockrell, George Pollexfen, Sir Richard Martin, Lord Ardilaun, Sir John Arnott, Goodbody (various), W.J. Goulding, Lord Iveagh, John Jameson, Whyte family of Balbriggan (various), Beamish (various), George Pollexfen, Sir John Power, Sir Henry Cochrane.[102]
Catholic petition against Home Rule, 1893.[103]	Charles & Richard Martin, James & John Talbot Power, John Smithwick.
Irish Unionist Alliance, prominent southern business leaders, 1913.[104]	Sir John Arnott, Cairnes (various),Sir Maurice Dockrell, Sir Robert Gardner, Sir William Goulding, Goodbody (various), Guinness (various), William Hewat, G.N. Jacob, Jameson (various), F.V. Martin, J. Mooney, Sir John Nutting, Pim (various), J.F. Stokes, Fane Vernon.
South Co. Dublin Unionist Registration Association, 1915.[105]	Viscount Iveagh, Sir Maurice Dockrell, Sir Stanley Cochrane, Andrew Jameson, Frank V. Martin, Sir John Nutting, James Talbot Power,
Irish Unionist Alliance, 1919–20.[106]	Sir John Arnott, Guinness (various), Odlum (various), W.P. Cairnes, C.E. Denny, George Shackleton.
Unionist Anti-Partition League, 1919.[107]	Sir John Arnott, John Good, Sir William Goulding, Guinness (various), Viscount Iveagh, Andrew Jameson, John Mooney, Sir Harold Nutting.

[100] *Irish Times*, 3 Dec. 1887.
[101] Unionist Convention Dublin 1892, Provinces of Leinster, Munster, and Connaught (Report of Proceedings) (NLI).
[102] *Irish Times*, 18 Jun. 1892.
[103] *Irish Times*, 24 Mar. 1893.
[104] *Irish Independent*, 17 Nov. 1913.
[105] *Irish Independent*, 4 Jun. 1915.
[106] Irish Unionist Alliance, 30th annual report, 1919–1920 (NLI).
[107] *Irish Times*, 28 Jan. 1919.

II

Servants of the Crown

CHAPTER V

Loyal to What? Identity and Motivation in the Southern Irish Protestant Involvement in Two World Wars

Ian d'Alton

I

The global conflagration which started in August 1914 spread its cancerous reach so far that, in the space of some 11 years in the twentieth century, some 175 million men and women fought in two great wars, and many little ones, across the globe. There were about 35 million fatal military casualties. Each of these lives was unique, exceptional, as was the reason why each went to war. It is nigh on a hopeless task to generalise, to collate and to correlate these reasonings into anything resembling a coherence. Nevertheless, this essay will attempt such in respect of a small peripheral community perched at the edge of Europe, well away from the principal theatres of war. These are the Protestants of what became the Irish Free State, numbering some 311,000 at the start of the Great War, and about 195,000 at the start of the Second World War. In 1914 they were about to be left beached by a rapidly outgoing unionist tide, or to be swamped by an incoming nationalist one, depending on perspective. How many went to war, and why – twice in a single generation – is the theme of this essay.[1] They were not forced to. And because motivation is, in essence, personal, there are two individuals who feature through this chapter. In the case of the Great War, it is Captain Norman Jerome Beauchamp Leslie, The Rifle Brigade, of Castle Leslie, Glaslough, in County Monaghan,[2] second son of Colonel (later Sir) John Leslie. Norman was an aristocratic rogue with a

---

[1] For another treatment of the first part of this essay, dealing with the Great War and the Anglo-Irish, see Ian d'Alton, 'Prisoners of War? Evoking an Anglo-Irish Perception of the Conflict of 1914–19', *Australasian Journal of Irish Studies*, 17 (2017), pp. 6–22.

[2] For Norman Leslie's papers, see NLI, MS 49,495/2/64-68; also Ian d'Alton, '"Lay Spring Flowers on Our Boy's Grave": Norman Leslie's Short War', in Terence Dooley and Christopher Ridgway (eds), *The Country House and the Great War: Irish and British Experiences* (Dublin, 2016), pp. 76–86.

raffish eye for several ladies – he was the last British officer to fight a duel in 1910 with a Turk, over said Turk's wife – and he was killed at Armentières on 19 October 1914.[3] For the Second World War, the exemplar is the author's uncle and godfather, Michael d'Alton, of Sandycove, County Dublin, who was second-in-command of a landing craft at D-Day in Normandy. Unlike Norman Leslie, Michael d'Alton survived his war, and was awarded the Légion d'honneur in 2014. He died in 2016.

While attempting to quantify Protestant military participation in both wars – which may give an indication of the relative pull of each war on the southern Protestant community – the focus of this essay is on how each queried loyalties, probed motivation, asked awkward political and cultural questions, provoked self- and community-examination. It analyses why the Great War still seems to loom larger in the southern Protestant collective consciousness than does the Second World War. War is cathartic; it 'sharpens the bleak light', in writer Elizabeth Bowen's words, and interrogates the notions of identity, belonging, and place – physical and metaphysical – that are examined here. This has value beyond the specific dynamics of this Lilliputian society. Because the southern Protestants' reaction to war, and their actions within it, questioned and challenged the dominant and orthodox narrative in southern Ireland we should perhaps see this in a positive light; if they represented a problem, they were also, in Eugenio Biagini's words about minorities in Ireland:

> 'part of the solution', not only because their existence forced policy makers to reckon with diversity and pluralism, but also because their historical analysis can help historical analysts to understand the making of a pluralist society and a functioning democracy.[4]

II

War numbers are a minefield. The late Keith Jeffery, an expert in this area, advised this writer about 'the folly of trying to extract any sort of precise statistics at all'. Jeffery favoured the use of phrases like 'quite a lot', or 'more

---

[3] Leslie's amatory escapades are recounted in Lord Carmichael, governor of Madras, to Norman Leslie, 14 Sep. 1912 (NLI, MS 49,495/2/64); also details of his duel with Yosoury Pasha (NLI, MS 49,495/2/64, folder 4); also Sir John Maxwell to Léonie Leslie, 22 Apr. 1910, re the duel (NLI, MS 49,495/2/66).

[4] Eugenio Biagini, 'Minority Studies and the Making of an "Alternative History" of Twentieth Century Ireland', paper delivered to the American Conference of Irish Studies, UCD, 13 Jun. 2014 (author's script), p. 2.

than you'd think', or 'a fair few'.[5] From recruitment figures during the Great War, it appears that, for all Ireland, Protestants accounted for 45 per cent of recruits, Catholics for 55 per cent. This compares with a proportionate population in the island of 26 per cent to 74 per cent, indicating that, taking the island as a whole, proportionately more Protestants joined up than Catholics. Estimates of the number of southern Protestant combatants are difficult to come by; but of the 210,000 or so Irishmen that David Fitzpatrick has suggested served,[6] it is reckoned that somewhere in the region of 12,000 were Protestants from the three southern provinces, or about 13 per cent of Protestant participation from the island. The figures can only be treated as broad-brush, though, as recruitment figures do not include officers (who were disproportionately Protestant); those who joined dominion regiments; or those who served in the Royal Navy.

How many of these died?[7] We do not know for sure, but the number of approximately 5,000 computed by Sexton and O'Leary in 1996, and repeated by Andy Bielenberg in 2013 in an important article on southern Protestant demographics in the 1920s, is probably not wildly inaccurate.[8] The significant point is that this figure would account for less than 5 per cent of the huge decline (some 33 per cent) in Protestant population between 1911 and 1926. The British departure after Irish independence in 1922, the effects of the *Ne temere* decree (the children of mixed marriages being brought up as Catholics), emigration, late marriage, and low fertility were much more influential factors in demographic change.[9] But the compartmentalised nature of southern Protestantism meant that the War affected different groups differently.

[5] Email, Keith Jeffery to the author, 27 Jun. 2014.

[6] The 210,000 were comprised of about 58,000 regular army personnel, the remainder recruits. See David Fitzpatrick, 'Militarism in Ireland, 1900–1922', in Thomas Bartlett and Keith Jeffery (eds), *A Military History of Ireland* (Cambridge, 1996), pp. 386, 388, quoted in Keith Jeffery, *Ireland and the Great War* (Cambridge, 2000), p. 7.

[7] For Ireland overall, the modern consensus lies between 27,000 and 40,000. Jeffery, *Ireland and the Great War*, pp. 33, 35. John Horne, 'Our War, Our History', in John Horne (ed.), *Our War: Ireland and the Great War* (Dublin, 2008), pp. 5, 6, estimates the number to lie between 27,000 and 35,000.

[8] Andy Bielenberg, 'Exodus: The Emigration of Southern Irish Protestants during the Irish War of Independence and the Civil War', *Past & Present*, 218 (2013), p. 221, quoting J.J. Sexton and Richard O'Leary, 'Factors Affecting Population Decline in Minority Religious Communities in the Republic of Ireland', in *Building Trust in Ireland: Studies Commissioned by the Forum for Peace and Reconciliation* (Belfast, 1996).

[9] I express my appreciation to Andy Bielenberg and Donald Wood for their valuable and informative comments on these numbers, contained in private email communications, Feb. to Mar. 2019.

One sub-community that rewards examination – principally for reasons of abundant evidence – is the Irish gentry. In this cadre can be found the most articulate grounding of the southern Protestant motivations for wartime participation. This was a nobility of the sword rather than of the robe.[10] Almost half of their eligible young men born between 1830 and 1929 who survived to adulthood were commissioned into the armed forces.[11] As increasingly they were what Edith Somerville called 'landless landlords',[12] position and place became concomitantly more important – the army and navy, like the Church of Ireland, had always been how they earned their crust, had status and meaning. George Birmingham suggested that the close involvement of the gentry in military and imperial service which took so many overseas – 'dazzled with England's greatness and the prospect of Imperial power' – resulted in a destructive absenteeism more lethal than spending the season in London or on English estates. The manoeuvring of military men was part of the ritual and theatre of Big House living, such as the 1899 army exercises that were held on the borders of Kilkenny and Queen's County, which went on for upwards of two weeks. This was more than just pretend war – it set the boundaries of friendship and formality, even marriage prospects and possibilities. The gentry might have been politically neutered and increasingly economically detached from Ireland by 1914, but it was still setting the style. And this applied as much to attitudes to war in general, and this War in particular.

The Great War was significant for the Anglo-Irish sense of belonging, since, however temporarily, it restored an identity with a seemingly sympathetic Ireland; or, at the least, the hope of empathy. As the brothers Ross-Lewin, offshoots of the County Clare gentry, put it, they 'cemented with their blood a new brotherhood of Irishmen all the world over, imbued with new thoughts, and new inspirations during the defence of their common Empire'.[13] It seemed that Ireland had moved beyond a utilitarian 'Dunraven moment', into a transcendence in which class and religion in Ireland could be subsumed into a higher unity.[14] But it could not be sustained. By the war's end, all this was in utter ruin.

If the Great War was a catastrophe for Norman Leslie, and a tragedy for his family and friends, it also had significant ramifications for the class that the Leslies represented. Even a cursory examination of *Burke's Landed Gentry*

---

[10] J. Wilson Foster, *Irish Novels, 1890–1940* (Oxford, 2007), p. 266.

[11] Nicholas Perry, 'The Irish Landed Class and the British Army, 1850–1950', *War in History*, 18/3 (2011), pp. 309–10.

[12] E.Œ. Somerville, *An Enthusiast* (London, 1921), Preface, unpag.

[13] The Brothers Ross-Lewin, *In Britain's Need* (Dublin, 1917), p. 7.

[14] See, for example, a description of the bonds created at the front between opposing political and social bedfellows: Colin Reid, *The Lost Ireland of Stephen Gwynn* (Manchester, 2011), pp. 140–3; *Church of Ireland Gazette*, 31 Jul. 1914; *Irish Times*, 17 Sep. 1914; Jeffery, *Ireland and the Great War*, p. 71.

of Ireland and *Burke's Peerage, Baronetage & Knightage* brings forth the sheer greatness of the Great War for the Anglo-Irish. From Abercorn to Wolseley, three-quarters of the families to whom Ireland was still significant had close military connections with the conflict.[15] This marked the class as fundamentally different from what Joe Lee has suggested was the 'relatively weak sense of identity with the war effort' that existed amongst the Irish generally, where only a little more than one-tenth of the men that could have served, did.[16] That this was a caste-led inclination and tradition is clearly demonstrated if one looks at the proportion of *Protestants* of different classes who joined up; in the Leslie's county of Monaghan, for instance, the Protestant townspeople and farmers showed a considerable reluctance to enlist, thus emphasising the gentry's separateness in joining the war to the extent they did.[17]

Were the Protestant gentry inordinately decapitated? Mark Bence-Jones thought so, characterising 1914 as 'not just the beginning of a war, but the end of a nation'.[18] Only a couple of months after its outbreak, Norman Leslie's father was writing to his wife with a catalogue of the casualties that had already occurred: 'Cecil Leslie's son wounded in the eye ... Lady Erne is perfectly satisfied that Harry Crichton is alive. I hope he is'. But Harry heir to the earl of Erne, did not come home.[19] In 1915, when 114 officers had already died, representing one-seventh of the eligible cohort of young men,[20] Douglas Hyde famously wrote:

> Nearly everyone I know in the army has been killed. Poor Lord De Freyne and his brother were shot the same day and buried in one grave ...

---

[15] This corroborates the conclusions of Terence Dooley, *The Decline of the Big House in Ireland: A Study of Irish Landed Families, 1860–1960* (Dublin, 2001), p. 122; of Patrick Buckland, 30 years earlier using a different sampling technique, in *Irish Unionism I: The Anglo Irish and the New Ireland, 1885–1922* (Dublin, 1972), p. 30; and of Perry, 'The Irish Landed Class', p. 328 (the most forensic analysis to date). The Centre for the Study of Historic Irish Houses and Estates (Maynooth University) is (2019) in the process of compiling a comprehensive database of the involvement of the gentry and noble classes of Ireland in both world wars.

[16] J.J. Lee, *Ireland 1912–1985: Politics and Society* (Cambridge, 1989), p. 23. Less than a quarter of those in non-agricultural occupations joined up. David Fitzpatrick, 'Home Front and Everyday Life', in Horne, *Our War*, p. 134.

[17] Terence Dooley, *The Decline of Unionist Politics in Monaghan, 1911–23* (Maynooth, 1988), pp. 8–9.

[18] Mark Bence-Jones, 'The Changing Picture of the Irish Landed Gentry', in *Burke's Landed Gentry of Ireland* (London, 1958); Robinson, *Bryan Cooper* (1931), both quoted in Dooley, *Decline of the Big House*, pp. 124–5.

[19] Jack Leslie to Léonie Leslie, undated, but probably around the second week of October 1914 (NLI, MS 49,495/2/41, folder 4).

[20] Perry, 'The Irish Landed Class', p. 329.

MacDermott of Coolavin, my nearest neighbour, has lost his eldest son shot dead in the Dardanelles. All the gentry have suffered. *Noblesse oblige.* They have behaved magnificently.[21]

If they seemed to have fallen in disproportionate numbers, one reason may have been that, like Leslie, many were of the officer class, and thus notable and noted. Required by honour and tradition to lead men over the top, they were first in the firing-line.[22] Talismanic they might have been, but the weaponry of older wars was of no use in the new dispensation. Leslie had with him the blade given to him by the duke of Connaught, futile against German bullets.[23] Edith Somerville's Dan Palliser, in her 1921 novel *An Enthusiast*, similarly expires with his father's Crimean sword uselessly in his hands, but this time against domestic enemies.[24]

Of gentry and noble families,[25] 1 in 4 or 5 suffered fatal casualties, compared with 1 in 30 families amongst all Irish combatants.[26] That represents substantial damage. Nevertheless, the corollary was that some three-quarters of them remained undisturbed by receipt of the dreaded orange telegram.[27] Fewer than 10 heads of families in *Burke*, or about one-fiftieth of the Irish total, lost their lives.[28] In very few cases was there a serious problem of succession, even if what was being succeeded *to* was perhaps of dubious quality.[29] Numbers

[21] Dooley, *Decline of the Big House*, p. 122; Laura Dooney, 'Trinity College and the War', in David Fitzpatrick (ed.), *Ireland and the First World War* (Dublin, 1986), p. 46.

[22] The nature of industrial killing in the Great War is well represented in Act 2 of Sean O'Casey's play *The Silver Tassie*. Terence Brown, *The Literature of Ireland: Culture and Criticism* (Cambridge, 2010), pp. 83–4. Norman's war diary is full of that suddenness when everything could change. See NLI, MS 49,495/2/64.

[23] See www.castleleslie.com/castle-hotel-normans-room.html# (accessed 1 May 2014). The sword was presented to Norman by the duke of Connaught, a lifelong admirer of his mother Léonie. See NLI, MS 49,495/2/66.

[24] Somerville, *An Enthusiast*, p. 133; David Fitzpatrick, 'The Logic of Collective Sacrifice: Ireland and the British Army, 1914–1918', *Historical Journal*, 38 (1995), pp. 1017–18.

[25] A measure that includes heads of families, sons, and close relations.

[26] Using the number of households from the 1911 Census, and total fatalities at about 30,000. Perry, 'Irish Landed Class', p. 328; Fitzpatrick, 'The Logic of Collective Sacrifice', p. 1018.

[27] See Claud Hamilton to the earl of Wicklow, 5 Nov. 1916, quoted in the National Library of Ireland Exhibition on the Great War (ongoing as at February 2019).

[28] All but one had brothers or sons to inherit titles, estates, and houses.

[29] While 24 families, or nearly 8 per cent, lost eldest sons, this did not unduly disturb the succession – all but three had either brothers or that son's son to succeed. The Big Houses were already in a precarious economic position for reasons that had little to do with the war. As Terence Dooley has succinctly put it: 'An economic

alone, however, do not comprehend the cumulative power of death within this small, interrelated, interbred community, where a loss for one family was a loss for many. Simply put, everyone knew everyone else, so that the scale was amplified and magnified through an intimate consanguine connectivity. All previous remembered conflicts, when compared with this one, were remote, unchallenging to the social and political order, ultimately optional.[30] Not the Great War. That War made all of them its prisoners.

That is not to say that they weren't *willing* prisoners. Duty always tugged at the gentry's sleeves and was usually responded to. Norman Leslie's father had served in his own faraway wars in Egypt and South Africa, and although aged nearly 60 at the outbreak of the War played his part in training men in Donegal.[31] This was, at least initially, an 'honour war'. Norman's sense of it was encapsulated in a letter published just as the war started. In it, he wrote of the sublimation of the person into a greater whole:

> let us forget individuals and let us act as one great British unit, mixed and fearless. Some will live and many will die, but count the loss not. It is better far to go out with honour than survive with shame.[32]

Motivation for enlistment, according to David Fitzpatrick, was seldom on the basis of ideology, or indeed a rational assessment of risks and rewards.[33] For the Irish gentry, I am not so sure, that is if duty and honour are defined as ideology, and the rational assessment that not to go would result in ostracisation and social shame. And it was an organic part of their sense of identity, of belonging. The literature illustrates this clearly. Those Irish McGonagalls, the brothers Ross-Lewin, were writing excruciating, but sincere, verse in 1917. Their simple credo is entitled *In Britain's Need*:[34]

> But our little Western Island
> Could never stand alone.
> And we share in the greatest Empire
> That the world has ever known.

---

entity can survive the loss of its management structure; but management cannot survive bankruptcy': Dooley, *Decline of the Big House*, p. 125. See also J.M. Hone, *Ireland since 1922* (London, 1932), p. 28.

30 Perry, 'Irish Landed Class', p. 328.
31 See numerous letters from John Leslie to his wife, 1917–18 (NLI, MS 49,495/2/41).
32 Quoted in Otto Rauchbauer, *Shane Leslie: Sublime Failure* (Dublin, 2009), p. 183.
33 David Fitzpatrick, 'Militarism in Ireland', in Bartlett and Jeffery, *Military History of Ireland*, pp. 389–90.
34 The Brothers Ross-Lewin, *In Britain's Need*, p. 51; [R.S. Ross-Lewin], *Poems by a County of Clare West Briton* (Limerick, 1907), pp. 7–9.

To Celt and Scot and Saxon
That Empire was decreed –
'Tis guarded by Irish soldiers
Who fight in Britain's need.

Excitement and adventure, fuelled by testosterone, were, initially at any rate, serious motivators also. Thomas Henn of Paradise in County Clare was a schoolboy in July 1914, and he remembers his brother and cousins joining up immediately – as he says, 'for the unreasoning adventure of it'.[35] Even professional soldier Norman Leslie caught the bug, writing sarcastically to his mother in September 1914: 'what fun it will be in November lying with our Mackintosh in a frozen turnip field!'[36] This was a *Boy's Own* war; a simple polarity, them and us, like the football match between Emyvale and Glaslough Church Lads' Brigades recounted by Norman to his mother Léonie in the 1890s.[37]

There were dissenting voices, of course, though not many, and often heard through the medium of the playwright, novelist, and poet. Lennox Robinson's play *The Big House*, written less than a decade after the war had ended, has the heroine's brother killed three days away from the Armistice. She lashes out at her conventional Anglo-Irish father: 'You and your King and your Empire! Much good they ever did Ulick, or me, or you'.[38] Echoing this in other fiction is Sidney Royse Lysaght's character, who declares that 'This war ... would disgrace hell ... you might as well call smallpox heroic', or Robert Graves's 'War was foundering of sublimities'.[39] Norman's brother Shane, while dutifully doing his bit, privately agreed.[40] Writing to his father in December 1914, he philosophised:

Warfare throws everything out of the ordinary and natural. Everything become[s] extraordinary or subternatural ... everything in war becomes

[35] T.R. Henn, *Five Arches: A Sketch for an Autobiography and 'Philoctetes' and Other Poems* (Gerrard's Cross, 1980), p. 64.
[36] Norman Leslie to Léonie Leslie, 28 Sep. 1914, quoted from PRONI, Leslie papers, 'Introduction', p. 73: www.nidirect.gov.uk/sites/default/files/publications/leslie-papers.pdf (accessed 21 Mar. 2019).
[37] Norman Leslie to Léonie Leslie, undated, but probably late 1890s; account of such a match (NLI, MS 49,495/2/42, folder 1).
[38] Christopher Murray (ed.), *Selected Plays of Lennox Robinson* (Gerrards Cross, 1982), p. 141 [Captain Montgomery Despard].
[39] S.R. Lysaght, *My Tower in Desmond* (London, 1925), p. 417; in Robert Graves's poem, *Recalling War*: www.theguardian.com/books/2008/nov/13/robert-graves-recalling-war-poem (accessed 21 Mar. 2019).
[40] 'Life, where is thy boasted sting?/Where thy victory, O Day?': 'Finis', *The Poems of Shane Leslie* (London, 1928), p. 96.

heroic or ridiculous ... the forces of war are not intended to be under human control ... Powers sinister direct all, envelop all, destroy all ... war is simply waste, waste of limb and life, waste of time and talent, waste of heroism and prudence, waste of all things useful and beautiful. And the same iron rain – it raineth upon the fit and the unfit alike.[41]

It led some to wonder, like that self-styled 'inglorious soldier', Monk Gibbon, a suburban southern Protestant, if this war, ultimately, had any purpose or objective other than prestige and subservience. Gibbon surmised that a war fought for such abstractions would be the most bloody and ruthless of all.[42] And bloody and ruthless it was; yet, in a perverse way, it had some coincident meaning for Norman's people; for, in the Ireland of 1914, they had little left but the increasingly empty prestige of lineage and the remnants of a false subservience on which to rest. In that wholly negative sense, the War provided purpose.

From the perspective of the wider Protestant and loyal community, it is instructive to see how the *Church of Ireland Gazette* approached the outbreak of war in 1914. In the days leading up to August, its narrative is one of emphasising Irish unity, north and south, Protestant and Catholic, in the face of a common enemy. It suggests that Ireland is 'happily circumstanced' in the crisis, since it is primarily agricultural and the threat of invasion is remote.[43] Leonard Strong captured this sense of distance in his memoir: 'In Sandycove the prospect of war had seemed fantastic'.[44] Frances Moffett, writing of Protestant life in Galway, detailed how little the war affected her family.[45] They are not untypical. And yet despite this remoteness and evidence that the Great War did not have a determining effect on Protestant demography, it has acquired an iconic status.[46] Why does it figure so prominently in the southern Protestant mythology, still overshadowing its part in the Second? Maybe the Great War – the epitome of heroic awfulness – offered an irresistible foundation myth for a society that saw itself as the victim of some preordained grand tragedy. It was as if the Easter Rising of 1916 had to be matched, somehow.

That was nurtured by the iconography of sacrifice that fully flowered after 1918. Sacrifice was all around Irish Protestants, in a way that it was

---

[41] Shane Leslie to John Leslie, 17 Dec. 1914 (NLI, MS 49,495/2/42, folder 4).

[42] Monk Gibbon, *Inglorious Soldier* (London, 1968), p. 256.

[43] *Church of Ireland Gazette*, 31 Jul., 7 Aug. 1914.

[44] L.A.G. Strong, *Green Memory* (London, 1961), p. 143.

[45] F. Moffett, *I Too Am of Ireland* (London, 1985), p. 84.

[46] See Moffett, *I Too Am of Ireland*, for what *isn't* said about the Great War; also Joan de Vere, *In Ruin Reconciled: A Memoir of Anglo-Ireland 1913–1959* (Dublin, 1990).

not for Catholics. Every Sunday was a mini-remembrance as, after services in their churches and cathedrals, those who were left eyed the tablets and rolls of honour and came up time and again against the names of those who had died. In St Ann's Church, Dawson Street, Dublin, the Roll of Honour is behind the altar and thus in the face of the congregation. In St Mary's Church, Dunmanway, County Cork, the memorial tablet is on the back wall of the church, always visible as people left after service.[47] Heather Jones has suggested that remembrance of the Great War came to stand proxy for something else.[48] The four years of that war were followed by four more years of a lesser. That lesser one did hugely more demographic and social damage to the southern Protestant community than the greater. Standing behind the war dead, then, were the many more ghosts of those who had fled. The final piece of the jigsaw, building on this sense of the great departed, but hanging it on the Great War, was the emergence of a seductive and subversive literature – both fiction and memoir. It speaks to regretful loss, of a Dostoyevskian sense of grand tragedy. Its exponents are the likes of Molly Keane, Annabel Davis-Goff, Barbara Fitzgerald, and William Trevor. If Jennifer Johnston, perhaps the mistress of this genre, admits that she is often seen as telling 'the same story ... over and over again',[49] it must be acknowledged that saying it over and over again does have an effect. Here is Elizabeth Bowen on the day after war was declared between Britain and Germany, seductive in a painterly and dimensional manner:

> August 5th was a white-grey, lean, gritty day, with the trees dark. The newspaper did not come ... about eleven we drove down the avenue in the large pony trap ... At Rockmills, my father – whose manner, I do remember, had been growing graver with every minute – stopped the pony and went into the post office. There was a minute to wait, with the pony stamping, before I again saw him framed in the low dark door. He cleared his throat and said: 'England has declared war on Germany'. Getting back into the trap he added: 'I suppose it could not be helped'. All I could say was: 'Then we can't go to the garden party?'[50]

---

[47] Great War memorials in Irish Roman Catholic churches are only to be found in the chapel at Clongowes Wood College, Co. Kildare, and Haddington Road Church, Dublin.

[48] Heather Jones, 'Church of Ireland Great War Remembrance in the South of Ireland: A Personal Reflection', in John Horne and Edward Madigan, *Towards Commemoration: Ireland in War and Revolution 1912–1923* (Dublin, 2013), pp. 74–81.

[49] In Edna Longley (ed.), *Culture and Diversity in Ireland: Proceedings of the Cultures of Ireland Group Conference* (Belfast, 1991), p. 10.

[50] Elizabeth Bowen, *Bowen's Court* (1942). The quotes following are from Elizabeth Bowen, *Bowen's Court & Seven Winters* (London, 1984), pp. 434–5.

She continues:

> The tremendous news certainly made that party, which might have been rather flat. Almost every one said they wondered if they really ought to have come, but they had come – rightly: this was a time to gather ... For miles around, each isolated big house had disgorged its talker, this first day of the war. The tension of months, of years – outlying tension of Europe, inner tension of Ireland – broke in a spate of words. Braced against the gale from the mountains, licking dust from their lips these were the unmartialled loyalists of the South. Not a family had not put out ... its generations of military brothers – tablets in Protestant churches recorded deaths in remote battles; swords hung in halls. If the Anglo-Irish live on and for a myth, for that myth they constantly shed their blood. So, on this August 1914 day of grandeur and gravity, the Ascendancy rallied, renewed itself.[51]

The subversion in Bowen's particular case lies in the fact that this was actually written a quarter of a century later, in the midst of a bomb-blitzed London in which she self-professedly had 'no feeling to spare'.[52] She was well aware of having to come up with some reason for placing her people in a particular mode of remembrance – and she did it with the phrase, 'It was an afternoon when the simplest person begins to anticipate memory'.[53] Metaphor is scattered with the abandonment of used shell-casings. Here is just one: 'The bye-roads had dried in the wind and were glaring white; the War already gave them an unreal look'.[54] This was the ghostliness that became the gentry's leitmotif; in one spare image the white-dried roads stand for the bleached bones of the yet-to-be-dead, 'the *youthful* dead shouldering past the old through St Peter's Gate'.[55]

Those, like Bowen, who fashioned the War in the memorial sculpture of the word did so in the imagery of the haunted and the haunting.[56] 'Ghosts rode with us' wrote Daisy, countess of Fingall, in 1937.[57] The boy Ulick in Robinson's play *The Big House* is a ghost even *before* he is killed, appearing

---

[51] Bowen, *Bowen's Court*, pp. 435–6.
[52] Elizabeth Bowen, 'London, 1940', in *Collected Impressions* (London, 1950), p. 220.
[53] Bowen, *Bowen's Court*, p. 436.
[54] Bowen, *Bowen's Court*, p. 435.
[55] Foster, *Irish Novels 1890–1940*, p. 342.
[56] Mrs Victor Rickard, *The Fire of Green Boughs* (Toronto, 1919), esp. pp. 22, 26, 120–2.
[57] Elizabeth (Daisy) Fingall, *Seventy Years Young: Memories of Elizabeth, Countess of Fingall* (New York, 1937), p. 386.

to his sister on the day that he enlists. It is said that Norman Leslie too was
seen as an apparition at Glaslough a week before he met his death.[58] Frances
Moffett wrote of seeing a young man of her acquaintance after he had been
killed at the Somme.[59] Predetermination is the cousin of prescience; here is
Molly Keane in her 1937 novel *Rising Tide*:

> It was November 1915 and the War had been going on for a year and four
> months, when Cynthia heard the news that Desmond had been killed. She
> had never really expected him *not* to be killed. She had felt quite fatally
> certain about it from the first ... They had each known quite well and
> each tried quite futilely to hide from the other the foreknowledge that
> this was going to happen. ... Cynthia had made herself hard over this
> so often that when she read the telegram and said, 'There's no answer,'
> she only felt a sort of dizziness.[60]

As Shane Leslie had divined, war itself had become monstrous, a behemoth
with a malign life of its own. At the end, Theseus was really fighting the
Labyrinth, not the Minotaur.[61] In the same way, the true enemy was not the
Hun, or old Fritz, or Abdul. It came to be war itself: in Leslie's words, 'a
nightmare which has no end or meaning possible'.[62]

David Fitzpatrick's 'logic of collective sacrifice' was grounded in ritual,
in camaraderie. It was seen in Trinity students joining up en masse and
exemplified by the 'Pals', 'D' Company of the 7th Royal Dublin Fusiliers
that enlisted en bloc in 1914, comprised of upper-middle-class Catholics and
Protestants (of which my paternal grandfather was one) and which distinguished itself (and nearly extinguished itself) in the Dardanelles in 1915. But
the problem of war was that while it could give purpose to identity, it could
also take it away.[63] For many southern Irish Protestants like the Leslies,
the symbolic end of their Eight Years War was on 12 June 1922. Then, the
bureaucrats in the War Office accomplished what the Kaiser and the Sultan
had not, the disbandment of several Irish regiments: the South Dublin

---

[58] Murray, *Selected Plays*, p. 155; Norman's ghostliness is a feature of Castle Leslie's
(now a boutique hotel) marketing: www.castleleslie.com/castle-hotel-normans-
room.html# (accessed 1 May 2014).

[59] Moffett, *I Too Am of Ireland*, pp. 83–4.

[60] M.J. Farrell [Molly Keane], *Rising Tide* [1937] (London, 1984), p. 103.

[61] The 'Theseus' reference is borrowed from Tim Smith-Lang, 'A Lost Cause', *Apollo*
(Mar. 2014), p. 101.

[62] Shane Leslie to John Leslie, 17 Dec. 1914 (NLI, MS 49,495/2/42, folder 4).

[63] The Clare soldier Bindon Blood could not even bring himself to write of the war,
because of the betrayal he felt. Bindon Blood, *Four Score Years and Ten* (London,
1933), p. xii.

Horse, the Leinsters and Munsters, the Royal Irish, the Connaughts, and the Royal Dublin Fusiliers.[64] The obsequies were held at Windsor Castle as the regimental insignia were surrendered into the bosom of the king's protection. The ceremony had all the characteristics of a funeral, from the baked meats as the regimental representatives (in the sad, angry words of the *Irish Times*) 'were entertained to luncheon on the completion of their pathetic errand' to the 'band in the quadrangle [which] played plaintive airs'.[65] For southern Protestants, it was perhaps the last great death of the Great War. The *Irish Times* leader-writer hoped for a Christ-like resurrection for the regiments. But it would never come.[66]

III

For southern Protestants, involvement in the Second World War carried more complex motivations. There is even less consensus as to the number of citizens of Éire that served in the British military forces; numbers vary from as high as 165,000 to as low as 38,000.[67] Geoffrey Roberts, drawing on Richard Doherty's work, has a median estimate of about 70,000.[68] While a formal denominational breakdown is not available, from a small sample of those interviewed for a University College Cork oral history project, Roberts suggests that possibly around 20 per cent were non-Roman Catholics; Steven O'Connor, author of the recent *Irish Officers in the British Forces, 1922–45*, contends that 'a large number of Irish Protestants joined up during the war and they were disproportionately represented among the volunteers from southern Ireland'.[69] O'Connor reckons that more than half of the Irish officers who served in the British forces were from a southern Protestant background; and the list of Irish generals from that tradition – the likes of Michael O'Moore

---

[64] Praise to these regiments is found in The Brothers Ross-Lewin, *In Britain's Need*, pp. 15, 24, 41, 55.

[65] See an editorial headed 'Lest We Forget', *Irish Times*, 11 Apr. 1922.

[66] *Irish Times*, 13 Jun. 1922. The report is given considerable prominence on page 3.

[67] The high figure is that of retired General Sir Hubert Gough. In 1946, he asserted that he had been told from a source in the army that the next-of-kin addresses for 165,000 soldiers were in southern Ireland – this has never been verified but the estimate is mentioned in Richard Doherty's and Brian Girvin's books.

[68] Geoffrey Roberts, 'Neutrality, Identity and the Challenge of the "Irish Volunteers"', in Dermot Keogh and Mervyn O'Driscoll (eds), *Ireland in World War 2: Diplomacy and Survival* (Cork, 2004), p. 274. See also Richard Doherty, 'Irish Heroes of the Second World War', in Brian Girvan and Geoffrey Roberts (eds), *Ireland and the Second World War: Politics, Society and Remembrance* (Dublin, 2000), pp. 92–3.

[69] Email to the author, 3 Jul. 2014.

Creagh, the Cunninghams, Somerville, Montgomery, Tim Pile, Freddie Loftus-Tottenham, David Dawnay, and so on – is impressive.[70] In contrast, though, Aidan McElwaine contends that 'The Anglo-Irish community does not appear to have been over-represented amongst the Eire volunteers'.[71] On these bases southern Protestant military participation ranged between 4,600 and 14,000. When relative population sizes are taken into account, it is likely that a somewhat *greater* proportion of the southern Protestant population served in the second war than had in the first.[72]

A much lower death rate in the Second World War – 4.5 per cent compared with 14 per cent in the First – may go some way towards explaining why that extent of southern Irish Protestant entanglement in the Second World War seems underestimated in the popular mind. The number of Protestant dead from the 26 counties may thus lie between just above 200 to 650 or so. Even at the top end, deaths would have been only one-seventh of the 5,000 or so for the Great War figure.[73] The rolls of honour found in the churches and cathedrals of the Church of Ireland and in institutions like the Kildare Street and University Clubs back this up. But the gentry still stick out. Nicholas Perry suggests that

> their casualties were proportionately almost as high in the Second as the First, due in no small part to their enthusiasm for the RAF as an alternative ... to the cavalry as the dashing arm for fearless riders to hounds to join: only for the grim attrition of Bomber Command's Battles of the Ruhr & Berlin to winnow many out.[74]

Michael Maurice Austin d'Alton was 23 years old in June 1944. He travelled to Belfast, as most potential Irish recruits did, without let or hindrance (unlike those in other neutral states) to join the Royal Navy in which he participated in the Normandy landings. He was, according to his witness account given to the US Army Military History Department in 2004, 'I think a temporary acting sub-lieutenant. The lowest form of commissioned life ... I was ... appointed to combined operations to the tank landing craft portion of it, as second-in-command of LCT796 ... and ... my commanding officer was a lieutenant. An

---

[70] Richard Doherty, *Ireland's Generals in the Second World War* (Dublin, 2004), *passim*; Mark O'Brien, *The Irish Times: A History* (Dublin, 2008), p. 109; Eugenio F. Biagini, *Storia dell'Irlanda dal 1845 a oggi* (Bologna, 2014), p. 141.

[71] Geoffrey Roberts, 'Neutrality, Identity and the Challenge of the "Irish Volunteers"', in Keogh and O'Driscoll, *Ireland in World War 2*, pp. 274, 279.

[72] *Census of Population of Ireland, 1971*, vol. 9 (1977), p. 1.

[73] Doherty, 'Irish Heroes of the Second World War', p. 94.

[74] Email from Nicholas Perry to the author, 8 Jul. 2014.

Englishman, and a rather pugnacious Englishman'.[75] So, why and how could those like Michael d'Alton (and his sister, and his brother – the author's father) as citizens of a nominally neutral state justifiably offer themselves as combatants? Attitudes amongst the southern Protestant community generally towards the war, neutrality, and support for the Allied cause are dealt with extensively elsewhere in this volume by Joseph Quinn.[76] The concentration in this essay relates primarily to motivation, and the Volunteers Project Archive at University College Cork (UCC) throws up a welter of fascinating information about why southern Protestant combatants say they joined up.[77]

It seems that the communal psychology of southern Protestantism demanded a two-stage decision process. The first step required that fighting on the same side of the British was rationalised as an acceptable reflection of their sense of Irishness at the time: that is, an Ireland still, just, as a constituent part of the Commonwealth. That allowed them a 'bi-polarity', in Quinn's phrase – supporting the Allied cause while at the same recognising that Irish neutrality was sensible and pragmatic.[78] The identities exhibited by southern Protestants in 1939 were much more complex than Bernard Share's 1978 caricature as 'physically in occupation of decaying country houses and other crumbling enclaves, not living in contemporary Ireland at all'.[79] This description would have perplexed the likes of Michael d'Alton. While describing himself as 'coming from what you might call ... a West British background', he was not of the country house set. And he did not consider himself a 'West Briton', whatever that might mean. As Aidan McElwaine reported, 'he dislikes this label, preferring to describe himself as pro-British'.[80] The crucial signifier here was that being pro-British did not entail being anti-Irish. Southern Protestants had become more comfortable with this position, developed over close to two decades of Irish self-government. Within a stockade of economic and social exclusivity, they had invented for themselves after 1922 what we might call the 'Protestant Free State' – a

---

[75] US Department of the Army, 44th Military History Detachment, interview with M.M.A. d'Alton, 8 Jun. 2004 (Oral History 44-OPNORM 60-I-00 42; transcript courtesy of Mark d'Alton).

[76] See Chapter 8.

[77] The following is largely taken from the UCC Volunteer Project Sound Archive – official summary (kindly supplied to the writer by Dr Steven O'Connor by email, 3 Jul. 2014). Other references are noted hereunder. See also Richard Doherty, *Irish Volunteers in the Second World War* (Dublin, 2000), pp. 309–21 ('Reflections').

[78] *Irish Times*, 4, 6 Sep. 1939.

[79] Cormac Kavanagh, 'Irish and British Government Policy Towards the Volunteers', in Girvan and Roberts, *Ireland and the Second World War*, p. 85.

[80] Aidan McElwaine, 'The Oral History of the Volunteers', in Girvan and Roberts, *Ireland and the Second World War*, p. 115.

sort of parallel entity to the official one – which emphasised Ireland as a constitutional monarchy and its dominion status. That allowed loyalty, or at least tolerance, to function on two levels without much conflict. Elizabeth Dobbs,[81] who joined the Women's Royal Naval Service (the Wrens), suggested that her religion and background played an important part in her decision. She captures the relatively unstructured, instinctive sense of why 'Most Protestants felt a kinship, sort of something to do with England'.[82] Protestants, sidelined in southern Ireland, could still cleave to Empire as being the greater whole of which they could be part. That Empire came with values. The professed southern Protestant motivation for participation in both world wars was essentially allied to those with which they could empathise – liberty, tolerance, loyalty, respect for law and order, good humour, possibly ethnic superiority allied to a sense of righteousness. Indeed, if southern Protestants had one collective failing, it was this latter sort of moral smugness, of being 'better' than their Catholic countrymen. This was reinforced by a sense that, in return for an outward acceptance of the constitutional dispensation in 1922, Protestants had expiated their former sins; the responsibility for Irish history was no longer theirs to bear. They were thus less conflicted by guilt and moral ambiguity in the Second World War, easing the way into participation.

Once that generic and communal permissive bar had been crossed, the second stage in the process was down to individual reasoning. It is said that the pulls and pushes that had existed on individuals and groups in the Great War no longer carried as much purchase. In a formal sense, that seems to have been the case. It was perfectly possible to stay at home in relative safety and comfort – and many did. Geoff Roberts points out that 'decisions to volunteer and serve were mainly individual ... there is no sign of the "logic of collective sacrifice" evident in Irish recruitment to the British armed forces during the First World War'.[83]

The fact that there is little formal evidence of 'collective sacrifice' in the second war doesn't mean that it didn't exist. Michael d'Alton claimed that he was under no pressure to enlist. But moving within a south county Dublin Protestant community – middle class, business-oriented, with a complete social structure of churches, schools, boy scouts, rugby, golf and yacht clubs, professional associations (he had just qualified as a quantity surveyor), workplaces, the freemasons, and so on – his mind was surely formed and

---

[81] Elizabeth Dobbs, Monkstown, Co. Dublin, died on 2 May 2010: www.rip.ie/ showdn.php?dn=104295 (accessed 2 Jul. 2014).

[82] McElwaine, 'The Oral History of the Volunteers', pp. 115–16.

[83] Roberts, 'Neutrality, Identity and the Challenge of the "Irish Volunteers"', pp. 274–5.

informed by an informal camaraderie of shared interests and beliefs with his peer group.

What still held sway, though, in the Second World War, were, broadly, the same reasons that had been there in the First. As then, for each individual, there was seldom just one. A family tradition of military service was an important motivator, or at least a psychological facilitator. Given the Leslies' background, it was not surprising that Norman's nephew, Desmond, enlisted, joining the RAF; in his memoirs, he maintained that he was responsible for the destruction of many aircraft – unfortunately, most of them on his own side![84] Basil Baker's grandfather had been a general in the Connaught Rangers. John Jermyn from Cork was motivated to enlist because his uncle had been killed at Gallipoli: 'In some foolish way I thought that perhaps I should take his place'.[85] Excitement was another reason why young men will always go to war, imagining that they are immortal and that no bullet will ever have their name on it. Like Tom Henn 25 years previously, Corkman Brian Bolingbroke was attracted by such 'excitement'; but as neutral Ireland's armed forces were considered about as useful as a 'chocolate teapot', the prospect of decent naval service was a factor in his joining the British forces. John Rowlands from Dalkey wanted to see the world – Ireland was very constricted, he felt. R.J. Good from Kinsale joined up from a mixture of boredom and excitement. Interestingly, he 'had nothing against Germans, had never even met one – and didn't really care about England'.

What about money? From the responses given to the UCC volunteer project, it is what you would expect – those who came from poorer backgrounds cited it as a significant determinant in their decision to enlist. Given the general socio-economic composition of southern Irish Protestantism, it is a reasonable assumption that money was not the principal mover in their decisions to join up. Nevertheless, R.E. Jones from Cork, who was a salesman before the War, was not untypical of those Protestants who came from less well-off backgrounds: 'Always on for a bit of fun and excitement, and I wanted to advance myself, so took that chance. With [the] economic situation here, I was earning a pittance'. John Jacob, of Quaker extraction, claimed that he was the first of his family to go to war in 300 years: 'I was 24, the business I was in – feedings stuff – was slowly closing down as it wasn't able to import things'.

It is tempting to look for some sort of high-minded moral purpose in the southern Protestant motivation to fight. And, even allowing for caution in its articulation long after the event, it *is* there. Mirroring Norman Leslie, journalist Brian Inglis, from the upper-middle-class Protestant enclave of

---

[84]   Robert O'Byrne, *Desmond Leslie (1921–2001): The Biography of an Irish Gentleman* (Dublin, 2010), p. 38.
[85]   McElwaine, 'The Oral History of the Volunteers', pp. 107–8.

Malahide, was minded to join up by what he simply called 'duty'.[86] Arthur Jones, a Dublin electrician, 'was practical and idealistic in some ways. In WWI Germany was stumbling for her place in the sun, nothing perniciously evil, it was different in WWII it was evil, a crusade'. For others, that crusade was shot through with a healthy dose of practical patriotism. Simply put, they might have believed, in Michael d'Alton's words, 'that that bloody little monster from Germany had to be stopped';[87] but that was because Ireland would inevitably be next on Hitler's hitlist. John Jermyn was convinced that the German juggernaut would, if not halted, overwhelm Ireland; Hitler only had to send 'a platoon of girl guides to take Ireland', he said. John Jacob 'was certain that if the Germans did conquer Britain, they would not stop at Holyhead or Fishguard'.[88] Brian Bolingbroke felt that 'I thought Nazi Germany was an appalling thing, and would hate to have thought that we'd live under Nazi rule for the rest of my life'. Bringing all these motivations together was Maureen Deighton from Limerick, who had practically the full deck of cards: 'It was the done thing – the right thing to do, you were fighting evil, I was fancy free, I was young, I had a bit of education. Mostly it was because everyone else was'.

The annoyances of official neutrality – war on the home front between Smyllie of the *Irish Times* and the censor is perhaps the best known example – did not dent what everyone knew; that the south was, in the words of Aengus Nolan and Dermot Keogh, 'on the side of the allies … but quietly'.[89] Terence Brown's surmise that for the Anglo-Irish community 'neutrality was a bitter pill to swallow', is not really borne out by the evidence.[90] A debate in the Senate at the outbreak of war is prototypical. Of the southern Protestant senators who spoke, James Douglas, Robert Rowlette, and E.H. Alton favoured neutrality from a practical viewpoint, while only Sir John Keane spoke against.[91] The southern Protestant volunteers in the UCC project reflected this balance: Brian Bolingbroke thought that 'Generally I had no objection to Ireland being neutral and thought it was the right thing to do … Neutrality was a good thing. It saved this country the appalling devastation I saw in Britain'. Frank McLoughlin thought that 'We were better off out of it'. John

[86] Brian Inglis, *West Briton* (London, 1962), pp. 39–45.

[87] *Irish Times*, 6 Jun. 2014, interview with Michael d'Alton marking the 70th anniversary of the Normandy D-Day landings. Also McElwaine, 'The Oral History of the Volunteers', p. 116; interviews by Kevin Myers, *Irish Times*, 6 Jun. 1984.

[88] McElwaine, 'The Oral History of the Volunteers', pp. 115–16.

[89] Dermot Keogh and Aengus Nolan, 'Anglo-Irish Diplomatic Relations in World War II', *Irish Sword*, 19 (1993/4), p. 124.

[90] Terence Brown, *Ireland: A Social and Cultural History* (London, 1981), p. 173.

[91] Seanad Debates, 2 Sep. 1939: http://debates.oireachtas.ie/seanad/1939/09/02/00004. asp (accessed 4 Jul. 2014); *Irish Times*, 3 Sep. 1939.

Jacob's view was that 'Neutrality only possible thing – we were a young state'. Michael d'Alton's take on neutrality was similar: 'I thoroughly agreed with it. If it had joined it would have been counter-productive and would have enabled Germany to invade from the west without international condemnation'. '"We'd be more of a liability than an asset", he has said: "Far more forces would have had to be devoted to our protection that were needed elsewhere"'.[92] All this is summed up in the joke about the two Irish soldiers cowering in a foxhole in North Africa, under intense mortar and machine-gun fire, and they are arguing politics, of course, as Irishmen do anywhere, and one shouts to the other, "Well, you can say what you like about De Valera, but at least he's kept us out of *this* war"'.[93]

The Second World War saw a small but significant trickle of southern Protestants into the Irish Defence Forces.[94] Several Protestant schools which had a strong British military tradition – St Columba's, St Andrew's, and Wilson's Hospital – recorded past pupils joining the Irish army, although the vast majority of those who took up a military career in the interwar years and during the Second World War did so in the British forces.[95] TCD's Officer Training Corps, founded in 1908 and disbanded in 1922, was reconstituted as part of the Irish Defence Forces' reserve in 1930. And there were southern Protestants like John Richards-Orpen, who had decided that 'as their homes and families were in Ireland they should offer their services to their own country's defence'. Some southern Protestants joined *Na Caomhnóiri Aitúila*, the Local Security Force. Nevertheless, this trend should not be exaggerated. Those who actively participated in the Irish forces represented a small minority of the minority, always unstable; for instance, Trinity's reconstituted Officers' Training Corps went out of existence during the Second World War.[96] For many, the British forces were still 'our Army' and 'Our Navy'. As late as 1954, Elizabeth Bowen, in her novel *A World of Love*, was articulating a perceived southern Protestant mild bemusement that Ireland even *had* an army.[97]

Generational change and the years of the 'Protestant Free State' had moved southern Protestant attitudes on from the relative simplicities of the Great

---

92 *Irish Times*, 6 Jun. 2014.
93 See http://ww2talk.com/forums/topic/1179-irishmen-in-ww2/ (accessed 16 Feb. 2018).
94 Nora Robertson, *Crowned Harp: Memories of the Last Years of the Crown in Ireland* (Dublin, 1960), p. 153.
95 Steven O'Connor, *Irish Officers in the British Forces, 1922–45* (Basingstoke, 2014), pp. 64–72.
96 Roger Willoughby, *A Military History of the University of Dublin and its Officers' Training Corps, 1910–22* (Limerick, 1989), p. 5.
97 Kavanagh, 'Irish and British Government Policy towards the Volunteers', p. 84; Elizabeth Bowen, *A World of Love* (New York, 1978), p. 183.

War. Again, looking at the *Church of Ireland Gazette*, the sense of distance that it offered in 1914 bears a surface comparison with something similar in September and October 1939. But there is a subtle difference in tone in 1939, with a new distance from Britain, too. The *Gazette*'s correspondence at the start of the Second World War has a few letters hostile to Irish neutrality; but there are many more on the subject of pacifism, including letters from the TCD academic A.A. Luce (against) and the rector of Howth (for). There is a serious debate as to whether the true Christian can, and should, fight. The *Gazette* wrote approvingly of de Valera on 6 October 1939: 'the main task, which may be called the implementation of neutrality, is being surveyed with courage and energy'.[98] Despite what might now be accepted as the morality and necessity of the war against Nazi Germany, all this indicates a much more conditional attitude than appears to have been the case 25 years before. There is relatively little soul-searching about the southern Protestant condition – here we have briskness, getting on with things as they are, an engagement with the contemporary. In reality, that community had little choice. Both world wars, though, were important markers in defining Protestantism's identity and relationships within a triangulation of Britain, Ireland, and themselves. Four years after the first's end, Ireland departed from the United Kingdom. In a coincidental symmetry, four years after the second, Ireland finally left the Commonwealth. In neither case could the erstwhile loyalists of the south – martialled or unmartialled – have prevented what had happened. They had done their bit, but they were already ciphers in 1922, and virtually unnoticed in 1949. Perhaps that was all to the good. The life-span of overly visible and aggressive minorities in most countries tends to be quite short.

[98] See *Church of Ireland Gazette*, 1, 8, 22 Sep., 13, 20, 27 Oct., 3, 10 Nov. 1939.

CHAPTER VI

'The future welfare of the Empire will depend more largely on our women and girls': Southern Loyalist Women and the British War Effort in Ireland, 1914–1922

Fionnuala Walsh

The outbreak of war in August 1914 created an unprecedented unity within Ireland, and between Ireland and Great Britain. A conditional and suspicious unity, perhaps, but one which nonetheless drew nationalists and unionists together.[1] The *Irish Times* stated that 'In this hour of trial the Irish nation has found itself at last. Unionists and Nationalists have ranged themselves together against the invader of their common liberties'.[2] R.B. McDowell described this as southern unionism's 'finest hour', presenting an opportunity for them to 'throw themselves into serving the empire in a time of peril, proudly sharing the fears, hopes and sacrifices of their fellow subjects in Great Britain'.[3] Between 1914 and 1918 about 206,000 Irishmen served in the British military, comprising between a quarter and a third of the available young men in Ireland.[4] At the same time, thousands of Irish women joined the British Red Cross, St John Ambulance Association, the Irish War Hospital Supply Depot, and many other voluntary organisations, offering their time and labour unpaid.[5] Many of those involved felt a strong identification with the British war effort and a desire to prove their loyalty to Britain. This chapter

---

[1] Adrian Gregory and Senia Pašeta (eds), *Ireland and the Great War: 'A War to Unite Us All'?* (Manchester, 2002), p. 2.

[2] *Irish Times*, 5 Aug. 1914

[3] R.B. McDowell, *Crisis and Decline: The Fate of the Southern Unionists* (Dublin, 1997), p. 53.

[4] David Fitzpatrick, 'Ireland and the Great War', in Thomas Bartlett (ed.), *The Cambridge History of Ireland*, vol. 4, *1870 to the Present* (Cambridge, 2018), p. 231; Keith Jeffery, *1916: A Global History* (London, 2016), pp. 110–11.

[5] More than 13,000 Irish women served under the joint committee of the British Red Cross and St John Ambulance Association from 1914 to 1918. British Red Cross Archives, membership records for the Great War. I am grateful to the

examines the participation of Irish women in the war effort and how war service provided an outlet and focus for southern loyalist identity in this period, before briefly exploring the post-war experience of such women during the War of Independence and Civil War.

What do we mean by southern loyalist identity? And how do we define loyalism? In a recent article, Brian Hughes draws on the criteria set out by the Irish Grants committee: 'disbanded members of the RIC, ex-servicemen, and civilians believed to have been loyal to the British connection'.[6] If applying this to women, members of war relief organisations and the families of British army soldiers were categorised as loyalists. However, Hughes questions how we reconcile behaviour with allegiance.[7] Irishmen enlisted in the British forces for a mixture of motives, not all of which involved loyalty to the Crown. Occupation, for example, affected recruitment to the wartime British army to a greater degree than religion: Protestants in rural Ulster were less likely to enlist than Belfast Catholics.[8] There were also many diverse motivations for Irishwomen to participate in war relief activities, including personal, associational, and political factors. Although women's mobilisation was often linked to the 'service of the Empire', not all women active in the war effort were motivated by imperial zeal, or indeed were really loyalists at all.[9] Many were constitutional nationalists following John Redmond's call to support Britain in exchange for Home Rule. For others, politics and patriotism came second to humanitarian concerns about relieving the distress caused by the war, or the desire to use war work as a means to advance the suffrage cause. Most relief work was performed in work parties or sphagnum moss collecting groups, providing a supportive associational environment. Many women found fulfilment in the companionship of working with others, and a sense that their lives had meaning and purpose.

The relationship between religion and loyalism is complex. Despite contemporary assumptions of the link between Protestantism and loyalism, there were sizeable numbers of Protestant nationalists active in the Irish revolution.[10]

British Red Cross Archives for providing me with this data and to Daniel Purcell for his assistance with the data analysis.

[6] Brian Hughes, 'Loyalists and Loyalism in a Southern Irish Community, 1921–1922', *Historical Journal*, 59/4 (2016), p. 1076.

[7] Hughes, 'Loyalists and Loyalism', p. 1077.

[8] Catriona Pennell, *A Kingdom United: Popular Responses to the Outbreak of the First World War in Britain and Ireland* (Oxford, 2012), pp. 192–3.

[9] *Irish Life*, 21 Aug., 27 Nov. 1914; 21 Jan., 16 Jun. 1916.

[10] Valerie Jones, *'Rebel Prods': The Forgotten Story of Protestant Radical Nationalists and the 1916 Rising* (Dublin, 2016); Conor Morrissey, *Protestant Nationalists in Ireland, 1900–1923* (Cambridge, 2019).

There were also Catholic loyalists. Nonetheless, most of those active in Red Cross voluntary work for the war effort belonged to the Protestant churches, and Protestants dominated the leadership of the Red Cross and St John Ambulance Association in wartime Ireland. Women from the Protestant denominations made up almost 90 per cent of a sample of 137 women who acted as Red Cross work party leaders or divisional commandants in the British Red Cross and St John Ambulance Association. The strong influence of the Protestant churches in war relief work is further evident in the 18 clergymen's wives among Red Cross leaders.[11]

The Protestant churches played an important role in promoting women's participation in the war effort. Following the outbreak of the war, John Henry Bernard, archbishop of Dublin, exhorted women to ignore 'domestic politics; they can wait a happier hour' and to divert their energies into persuading men to enlist in the army.[12] Appeals and praise for women's war work were common in the *Church of Ireland Gazette*. In August 1914, the bishop of Ossory placed the nursing work of women on equal footing with the army service of men, while the Armagh diocesan synod in November 1915 recorded its 'profound admiration of the work done by women of the country, both at home and abroad'.[13] The Presbyterian and Methodist churches also highlighted the contribution of their women members to the war effort. Church-led activities included work parties organised by Presbyterian women to make comforts for the front and the provision of recreation rooms for soldiers and sailors in Dublin and Queenstown, which were staffed by Methodist women, who also paid regular visits to soldiers in hospitals.[14] The Presbyterian Church recognised the role women could perform on the home front and that this, together with the

---

[11] *The Red Cross in Ireland: an account of the Red Cross work of the St John Ambulance Brigade and the British Red Cross Society in the provinces of Leinster, Munster and Connaught from August 1914 to November 1918* (Dublin, 1920); 'Memoranda on Red Cross in Ireland' in *Reports by the Joint War Committee and the Joint War Finance Committee of the British Red Cross and the Order of St John of Jerusalem in England on Voluntary Aid rendered to the sick and wounded at home and abroad and to British prisoners of war, 1914–1919* (London, 1921), p. 670.

[12] John Henry Bernard, 'God save the King – Kilkenny, 6 Sept 1914', in *In Wartime* (London, 1917), p. 12.

[13] *Church of Ireland Gazette*, 14 Aug. 1914, 5 Nov. 1915. See also J.A. Maconchy (ed.), *Journal of the General Synod of the Church of Ireland Holden in Dublin MDCCCCXVII* (Dublin, 1917), p. liii.

[14] *Minutes of the Proceeding of the General Assembly of the Presbyterian Church in Ireland, 1916–1920*, vol. 13 (Belfast, 1920), p. 82; *Annual Report of the Methodist Home Mission and Contingent Fund and of the General Mission (Ireland)* (Dublin, 1915), pp. 29–32.

sacrifice of soldiers, was helping to 'hasten the triumph of our cause'.[15] Similarly, the Methodist conference in 1915 noted how both Irishmen and Irishwomen were 'playing a noble part' in what they described as a 'fierce struggle between light and darkness, liberty and tyranny, Christ and Belial'.[16] The use of this rhetoric to describe the war is illustrative of how war service was promoted as an essential sacrifice, as a war of religion and civilisation.[17] Imperialist and loyalist rhetoric is also apparent. The 1917 report of the General Synod of the Church of Ireland mentioned the 'many sons and daughters' of the church 'in the service of the Empire'.[18] There were many similar examples of references to the mobilisation of men and women from the different churches on behalf of Britain and the imperial war effort.[19] Such praise and promotion of women's war work created an environment that encouraged and motivated Protestant women to become involved in war relief organisations.

Much of the war relief work by Protestants was organised through the two largest Anglican women's organisations, the Mothers' Union and Girls' Friendly Society. These were Irish branches of British-based organisations with a strong imperial ethos and close links to the Anglican Church. The Irish branch of the Mothers' Union was founded in Ireland in 1887, and by 1892 there were committees in every diocese.[20] The membership consisted of married mothers, mostly from the middle class. It aimed to organise 'in every place a band of mothers who will unite in prayer and seek by their own example to lead their families in purity and holiness of life'.[21] There was significant overlap in leadership with the Girls' Friendly Society, established in Ireland in 1877 to nurture young Church of Ireland girls by training them in religious principles and domestic duty.[22] Consisting

[15] Minutes of the Proceedings of the General Assembly of the Presbyterian Church in Ireland, held at Belfast, June 1918, p. 564.

[16] Minutes of the One Hundred and Forty-sixth Conference of the People Called Methodists (Dublin, 1915), p. 130.

[17] Similar attitudes prevailed among the churches in France. See Adrian Gregory and Annette Becker, 'Religious Sites and Practices', in Jay Winter and Jean-Louis Robert (eds), Capital Cities at War: Paris, London, Berlin 1914–1918, vol. 2: A Cultural History (Cambridge, 2007), pp. 383–427 (at p. 391).

[18] Maconchy, Journal of the General Synod of the Church of Ireland, p. 82.

[19] Church of Ireland Gazette, 14 Jun. 1918; Minutes of the One Hundred and Forty-sixth Conference of the People Called Methodists, p. 130; Minutes of the Proceeding of the General Assembly of the Presbyterian Church in Ireland, 1911–1915, vol. 12 (Belfast, 1915), pp. 1085, 1122.

[20] Diana McFarlan, The Mothers' Union in Ireland: A Centenary History, 1887–1987 (Dublin, 1987), p. 5.

[21] Lady Isabel Talbot de Malahide, Foundations of National Glory: Mothers' Union Addresses (London, 1915), p. 21.

[22] Maria Luddy, Women and Philanthropy in Nineteenth Century Ireland (Cambridge, 1995), p. 60.

mostly of working-class girls, it was one of the largest women's organisations in early twentieth-century Ireland. In 1915, it had a membership of 16,010 women dispersed across 510 parishes and 234 branches.[23] Both it and the Mother's Union were essentially conservative organisations with traditional ideas of women's roles in the domestic and public spheres. They were both closely associated with the Church of Ireland hierarchy, with the archbishops of Armagh and Dublin serving as patrons. However, the real power rested with the Central Council, which was entirely composed of women, the majority from the aristocracy. The organisational structure and experience of the two associations enabled them to provide a nationwide network of charitable endeavour in wartime.

The Mothers' Union and Girls' Friendly Society both diverted their usual work to war relief activities.[24] The type of voluntary work performed by members was typical of the most common forms of war-related activity for Irishwomen: knitting comforts for soldiers, sending parcels to prisoners of war, and manufacturing and providing medical supplies for the Red Cross and similar organisations. Some diocesan committees organised war work themselves, while in other cases members individually joined organisations such as the Red Cross. Several of the diocesan presidents of the Mothers' Union, for example, played a prominent leadership role in the war effort. Lady Farnham, president of the Kilmore Mothers' Union until 1915, was centrally involved in the Irishwomen's Association, which provided parcels for Irish prisoners of war, while Lady Clonbrock, president of the Killaloe diocesan branch, led several local endeavours in Galway such as providing comforts for soldiers serving with the Connaught Rangers.[25] These women were active unionists: Lady Farnham was a member of the Ulster Women's Unionist Council while Lady Clonbrock was involved in collecting funds for the Irish Unionist Alliance (IUA) and in organising a petition to the British government against Home Rule from Galway women.[26]

---

[23] *Thirty-ninth Report and Associates List of the Girls' Friendly Society in Ireland for Year Ending 31st December 1915* (Dublin, 1916), p. 3.

[24] Minute book of the organising committee of the Mothers' Union of Ireland 1912–21 (Representative Church Body Library, MS 749); Minute books of the Central Council and executive committee of the Girls' Friendly Society, 1914–1918 (Representative Church Body Library, MS 578); *Thirty-ninth Report and Associates List of the Girls' Friendly Society in Ireland.*

[25] Letters and other material relating to Lady Farnham's charitable work in Co. Cavan during the Great War and materials relating to the Girls' Friendly Society and Mothers' Union (NLI, MS 18,616/2-8); Report of the Galway War Fund Association, 1917–18 (NLI, MS 35,796(4)).

[26] NLI, MS 18,616/8; *Belfast News-letter,* 3 Apr. 1918; NLI MS 35,796(2). See, for example, Receipt from the IUA to Lady Clonbrock for £93 contributed to the IUA, 10 Dec. 1910; petition signed by Galway women addressed to the British parliament opposing Home Rule, undated.

The religious work of the Mothers' Union and Girls' Friendly Society took
on increasing significance in the war years. Cordelia Moyse has described how
the Mothers' Union in Britain saw the Great War as an affirmation of the
spiritual vocation of women. They viewed women's particular wartime contribution as advocating a life of Christian faith grounded in regular prayer and
worship.[27] Lady Talbot de Malahide, president of the Dublin diocese Mothers'
Union, argued in 1915 that 'at a time like this in the world's history ... the
advantage of a united effort to bind women together in a common cause,
is more widely felt than ever'.[28] The Cork, Cloyne and Ross diocesan union
noted that members received 'great help and spiritual support in those war
years'.[29] Mother's Union members were called upon to remember their special
responsibility towards the moral welfare of soldiers, and in preparing the
domestic sphere for the soldiers' return.[30] The Girls' Friendly Society similarly
described their work as of 'greater importance now than it has ever been before'
and argued that the 'future welfare of the Empire will depend more largely
on our women and girls and be more deeply marked by their influence and
example than it has been in the past'.[31] The Society viewed the involvement of
its members and associates in the war effort as affirmation of the important
place of the organisation in Irish society.[32] Involvement with the Mothers'
Union or Girls' Friendly Society helped to develop a sense of community
among Anglican women in Ireland, but also served as a connection to Britain
and to the British Empire.[33]

Religion evidently played a significant role in promoting and supporting
women's war service, linking it to ideals of sacrifice and duty, and provided
a sense of community for loyalist women. Co-operation, however, between
Catholic and Protestant women proved difficult to sustain. The disproportionate representation of Protestants among the leadership of the Red Cross
divisions was noted with anxiety by the *Irish Catholic*, who were concerned
that the British Red Cross included Protestant proselytisers who were preying
upon the vulnerable wives of absent soldiers. The St John Ambulance
Association was treated with particular suspicion, with one anonymous letter

---

[27] Cordelia Moyse, *A History of the Mothers' Union: Women, Anglicanism and
Globalisation, 1876–2008* (Woodbridge, 2009), pp. 102–3.

[28] Talbot de Malahide, *Foundations of National Glory*, p. 49.

[29] McFarlan, *The Mothers' Union in Ireland*, p. 12.

[30] *Church of Ireland Gazette*, 4 Dec., 11 Dec. 1914; 27 Jul. 1917.

[31] *Thirty-ninth Report and Associates List of the Girls' Friendly Society in Ireland*,
p. 3.

[32] *Thirty-ninth Report and Associates List of the Girls' Friendly Society in Ireland*,
p. 3; see also *Church of Ireland Gazette*, 25 Jun. 1915.

[33] Oonagh Walsh, *Anglican Women in Dublin: Philanthropy, Politics and Education
in the Early Twentieth Century* (Dublin, 2005), p. 150.

writer describing it as a 'Protestant imitation of a Catholic religious order' and warning *Irish Catholic* readers to stay clear of the association for fear of its proselytising intentions.[34]

Philanthropy was far more common among lay Protestant women than lay Catholics in early twentieth-century Ireland, owing to the significant number of Catholic nuns who amounted to what Oonagh Walsh describes as a 'ready-made philanthropic army'.[35] Nonetheless, the war brought a growing awareness of the roles Catholic women could perform in society. Many Catholic women participated in church-led activities to support the war effort, particularly in assisting the 3,000 Belgian Catholic refugees who settled in Ireland.[36] Priests encouraged their congregations to subscribe to funds established for the Belgians' relief.[37] Lay Catholic women assisted with the Sunday collections and organised fundraising events for the refugees themselves.[38] May Starkie, a Dublin Catholic, was preoccupied with the war effort: working daily at a Red Cross depot manufacturing hospital supplies, organizing a club for soldiers' wives, and assisting with an Alexandra College Guild scheme to provide a hostel for young girls working in munitions factories.[39] She was married to William Starkie, resident commissioner of national education in Ireland, and belonged to the upper-class Dublin social scene. Both William and May Starkie were unionists and strong supporters of the war effort. May Starkie's 1916 pamphlet, *What is Patriotism: The Teaching of Patriotism*, was interpreted as propaganda in support of conscription and made the couple increasingly unpopular with the Irish public and the Catholic Church.[40]

Loyalist women were also active in the war effort through their own unionist organisations. Diane Urquhart has published extensively on the

---

[34] *Irish Catholic*, 24 Oct., 28 Nov. 1914.

[35] Walsh, *Anglican Women in Dublin*, p. 87.

[36] Richard S. Grayson, *Dublin's Great Wars: The First World War, the Easter Rising, and the Irish Revolution* (Cambridge, 2018), p. 30.

[37] Resolutions passed at annual meeting of the Catholic hierarchy in Maynooth, 13 Oct. 1914, *Irish Catholic Directory and Almanac for 1915*, p. 541; Letter from Robert Browne, bishop of Cloyne, 20 Mar., *Irish Catholic Directory for 1916*, p. 504; *Irish Catholic*, 28 Nov. 1914.

[38] Mrs Breda Morgan-Browne to Archbishop Walsh, 12 Oct. 1914 (Dublin Diocesan Archives, Walsh/1914/387/2/Laity). See, for example, *Kildare Observer*, 14 Nov. 1915.

[39] Enid Starkie, *A Lady's Child* (London, 1941), p. 200. See also May Starkie to Archbishop Walsh, 19 Nov. 1914 (Dublin Diocesan Archives, Walsh/1914/387/2/Laity).

[40] Jacqueline A. Hurtley, 'Starkie, William Joseph Myles', in James McGuire and James Quinn (eds), *Dictionary of Irish Biography* (Cambridge, 2009): http://dib.cambridge.org/viewReadPage.do?articleId=a8263. See also May C. Starkie, *What is Patriotism: The Teaching of Patriotism* (Dublin, 1916), pp. 8–9.

Ulster Women's Unionist Council during this period, showing how the council responded to the war by initially suspending political agitation in favour of war relief work.[41] Southern Unionist women's organisations feature less prominently in the historiography of Irish Unionism. In his study of southern unionism, R.B. McDowell refers briefly to the Dublin Women's Unionist Club.[42] It had 3,000 members in April 1914, which had apparently increased to 4,500 by February 1915. Leading members included Margaret Dockrell, wife of the later Unionist MP Sir Maurice Dockrell, and Lady Caroline Arnott, wife of Sir John Arnott, the owner of the department store and the *Irish Times* newspaper. At the outbreak of war, the club suspended political action and diverted its attention to war relief activities. For example, members contributed subscriptions for a motor ambulance for the front in February 1915.[43] There were also various ladies' branches of the IUA in provincial Ireland. One such branch was only established in County Kerry in 1916, indicating that the war had not halted all such political activity.[44] Southern unionist women joined other war relief organisations and appear to have been less particular than Ulster women about maintaining a distinct unionist identity. In the south of the country, women from various political backgrounds worked together in many of the war relief organisations: the volunteers at the sphagnum moss depot at the Royal College of Science in Dublin were described as a mix of unionists and 'nationalists of one kind or another'.[45]

The partition of Ireland had been accepted in principle by the Ulster Unionist Council in 1916 and a growing partitionist mindset is evident during the war years. As noted by Senia Pašeta, 'partition was a well-established fact of war relief'.[46] The Ulster Women's Unionist Council had an extensive

---

[41] Diane Urquhart (ed.), *The Minutes of the Ulster Women's Unionist Council and the Executive Committee, 1911–1940* (Dublin, 2001); Diane Urquhart, '"The Female of the Species is More Deadlier than the Male"? The Ulster Women's Unionist Council, 1911–40', in Janice Holmes and Diane Urquhart (eds), *Coming into the Light: The Work, Politics and Religion of Women in Ulster, 1840–1940* (Belfast, 1994), pp. 93–125; Diane Urquhart, *Women in Ulster Politics, 1890–1940: A History Not Yet Told* (Dublin, 2000).

[42] McDowell, *Crisis and Decline*, p. 48.

[43] Senia Pašeta, 'New Issues and Old: Women and Politics in Ireland, 1914–1918', *Women's History Review*, 27/3 (2016), p. 4; Patrick Buckland, *Irish Unionism II: Ulster Unionism and the Origins of Northern Ireland, 1886–1922* (Dublin, 1973), p. 96.

[44] McDowell, *Crisis and Decline*, p. 63.

[45] Clara Cullen, 'War Work on the Home Front: The Central Sphagnum Depot for Ireland at the Royal College of Science for Ireland, 1915–19', in David Durnin and Ian Miller (eds), *Medicine, Health and Irish Experiences of Conflict, 1914–45* (Manchester, 2017), p. 165.

[46] Pašeta, 'New Issues and Old', p. 12.

role in organising and directing war relief work in the northern province, organising its own voluntary activities and expressing reluctance to co-operate with southern organisations.[47] There were separate Red Cross committees and sphagnum moss associations for Ulster and for southern Ireland. There is no evidence of communication between the sphagnum department co-ordinated by the Royal College of Science and the Ulster Sphagnum Moss Association, established by the Ulster Women's Unionist Council.[48] Although the Irish War Hospital Supply Depot had been established in Dublin in 1915, the organisers of the Belfast War Hospital Supply Depot travelled to London in 1916, rather than Dublin, to learn 'all about the running' of a depot. It was reported in the magazine *Irish Life* that their depot was run on 'identically the same lines as the London one'.[49] This was just one of several examples of missed opportunities for collaboration between UWUC-led organisations and similar bodies in the south. In the aftermath of the Easter Rising, the UWUC became increasingly concerned that their political agenda was being damaged by the prioritisation of their war work. This resulted in greater determination to maintain a distinct Ulster identity for their war work and to resist collaboration with others.

The Easter Rising also created great anxiety for unionists in southern Ireland. In June 1916, the Dublin Women's Unionist Club issued a women's petition calling on the Imperial Parliament to 'safeguard the liberties of the minority in the three southern provinces', fearful that the growth of republicanism would lead to sectarian violence.[50] After the Rising, the Protestant churches were anxious to emphasise their loyalty to Britain. The Methodist and Presbyterian assemblies condemned the rebellion at their 1916 annual conferences and assured the king of their 'unabated loyalty' to the 'throne and constitution of the United Kingdom'.[51] In a 1918 memoir, Katherine Tynan, a popular writer living in County Mayo, described her distress after the Rising:

> I had come to believe that affection for England and love of Ireland could quite well go hand in hand. I was enthusiastically pro-Ally. Both my boys were pledged to the War – by their own choice. ... We had grown up to the love of Ireland; and now came this sharp, bitter cleavage, in

47 Letter from W. King Stevenson (UWGF hon. treasurer) to Mrs Ainsworth Barr (UWGF hon. secretary), 6 May 1918 (PRONI, D/1507/A/27/8).
48 'Red Cross work at the Royal College of Science' (1919) (IWM, L.R. 121/1).
49 *Irish Life*, 18 Feb. 1916; 16 Nov. 1917.
50 Pašeta, 'New Politics and Old', p. 4.
51 *Minutes of the One Hundred and Forty-seventh Conference of the People Called Methodists, in Belfast June 1916* (Dublin, 1916), p. 112; *Minutes of the Proceeding of the General Assembly of the Presbyterian Church in Ireland, 1916–1920*, vol. 13, p. 20.

which, with incredible rapidity, the great body of the Irish were massing themselves in a hostility against England – and England, a great part of her, against Ireland. It was a tragedy many shared with us.[52]

It became more difficult in the turbulent years after the Rising for loyalty to the Union and the Empire to coexist with a sense of Irish identity.

Opposition to the war became more evident after the Easter Rising, and women associated with the relief effort experienced increased hostility. In 1917, Elsie Henry, quartermaster of the Irish War Hospital Supply Depot, recorded physical assaults endured by the voluntary workers of the sphagnum moss depot in Kilgarvan, County Kerry. She described an 'active bitterness' and anti-English feeling.[53] However, there was a parallel surge of voluntary support for the war effort in 1917 and 1918, evident in the output of the Irish War Hospital Supply Depot. Thirteen new sub-depots were established in the latter half of the war, indicating continued levels of enthusiasm for the organisation and the war effort.[54] The high outputs for 1918 are noteworthy given the high infection rates of the influenza epidemic in Ireland from spring 1918. An estimated 900,000 people were infected by the epidemic in Ireland and approximately 23,288 people died from influenza or from associated pneumonia from 1918 to 1919.[55]

The reports of Red Cross fundraising also suggest continued levels of support for the war effort after the Rising. Ireland's contributions to the Red Cross 'Our Day' appeal in 1917 and 1918 were particularly high – higher per capita than elsewhere in the United Kingdom. The 1917 contribution was described as 'exceptionally fine' by the report of the Joint Committee of the British Red Cross and St John Ambulance Association.[56] Ireland contributed £111,257 in 1917, making up 24.6 per cent of the total United Kingdom contribution.[57] The 1917 contribution from the southern provinces was five times that of 1916 while there was a further 25.8 per cent increase in 1918 in the amounts raised in Ireland for the Red Cross.[58] The Red Cross 'Our Day' fundraising

---

[52] Katherine Tynan, *The Year of the Shadow* (London, 1919), pp. 204–5.

[53] Elsie Henry, '13 Apr. 1917', in Clara Cullen (ed.), *The World Upturning: Elsie Henry's Irish Wartime Diaries, 1913–1919* (Dublin, 2013), p. 186.

[54] *Annual Report of the Irish War Hospital Supply Depot 1917–1918*, p. 36.

[55] Ida Milne, *Stacking the Coffins: Influenza, War and Revolution in Ireland, 1918–19* (Manchester, 2018), pp. 59–60.

[56] *Reports by the Joint War Committee and the Joint War Finance Committee of the British Red Cross Society and the Order of St. John of Jerusalem, 1914–1919* (London, 1921), p. 21.

[57] 'Memorandum on Red Cross Work in Ireland', p. 725.

[58] Figures for southern Ireland derived from *The Red Cross in Ireland*, p. 38 and the figures for Ulster from 'Memorandum on Red Cross Work in Ireland', p. 731.

in Ireland was organised by Sir John Lumsden, vice-chairman of the Joint Voluntary Aid Detachment committee for Ireland. Lady Arnott organised a pageant in Dublin in October 1917, which was claimed to be successful in stimulating 'public interest and generosity'.[59]

There was a competitive aspect to fundraising. In 1917, the committee for southern Ireland issued a 'friendly challenge to Ulster, which was accepted in an equally friendly spirit, and North and South at once entered into the contest with the right good-will'.[60] While such 'friendly challenges' may have had particular connotations in an increasingly divided Ireland, similar comparisons were made in *The Times* between the relative contributions of Glasgow and London to the War Loan.[61] The surge in support for the Red Cross in Ireland in 1917 and 1918 suggests that the political tensions may have spurred loyalist communities to reaffirm their allegiance to the British state and their patriotism through civil mobilisation. Adrian Gregory has drawn a similar inference from the particularly high contribution of Glasgow to the war savings scheme in early 1918, arguing that the 'disloyalty tag' associated with Glasgow acted as an incentive for its population to attempt to demonstrate 'conspicuous loyalty'.[62] Army enlistment also remained high in Ireland, despite the widespread public opposition to conscription. Nearly 10,000 Irishmen enlisted in the British forces in the final three months of the war.[63]

The southern loyalist community suffered a 'crisis of identity' and a 'deeply felt loss of status and confidence' in the turbulent years that followed the Armistice in 1918.[64] The success of Sinn Féin in the December 1918 election indicated the extent of the political transformation in Ireland over the course of the war. Over the next three years, the IRA and the British military forces were engaged in continual fighting and often brutal reprisals against the wider community.[65] Over 3,500 people were killed in the War of Independence and the Civil War that followed the Anglo-Irish Treaty.[66] Partition became a legal reality under the 1920 Government of Ireland Act, accentuating the sense of loss and displacement for southern loyalists. The Farnhams, for example, were horrified that their Cavan estate was now in the disloyal south rather than the northern state.[67] During the 1919–23 conflict many southern loyalists

[59] *The Red Cross in Ireland*, p. 22.
[60] *The Red Cross in Ireland*, p. 22.
[61] Gregory, *The Last Great War*, p. 228.
[62] Gregory, *The Last Great War*, p. 228.
[63] Thomas Bartlett, *Ireland: A History* (Cambridge, 2010), p. 383.
[64] Hughes, 'Loyalists and Loyalism', p. 1076.
[65] Fearghal McGarry, 'Revolution, 1916–1923', in Bartlett, *Cambridge History of Ireland*, vol. 4, pp. 269–79.
[66] McGarry, 'Revolution, 1916–1923', pp. 280–2, 291.
[67] Buckland, *Ulster Unionism II*, pp. 119–21. See also Chapter 13.

endured physical violence, intimidation, boycotts, arson, and other attempts to persuade them to leave Ireland. Although the numbers killed were comparatively small by international standards, there was enough violence to create what Hughes describes as an 'atmosphere of terror well beyond the reality'.[68] Women were less likely to be murdered or physically assaulted (some did have their hair forcibly cut as retaliation for interacting with soldiers) but they nonetheless suffered greatly from the fear of attack and the psychological effects of violence and raids on their homes.[69] The next section moves from discussing the public role of loyalist women in the war effort to examining how they were affected by the subsequent political upheaval. These often private and domestic experiences are typically less visible in the historical record than the accounts of war work but can be glimpsed through the Irish Grant Committee application records, an invaluable source for understanding southern loyalism in this period.

The volume of southern Irish refugees arriving in Britain during the War of Independence and Civil War led to the establishment of the British Treasury-funded Irish Distress Committee in 1922, which provided compensation to those obliged to leave. In 1923, it became the Irish Grants Committee, with a remit including southern Irish loyalists remaining in Ireland. A second grants committee met in 1926 to provide compensation for loyalists for loss and injuries sustained after the truce, between July 1921 and May 1923. There were over 4,000 applications in total, of which 2,237 received awards.[70] Although men appear more frequently to have completed applications, there are many submitted by women, and it is some of these that will be discussed below.[71] Hughes has noted the problems inherent with using compensation files as hard evidence of experience, arguing that they can be open to 'embellishment, reconstruction, or fictionalisation', with accounts liable to be skewed in the hope of financial gain.[72] Both the extent of the injury or loss suffered and

---

[68] Brian Hughes, *Defying the IRA? Intimidation, Coercion, and Communities during the Irish Revolution* (Liverpool, 2016), p. 128.

[69] Hughes, *Defying the IRA?*, pp. 140–2; Gemma Clarke, *Everyday Violence in the Irish Civil War* (Cambridge, 2014), p. 192. The subject of sexual violence against women during the Irish revolutionary period is a significant and expanding area of scholarship. See, for example, Linda Connolly, 'Sexual Violence and the Irish Revolution: An Inconvenient Truth?', *History Ireland*, 27/6 (2019), pp. 34–8 and Justin Dolan Stover, 'Families, Vulnerability and Sexual Violence during the Irish Revolution', in Ciara Meehan and Jennifer Evans (eds), *Perceptions of Pregnancy from the Seventeenth to the Twentieth Centuries* (Basingstoke, 2017), pp. 57–75.

[70] Hughes, 'Loyalists and Loyalism', p. 1078; McDowell, *Crisis and Decline*, pp. 131–2, 155.

[71] Hughes's case study of Arva, Co. Cavan reveals that men made up 76 per cent of applicants to the scheme in that area. *Defying the IRA?*, p. 102.

[72] Hughes, 'Loyalists and Loyalism', p. 1078.

the declarations of loyalty to the government of the United Kingdom were potentially exaggerated, or, less frequently, entirely fabricated.[73]

Margaret White's claim for compensation, for instance, was dismissed as a 'tissue of falsehoods' by the Irish Grants Committee, while even one of her referees admitted that her primary claim was untrue. White, living in County Tipperary, had married a member of the Auxiliary Division of the RIC in 1922 and had claimed that the couple's attempt to open a provisions store following his disbandment had failed due to IRA raids, forcing them to flee to England. Her husband, with whom she was no longer living, responded that he had never intended to remain in Ireland: her application was the first he heard of the provisions store, and that her allegations of IRA intimidation on their wedding day were entirely false.[74] Assertions of loyalty were also questioned. A note attached to the rejected application of Annie Ringwood, a Catholic from Queen's County, declared that 'we are informed that these people are not loyalists'. Ringwood and her daughters had sought compensation for farm damage, allegedly on account of refusing to give money to the Republicans.[75] The files nevertheless provide an unparalleled insight into the experience of self-proclaimed loyalists in the aftermath of the Great War.

The significant hardship faced by many loyalist families and the limitations of the compensation claim system were noted in a letter by the Anglican rector of Church Hill, Donegal, Reverend Alexander Munro, in support of Margaret Keeney's application for support in 1928: 'We all suffered because of our loyalty to England, not at a particular moment but for life long loyalty to an ideal, but we have had a rude awakening and I do not think anything compensates under the circumstances'.[76] Keeney's family suffered intimidation and damage to their property from the IRA in Donegal, owing to her husband's prior employment with the RIC and her son's refusal to support the IRA. After several attacks on their home they fled to Scotland but her husband died in 1924, his health having been affected by the previous traumatic years. Keeney received £50 (c.£2,000 in modern currency).[77] Although Keeney was a Catholic, Munro nevertheless provided her with a reference for her compensation claim, indicating his recognition that IRA intimidation was not confined to the Protestant community.[78]

---

[73] McDowell, *Crisis and Decline*, pp. 156–7.
[74] Margaret White claim (TNA, CO 762/156/5).
[75] Annie Ringwood claim (TNA, CO 762/194/3). Census return for Ringwood family of Cappalinnan, Queen's County in 1911: http://census.nationalarchives. ie/ (accessed 24 May 2019).
[76] Margaret Keeney claim (TNA CO 762/187/20).
[77] Margaret Keeney claim (TNA CO 762/187/20).
[78] Keeney family census returns for 1911: http://census.nationalarchives.ie/ (accessed 24 May 2019).

Public support for the British army during the Great War was viewed with suspicion by the IRA and was used as justification for their raids and assaults. Ex-servicemen and their families appear to have been particularly liable to assaults and intimidation. In Hughes' case study of Arva, County Cavan, the most common evidence of loyalism offered was connection to the Crown forces. The majority were either involved in helping the Royal Irish Constabulary or had family members who had served in the British army.[79] The experience of ex-soldiers during the War of Independence has been the subject of some debate, with Jane Leonard and Paul Taylor offering contrasting interpretations of the extent to which British army veterans were targeted by the IRA.[80] It seems probable that, as Hughes suggests, the truth is somewhere is the middle. In Hughes' view, Taylor underestimates the impact of revolutionary violence on ex-servicemen.[81] Unemployment levels among Irish ex-servicemen were also exceptionally high: 40,000 former soldiers were reported to be unemployed and without any means of subsistence by January 1920.[82] Many depended on the British Legion and the Southern Irish Loyalists Relief Association for basic support, making them more likely to be targeted for their link to the Crown forces and other loyalist bodies.[83] Some ex-servicewomen also faced difficult homecomings. One former member of the Women's Army Auxiliary Corps sold her farm in County Kildare after the war and moved to Australia, reportedly because she was unable to cope with the 'prevailing disloyalty'.[84]

Elizabeth Cordner argued in her application for compensation that there 'was no mistaking that we were not the sort of people wanted here'. Her brothers had served in the British army during the war and her husband's younger brother had been killed in Flanders. Her husband William, a Belfast Presbyterian, had run a successful motor car company in Waterford but was forced to abandon it and move to Belfast owing to the boycott of their business, on account of her 'husband's strong views on the Union being well-known'.[85] Mary Skerritt

---

[79] Hughes, 'Loyalists and Loyalism', p. 1089.

[80] Jane Leonard, 'Getting Them at Last: The IRA and Ex-Servicemen', in David Fitzpatrick (ed.), *Revolution? Ireland, 1917–1923* (Dublin, 1990), pp. 118–29; Paul Taylor, *Heroes or Traitors? Experiences of Southern Irish Soldiers Returning from the Great War, 1919–1939* (Liverpool, 2015), pp. 1–79, 243–5.

[81] Hughes, *Defying the IRA?*, pp. 131–2.

[82] French to Walter Long, 17 Jan. 1920 (IWM, JDPF 8/15).

[83] Michael Robinson, '"Nobody's Children"? The Ministry of Pensions and the Treatment of Disabled Great War Veterans in the Irish Free State, 1921–1939', *Irish Studies Review*, 25/3 (2017), p. 321.

[84] *Old Comrades Gazette*, 6 (Dec. 1920) (IWM, WWS Army 3.26/16).

[85] Elizabeth Cordner claim (TNA CO 762/139/2); Cordner 1911 family census returns: http://census.nationalarchives.ie/ (accessed 24 May 2019).

suffered the destruction of her home in Clare in 1920 as the IRA searched for her brother who was an ex-serviceman. She claimed that she and her brother were ardent loyalists: 'He has been such a loyal subject to the British Empire and always loyal to the colours. During the time the British subjects were in the country I catered for them with dinners and teas when we were opposed to do so and through all that I supplied them and I will always stand loyal to the colours'.[86] R.B. McDowell has observed how friendly interactions with the Crown forces were 'normal social behaviour' for loyalists but nonetheless brought them into direct conflict with republican sentiment and policy.[87]

Many of the women targeted by the IRA had been active in the war effort. The affected families occasionally drew on this war relief activity to demonstrate their long-standing loyalty to the British Empire. One applicant mentioned her 'deep personal interest in Red Cross work' as evidence of her loyalism.[88] Others, however, neglected to mention their war service, perhaps seeing it as insignificant compared with the military service of their menfolk, or as so commonplace as not to merit mention. Sarah Trinder, an Anglican farmer's wife, had volunteered with the Irish War Hospital Supply Depot in Cork during the war. Their farm was raided on a night in 1923. The trauma led to her husband suffering heart trouble, from which he died in 1928, leaving Sarah a widow aged 46. Her application mentions that they were 'well-known loyalists', which singled them out for 'continuous billeting, looting and annoyance by armed gangs' but provides no details of this conspicuous loyalty. Nevertheless, she received £250 (c.£14,000 in modern currency) in compensation.[89] Deborah E. Ball from King's County was described as having actively 'supported British rule in Ireland' by the rector in her parish. Although not mentioned in her application, she had volunteered with the Irish War Hospital Supply Depot, collecting sphagnum moss for over two years during the Great War. In 1922, her home was raided by the IRA and she was tied up outside for three hours. She subsequently fled the country. She received the substantial sum of £4,020 (c.£227,000 in modern currency) in compensation for the shock she suffered during the ordeal and the financial loss incurred by being obliged to sell her home.[90]

Ursula Bingham and her husband Denis, a gentleman farmer from County Mayo, were also targeted for their support for the war effort. The couple had

[86] Mary Skerritt claim (TNA, CO 762/43/5).

[87] McDowell, *Crisis and Decline*, p. 87.

[88] Hughes, *Defying the IRA?*, p. 129.

[89] Sarah Trinder claim (TNA, CO 762/194/18); Great War membership file for Sarah Trinder (British Red Cross Archives); Trinder family 1911 census return: http://census.nationalarchives.ie/ (accessed 24 May 2019).

[90] Deborah Ball claim (TNA, CO 762/110/11); Great War membership file for Deborah Ball (British Red Cross Archives).

assisted with recruiting for the British forces and Ursula's application for compensation included a letter from the Controller of Recruiting attesting to their public support for the British army during the Great War. Their home in Mayo had been raided several times by armed men in 1921 and 1922, including a 'terrifying night-time search' in May 1922. These raids were due to suspicion that the Binghams had passed information to the RIC about local IRA activity in April 1921. Indeed, the local RIC District Inspector praised the couple for 'their loyalty and willingness at all times to give every assistance to the Crown forces, often under trying circumstances'. The raids and tension took a toll on Ursula's health and she underwent a hysterectomy in October 1922. By February 1928, they were living in very 'straitened circumstances' and were in debt. She was awarded £600 (c.£33,000 in modern currency).[91] Mary Cahill in Kilkenny, whose husband was killed in action in the Great War, felt that she was singled out for her refusal to sign the anti-conscription pledge in 1918. She was then threatened by Sinn Féin and in September 1922 her house was raided by the IRA. Cahill, feeling obliged to leave Ireland, moved to France.[92]

Mary Cahill was one of many loyalists who emigrated in the years that followed the 1918 Armistice, feeling that there was no place for them in the emerging state. Historians continue to debate the extent of this 'exodus' and to question where responsibility for it should lie. As noted by Hughes, however, it was the perception of what 'was happening among those on the ground that is most important'.[93] McDowell's study of southern loyalism concludes that the pressure exerted on unionists between 1919 and 1923 accounts at least in part for the 'striking fall' in the Protestant population between 1911 and 1926.[94] He remarks that 'contemplation of historical trends' does little to mitigate the pain from loss and injury, and indeed statistical analysis of the demographics of the Protestant or loyalist populations reveal little about the lived experience of everyday violence.[95] It is evident from the compensation applications that the sense of displacement combined with the threats and terror created significant trauma and a sense of being outsiders.

During the Great War, war service acted as an outlet for southern loyalist identity. Men and women demonstrated their patriotism and support for Britain through enlistment in the military services and voluntary work on the home front. There was a strong communal and associational element to war relief activity, which together with the Home Rule crisis and the Easter Rising

---

[91] Ursula Bingham claim (TNA, CO 762/156/7); Bingham family 1911 census returns: http://census.nationalarchives.ie/ (accessed 24 May 2019).
[92] Mary Cahill claim (TNA, CO 762/156/4).
[93] Hughes, *Defying the IRA?*, p. 128.
[94] McDowell, *Crisis and Decline*, pp. 136, 164. For more discussion of the declining numbers, see Chapter 2.
[95] McDowell, *Crisis and Decline*, p. 159.

strengthened a separate southern loyalist identity. Co-operation with the wider Irish population, already strained in wartime, effectively ceased once the Great War ended. The brief discussion of some of the female applicants to the Irish Grants Committee yields insight into loyalist women's specific experience during the conflict which followed, and the links between war service and their subsequent isolation. Offering refreshments to British army soldiers and engaging in friendly interactions with them were all norms of behaviour during the Great War, but suddenly became the subject of suspicion and antagonism in the tumultuous years that followed. In wartime, the families of soldiers received support and sympathy but suffered in the aftermath when this war service was given new meaning and ideological motivation. Everyday actions became politicised and used as justification for retribution and violent attacks from their local communities. Although they contributed to an atmosphere of intimidation and hostility, such incidences of violence were comparatively rare, and many loyalists encountered a warmer response from the fledgling Irish state than initially feared. There was government support for public events to mark Armistice Day, for example, throughout the 1920s and 1930s.[96] Nevertheless, the revolutionary upheaval took its toll, and within a decade of the 'unprecedented unity' created by the outbreak of European war in 1914 a significant minority of loyalist families had left Ireland, believing that there was no home for them in the Irish Free State.

---

[96] Keith Jeffery, 'Irish Varieties of Great War Commemoration', in John Horne and Edward Madigan (eds), *Towards Commemoration: Ireland in War and Revolution 1912–1923* (Dublin, 2013), p. 118.

CHAPTER VII

Southern Irish Loyalists and Imperial Service

Seán William Gannon

Significant Irish enlistment in Britain's imperial services commenced in the mid-1850s, when Ireland's elite educational infrastructure began exploiting the opportunity provided by the introduction of recruitment by competitive examination for India's civil and medical services. The appointment of an 'old boy' to the Indian Civil Service (ICS) quickly became a prize coveted by Ireland's expanding network of fee-paying intermediate colleges, while Irish universities reoriented their curricula to cover the subjects examined. The second half of the nineteenth century also saw increasing Irish interest in the employment opportunities provided by the emergent British Colonial Service (BCS), and elite educational institutions there too played a pivotal role, notwithstanding its recruitment through patronage. Intermediate colleges such as Portora Royal, St Columba's, and Clongowes Wood, and universities such as TCD and the Queen's Colleges, cultivated a pro-Empire outlook and an ethos of imperial service.[1] Thus, by the turn of the twentieth century, when territorial acquisitions in Africa saw the BCS develop into a major overseas service, Irishmen could be found serving as administrators, doctors, lawyers, engineers, and policemen throughout Britain's dependent empire, and this remained the case in 1919 as the Irish War of Independence broke out. Southern Ireland's secession from the United Kingdom three years later fatally holed its imperial connection.[2] Nevertheless, Irishmen continued to enlist in

---

[1] On Irish elite education and imperial service, see Kevin Flanagan, 'The Rise and Fall of the Celtic Ineligible: Competitive Examinations for the Irish and Indian Civil Services in Relation to the Educational and Occupational Structure of Ireland, 1853–1921', D.Phil. thesis, University of Sussex, 1977, pp. 450–7; David Dickson, Justyna Pyz, and Christopher Shepard (eds), *Irish Classrooms and the British Empire: Imperial Contexts in the Origins of Modern Education* (Dublin, 2012).

[2] For convenience and clarity, the terms 'southern Ireland' and 'southern Irish' are used throughout this essay with reference to the 26 counties, which, during

Britain's imperial services in significant numbers and were well represented at all levels and across all sectors until the Colonial Office's closure in 1966.

Given the centrality of Ireland's elite education system to British imperial services' recruitment in the second half of the long nineteenth century, the overwhelming majority of Irish enlistments was drawn from amongst the demographics that could afford it, namely the Protestant gentry and the Protestant and Catholic middle classes.[3] In fact, over 80 per cent of Irish Civilians (as covenanted Indian civil servants were called) and 75 per cent of Irish BCS officers recruited between 1870 and 1914 came from the Protestant middle class.[4] The sons of professionals, merchants, high- and middle-ranking Crown servants, and large farmers, they saw in imperial service an opportunity for 'good pay, the promise of rapid promotion, challenge, adventure, prestige, and the satisfaction of leadership'.[5] Ireland's burgeoning Catholic middle class provided a steadily increasing proportion of similarly motivated enlistments during this time so that, by 1919, Catholics accounted for approximately 30 per cent of Irish ICS and BCS recruits. And while recent research on Irish imperial agency has confuted the view that Irish nationalism and British imperialism were, by definition, dichotomous, a majority of Irish imperial servants recruited from pre-revolutionary Ireland was drawn from its unionist minority – Protestants and so-called 'Castle Catholics' who supported the constitutional status quo.[6]

the period explored, comprised the Irish Free State (1922–37), Éire, or Ireland (1937–49), and the Republic of Ireland (1949–).

[3] While the Catholic gentry was less well represented, it provided some of the best known amongst Irish imperial servants – for example, Anthony McDonnell and Michael O'Dwyer of the ICS.

[4] These (and otherwise unreferenced statistics cited below) are abstracted from an analysis of a wide range of sources, primarily *The India Office List* (London, 1886–95); *The India List and India Office List* (London, 1896–1906): *The India Office List* (London, 1907–37); *The Colonial Office List for 1862–1925; or General Register of the Colonial Dependencies of Great Britain* (London, 1992); *Colonial Office List, 1925* (London, 1925); *The Dominions Office and Colonial Office List* (London, 1926–40); *Colonial Office List* (London, 1946–66); Royal Irish Constabulary General Registers of Service (TNA, HO 184/1-43); *Census of Ireland, 1901* and *1911*: http://census.nationalarchives.ie/; Irish civil registration records: www.irishgenealogy.ie.

[5] Scott B. Cook, 'The Irish Raj: Social Origins and Careers of Irishmen in the Indian Civil Service, 1855–1914', *Journal of Social History*, 20/3 (1987), pp. 507–29 (at p. 511).

[6] See, for example, S.B. Cook, *Imperial Affinities: Nineteenth Century Analogies and Exchanges between India and Ireland* (London, 1993); Keith Jeffery (ed.), *'An Irish Empire'? Aspects of Ireland and the British Empire* (Manchester, 1996); Kevin Kenny (ed.), *Ireland and the British Empire* (Oxford, 2004); Patrick O'Leary, *Servants of the Empire: The Irish in the Punjab, 1881–1921* (Manchester, 2011); Barry

Ireland's unionist minority continued its tradition of imperial service after southern Irish independence. Together with the intra-imperial Home Ruler residuum (pre-1922 constitutional nationalists who still believed in Ireland's place within a worthy British Empire and were seen by 'the "plain people" of Ireland' … [as] ex-unionist'), they then formed what Colonial Office under-secretary Sir John Shuckburgh termed a southern Irish 'loyalist class', which provided the mainstay of imperial services' enlistment throughout the interwar and Second World War years.[7] However, during the Irish Revolution and aftermath this 'loyalist class' itself formed part of a broader societal estate, which, in the context of colonial Kenya, Bethwell Ogot termed a 'loyalist crowd'. In a pioneering analysis published just nine years after Kenyan independence, Ogot applied George Rudé's 'sociological approach' towards 'the crowd' in the French Revolution to Kikuyu loyalists, challenging their monolithic characterisation by former Mau Mau as 'despicable collaborators', and presenting instead several distinct categories of loyalism with individual agendas ranging from 'humiliating necessity … [to] honourable choice'.[8] The 'loyalist crowd' in revolutionary Ireland was similarly diverse. Essentially (although not entirely) republican-defined, it comprised members of perceived socio-political outgroups such as Protestants, Crown servants (particularly policemen), and serving and demobilised British armed forces personnel.

This essay takes as its subject the cohort of this 'loyalist crowd' who opted for imperial service. It first examines the impact of the Irish Revolution on their decisions to so do and investigates their loyalist credentials. It then explores the persistence of southern Irish loyalist enlistment in the later post-revolutionary era.

Crosbie, *Irish Imperial Networks: Migration, Social Communication and Exchange in Nineteenth-Century India* (Cambridge, 2012); Timothy G. McMahon, Michael de Nie, and Paul Townend (eds), *Ireland in an Imperial World: Citizenship, Opportunism, and Subversion* (Basingstoke, 2017); Seán William Gannon, *The Irish Imperial Service: Policing Palestine and Administering the Empire, 1922–1966* (Cham, 2019).

[7] R.B. McDowell, *Crisis and Decline: The Fate of the Southern Unionists* (Dublin, 1997), p. 163; John Shuckburgh, Departmental minute, 20 Aug. 1940 (TNA, CO 877/20/4).

[8] Bethwell A. Ogot, 'Revolt of the Elders: An Anatomy of the Loyalist Crowd in the Mau Mau Uprising, 1952–1956', *Politics and Nationalism in Colonial Kenya* (Nairobi, 1972), pp. 134–48 (at pp. 135–7). For more recent studies of loyalism in colonial Kenya, see Daniel Branch, *Defeating Mau Mau, Creating Kenya: Counterinsurgency, Civil War, and Decolonization* (Cambridge, 2009); David M. Anderson, 'Making the Loyalist Bargain: Surrender, Amnesty and Impunity in Kenya's Decolonization, 1952–63', *International History Review*, 39/1 (2017), 48–70.

Escaping from under its government

That research on Irish imperial agency has to date been almost entirely confined to the eighteenth and long nineteenth centuries speaks to a historiographical assumption that Irish interest in imperial service was 'virtually destroyed' by what Scott Cook termed 'the twin jolts of the First World War and the Irish political upheaval that followed'.[9] Cook wrote with specific reference to the ICS and there the number of southern Irish appointments certainly sharply declined in the post-independence period. For example, TCD, the ICS's principal Irish recruitment ground in the twentieth century, produced just 23 Civilians between 1922 and 1938 (when ICS recruitment ceased), half the figure for 1902–21.[10] The role of the Irish Revolution in this downward trend is, however, unclear, as the drop-off in ICS enlistments was not a localised Irish trend but reflected a general crisis in 'British' recruitment occasioned by the service's creeping 'Indianisation', which diminished its attractiveness as a career.[11] What is clear is that Ireland's revolutionary upheaval did not end Irish interest in the BCS. In fact, enlistment from southern Ireland so continued that, with the exception of the Colonial Administrative Service, Irish representation was maintained across all BCS branches and in certain of them actually increased.[12]

While the evidence suggests that the decisions of Irish loyalists to enlist in the BCS were informed by a confluence of contributory factors including economics, career prospects, endo-recruitment (a family history or tradition of imperial service), and the quest for adventure, those taken during the Irish Revolution and aftermath were oftentimes enshrouded in politics. In January 1922, the *Church of Ireland Gazette* noted the anger felt by many Irish Protestants at the 'nefarious selling of the pass' that, for them, the Anglo-Irish Treaty represented, and this applied equally to Catholic unionists, who were similarly confounded by the old order's peremptory change.[13] And while most

---

[9] Cook, 'Irish Raj', pp. 511–12.

[10] Seton to Barnard, 14 Oct. 1922 (TCD, MUN/V/5/22/280-81); *Dublin University Calendar, 1946–47* (Dublin, 1947), pp. 479–82.

[11] As early as August 1922, the *Irish Times* was remarking that the ICS, 'formerly a prize for the best brains of Trinity College', no longer held much prospect when just one-quarter of the candidates sitting that year's competitive examination in London were 'white men': *Irish Times*, 5 Aug. 1922.

[12] For example, Irish lawyers accounted for 13 per cent of the Colonial Legal Service in the pre-independence period, while southern Irish lawyers alone constituted 16 per cent of the service between 1922 and 1966.

[13] *Church of Ireland Gazette*, 20 Jan. 1922. The *Gazette* was one of the two 'leading organs of Southern unionist opinion', the other being the *Irish Times*. McDowell, *Crisis and Decline*, p. 122.

former unionists embraced this change or settled into a state of what Kurt Bowen termed 'indignant marginality' within the new Irish Free State, others felt so politically, socio-culturally, or otherwise alienated that they opted to leave, and some saw in British imperial service an avenue through which to so do.[14] Indeed, so commonplace was contemporary loyalist recourse to colonial service that, three years after the Free State's foundation, the Colonial Office's de facto director of recruitment Ralph Furse observed that 'while it may be regrettable ... the majority of the best candidates from the [Irish Free State] who have come to us have mainly done so because they wished to escape from being under [its] Government'.[15]

Surviving personal testimonies provide insights into the issues they perceived as in play. Some, such as Henry Blackall, viewed the emergent Ireland with utter disdain. A Catholic unionist from Gardenhill, Limerick (his father claimed descent from 'a Cromwellian adventurer' while his mother's family 'belong[ed] to the Irish peerage'), he was dismayed by the result of the December 1918 general election and consequent convening of the First Dáil, which, to his mind, heralded the inevitable end of British rule: he joined the Colonial Legal Service in autumn 1919.[16] So too with Martin Mahony, who was serving as an officer with the King's African Rifles when southern Irish independence was won. The Downside and Oxford-educated son of a Catholic Cork businessman and banker, he nursed a violent hatred of Irish republicans and abhorred the new Ireland in which their revolution resulted. ('Personally, all my sympathies are with Ulster for valuing her civilisation and working to stand out').[17] When Ireland's slide into civil war did not lead to the British reconquest he desired, he decided to make his life in the Empire: he served another tour with the army in Kenya before joining the Colonial Administrative Service in 1925.[18] Others, like Edward Lumley, a self-described 'lower-middle-class' King's County Methodist, were unsettled

---

[14] Kurt Bowen, *Protestants in a Catholic State: Ireland's Privileged Minority* (Kingston and Montreal, 1983), p. 58.

[15] Ralph Furse, Departmental minute, 7 Nov. 1925 (TNA, CO 877/3, 'Applications for colonial positions from persons resident in Irish Free State').

[16] Henry Blackall, Foreword to collection, 10 Jul. 1968 (Oxford, Bodleian Library, Commonwealth and African Studies (CAS), MS Brit. Emp. s.447, Henry Blackall collection).

[17] Martin Mahony to Thomas Mahony, 1 Feb. 1922 (Bodleian Library, CAS, MS Afr. s.487, Martin Mahony collection).

[18] The extent of Mahony's hatred of Irish republicans is laid bare in his diaries. He prayed for a renewal of war, 'and this time I hope [the British] exterminate the whole brood of Sinn Feiners, men women and children', for whom 'honour, truth and "playing the game" are not only unknown, but absolutely foreign to their natures'. News of Sir Henry Wilson's assassination in June 1922 roused him into 'a state of impotent fury ... [I] pray that when the day of vengeance comes,

by the passions that the revolutionary period unleashed. Although 'moved to [the] decision by a variety of considerations', he was 'finally tilted' towards the Colonial Administrative Service in 1923 by his desire to escape 'the political environment of fanaticism and strife' he had endured during his previous four years as a TCD student.[19] Yet more, such as Michael O'Connor, a Catholic University College Dublin-trained doctor who joined the Malayan Medical Service in the mid-1920s, felt that they had no prospects in the Irish Free State. A veteran of the Royal Irish Regiment, he believed that his status as a British ex-serviceman made him 'anything but *persona grata* to those in authority' in an Ireland that was 'still licking her wounds after the grim regime of the Black and Tans and the civil war that followed'.[20] Similarly, with ex-unionists: 'many Protestants (and some Catholic ex-unionists) thought that they might easily become the victims of [employment] discrimination' on account of their historical politics, and the BCS provided an alternative route to professional success.[21]

Similar feelings were commonplace amongst former members of the RIC, some 300 of whom joined the imperial services during the revolutionary endgame and aftermath. Ex-inspector-general Joseph Byrne secured the governorship of the Seychelles in compensation for his effective dismissal in 1920 (for 'loss of nerve' and suspected Sinn Féin sympathies).[22] But most were seeking to remove themselves from an Ireland in which they considered their lives at the time irrecoverable because of their central counter-revolutionary role. Fears for personal safety or the prospects of a future livelihood were compounded in spring 1922 by the emergence of localised expulsion campaigns mainly conducted by elements of the anti-Treatyite IRA.[23] By June,

---

as surely it must, I may be there to lend a hand'. Diary of Martin Mahony, 17 Jan., 3 Feb., 9 Jul. 1922 (Bodleian Library, CAS, MS Afr. s.487).

[19] E.K. Lumley, *Forgotten Mandate: A British District Officer in Tanganyika* (London, 1976), p. 177.

[20] Michael O'Connor, *The More Fool I: A Piece of Autobiography* (Dublin, 1954), p. 12.

[21] For Protestants, this was subsequently seen to be proved by the introduction of the Irish language requirement in certain sectors: McDowell, *Crisis and Decline*, pp. 164–5.

[22] Eunan O'Halpin, 'Sir Warren Fisher and the Coalition, 1919–1921', *Historical Journal*, 24/4 (1981), pp. 907–27 (at pp. 917–19). Byrne subsequently served as governor of Sierra Leone and Kenya.

[23] See, for example, Seán Gannon, '"Very Cruel Cases": The Post-Truce Campaign against the Royal Irish Constabulary in County Limerick', *Old Limerick Journal*, 51 (2016), pp. 15–25; Cormac Ó Comhraí, 'The Campaign against Ex-Policemen in Galway, 1922', paper delivered at 'Outsiders in Independent Ireland, 1922–49' conference, Maynooth University, 5 Sep. 2014 (I am grateful to the author for providing me with a copy of this paper). See also Brian Hughes, *Defying the IRA?*

the assistant under-secretary at Dublin Castle was complaining of 'a concerted movement for a wholesale expulsion' of RIC personnel and/or their families.[24] And although this was in hindsight ultra-alarmist, the radius of threat which emanated from those many expulsions that did occur created a climate of panic amongst ex-RIC, as a result of which thousands took temporary or permanent flight. Of those who took up imperial employment, almost all remained in policing. For while the constabularies of England and Wales were disinclined to accept applications from ex-members of a paramilitarised and generally discredited service, colonial forces sought them out.[25] The Indian Police Service, for example, actively recruited a number of ex-RIC on the basis that they were 'tactful – and painfully experienced – in handling crowds',[26] while the Shanghai Municipal Police agreed to accept 'loyal Catholic unemployed RIC'.[27] However, the great majority joined the British Section of the Palestine Gendarmerie, a 760-strong striking force/riot squad raised in spring 1922 almost entirely from RIC sources as a reinforcement for the locally recruited police force of Britain's recently acquired Palestine Mandate. Significantly, perhaps, in the context of southern Irish loyalist migration, Irish Protestant policemen were well over-represented in this British Gendarmerie's original draft, accounting for 40 per cent of the ex-RIC who enlisted at a time when they comprised approximately 20 per cent of the Old Force's rank-and-file.[28]

The Colonial Office occasionally facilitated loyalist migration to the colonies. For example, a number of lawyers joined the Colonial Legal Service in 1921 and 1922 after the Irish chief secretary, Sir Hamar Greenwood, successfully petitioned the colonial secretary, Lord Milner, to consider Irish Bar members for overseas appointments. 'These gentlemen', Greenwood pleaded, 'have had a bad time and will have a worse time owing to the cessation of much of the work of the Courts in Ireland. They have loyally refused to touch the Sinn

Intimidation, Coercion, and Communities during the Irish Revolution (Liverpool, 2016), pp. 192–200.

[24] Alfred Cope to Michael Collins, 22 Jun. 1922 (NAI, TSCH3/S1842).

[25] Most significantly, in Jan. 1922, the commissioner of the London Metropolitan Police Sir William Horwood rejected a request to take on ex-RIC, partly because their Irish service was, 'even previous to Sinn Fein activities ... more of a military nature than that of a civilian police force'. William Horwood to Winston Churchill, 25 Jan. 1922 (TNA, HO 45/24754). My thanks to Dr Brian Hughes for this reference.

[26] Michael Silvestri, *Ireland and India: Nationalism, Empire and Memory* (Basingstoke, 2009), pp. 68–9.

[27] John Pook to Kenneth McEuen, 14 Nov. 1922 (Shanghai Municipal Council Archives, U1-3-1708). My thanks to Prof. Robert Bickers for this reference.

[28] On the RIC's denominational breakdown, see Elizabeth Malcolm, *The Irish Policeman, 1822–1922: A Life* (Dublin, 2006), pp. 56–7, 61–3.

Fein courts and they suffer for it'.[29] In spring 1922, Milner's successor, Winston Churchill, was the prime mover in efforts to secure policing positions for disbanded RIC personnel in the Empire. As noted above, he had success in the Palestine Mandate, which he hoped 'would afford shelter' from the dangers he believed they were facing at home, but little across the dominions, where horror at the 'sheer nature of the violence and the role played by the Black and Tans ... conjured up scenes of barbarity and brutality which no dominion police force wanted to be associated with'.[30] Furthermore, Furse adapted the BCS's regulations on recruitment to encourage Irish loyalist enlistment. Under existing regulations, candidates from Britain's distant dominions, who could not be expected to travel to London for interview, were compelled to make their applications through their local governor-general: he assessed the applications and reported to the Colonial Office on their merit. However, fearing that Irish loyalists unsympathetic to the new Dublin government would 'be less ready to apply' had they to do so under its auspices, Furse allowed southern Irish candidates to apply directly to him. As Shuckburgh noted, 'Irish Free State conditions are peculiar, and we must sometimes make allowances accordingly'.[31] The unavailability of BCS application forms and desk diaries for 1920 to 1926 precludes a calculation of the number of Irish men and women who applied for the BCS during this time. However, an analysis of the Colonial Office List and other sources indicates that around 200 were ultimately successful (excluding 250 British Gendarmerie recruited externally).

'We were all regarded by the IRA as adherents of the "British enemy"'

The loyalist allegiances of contemporary Irish BCS recruits were often more complex than republicans allowed. Most, certainly, were loyalists by birth. The Protestant gentry remnant maintained a small but observable presence. Meanwhile, 67 per cent of those recruited by the BCS's non-policing branches

---

[29] Hamar Greenwood to Alfred Milner, 24 Aug. 1920 (TNA, CO 877/1, 'Legal vacancies in Colonial Service').

[30] Keith Middlemas (ed.), *Thomas Jones: Whitehall Diary*, vol. 1, *1916–1925* (Oxford, 1969), 7 Dec. 1921, p. 183; Kent Fedorowich, 'The Problems of Disbandment: The Royal Irish Constabulary and Imperial Migration', *Irish Historical Studies*, 30/117 (1996), pp. 88–110 (at p. 101).

[31] The relaxation of this regulation was facilitated by the fact that Irish candidates could travel without difficulty to London, while any additional vetting required could be carried out through the Colonial Office's network of local Irish contacts. John Shuckburgh, Departmental minute, undated (c.Oct. 1925) (TNA, CO 877/3, 'Applications for colonial positions from persons resident in Irish Free State').

were Protestant at a time when Irish Protestantism essentially 'stood for the Union'.[32] Moreover, many Catholic recruits came from staunchly unionist stock. The ideological commitment of families from both sides of the denominational divide to the constitutional status quo was frequently demonstrated through involvement in unionist politics or strong traditions of domestic or imperial Crown service, while the leanings of recruits themselves was evidenced by membership of loyalist organisations and clubs, or their active retention of Crown subject status. Henry Blackall was typical: a self-described 'Unionist by tradition and conviction', he was a member of both Dublin's Kildare Street Club ('the holy of holies in the Dublin [loyalist] social register') and the Irish Loyalist Imperial Federation, a reconstitution of the Irish Unionist Alliance comprising 'loyal South Irish-born subjects of the King, who prize their birth-right status as British subjects and are determined to hand it on unimpaired'.[33] He derided what he termed 'Mr De Valera's invented Eire citizenship' and refused to 'become a citizen of the Irish Free State or, worse still, of the Irish Republic'.[34] Like many of his compatriot colleagues, Blackall ultimately applied for British citizenship under the terms of the British Nationality Act 1948.

Others who joined the BCS at this time had their loyalist identities thrust upon them by circumstance, being branded as such by republicans without reference to their personal political convictions. Some, like Captain William Fitzgerald, were Catholic Redmondite Home Ruler ex-servicemen discomfited by the 'outsider' status that a British war record potentially conferred. Sensing local republican hostility, he revised his intention to resume the legal studies he had interrupted to join the Durham Light Infantry in 1914 in favour of an urgent application to the BCS: 'I am very anxious to obtain immediate employment ... I am willing to go to any colony and undertake any duties'.[35] Fitzgerald, who believed that republican hostility towards his war service would be exacerbated by the 'great assistance' he provided at local recruitment

---

[32] *Church of Ireland Gazette*, 6 Jan. 1922. See also James Alley, 'Irish Methodism and Political Change', in Alexander McCrea (ed.), *Irish Methodism in the Twentieth Century: A Symposium* (Belfast, 1931), pp. 9–24 (at p. 18).

[33] Blackall, 'British nationality: correspondence with Home Office re. my claim to retain it', Explanatory note, 10 Jul. 1968 (Bodleian Library, CAS, MS Brit. Emp. s.447); Brian Inglis, *West Briton* (London, 1962), p. 19; 'Irish Loyalist Imperial Federation: Its Object', undated (c.1934) (PRONI, D989/B/3/26). On loyalism and the post-1922 Kildare Street Club, see R.B. McDowell, *Land and Learning: Two Irish Clubs* (Dublin, 1993), pp. 98–9.

[34] 'British nationality correspondence', Explanatory note, 10 Jul. 1968; 'Blackall to Home Office, 12 Feb. 1949 (Bodleian Library, CAS, MS Brit. Emp. s.447).

[35] Captain W. James Fitzgerald, Fitzgerald to Ralph Furse, 3 Jul. 1919 (TNA, CO 429/112).

meetings when on home leave, went to Nigeria as an assistant district administrative officer in autumn 1919.[36] The wisdom of his decision to leave was, to
his mind, demonstrated one year later, by the IRA's killing of his brother
John. A British ex-serviceman recently recruited as a Colonial Police Service
cadet, he was, as was the norm, performing RIC service to gain policing
experience pending his first posting when was shot dead on Bloody Sunday
(21 November 1920), just two weeks before he was due to sail.[37]

Michael O'Connor also believed himself branded a loyalist on account of
his British army service, his strong Irish nationalist views notwithstanding.
He, by his own account, applied for Malaya on being told that he had 'been
diagnosed as an agent of Dublin Castle during the troubled period' and slated
for 'liquidation'.[38] Others, like Edward Lumley, were Irish Protestants uncaring
of the unionist cause. However, he felt that his TCD student status had cast
him as a loyalist in republican eyes. 'We were all regarded by the IRA as
adherents of the "British enemy" and more than one of our alumni had been
murdered'. The creation of the Irish Free State, which Lumley unquestioningly
accepted, brought him little personal respite, as 'the IRA then turned its
wrath against the new Irish Government, and all who rendered it obedience
was suspect'.[39] But chief amongst those who had 'loyalism' thrust upon them
during the revolutionary period were Catholic nationalist policemen, who,
by 1919, comprised so significant a majority of the RIC that the force was
widely regarded in Ulster unionist circles as 'a Catholic nationalist body
directed from Dublin'.[40] Catholic nationalist RIC personnel frequently formed
the frontline against a revolution, the aim, if not the means, of which many
broadly agreed with, earning themselves a place in the Irish nationalist
historical imagination as the 'extremely effective agent[s] of Imperial ideas
and ... nucleus of Imperialism' in Ireland.[41]

Unsurprisingly, serving Irish colonial servants were also branded by
republicans as 'loyalists', and some even found themselves suspected as spies.
For example, in March 1922, Nigerian police commissioner Francis Garvey was

---

[36] Vere R. Hunt, 'Statement respecting Captain William Fitzgerald', 12 Jul. 1919
     (TNA, CO 429/112).
[37] The reason for which Fitzgerald was targeted remains unexplained, although he
     had survived another assassination attempt some weeks previously while serving
     as a Defence of Barracks Sergeant in Clare. See Jane Leonard, '"English Dogs" or
     "Poor Devils"? The Dead of Bloody Sunday Morning', in David Fitzpatrick (ed.),
     Terror in Ireland, 1916–1923 (Dublin, 2012), pp. 102–40 (at p. 106).
[38] O'Connor, *The More Fool I*, p. 16.
[39] Lumley, *Forgotten Mandate*, pp. 174, 177.
[40] Malcolm, *Irish Policeman*, p. 217.
[41] Cormac K.H. O'Malley and Anne Dolan, *No Surrender Here: The Civil War Papers
     of Ernie O'Malley, 1922–1924* (Dublin, 2007), p. 429.

served an expulsion order while on home leave in Mayo giving him 24 hours to 'clear out', while Norman Jewell of the East Africa Medical Service narrowly escaped an attempt on his life while on furlough in Dublin.[42] Although Jewell had, by his own account, 'taken no part in any [intelligence] activities and had friends on both [Crown and republican] sides', his lodgings were raided on Bloody Sunday by 'a group of men looking for me to kill me'. Fortunately, he had vacated three days previously to begin his return journey to Kenya.[43] Both men believed that their receipt of mail bearing the British government's official frank had made them marked men, and other compatriot colleagues raised similar concerns. Consequently, the Crown Agents for the Colonies introduced the use of plain stamped envelopes for all correspondence to Irish addresses from May 1922. The Colonial Office followed suit in September, albeit it only in cases where it was requested by an addressee.[44] Its principal officer, John Flood, described the concerns of Irish colonial servants as 'amply justified', although he felt that it was 'only in the wilds that there is much risk and even then the most that is likely to happen would be a notice to clear out at once'. However, he cautioned that Churchill's involvement in Irish affairs represented 'an additional element of danger' in this regard, adding that if he himself (a strong loyalist from Cavan) had 'been captured by Irregulars' while in Ireland he was 'pretty sure that [his] "colonial office pass" would have proved a pass to the next world'.[45]

'The Southerner may or may not be loyal in his sympathies'

Sir John Shuckburgh's 'loyalist class' continued to provide a substantial majority of southern Ireland's BCS recruits during the rest of the interwar years. The country's Protestant communities were greatly over-represented: they provided 73 per cent and 60 per cent of those recruited into the BCS's

[42] John Flood, Departmental minute, 2 Sep. 1922 (TNA, CO 323/895/20).

[43] Jewell's claim that 'some who were in the Colonial Service like me, were shot' that morning is probably a reference to John Fitzgerald. See Norman Parsons Jewell, *On Call in Africa in War and Peace, 1910–1932* (Hove, 2016), pp. 126–7.

[44] The Colonial Office subsequently adopted this practice in correspondence relating to Irish Grants Committee compensation claims, which might 'contain a précis of reasons for which an applicant has left Ireland', and result in his/her relatives receiving 'unwelcome attention'. Colonial Office Departmental minute, 16 Apr. 1924 (TNA, CO/323/895/30).

[45] John Flood, Departmental minute, 2 Sep. 1922 (TNA, CO/323/895/20). The RIC Tribunal employed a similar subterfuge during this time, as did the British armed forces throughout the interwar years. See L.N.B. Odgers to D.I.G (Finance), 7 Jul. 1922 (TNA, HO 351/96/001438/14); Steven O'Connor, *Irish Officers in the British Forces, 1922–45* (Basingstoke, 2014), p. 109.

non-policing sectors from 1926 to 1929 and 1930 to 1939 respectively (and 40 per cent of those who enlisted in the colonial police between 1926 and 1939), at a time when non-Catholic Christian denominations accounted for between 7 per cent and 5 per cent of the population. Informing the decisions of Irish Protestants to enlist was the persistence of an Anglophile communal culture which cast them as 'Imperial Irishmen' and strongly valued imperial service. The morning after the Anglo-Irish Treaty was signed, the *Irish Times* declared that for southern Protestant loyalists 'Ireland does not exist, and will never exist apart from the Empire which the blood of their sires and sons has cemented', and the imperial attachment that such sentiment represented became a marked aspect of post-1922 Irish Protestant identity, filling (at least partly) the void left by political unionism's demise.[46] The influence of elite education endured. Approximately 14 per cent of Irish Protestant BCS recruits acquired their intermediate education at English public schools (seen by Furse as hothouses for the cultivation of the BCS's *beau idéal*), while a majority of the remainder received what Roy Foster called the 'Anglicized educations' then provided in Irish Protestant schools.[47] Although nurturing a specifically Irish identity, fee-paying intermediate colleges such as St Columba's, St Andrew's, and the Erasmus Smith High School, continued to promote British Crown service and maintained a distinctly imperial outlook until after the Second World War. This was evidenced in their student magazines, the 'Notes on old boys' and 'Obituaries' sections of which routinely documented with pride the imperial careers of past pupils and featured occasional articles and letters describing the joys of colonial life.[48] The inculcation of imperial affinities continued at TCD, where 68 per cent of Irish graduates appointed to the BCS in the interwar years earned their degrees. Although not entirely the irredeemably pro-British enclave sometimes described, 'former unionists' continued to comprise the great majority of its staff and, facilitated by 'the ambiguities inherent in Dominion status and the Commonwealth concept', an imperial atmosphere persisted, and imperial service was actively promoted.[49]

---

[46] *Irish Times*, 7 Dec. 1921. See also *Church of Ireland Gazette*, 21 Sep. 1923, 5 Jun. 1925. On the varieties of Irish Protestant responses to southern Ireland's independence, see Ian d'Alton and Ida Milne (eds), *Protestant* and *Irish: The Minority's Search for Place in Independent Ireland* (Cork, 2019); Caleb Wood Richardson, *Smyllie's Ireland: Protestants, Independence, and the Man Who Ran the* Irish Times (Bloomington, IN, 2019).

[47] R.F. Foster, *Paddy and Mr Punch: Connections in Irish and English History* (London, 1993), p. 27.

[48] For examples, see *Erasmian*, 19/7 (1925), 19/8 (1926), 21/1 (1930), 22/3 (1931); *Columban*, 60/2 (1939), 61/3 (1940).

[49] For example, the Union flag flew over the college (albeit alongside the tricolour) until 1935; 'God Save the King' was played at the conclusion of Commencements

From the Colonial Office's perspective, loyalty actually became a *sine qua non* for southern Irish BCS recruitment during this time. London had long been sensitive to what Barry Crosbie has termed 'perceived threats to the British Empire coming from within the imperial bureaucratic edifice itself', not least from Irish republicans.[50] In 1926, the Royal Navy imposed an embargo on southern Irish recruitment after intelligence that 'a certain number of Irish rebels may possibly endeavour to join His Majesty's Navy whose real motive is espionage, sabotage, or propaganda'.[51] Restrictions were relaxed over time. However, fears resurfaced in the mid-1930s ('ten years ago there was the prospect of the traditional enmity being forgotten, but since then enmity has greatly revived'), and again during the Second World War, when the secretaries of state for War and the Dominions opposed plans for an Irish Brigade due to 'the possibility that completely Irish units … might become a fertile breeding ground for subversive agitation by the IRA and other disloyal elements'.[52] Similarly, at the Colonial Office, where there were concerns as to whether candidates from southern Ireland, immersed in what officials perceived to be an anti-British and increasingly republican culture, could serve loyally imperial interests.[53] Thus, just three years after the Irish Free State's foundation, Flood advised Furse against accepting Irish Free State army doctors for colonial service, warning that they would be 'totally unsuited for any service under the Crown' because of their probable politics.[54]

Their solution to what they termed the problem of Irish 'right-mindedness' was the active encouragement of recruitment from TCD, still seen as the *ancien régime*'s southern Irish last stand. However, with the outbreak of the

until 1939; the British Army was routinely referred to as 'the home forces', in TCD board minutes during the Second World War; and the King was toasted at college dinners until 1945. R.B. McDowell, *Trinity College Dublin, 1592–1952: An Academic History* (Cambridge, 1982), pp. 430, 432. See also Tomás Irish, 'Ostriches and Tricolours: Trinity College Dublin and the Irish State, 1922–45', in d'Alton and Milne, *Protestant* and *Irish*, pp. 122–36.

50 Crosbie, *Irish Imperial Networks*, p. 228.
51 O'Connor, *Irish Officers*, pp. 109–10.
52 Troup, Departmental minute, 30 Apr. 1936 (TNA, ADM 178/144); O'Connor, *Irish Officers*, p. 117.
53 This culture was seen to be manifested in the practical assertions of national sovereignty by the 1922–32 Cumman na nGaedheal government (denounced by the Irish Unionist Alliance as 'studied disloyalty'), Fíanna Fáil's 'constitutional revolution' of the 1930s, and Irish neutrality during the Second World War. *Notes from Ireland*, 4/31 (1926).
54 John Flood, Departmental minute, 19 Nov. 1925 (TNA, CO 877/3, 'Applications for colonial positions from persons resident in Irish Free State'). On the presumed 'disloyalty' of Irish Free State army personnel, see Richard Walton, Departmental minute, 13 Oct. 1936 (TNA, ADM 178/144).

Second World War, its graduates too had their loyalty questioned. Although the college remained the acknowledged 'principal training ground of those elements in Éire which still support the maintenance of the connection' with Britain, the perceived danger of wartime republican infiltration saw the Colonial Office proceed extremely cautiously with all southern Irish recruitment.[55] This change in attitude was illustrated in 1940 by the manner in which nine Irish Colonial Administrative Service applicants were treated, seven of them southern Irish TCD graduates. At a time of rising Anglo-Irish tensions over the issue of Irish neutrality, and in the midst of the IRA's 'Sabotage Campaign', Furse's deputy (and brother-in-law), Francis Newbolt, believed that while the Colonial Office 'presumably need have no scruples about the genuine Northerner ... the Southerner may or may not be loyal in his sympathies', and the chairman of the Colonial Service Appointments Board (CSAB) agreed, warning Furse that they should 'have to be very careful', as 'even if the attitude of the candidate himself was all right, the influence of his relations might make things difficult'.[56] Furse and his officials believed that southern Irish candidates therefore required a more thorough vetting than the Colonial Office could provide, leading Newbolt to suggest the creation of 'some sort of "secret service" agency' operating out of the office of the British high commissioner in Dublin, which would 'probe into the antecedent "loyalty" of each individual case'.[57] In the event, Furse asked MI5 and Scotland Yard to vet the seven candidates from south of the border. Although all received clean bills, Scotland Yard advised against their admission to England for interview, as encouraging travel between Britain and Ireland ran the risk of IRA infiltration. This warning was taken so seriously by Newbolt that he professed himself disinclined to consider any southern Irish applications at all: 'we [cannot] afford to take the smallest risk of admitting a possible Quisling to the Colonial Service'.[58] But, determined to maintain what the British high commissioner in Dublin, Sir John Maffey, termed TCD's 'old imperial interests', Furse decided to process the outstanding applications while taking steps to reduce the risk of IRA infiltration.[59] In the event, Maffey's political secretary, Maurice Antrobus, vetted the candidates through investigation and interview, and informed Scotland Yard of the identities of those selected to travel to London to appear before the CSAB. Two of the seven southern TCD

[55] John Shuckburgh, Departmental minute, 5 Feb. 1940 (TNA, CO 877/20/4).
[56] A.F. Newbolt, Departmental minute, 26 Jan. 1940; Ralph Furse, Departmental minute, 24 Jan. 1940 (TNA, CO 877/20/4). The CSAB was a (theoretically) independent body which made the final decision on the recruitment of BCS candidates selected by the Colonial Office itself.
[57] A.F. Newbolt, Departmental minute, 26 Jan. 1940 (TNA, CO 877/20/4).
[58] A.F. Newbolt, Departmental minute, 19 Aug. 1940 (TNA, CO 877/20/4).
[59] John Maffey to C.J. Jeffries, 12 Sep. 1940 (TNA, CO 877/20/4).

applicants were ultimately appointed. The facts that they were the sons of a Church of Ireland bishop and a distinguished, long-serving colonial servant were seen to underwrite their loyalist credentials.

On his return to the Colonial Office after active service in the Great War, Furse had prioritised the applications of demobilised soldiers, believing that British armed forces enlistment demonstrated the loyalty required in colonial servants, and he was still of this view in 1940.[60] There was, in fact, broad agreement amongst Colonial Office officials on this point, and it was therefore decided that the 'Antrobus scheme' need not apply to 'those citizens of Éire who, by joining [HM] Forces, have shown themselves non-neutral'.[61] Second World War military service remained the key (albeit rather poor) indicator of British loyalty in the war's aftermath as well. Consequently, applicants who had not voluntarily enlisted were required to show evidence of theirs. To this end, the colonial secretary, Arthur Creech Jones, approved in January 1948 an arrangement whereby southern Irish BCS candidates were obliged to submit to interview by the CSAB to have their 'right-mindedness' assessed. So strongly did the CSAB's chairman, Sir Percival Waterfield, feel about the issue that he recommended that even candidates for short-term temporary contracts introduced after the war have their loyalty tested. As the CSAB dealt only with career (viz. permanent, pensionable) appointments made by the Colonial Office itself, objections were raised by officials who felt that assessing southern Irish 'right-mindedness' was not really Sir Percival's role. However, while Newbolt, who had succeeded Furse as director of recruitment two years earlier, agreed that contract employment was not the concern of the CSAB, he felt that there was 'something to be said for sticking to the ruling' that loyalty be assessed by the board:

> I think myself it is better that the onus in this matter ... should be on the Board rather than on individual members of the recruiting staff here ... If an Irish 'wrong-un' should ever slip through, and become the cause of trouble in a Colony, I should prefer that the blood should be on the heads of the Board, and not ours![62]

This extraordinary arrangement, therefore, remained in place, and when, or indeed if, it was rescinded prior to the closure of the Colonial Office in 1966 is unclear. To be fair to officials, the persistence of militant Irish republicanism in the form of a rump Sinn Féin/IRA presented a legitimate concern, and they

---

[60] Resultantly, approximately two-thirds of southern Irishmen recruited between 1919 to 1926 were British ex-servicemen.

[61] Moult, Departmental minute, 4 Apr. 1940 (TNA, CO 877/20/4).

[62] A.F. Newbolt, Departmental minute, 17 May 1950 (TNA, CO 877/20/4).

had a relatively recent example of perceived in-house Irish 'disloyalty' on which to draw – the anti-government judicial activism of Palestine's chief justice, Sir Michael McDonnell, which had forced his 'retirement' from the Colonial Legal Service in 1936.[63] Yet, in the final analysis, their anxieties about Irish disloyalty were rooted in the absurd colonial cliché of the Irish as natural subversives, opposed (as a 1922 British military intelligence summary put it) 'not so much to the British Government as to any form of Government, National or Local' and, by extension, imperial.[64]

Conclusion

Unlike loyalists in colonial Kenya, who 'claimed the political victory and filled the ranks of the new African government' at independence in 1963, the 'loyalist crowd' in revolutionary Ireland suffered effective political defeat.[65] The remnant of the intra-imperial Home Rule tradition presented a qualified exception; although the movement had been electorally obliterated by Sinn Féin, its ambition of limited Irish self-government had been (over)-achieved, while dominion status satisfied the 'colonialists' who remained committed to Ireland's place in the Empire.[66] But unionism was rendered an anachronism overnight. Many of its erstwhile adherents quickly (and, indeed, comfortably) accommodated themselves to the new dispensation, feeling duty-bound 'to support, even if [they could not] love, [its] lawfully constituted authority', or simply resigned to the fait accompli.[67] However, others, 'hurt and sore because those ideals of government which [they] valued and to which [they] were loyal, [had] been superseded', did so very ambivalently, or refused to do so outright.[68] 'Loyalty', as the *Church of Ireland Gazette* explained, 'is an affair

---

[63] See 'Position of the Chief Justice Sir Michael McDonnell; his eventual early retirement from the post', 1936–7 (TNA, CO 733/313/1).

[64] Paul McMahon, *British Spies and Irish Rebels: British Intelligence and Ireland, 1916–1945* (Woodbridge, 2008), p. 168.

[65] Anderson, 'Making the Loyalist Bargain', p. 49.

[66] Defined as 'an Irish nationalist who believed in the British Empire', the term 'colonialist' was coined by Fergus Linehan in his fictionalised account of his father William's career as a senior BCS administrator in Malaya. Fergus Linehan, *Under the Durian Tree* (Dublin, 1995), p. 6.

[67] Canon George Chamberlain, Armistice Day sermon 1923, published in *Church of Ireland Gazette*, 23 Nov. 1923. Irish Unionist Alliance diehards took a similar view, warning that it was 'the duty of all law-abiding citizens to do nothing in any way to hinder the [new] lawfully constituted authority'. *Notes from Ireland*, 12/29 (1923).

[68] Chamberlain, Armistice Day sermon, 1923. Their hurt was compounded by a belief that they had been abandoned by Britain to their fate in what Lord Midleton

of the heart, and it is not possible to force the heart to follow the hand'.[69] The most disillusioned left Ireland in consequence, while more opted for 'internal' exile amongst the ruins of the old 'County Set' or in other (overwhelmingly Protestant) loyalist micro-communities, themselves on the cusp of a terminal decline. The RIC was similarly worsted. Hundreds of Irish members were killed or wounded and thousands more temporarily or permanently displaced during what David Fitzpatrick termed Ireland's 'revolutionary ordeal', and it was disbanded as part of the peace.[70] And although a majority of those disbanded quietly (and, oftentimes, easily) remade their lives in post-revolutionary Ireland, they became the primary long-term losers in the 'political and propaganda wars' over the manner in which the Irish Revolution was 'remembered, interpreted and commemorated and, ultimately, justified'.[71] The extent to which independent Ireland provided a cold house for British ex-servicemen remains a matter of scholarly debate. However, they undoubtedly suffered disproportionately during the 1919 to 1922 period.[72]

The precise nature and scale of the 'flight' in which the defeat of the 'loyalist crowd' resulted is, historiographically, highly contentious.[73] But it is beyond question that a minority endured enforced or involuntary self-imposed exile during the Irish Revolution and aftermath. Britain's imperial services provided a haven for a minority of this minority. But they also offered a route out for others who left uncoerced, mainly diehard ex-unionists unwilling to remain on

---

described as 'one of the most deplorable desertions of their supporters of which any [country] has ever been guilty'. Earl of Midleton, *Records and Reactions, 1856–1939* (London, 1939), p. 264. See also Michael O'Dwyer, *India as I Knew It, 1885–1925* (London, 1925), p. 6; Arland Ussher, *The Face and Mind of Ireland* (London, 1949), pp. 53–4.

[69] *Church of Ireland Gazette*, 21 Sep. 1923.

[70] David Fitzpatrick, *Descendancy: Irish Protestant Histories since 1795* (Cambridge, 2014), p. 190. For a survey of RIC deaths, see Richard Abbott, *Police Casualties in Ireland, 1919–1922* (Cork, 2000).

[71] Malcolm, *Irish Policeman*, p. 213.

[72] See, for example, Jane Leonard, 'Getting Them at Last: The IRA and Ex-Servicemen', in David Fitzpatrick (ed.), *Revolution? Ireland, 1917–1923* (Dublin, 1990), pp. 119–29; Paul Taylor, *Heroes or Traitors? Experiences of Southern Irish Soldiers Returning from the Great War, 1919–1939* (Liverpool, 2015); Hughes, *Defying the IRA?*, pp. 131–2, 179–83.

[73] See, for example, Peter Hart, *The I.R.A. at War 1916–1923* (Oxford, 2003), pp. 223–58; Andy Bielenberg, 'Exodus: The Emigration of Southern Irish Protestants during the Irish War of Independence and the Civil War', *Past & Present*, 218 (2013), pp. 199–233; David Fitzpatrick, 'Ethnic Cleansing, Ethical Smearing and Irish Historians', *History*, 98/239 (2013), pp. 135–44; Fitzpatrick, *Descendancy*, pp. 157–240; Gemma Clark, *Everyday Violence in the Irish Civil War* (Cambridge, 2014), pp. 98–153; Hughes, *Defying the IRA?*, pp. 171–204.

in an Ireland they saw through a glass darkened by disappointment, suspicion, and/or spite. According to R.B. McDowell, those who remained became 'exhilarated by the imperial ideal', and the persistence of BCS enlistment in the interwar and Second World War periods illustrated the importance of the continuing imperial connection for the 'loyalist class'.[74] Emblematised by the reconstitution of the Irish Unionist Alliance as the Irish Loyalist Imperial Federation, this connection could surrogate for the embers of the unionist impulse or substitute for it per se. Hence, Ireland's withdrawal from the British Commonwealth in 1949, which, as one ex-unionist put it, 'finally unscrewed the Crown from the Harp', signalled southern Irish loyalism's inexorable extinction.[75] As the regulations on right-mindedness exemplified, it thereafter increasingly constituted less a communal 'attitude of mind' than a chimera exogenously defined.[76]

---

[74] McDowell, *Crisis and Decline*, p. 21.
[75] Nora Robertson, *Crowned Harp: Memories of the Last Years of the Crown in Ireland* (Dublin, 1960), p. 181.
[76] McDowell, *Crisis and Decline*, p. 163.

CHAPTER VIII

'It was the done thing': Southern Irish Protestants and the Second World War

Joseph Quinn

The presence of a sizeable southern Irish contingent within the British forces for the duration of the Second World War is among the most interesting aspects of the fraught relationship between neutral Éire and wartime Britain.[1] Many leading authors on the subject, including Robert Fisk and Clair Wills, have acknowledged the significance of voluntary manpower from southern Ireland in aiding Britain's war effort.[2] The military historian and former Irish army officer J.P. Duggan also notes that in the context of the Allied struggle against Nazism Éire had little to be ashamed of. He pays tribute to the thousands of Irishmen who had fought and died 'at the tip of the spear – that's where they generally were – on the battlefields' and had eight Victoria Crosses to prove it.[3] However, the service of southern Irish personnel in British uniform also reflected the very divided and highly stratified nature of Irish society post-independence, and, quite often, these divisions could be identified along generational, rather than political lines. Two retired Irish army Generals, Patrick Hogan and Patrick Daly, who both served in the Irish army during the Emergency, stated that senior officers tended to be pro-British, while junior officers inclined towards Nazi Germany.[4]

The neutral policy adopted by southern Ireland, or Éire, was an understandable alternative to the prospect of war, emulated by many other European nations, the majority of which, like Ireland, were smaller or less

---

[1] The period in which the Second World War took place is commonly referred to in the Republic of Ireland as 'the Emergency'. Both terms will be used, where appropriate, within this chapter.

[2] Robert Fisk, *In Time of War: Ireland, Ulster and the Price of Neutrality* (Dublin, 1983), p. 105; Clair Wills, *That Neutral Island: A History of Ireland during the Second World War* (London, 2007), p. 51.

[3] J.P. Duggan, *Neutral Ireland and the Third Reich* (Dublin, 1985), pp. 258–9.

[4] Benjamin Grob-Fitzgibbon, *The Irish Experience during the Second World War: An Oral History* (Dublin, 2004), p. 200.

militarily powerful than the major belligerents.[5] Though unpopular with the Allied powers, especially in Britain and the USA, one of the main issues on which Irish neutrality was predicated was the necessity of ensuring internal security and preventing a renewal of civil war. Both the IRA and former Blueshirts, whose respective supporters espoused the opposing political ideologies of the day, posed a direct threat to the stability of the state, and it was a matter of crucial importance for Éire's Taoiseach, Eamon de Valera, to unify the Irish nation behind a policy which ensured that no faction would be motivated towards insurrection.[6] De Valera also knew it was inevitable that Irish nationals would take sides in the event of war.[7] For this reason, a broad cross-section of southern Irish society had supported neutrality, ranging from dyed-in-the-wool republicans committed to national reunification to former unionists in southern Ireland whose sons were serving as officers in the British army.[8] In the case of the latter group, who were to be found mainly among the southern Irish Protestant community, there was probably a special sensitivity about the misfortunes such a renewal of hostilities might bring upon their people.[9] An anxiety not to revisit the Civil War of 1922 to 1923 goes some way to explaining why the policy of neutrality was welcomed by members of this community.

The Irish Protestant community, though ceasing to be unionist, had resolutely upheld a mainly pro-British view in Irish society during the interwar years.[10] Throughout the course of the Emergency the position of southern Irish Protestants was similarly pro-British and pro-Allied, reflecting those feelings of loyalty to Britain demonstrated by Irish Protestants prior

---

[5] Neville Wylie, 'Introduction: Victims or Actors? European Neutrals and Non-Belligerents, 1939–1945', in Neville Wylie (ed.), *European Neutrals and Non-Belligerents during the Second World War* (Cambridge, 2002), p. 25.

[6] The latter faction, the Blueshirts, otherwise known as the Army Comrades Association, had become dormant by 1939. It was composed of Irish policemen, ex-soldiers who had fought during the Irish Civil War (1922–3) and other disaffected groups. Their ideology was a peculiar form of quasi-fascism which drew some influence from Mussolini's Blackshirt movement.

[7] Brian Girvin, *The Emergency: Neutral Ireland, 1939–45* (London, 2006), p. 63.

[8] Fisk, *In Time of War*, p. 413; John Bowman, *De Valera and the Ulster Question* (Dublin, 1983), p. 208.

[9] Paul Taylor addresses the treatment of members of the Protestant landed classes during the Irish Revolution and Civil War period. See Paul Taylor, *Heroes or Traitors? Experiences of Southern Irish Soldiers Returning from the Great War, 1919–1939* (Liverpool, 2015), pp. 60–1.

[10] R.B. McDowell produced a partially autobiographical account of the position of southern Irish Protestants and ex-unionists in Ireland after independence, especially regarding Great War remembrance. See 'Afterword', in R.B. McDowell, *Crisis and Decline: The Fate of the Southern Unionists* (Dublin, 1997).

to independence. Nevertheless, the ideological stance expressed by many within the Protestant population in the southern Irish state was tempered by a general respect for the government's policy of neutrality. Even the formerly unionist *Irish Times*, under the editorship of R.M. Smyllie, carried out a careful balancing act, voicing subdued tones of sympathy for Britain's war effort and support for Irish members of the British forces fighting overseas, while simultaneously maintaining a wholehearted defence of Irish neutrality and general support for de Valera's foreign policy.[11] In addition, a small lobby group composed of retired southern Irish army and naval officers, led by the primary architect of the 'Curragh Incident', the Waterford-born General Sir Hubert Gough, registered strong public objections against the consistent antagonism of the Stormont governments of Lord Craigavon and John M. Andrews towards Éire. They were later able to draw upon the service of the many tens of thousands of southern Irish volunteers in the British forces, compared with a smaller number from Northern Ireland, and strenuously defended the sovereign right of the southern Irish state to adhere to a neutral policy, though they hoped that Ireland could one day, herself, voluntarily join the war on the Allied side.[12]

The presence and significance of southern Irish Protestants in the British armed forces during the Second World War is evidenced by the senior positions held by Irish Protestant officers. The Dublin-born Cunningham brothers are among numerous examples of Church of Ireland Protestants who had risen to senior positions within their respective services by the outbreak of war. General Sir Alan Cunningham commanded the British Commonwealth forces which defeated the Italian armies in the East African Campaign and would briefly command the British Eighth Army in Egypt before being appointed as the last British High Commissioner of Palestine in 1946. His brother, Admiral Sir Andrew Cunningham, rose to become the most senior Royal Navy commander of the war; he commanded the British Mediterranean Fleet, winning victories against the Italian Navy at Taranto and Cape Matapan, and later became Admiral of the Fleet, eventually rising to the position of First Sea Lord in 1943.[13] According to Steven O'Connor, a family tradition of military service resonated most strongly among the old Irish landed classes who, until the Great War, provided the overwhelming

---

[11]   See Mark O'Brien, *The Irish Times: A History* (Dublin, 2008). See also Tony Gray, *Mr Smyllie, Sir* (Dublin, 1991).

[12]   Philip Ollerenshaw, *Northern Ireland in the Second World War: Politics, Economic Mobilisation and Society, 1939–45* (Manchester, 2013), p. 146.

[13]   For more on Irish-born military commanders in the British forces during the Second World War, see Richard Doherty, *Ireland's Generals in the Second World War* (Dublin, 2004).

majority of Irish officers for Britain's armed forces.[14] The Second World War also saw many younger members of the southern Protestant community take up a leading role in the British forces, especially in traditional roles such as officers or subalterns in Britain's army and navy.

This chapter will assess the attitude of the southern Protestant community in neutral Ireland during the war, reflected by British mail censorship reports and a sample of editorials from the *Irish Times* and the *Church of Ireland Gazette*. It explores efforts made to lobby the British government by a group of influential London-based Irish and Anglo-Irish ex-British officers who defended neutral Ireland and also campaigned for the welfare and recognition of Irish personnel in the British forces. It next examines southern Irish Protestants in the British forces, exploring the motivations of some of the southern Protestant volunteers who served, and highlighting the overall impact that family military tradition and the involvement of relatives in the Great War had upon those who joined up. Lastly, this chapter, with the aid of oral history testimonies, explores the experiences of a sample of southern Irish Protestant veterans, evaluating their opinions on Irish neutrality, along with their perceptions of place within southern Irish society.

Southern Irish Protestant Opinion in Ireland

Neutrality had the potential to put the southern Irish Protestant community in a difficult position. On the one hand, many felt connected to the United Kingdom and keenly supported Britain and the Empire in the war against Germany; on the other hand, many wholeheartedly agreed with de Valera's decision to keep Éire out of the war.[15] Some Protestant politicians in southern Ireland, such as Major James Myles, a Great War veteran and an independent deputy representing Donegal in Dáil Éireann, voiced support for the policy, stating that the Emergency powers were not only necessary, but should be properly used.[16] During a visit to Dublin in 1940, the southern Irish writer and former Unionist MP Herbert Shaw discovered that 'even former Unionists who were prepared without hesitation to send their sons into the British Army, held no other policy to be possible'.[17] Later, in 1943, during a conference for Irish workers in Britain, a retired Irish British army officer, Captain Henry

---

[14] Steven O'Connor, *Irish Officers in the British Forces, 1922–45* (Basingstoke, 2014), p. 42.

[15] Ian d'Alton cites the example of three Protestant senators who spoke in favour of neutrality in September 1939. See Chapter 5.

[16] Girvin, *The Emergency*, p. 65.

[17] Fisk, *In Time of War*, p. 413.

Harrison, declared: 'I am a defender of Ireland's neutrality under existing circumstances, but if it were not for my age I would be fighting the Germans at the present moment'.[18] It is this duality in the southern Irish Protestant and former unionist viewpoint that would become the defining feature of the community's stance during the war period.

Throughout the Second World War there was also considerable curiosity in London about Éire's position, especially relating to the division of opinion in Ireland between those who recognised the moral ascendancy of Britain in the war and those who questioned whether southern Ireland was justified in remaining neutral. The future *Irish Times* Features editor, W.J. White, in reference to a 'dwindling but still influential minority' who were still in occupation of 'decaying country houses and other crumbling enclaves', commented that among this group there were very often utterances of solidarity with the British armed forces: 'They talk of *our* Navy, or *our* Air Force, meaning those of England'.[19] There was clearly support for Britain's war effort emanating from the southern Protestant community, but this would be mixed with support for Éire's neutral position, which may well have caused some confusion among some British observers unable to comprehend that these positions could coexist. The most reliable method for the British to determine attitudes or survey the opinions of Irish nationals at home or abroad in Britain was to read their mail. Late in 1941, Churchill's War Cabinet received postal censorship reports based on detailed examinations of intercepted mails sent between the two countries, mainly from Irish correspondents living in Britain writing to their families back home. What would be heavily emphasised in the postal censorship report, sent to the cabinet at the start of October 1941, was that 'many young Irishmen and women were serving in the Allied forces' and that this fact was 'not sufficiently recognised in England'.[20]

A few days earlier, in a letter to the editor of *The Times*, General Sir Hubert Gough had argued that tens of thousands of Irish were serving in the British forces, and called for the formation of an Irish Brigade as a tribute to this fact.[21] Gough, often prone to exaggeration, was, on this occasion, correct; according to the official statistics maintained by British army recruiting authorities in Northern Ireland, exactly 10,158 male recruits from neutral Éire were recorded as having enlisted in all three branches of the British forces between August 1940 and August 1941, bringing the total number of southern

---

18   Ian S. Wood, *Britain, Ireland and the Second World War* (Edinburgh, 2010), p. 165.
19   Bernard Share, *The Emergency: Neutral Ireland, 1939–45* (Dublin, 1987), p. 7.
20   'Postal Censorship Report: 'Insufficient recognition of Eire's voluntary effort', 1 Oct. 1941 (TNA, PREM 3/129/5).
21   *The Times*, 26 Sep. 1941.

Irish recorded as serving in the combined forces to over 40,000.[22] As part
of his deliberation on Gough's proposal to form a brigade in honour of the
voluntary enlistment of the southern Irish, Churchill sounded out various
government departments, and had requested an evaluation of Irish public
opinion on the matter. As part of the postal censorship report delivered to
the War Cabinet, there were excerpts taken from the letters of two individuals
from Dublin, proclaiming themselves to be 'loyalists' or 'loyal British subjects',
who complained bitterly regarding the manner in which they were being
perceived in Britain on account of Éire's neutrality. The first letter, addressed
to a recipient in Suffolk, was checked in August 1941:

> It's hard that we, the loyal British subjects in Eire, must suffer with
> Government for not going into war – every single relation of mine and
> yours is serving – and our only thought is for the British Empire – and
> that most of our friends who think we are such 'rats' in England – Of
> course the average Irish person has always hated England, and their
> argument is why be friendly now – it's a short-sighted policy we know
> – and neutrality has its drawbacks – (We never see a news reel for
> instance) – We, in the South of Ireland, are disgusted with the people
> in the North of Ireland. The percentage of volunteering for military
> service in England is much higher here than in the North – all our
> young friends, girls and men, have gone, but, no one knows that and we
> get slated here – while the North gets all the benefits of being in the
> Empire and have been awfully slack about doing their bit.[23]

A second letter speaks of the humiliation endured by the minority in Éire at
the hands of their own kinsfolk in Britain:

> We tiny minority of loyalists must accept our Government's ruling.
> What else in God's name can we do except suffer in our hearts, send
> our sympathies, eatables, pray for you in our Protestant Churches (only
> 3%) and writhe at the insults, sneers, digs and reproaches hurled at us
> over the air in your papers and by our British friends, and pray that

---

[22] PRONI, CAB/3A/57. There is no separation between Northern Ireland and Éire
for the period 1939–40, which implies that the total figures of recruits are
imprecisely distributed. However, for the same reasons, the figures for recruits
from neutral Éire in August 1941, recorded separately after August 1940, can be
taken as accurate.

[23] 'Postal Censorship Report: Insufficient recognition of Eire's voluntary effort',
1 Oct. 1941 (TNA, PREM 3/129/5).

when this war is over the truth of the number of Southern Irish boys in your forces may be published in blazing figures.[24]

Reports such as these afford the observer a fascinating insight into the thoughts and feelings of southern Irish Protestants, or self-professed 'loyalists' living in southern Ireland. It clearly influenced Churchill's decision to form the 38th Irish Brigade, in spite of the opposition that he would face from the government of Northern Ireland. Whether or not the opinions expressed in these letters reflected the wider opinion among the Protestant community in southern Ireland is more difficult to determine.

Brian Girvin observes that virtually every Irish newspaper, journal, or periodical that represented the diverse sections of Irish public opinion had signalled support for neutrality in September 1939, and this had even included publications like the *Irish Times* and the *Church of Ireland Gazette*, both of which had editorialised their approval of de Valera's policy.[25] The latter publication, which was unashamedly pro-British in tone, began by publishing several pieces which denounced Nazism as a 'doctrine of physical force and brutality', and with indirect reference to the invasion of Poland – 'enslaving a great country by tyranny and oppression' – the editorial confidently predicted that 'Germany will be compelled once again to drink the cup of defeat'.[26] The next issue of the *Gazette*, published almost two weeks into the war, posted a front-page advert for air-raid shelter construction and, in further connection with air-raid precautions, cautiously advised their readers to be supportive of neutrality, but also vigilant and prepared for war:

> As for our neutrality, that is a matter upon which it is unwise to say too much at present. Most people must see that to preserve it is the best protection against internal disturbance, and that as a member of the British Commonwealth we are free to decide for ourselves how, in view of whatever special circumstances may exist, we should act at the present moment. This is not to suggest for an instant that we, as individuals, can be indifferent to the issues at stake in the war, but we do suggest that until an admittedly delicate situation has cleared itself up a little it would be improper to embarrass the Government in its task of doing what it thinks is best. In any case, it would be idiotic to conclude that our neutrality makes it unnecessary to train ourselves in air raid precautions. Neutrality can be ended voluntarily, it can be ended by a

---

[24] 'Postal Censorship Report: Insufficient recognition of Eire's voluntary effort', 1 Oct. 1941 (TNA, PREM 3/129/5).

[25] Girvin, *The Emergency*, p. 62.

[26] *Church of Ireland Gazette*, 8 Sep. 1939.

declaration of war by another Power, or it can be violated without such a declaration. For what may come we must be prepared.[27]

In early October 1939, the *Gazette* assessed how well the state was adjusting to neutrality, commenting on de Valera's realism in his distinction between 'national and personal neutrality', alluding to his statement that there were 'no neutrals in Ireland'. Aside from criticism of the clumsy handling of certain aspects of neutrality policy, particularly censorship, the *Gazette*'s view of the de Valera government was positive and they noted that neutrality 'is being surveyed with courage and energy'.[28]

The editorials of the *Irish Times*, which still maintained a substantial Protestant readership, with a largely Protestant staff, can also offer a representative view of Irish Protestant opinion. Throughout the war, the newspaper, under the stewardship of R.M. Smyllie, had adopted a notably pro-British standpoint while being simultaneously supportive of neutrality.[29] When war commenced, followed shortly by the announcement of neutrality, the *Irish Times* plainly outlined their position on both matters: 'while the sympathies of this newspaper need no advertisement, we recognise the wisdom of Mr de Valera's decision, and shall give it our loyal support'.[30] An editorial on 4 September 1939, the day after Britain declared war on Germany, declared:

> Ireland faces the uncertain future with a heavy heart. She is a tiny nation, whose sole interest is peace, but her geographical position, her economic system, and to a large extent, her history, have placed her at the mercy of a warring world. Mr de Valera has proclaimed a policy of strict neutrality. In all the circumstances, it is the only policy that the Irish Government could pursue.[31]

Despite the paper's pledge of support for neutrality, *Irish Times* staff were soon subject to the rigours of strict censorship under the Emergency Powers Act 1939. Nonetheless, the paper continued to articulate a pro-British view and indeed lent whatever moral support it could to Britain's war effort. It published advertisements for vacancies in the British armed services and circulated the wartime addresses of King George VI to the British army and

---

[27] *Church of Ireland Gazette*, 15 Sep. 1939.
[28] *Church of Ireland Gazette*, 6 Oct. 1939.
[29] O'Brien, *The Irish Times*, p. 101.
[30] *Irish Times*, 6 Sep. 1939.
[31] *Irish Times*, 4 Sep. 1939; see also Gray, *Mr Smyllie, Sir*, p. 144.

Royal Navy, which were published, to the irritation of the censor, as 'the navy and the army', and featured letters to the editor referring to 'Our Tommies'.[32]

For the duration of the war, the paper was keen to highlight the large numbers of Irishmen who had joined the British forces, not least because a number of its own employees had enlisted: Johnny Robinson, who joined the Royal Navy, Brian Inglis, who served in the Royal Air Force, James Pettigrew, the Fleet Air Arm; even Smyllie's younger brother Donald joined up, making the war a deeply personal matter for a number of the newspaper's staff.[33] In 1941, they informed their readers, much to the horror of the censor, of the safe recovery of Robinson, whose ship, HMS *Prince of Wales*, was torpedoed and sunk by Japanese bombers. Appearing under the headline, 'ACCIDENT IN THE PACIFIC', the paragraph read: 'the many friends of Mr. John A. Robinson, who was involved in a recent boating accident, will be pleased to hear that he is alive and well'.[34] The *Irish Times* would continue openly to flout or circumvent strict censorship regulations to emphasise the importance of supporting Irish servicemen in the British forces, as they did, for instance, in November 1939, urging readers to provide materials to Irish soldiers serving in France during the approaching winter:

> Even if there were no Irish soldiers fighting on behalf of the democracies, the task would be laid upon us; but there are many thousands of Irishmen from North and South in the ranks to-day who have a right to claim our services in this matter.[35]

The paper later went further. Another editorial argued that it was absurd for people in Ireland to behave 'as indifferent to the fortune of Great Britain as, say, the inhabitants of Nicaragua', since, as the editorial noted, 'for one thing, there can be very few families in Eire that have not some relatives or friends in one or other of the British services'.[36] The fortunes of the paper fluctuated during wartime: circulation stood at over 25,000 in 1939, dropped to below 20,000 in 1942, but gradually rose to 27,000 by 1945.[37] Though the censor permitted occasional infractions of regulations at the beginning of the war, the paper soon risked being subject to the full force of press censorship and loss of editorial independence. This came in December 1942, when the newspaper staff were ordered to submit all copy to the censor in advance

---

[32] O'Brien, *The Irish Times*, p. 103.

[33] O'Brien, *The Irish Times*, p. 103; Gray, *Mr Smyllie, Sir*, p. 144.

[34] *Irish Times*, 17 Dec. 1941. See Tony Gray, *The Lost Years: The Emergency in Ireland, 1939–45* (London, 1997), p. 158.

[35] *Irish Times*, 12 Sep. 1939.

[36] *Irish Times*, 28 Sep. 1939.

[37] O'Brien, *The Irish Times*, p. 107.

of publication until the end of the war.[38] This proved particularly difficult
when it came to a ban on the publication of the details of war fatalities, as
Girvin observes. Hugh Gore-Booth, son of Lady Gore-Booth, who was killed
in action on the island of Leros in 1944, was a keen Irish language enthusiast
and a proud Irishman, but when drafting his obituary his grieving mother
was obliged to omit the circumstances of his death along with the fact that
he was a serving member of the British army.[39] In spite of the newspaper's
clear support for Britain, many of the *Irish Times* staff had felt quite strongly
that de Valera had been absolutely correct in his judgement to keep southern
Ireland out of the war. Certain senior staffers, particularly Alec Newman and
Lionel Fleming, became especially vociferous in their argument that it was
the firm duty of all Irish nationals, 'Protestant and Catholics, Unionists and
Republicans alike, to defend neutrality against all aggressors – the British, if
necessary, as well as the Germans'.[40]

At the end of the war, for VE Day, the front page cover of the *Irish Times*
featured an assembly of photos of key Allied leaders in a V shape – famously
known as Smyllie's 'V for Victory' – which would be the editor's last act
of defiance against the censor.[41] However, within days, the paper mounted
a tactful defence of de Valera and Éire's neutral policy in the aftermath of
Winston Churchill's remarks that the Dublin government had frolicked with
'the Germans and later with the Japanese to their heart's content': the editorial
would describe Churchill's comments as 'a slight overstatement', noting that
everyone, including the British Prime Minister, was fully aware that 'Ireland's
neutrality was wholly benevolent in respect of the United Nations'.[42] In 1946,
Smyllie realised that there was a pressing need to explain the rationale behind
Irish neutrality to foreign observers and to raise awareness of the efforts which
Ireland's volunteers had made for the Allied cause. In a well-known article,
'Unneutral neutral Ireland', published in *Foreign Affairs*, he argued that Éire,
even as a neutral country, had rendered largely unrecognised services to the
Allies in supplying food, information, and, above all, manpower to aid the
war against Nazi Germany, citing the service of between '150,000 and 180,000
young Irishmen under a British flag ... every one of them was a volunteer'.[43]
Of all southern Irish Protestants who sympathised with Britain's war effort,
while also signifying their loyalty to the neutral Irish state, Smyllie's was
surely the most interesting contribution.

---

[38] Donal Ó Drisceoil, *Censorship in Ireland, 1939–1945: Neutrality, Politics and Society* (Cork, 1997), pp. 162–5.
[39] Girvin, *The Emergency*, p. 279.
[40] Gray, *Mr Smyllie, Sir*, p. 144.
[41] *Irish Times*, 8 May 1945. See Gray, *The Lost Years*, pp. 234–5.
[42] *Irish Times*, 15 May 1945.
[43] R.M. Smyllie, 'Unneutral Neutral Ireland', *Foreign Affairs*, 24 (1946), pp. 317–26.

General Hubert Gough and the 'Irish Lobby' in London

In August 1941, General Sir Hubert Gough, together with two Irish ex-British army officers, Captain Henry Harrison and Maurice Healy, drafted a letter to the Canadian wartime premier, William Mackenzie King, in which they denounced the raising of a 'Local Defence Volunteer Force analogous to the British Home Guard' in Northern Ireland. They argued that the Ulster Home Guard was, in an identical fashion to the Ulster Volunteer Force (UVF), 'recruited along politico-sectarian lines and is maintained free from British military discipline'.[44] This would become part of a wider campaign in which Gough, and a number of Irish and Anglo-Irish ex-army and navy officers who were sympathetic to neutral Éire, including Churchill's cousin Sir Shane Leslie and the famous aviator Colonel James Fitzmaurice, would oppose Lord Craigavon's Ulster Defence Volunteers and other sectarian policies of the Northern government, which they regarded as damaging to Anglo-Irish relations. Earlier, in September 1940, Gough sent a letter of protest, signed by all his supporters, to the British prime minister Winston Churchill. This provoked a considerable outburst from the elderly Craigavon when the issue was raised in the House of Commons of Northern Ireland: 'Craigavon lumbered to his feet, got hold of the dispatch box and said: "Mr Speaker, Sir – General Gough has gone off"'.[45] In the end, Gough's objections to the formation of a Home Guard force in Northern Ireland, made up almost exclusively of volunteers from the unionist community and operating a recruitment policy that appeared to exclude Catholic recruits entirely, would fall on deaf ears.

After Craigavon's death, his political successor, John Miller Andrews, attempted to extend conscription to Northern Ireland in May 1941. Gough, Harrison, and Healy, seeing an opportunity to derail Stormont's proposal, immediately leant their support to the opposition by suggesting that the Commonwealth war effort could only be damaged by the imposition of conscription as it would lead to 'domestic conflict and bloodshed', the ramifications of which would be felt 'wherever there are Irish people, or Catholics, or lovers of freedom'.[46] In August 1941, Gough and his colleagues became conspiratorial, claiming the 'existence of a powerful section of opinion in Britain and Northern Ireland which had long looked forward to the recurrence of a world war as furnishing an opportunity for re-conquest of a self-governing Ireland by Ulster protestant levies, operating from Northern Ireland with

---

[44] Gough, Harrison, and Healy to MacKenzie King, 21 Aug. 1941 (PRONI, CAB 9CD/174/3).
[45] Fisk, *In Time of War*, pp. 450–1.
[46] Ollerenshaw, *Northern Ireland in the Second World War*, p. 165.

the full support of the British Army'.[47] The idea of an invasion of southern
Ireland, aided by the Unionist north, was far from a conspiracy theory; it
had been entertained by Churchill's War Cabinet during 1940. Indeed, from
1940, the Irish government and their military chiefs had also anticipated a
British invasion of Éire, launched from Northern Ireland, something of which
Gough was probably aware.[48] Hence, an ostensible motive for his attack on
the Unionist government of Northern Ireland was the belief that Éire should
be coaxed into the war on Britain's side through conciliatory methods. Gough
believed that there was sufficient evidence of Irish 'goodwill' to demonstrate
that Éire had been a worthy friend of Britain:

> Recruits for H.M. [British] Armed Forces have been coming freely
> and spontaneously from Ireland since the war began. We have reason
> to believe that Ireland – population less than 3,000,000 – has sent
> some 120,000 voluntary recruits, whilst Northern Ireland – population
> about 1,250,000 – has sent some 1,900. Ireland's neutrality forbids the
> existence of British recruiting agencies in Ireland such as freely exist
> in Northern Ireland, side by side with British military and other units
> – a circumstance which makes these approximate figures all the more
> remarkable. Ireland's 120,000 are predominantly Nationalist Catholics
> of identical type with the Nationalist Catholic minority in Northern
> Ireland, whose unhappy plight and enforced separation from the parent
> Ireland form the principal factor that determined Ireland's neutrality.
> This outstanding fact, pregnant with invaluable implications as to the
> essential and sincere goodwill of strictly neutral Ireland towards Britain
> and the Commonwealth, is either intentionally withheld from the British
> and World public, or else is overlooked and left unmentioned by news
> services and propaganda agencies. Nor is it mentioned in the speeches
> of Ministers nor in the reports of Parliamentary Debates. We cannot
> forbear the comment that in our opinion the total eclipse of this very
> striking fact is as amazing and as significant as it has been infelicitous.[49]

There is no evidence to substantiate the figures provided by Gough; recruiting
figures maintained by the British military authorities in Belfast clearly show
that over 71,000 recruits from across the island joined in the Northern
Ireland district, with approximately 45,000 men and women coming from

---

[47] Gough, Harrison, and Healy to MacKenzie King, 21 Aug. 1941 (PRONI, CAB
9CD/174/3).
[48] Wills, *That Neutral Island*, pp. 87–90.
[49] Gough, Harrison, and Healy to MacKenzie King, 21 Aug. 1941 (PRONI, CAB
9CD/174/3).

southern Ireland against 26,000 from the six counties.[50] Andrews may have known the truth, but was more impulsive than rational about his response to these allegations. Outraged by Gough's spectacular condemnation of the state of wartime politics in the six counties, he resolved to defend the honour of Northern Ireland to his counterpart in Ottawa. Andrews consulted his colleagues in cabinet, especially his close confidants Richard Dawson Bates and Sir Basil Brooke, asking whether he should publish a response to Gough's claims.[51] Brooke would advise against doing so unless 'Gough's letter has received publicity itself', noting that Gough sufficiently demonstrated his ignorance of Irish affairs.[52] However, it was on the point of the sectarian-based composition of the Ulster Home Guard that Gough and his colleagues made the strongest impression. In the wake of the controversy surrounding Gough's letter, Churchill took soundings from the departmental heads of the Home Office, War Office, and Dominions Office. Although he wanted to let the matter drop, reports that Catholics were being harassed at roadblocks by Ulster Home Guard personnel and rumours that Catholics trying to join the Home Guard were being turned away proved unhelpful. This matter was raised by the Roman Catholic archbishop of Westminster, Dr Bernard Griffin, who had written to Downing Street in support of Gough's arguments.[53] Griffin later delivered a controversial homily, in November 1944, which compared the persecution of Catholics in Germany and Poland by the Nazis to the anti-Catholic sectarianism in Northern Ireland.[54]

Gough claimed the spotlight again when, in September 1941, he published an editorial in *The Times* in which he highlighted that 'very large numbers of Irishmen have joined H.M. Forces since the outbreak of the war' and that their enlistment was their 'own spontaneous and unsolicited act'. He cited the experiences of British army officers who had commanded Irish troops and suggested that existing Irish units should be 'regrouped into an Irish brigade or division'.[55] This letter was typical of the type which Gough published in *The Times* on the subject of volunteers from southern Ireland in the British forces, and he campaigned actively for their welfare and for greater recognition of

---

[50] Statistics for Northern Ireland and Eire recruits (male and female separately), 1940–45 (PRONI CAB/3A/57).

[51] Andrews to Dawson Bates; Andrews to Brooke, 17 Sep. 1941 (PRONI, CAB 9CD/174/3).

[52] Brooke to Andrews, 19 Sep. 1941 (PRONI, CAB 9CD/174/3).

[53] David R. Orr, *Duty without Glory: The Story of Ulster's Home Guard in World War 2* (Newtownards, 2008), p. 55.

[54] Brian Barton, 'Northern Ireland in the Second World War', in Brian Girvin and Geoffrey Roberts (eds), *Ireland in the Second World War: Politics, Society and Remembrance* (Dublin, 2000), p. 71.

[55] *The Times*, 26 Sep. 1941.

their contribution to the British war effort. For instance, during the opening years of the war, he was concerned that there was no facility for Irish service personnel to meet and rest in London. Soon he formed a committee and with the help of an initial donation of £1,000 from the Guinness family, the Shamrock Club opened in March 1943.[56] The club's patrons included a number of senior British service officers of Irish birth, including Air Commodore John C. Quinnell, and those of Anglo-Irish lineage, such as Admiral of the Fleet, William Boyle, the 12th Earl of Cork and Orrery, and it was supported with generous donations from Irish veterans who had served in the disbanded Irish regiments during the Great War.[57] Gough's editorial inspired an enthusiastic response from Churchill, who wrote a short memo to the War Office, observing that 'we have Free French and Vichy French, so why not Loyal Irish and Dublin Irish?'[58] At a meeting of the War Cabinet, on 9 October 1941, he told his cabinet colleagues that there had been a number of 'indications that public opinion in Ireland would be gratified if some action was taken which acknowledged the considerable help, which we were receiving, by the enlistment in our forces of volunteers from Southern Ireland' and requested that the secretary of state for war, David Margesson, consider forming an Irish Brigade in the British army.[59]

Andrews complained bitterly about the proposal in a letter to Churchill. He strongly objected to the fact that the new brigade was being formed using regimental battalions of the Royal Irish Fusiliers, the Royal Inniskilling Fusiliers, and the London Irish Rifles, all of which had territorial affiliations to Northern Ireland, as well as the use of the title 'Irish Brigade', which he felt was synonymous with the formation that fought against England 'in the days of Marlborough'. He also listed nefarious examples of Irish brigades since Sarsfield, including Major John McBride's brigade which fought alongside the Boers in the South African War, Roger Casement's brigade in the First World War, and the more recent example of O'Duffy's Blueshirts in the Spanish Civil War.[60] In spite of the significant opposition mounted by the Stormont government, the 38th (Irish) Brigade officially came into existence in January 1942. A distinguished Irish officer, Brigadier The O'Donovan, an Irish Fusilier who was decorated with the Military Cross for bravery in France during the Great War, was chosen to command the brigade. This Irish

[56] Anthony Farrar-Hockley, *Goughie: The Life of General Sir Hubert Gough* (London, 1975), pp. 372–3.
[57] Hubert Gough, *Soldiering On: Being the Memoirs of General Sir Hubert Gough* (London, 1954), p. 250.
[58] Prime Minister's Personal Minute, 6 Oct. 1941 (TNA, PREM 3/129/5).
[59] Extract from Conclusions of a Meeting of the War Cabinet: 'Proposed Formation of an Irish Brigade', 9 Oct. 1941 (TNA, CJ 1/85).
[60] Andrews to Churchill, 12 Dec. 1941 (TNA, PREM 3/129/5).

Protestant, who hailed from Gaelic aristocracy, confided to his friend and fellow 'Faugh', Kendal Chavasse, that when 'the formation of the Brigade was given to him, he felt the mantle of Sarsfield had fallen upon his shoulders'.[61] The brigade acquired a distinctly Irish identity: an official brigade songbook was commissioned with both nationalist marching ballads such as 'Kevin Barry', 'The Soldier's Song', 'The Boys who Beat the Black and Tans', and loyalist ballads such as 'The Sash my Father Wore', 'The Ulster Volunteers' and 'The Ould Orange Flute'. The Drum and Fife band of the brigade famously played these nationalist and loyalist ballads to Pope Pius XII in St Peter's Square in June 1944.[62]

Gough's 'Irish lobby' in London proved to be highly effective at influencing British government policy to the advantage of neutral Ireland, and they were probably helped in this regard by Churchill's complex and paradoxical relationship with the country.[63] It should be noted that Gough, despite his apparent alignment with the cause of neutral Éire during the war and sympathies with the southern Irish position, is considered by some authors, including Brian Girvin, to have been 'a lifelong unionist'.[64] It is, however, clear that the position of a number of influential southern Irish Protestants, members of the Anglo-Irish community, and certain retired senior officers of Irish birth or descent in London, was focused on the question of how to lure neutral Ireland back into the British fold. To this end, Gough, Healy, and Harrison had formed a united front with an alliance of 'Irish and Anglo-Irishmen with a strong military or naval background, academics, writers and critics, such as Stephen Gwynn and Denis Ireland', who all played a central role in lobbying the Churchill government in defence of neutral Éire and the benefit of Irish service personnel in the British forces. These men were later central to the creation of the Commonwealth Irish Association in 1942, a doomed venture which aimed to keep southern Ireland in the British Commonwealth, establish improved relations between Dublin and London, and promote a form of unity between the two jurisdictions of Ireland.[65]

Regardless of their achievements and failures, the work of Gough and his supporters would have been utterly impossible had it not been for the presence of a sizeable contingent of southern Irish in the British forces – a contingent that included a large number of young members of the southern

---

[61] Richard Doherty, *Clear the Way: A History of the 38th (Irish) Brigade* (Dublin, 1993), p. 7.

[62] Keith Jeffery, 'The British Army and Ireland since 1922', in Thomas Bartlett and Keith Jeffery (eds), *A Military History of Ireland* (Cambridge, 1996), p. 444.

[63] Paul Bew, *Churchill and Ireland* (Oxford, 2016), p. 182.

[64] Girvin, *The Emergency*, p. 258.

[65] Ollerenshaw, *Northern Ireland in the Second World War: Politics, Economic Mobilisation and Society, 1939–45*, p. 146.

Irish Protestant community. Indeed, at the end of the war, in 1946, in another daring letter to *The Times*, Gough would claim that, according to trustworthy sources, the War Office registered over 165,000 next-of-kin addresses in neutral Éire by July 1944.[66] If this as yet unverified figure is correct, each of these 165,000 Irish servicemen and women proved to be a valuable bullet in Gough's propaganda war against the Stormont government.

Irish Protestant Service Personnel in the British Forces

There are many thousands of families on the island of Ireland whose relations served in one or both world wars, forming part of a military tradition which, in some cases, stretches back centuries. This is what Steven O'Connor has identified as the family military tradition, the 'hereditary soldier', and he observes that this was especially strong in Ireland, particularly among the sons of landowners for whom becoming an officer originated in a family strategy that aimed at maintaining 'their social and economic position within the landed gentry'.[67] The family tradition of military service in Ireland was by no means confined to the landed classes, however, and it extended to all classes of Irish society. Bernard Kelly also indicates that the desire to continue a family tradition in British military service was a 'powerful motivation to enlist', and he outlines that the practice of 'following the family path to the recruiting office' was an established process, known as 'endo-recruitment'. He also notes that the greatest influence on the Irish volunteers who joined the British forces from 1939 onwards was the enlistment of the preceding generation in the Great War in large numbers.[68] Just over 200,000 Irish had fought in the conflict, around half of whom returned to Ireland after 1918.[69] Geoffrey Roberts points out a distinction in terms of the motives which propelled voluntary enlistment during the Second World War, arguing that 'decisions to volunteer and serve were mainly individual' and that there is little outward evidence of David Fitzpatrick's '"logic of collective sacrifice" evident in Irish recruitment to the British armed forces during the First World War'.[70] At the same time, despite neutrality, many who had made a 'personal

---

[66] *The Times*, 3 Apr. 1946.

[67] O'Connor, *Irish Officers in the British Forces*, p. 42.

[68] Bernard Kelly, *Returning Home: Irish Service Personnel after the Second World War* (Dublin, 2012), p. 29.

[69] Taylor, *Heroes or Traitors?*, pp. 11–13.

[70] Geoffrey Roberts' observations are based on his study of the UCC Volunteers Project Archive of oral history testimonies from Irish ex-service personnel of the Second World War. See Geoffrey Roberts, 'Neutrality, Identity and the Challenge of the "Irish Volunteers"', in Dermot Keogh and Mervyn O'Driscoll (eds), *Ireland*

decision' to enlist had little difficulty 'in reconciling their Irish identity with fighting in the British armed forces or contributing on the equally vital home front against Nazism'.[71]

Albert Sutton, who served in the Royal Air Force (RAF), came from a working-class Church of Ireland family background in Dublin that was 'strongly Unionist' and also had a tradition of service in the military, as well as the police. His father served in the Dublin Metropolitan Police and was involved in the arrests of rebels during the Easter Rising, and later took part in counterinsurgency activities in the city during the War of Independence. This became the profession that many male family members entered. Albert had two uncles in An Garda Síochána, one of whom served in France in the Royal Dublin Fusiliers during the Great War and had suffered so terribly from the after-effects of a gas attack that Albert found it surprising that he was accepted into the force; this uncle became a Garda sergeant whereas his other uncle rose to the rank of chief superintendent. Albert acknowledged the influence of his family's past military service, but did not describe it as his primary motivation for joining the British forces; the family's strongly unionist identity appeared to be far more of a motivator than any other factor.[72] The family military tradition involving service in the British army was, nevertheless, a central component in the family backgrounds of many RAF recruits, including Sidney James Gray, a Church of Ireland member from Bray, who enlisted in 1943 and became one of thousands of Irish airmen who served in Bomber Command:

> I think it was ... because all my mum's family had been Gloucester's, Gloucester Regiment, and my great-granddad, he was a Sergeant-Major, and they travelled the world, like Malta, with the Gloucester's and we were living then in Ireland. We were always very British, you know, pro-British, loved the British, and we thought it was a terrible thing and although they remained neutral through the war, they did certainly supply thousands of people to the forces. I know there was a hell of a lot in the RAF, and there was a hell of a lot in the Army, weren't there ... In Ireland you got like many Roman Catholics, and Protestants. And the majority of Protestants were always very pro-British.[73]

in World War Two: Diplomacy and Survival (Cork, 2004), pp. 274–5 and David Fitzpatrick, 'The Logic of Collective Sacrifice: Ireland and the British army, 1914–1918', *Historical Journal*, 38/4 (1995), pp. 1017–30.

71   Mervyn O'Driscoll, *Ireland, Germany and the Nazis: Politics and Diplomacy, 1919–1939* (Dublin, 2004), p. 283.

72   Interview with Albert Sutton, Zampano Productions, Jan. 2014.

73   Interview with Sidney James Gray (IWM, SA 30391/3).

Among a collection of one hundred ex-service personnel interviewed for oral history projects, whose motives are analysed in the Volunteers' Motivations Database,[74] 40 per cent of the total joined the RAF, with 14 per cent citing family military tradition as a motive. Gray's testimony alludes to another crucial factor in this respect, which is examined within the Volunteers' Motivations Database: a total of 17 per cent of the interviewees reported a defined affiliation, or sense of loyalty, to Britain and the cause for which she fought the war. This cannot be delineated upon merely religious or ethnic lines, as only 9 per cent of those who responded in this way were from a Church of Ireland background, with the remainder being Catholic, other faiths, or non-believers.[75] Jeremy Jenkins' study, which comprised interviews contained in the University College Cork Volunteers Project Archive,[76] found that 9 per cent of that cohort expressed an affiliation to Britain and the war effort.[77] Pro-British sympathy, however, did not exist on its own as a motivator. Albert Sutton also clarified that his family had strong pro-British sympathies, which did lie at the heart of his reasoning for joining up, but was not as powerful as the social influence among his peer group in the Dublin Protestant community.[78] His lifelong friend Kenneth MacLean, a Dublin working-class Protestant whose family held similar pro-British sympathies, enlisted in the British army, serving in the Burma Campaign; Kenneth and Albert had both joined the British forces during the same period in 1941.[79] The Volunteers' Motivations Database shows that 35 per cent of those who enlisted, of whom 17 per cent were southern Irish protestants, did so mainly

74 Volunteers' Motivations Database, 2015. This database is composed of oral history testimonies taken from a sample of one hundred Irish veterans of the Second World War. The database includes entries taken from the University College Cork Volunteers Project Archive (UCCVPA), supplemented by 45 additional interviews. The chart, 'Motivational Factors', outlines a selection of the top 15 motivating factors as expressed by the interviewees.

75 Volunteers' Motivations Database, 2015, 'Motivational Factors: Southern Irish Protestants'. Figure 8.1 is based on an analysis of the motivations of 31 southern Irish Protestants, separated from the 69 other participants, providing indicators of motivations as a percentage of the wider group of 100.

76 UCCVPA was created in 1995 by Prof. Brian Girvin and Prof. Geoffrey Roberts. Led by Tina Neylon, 56 Irish ex-service personnel who served in the British forces during the Second World War were interviewed. In addition to examining motivations and details of service, the project also queried participants' views on Irish neutrality.

77 Jeremy Jenkins, '"This a private shindy or can any bloke join in?": Why Neutral Irish Volunteered for Service in the British Forces during the Second World War', *Irish Sword*, 28/114 (2012), pp. 419–53 (at pp. 433–4).

78 Interview with Albert Sutton, Zampano Productions, Jan. 2014.

79 Interview with Kenneth MacLean, 5 Nov. 2015.

because their peers were doing so, a finding which contradicts Roberts' idea of 'individual' decisions and adds some weight to the theory that collective or social pressures, as defined by Fitzpatrick, were a feature of Second World War enlistment, just as they were during the Great War.[80]

In certain cases, family tradition was extremely important in the decision-making process of some volunteers, including those from Church of Ireland backgrounds, and some even felt it their duty to enlist in honour of the service rendered by previous generations. Corkman John Bennett Jermyn joined the British army, enlisting in the Royal Artillery where he rose to the rank of Captain, but was dissatisfied with his initial choice and traded in this rank to become a lieutenant serving in No. 2 Army Commando, seeing action in Sicily, Yugoslavia, Albania, and Italy. Jermyn stated that his 'mother's only brother was killed in World War I, he was in the Royal Munsters and was 19, and in some token way I felt I should take his place'. There were some influences within his school to enlist, even a tradition of service in the British forces, and he claimed that many fellow pupils, including several of his school friends, joined up. Though he does not believe that it had any influence upon him, he stated that 'Church of Ireland people were more likely to be pro-British than Catholics'.[81] However, this assertion may have been more of an assumption than a reality, as the above indicators from the database suggest. Identity was also an important factor for Irish Protestant servicemen: Michael Maurice d'Alton, who joined the Royal Navy, served in the Combined Operations service, and participated in the Normandy landings as an officer on an LCT (landing craft tank), described himself as coming from 'a West-British background'. As well as having a family tradition of military service, he had two siblings who also joined the forces.[82] Some 30 per cent of database participants, with southern Protestants representing 12 per cent, had siblings serving in the British forces during the Second World War.[83]

In certain cases, a family tradition of military service was so entrenched that it seemed inevitable that members of the next generation would obtain commissions in the army. Billy Vincent, who served with the 2nd Battalion of the Royal Inniskilling Fusiliers and would fight within the 38th Irish Brigade in Italy, recalled that although his father would not serve as a soldier in the First World War due to a leg injury he did join the American Field Ambulance Services with the French army, while all his brothers 'went into the British

---

[80] Volunteers' Motivations Database, 2015, 'Motivational Factors: Southern Irish Protestants'.
[81] John Bennett Jermyn (UCCVPA L6).
[82] Michael Maurice d'Alton (UCCVPA S12).
[83] Volunteers' Motivations Database, 2015, 'Motivational Factors: Southern Irish Protestants'.

army because that was what they had done for many years before'.[84] Aleck Creighton also described himself as coming from 'an ordinary Anglo-Irish background'; his father had been a doctor who served as a medical officer in the First World War and there was a solid tradition of military service in his family. However, when it came to his own reasons for enlisting in the Irish Guards in the Second World War, Aleck stated that among the people that his family mixed with it was simply the 'done thing' to join up.[85] William Harvey-Kelly, who also came from a Church of Ireland military family, stated that his father and grandfather had both served as British army officers, along with many members of their respective generation of the family. He had been a pupil at Wilson's Hospital, a school with a long tradition of past pupils entering the British army or another branch of the British forces, and William would acknowledge that he, along with some of his contemporaries, had joined up in this very same manner.[86] Basil Baker, who served as a Sergeant in the North Irish Horse, and later became a career soldier in the British army, had a grandfather who had served in the Connaught Rangers and had risen to the rank of General – Baker's choice of career was defined by the legacy of soldiering in his family.[87] A family military tradition was a predominant motive among 54 per cent of the participants, 18 per cent of whom were southern Protestants, particularly among those who joined the British army, with many southern Irish Protestant officers following the path of fathers and grandfathers.[88] O'Connor further notes that southern Protestants accounted for more than half of all Irish officers who served in the British forces during the war.[89]

Irish Protestant women served in the British forces in considerable numbers. One of many Irish members of the Women's Auxiliary Air Force was Maureen Deighton, who had hailed from a Church of Ireland background in County Limerick. She experienced the bombing of two British cities during the war, London and Plymouth, and felt that joining up was the right thing to do: 'It was the done thing – the right thing to do, you were fighting evil, I was fancy free, I was young, I had a bit of education. Mostly it was because

---

[84] Interview with A.W.B. Vincent, 26 Apr. 2012.

[85] Interview with Aleck Creighton, Zampano Productions, Jun. 2011.

[86] Interview with William Harvey-Kelly, Zampano Productions, Jun. 2012. For details on the service of past pupils of Wilson's Hospital, see David Robertson, *Deeds Not Words: Irish Soldiers, Sailors and Airmen in Two World Wars* (Multyfarnham, 1998).

[87] Basil Baker (UCCVPA A21).

[88] Volunteers' Motivations Database, 2015, 'Motivational Factors: Southern Irish Protestants'.

[89] O'Connor, *Irish Officers in the British Forces*, p. 42.

everyone else was. If I'd stayed in England I'd have been called up'.[90] Deighton, who served as a Radar Operator posted at several stations around the coast of England between 1940 and 1945, also referred to her own Protestant background as a consideration in her decision to enlist, stating that 'me, and all my relations and friends in County Limerick joined up – all the men I knew in Ireland joined something and the women minded the farms ... it was the done thing to do something in war in my circle'.[91] Elizabeth Dobbs from Dublin, a member of the Church of Ireland, joined the Fleet Air Arm in London in 1942 as a student, citing many of the same reasons as Maureen Deighton. Dobbs stated that she joined the British Forces because she 'just wanted to', and felt that the navy was the best service and was keen to join the Women's Royal Naval Service (the Wrens), but was initially thwarted by the embargo that had been put in place on recruiting from southern Ireland; she had initially served in the St John Ambulance Brigade with a friend and worked as a nurse's aide in Surrey a year before joining up. Dobbs also explained that 'most Protestants felt – something to do with England' and members of her family were no exception. Her uncles fought in the Great War, one of whom was killed in action, and her brother would serve in the RAF during the Second World War, and she spoke of the encouragement of her parents, who 'went on and on and on about joining up'.[92]

Dobbs, the daughter of a clergyman, and whose family influenced her decision to join up, was accompanied by Brenda Graham, a Trinity College Dublin student, whose father had been a Royal Army Medical Corps officer in Flanders during the Great War and met her mother while serving on the Western front. The romanticism of this proved to be a strong influence on Brenda.[93] Her father established the St John Ambulance Corps in Dublin when the Second World War broke out, and it was through this organisation that both Brenda and Elizabeth had 'received first aid training and a knowledge of basic nursing care'. But the two girls had a desire for 'adventure and wanted to do something positive in the war'. They found life in neutral Ireland to be quite 'boring and restrictive and they "wanted to get away"', especially to be active in the world where they could experience the war. It was with Brenda and other companions that Dobbs began her service to the British war effort as a nursing aid in Botleys Park War Hospital in Surrey, prior to her enlistment in the Royal Navy, a form of service that would be provided by

[90] Maureen Deighton (UCCVPA A4).
[91] Maureen Deighton (UCCVPA A4).
[92] Elizabeth Dobbs (UCCVPA S10).
[93] Richard Doherty, *Irish Men and Women in the Second World War* (Dublin, 1999), p. 44.

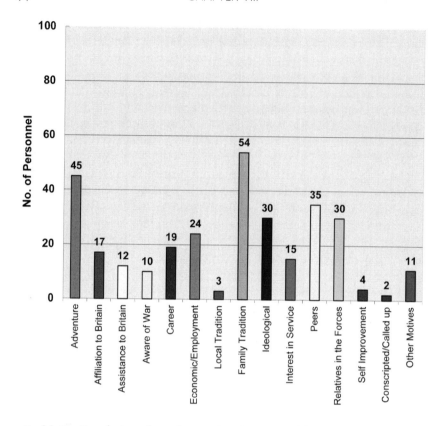

8.1 Motivation factors for volunteering among oral history interviewees
Source: UCC Volunteers Project Archive, supplemented by 45 additional
interviews. (Note: individual interviewees can offer more than one answer.)

many Irish women serving in other branches of the British forces.[94] In the case
of Brenda and Elizabeth, as with many Irish who volunteered, we see instances
where people enlisted because of the influence of their family backgrounds,
or their community. Like Elizabeth Dobbs, they state that joining the British
forces was often encouraged, even expected by those from an Irish Protestant
background; some 17 per cent of interviewees, of which southern Protestants
account for 9 per cent, stated that an affiliation with Britain through family
and community was a strong reason for enlisting (see Figures 8.1 and 8.2).[95]

---

[94] Doherty, *Irish Men and Women in the Second World War*, pp. 44–5; Elizabeth
Dobbs (UCCVPA S10).
[95] Volunteers' Motivations Database, 2015, 'Motivational Factors: Southern Irish
Protestants'.

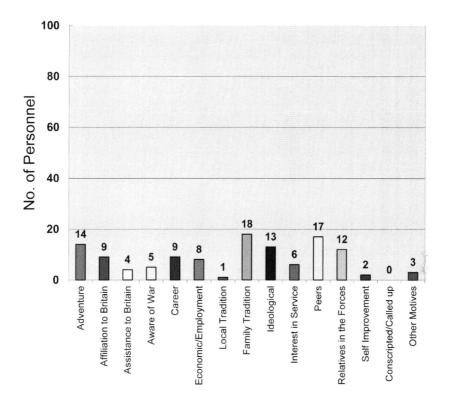

8.2 Motivation factors for volunteering among southern Protestant oral
history interviewees
Source: UCC Volunteers Project Archive, supplemented by 45 additional
interviews.

According to the available testimony, it seems that most Irish ex-service
personnel who offered an opinion on neutrality, including Irish Protestants,
agreed with the state's policy. Out of the 20 per cent of database participants
who, when asked, offered an approving view of Irish neutrality, some 8 per
cent were southern Irish Protestants; one southern Protestant ex-serviceman
expressed disapproval of the policy on moral or ethical grounds.[96] However,
it appears that most of the participants, including Protestants, were practical
about Irish neutrality, believing that the Irish state was unprepared to engage
in a major conflict, to ward off enemy naval and air attacks, or even to mobilise
Irish society to fight a war. Some Protestant volunteers valued neutrality
for the benefits it brought, including the protection of loved ones from the

---

[96] Volunteers' Motivations Database, 2015, 'Southern Protestant Views on Neutrality'.

horrors of war. One volunteer, David Baynham, argued strongly that Irish neutrality had 'kept all my friends and relations reasonably safe, I thought'.[97] Brian Bolingbroke 'had no objection to Ireland being neutral', feeling that it was right for the country: 'neutrality was a good thing – it saved this country the appalling devastation I saw in Britain'.[98] There was a minority of the volunteers who were opposed to Irish neutrality, represented by just one southern Irish Protestant volunteer, Arthur Jones.[99] This arose from a feeling that Éire stood aloof, allowing war to rage around its shores without providing sufficient assistance. As O'Connor observes, many of the volunteers had served in the Royal Navy and 'believed that the use of southern Irish ports would have made a significant difference in the struggle to sink German submarines operating in the Atlantic Ocean and to protect the convoys of merchant ships from the United States'.[100] Some Irish Protestant Royal Navy volunteers, such as Michael d'Alton, felt that Hitler was 'a little bloody monster' who had to be stopped, and that Ireland would have been threatened by Nazi Germany had the Allies not prevailed in the war. For this same reason, however, d'Alton also agreed with the neutrality of southern Ireland: 'I thoroughly agreed with it. If it [neutral Éire] had joined it would have been counter-productive and would have enabled Germany to invade from the west without international condemnation'.[101] John Jacob, who also served in the Royal Navy, held to the view that 'neutrality was the only possible thing – we were a young state'.[102] After having witnessed the destruction and horror of war, many might well have been glad also to return home to a country where their families had remained safe and above all at peace.

Conclusion

The Second World War was a critical moment for the southern Irish Protestant community and should be viewed as an important juncture at which one can assess how well members of the community had adapted to life in the new Irish state while simultaneously continuing their engagement with the country to which they had, historically, pledged their allegiance. Throughout the course of the war, southern Irish Protestants, on the whole, demonstrated sentiments that ran mostly in a pro-British vein, and were broadly supportive of the British

---

[97] David Baynham (UCCVPA 3L).
[98] Brian Bolingbroke (UCCVPA 1S).
[99] Arthur Jones (UCCVPA L11).
[100] Steven O'Connor, 'Why Did They Fight for Britain? Irish Recruits to the British Forces, 1939–45', *Études Irlandaises*, 40/1 (2015), pp. 59–70 (at p. 67).
[101] Michael Maurice d'Alton (UCCVPA S12).
[102] John Jacob (UCCVPA S4).

war effort. At the same time, they were very much defensive of neutral Éire and some even proved critical of their northern unionist counterparts. Their support for Irish neutrality was predicated upon a belief that neutral policy was the better and wiser course for southern Ireland, and more beneficial for their own community. There was probably some recognition that their community was safer in a neutral state, and that they would not have to suffer the privations endured by numerous other countries at war. Perhaps the very recent memory of the precarious position of the Protestant community during the Irish Civil War also prompted them to adopt this particular view. Another consideration was the possibility that southern Protestants had sufficiently adapted to life in the new Irish state for them to have comfortably adopted a sense of civic obligation, and possibly even a sense of loyalty. Most importantly, neutral Irish policy enabled them to serve the British war effort without fear of reprisal from any larger group. They would do so alongside many thousands of non-Protestant Irish comrades-in-arms who would account for the majority of southern Ireland's volunteer contingent in the British forces. It may well have been the recognition of this fact that prompted southern Irish Protestants, particularly those in British uniform, to defend the honour of Irish neutrality.

III

The Provincial Experience

CHAPTER IX

Henry Lawrence Tivy (1848–1929): The Rise and Fall of a Cork Loyalist

Alan McCarthy

Born into a patrician family in Cork, Henry Lawrence Tivy was a merchant prince who acquired the *Cork Constitution* newspaper in 1882 from the Savage family for £5,310 and later launched the weekly edition, the *Cork Weekly News*.[1] During this period, Tivy served as proprietor and co-editor at the *Constitution* alongside the like-minded William Ludgate. In 1915, he purchased the Dublin *Evening Mail* and *Daily Express*. These newspapers, where he collaborated with his sons, espoused Tivy's unionist politics, of which he remained an unshakeable proponent from the 1880s until his semi-retirement from public life in 1922. Throughout an eventful life he engaged in a host of philanthropic endeavours in Cork city, as well as a range of political and social pursuits which were also a hallmark of his wife and children's civic engagement. This chapter will assess Tivy's career, highlighting both his press career and his politics. It will chart the uneasy transition of unionist families such as the Tivys into the Irish Free State and consider their attempts to obtain compensation for losses sustained during the Civil War. Ultimately, it seeks to engage with the duality of H.L. Tivy's public life as a proud citizen of Cork and dedicated supporter of the Union between Britain and Ireland.

Background and Influences

The Tivy family had a lengthy association with the city of Cork, with one of their ancestors, George Tivy, receiving the Freedom of the City in 1686, while another ancestor, also George Tivy, received this honour in 1806.[2] H.L. Tivy was born into this affluent family on 30 October 1848. His father

---

[1] *Kerry Evening Post*, 28 Jan. 1882.
[2] George Tivy made a Freeman of Cork in 1686 (Cork City and County Archives [CCCA], U116/B/1, Tivy family papers); George Tivy made a Freeman of Cork in 1806 (CCCA, U116/B/23, p. i).

was also named Henry Lawrence, while his mother was Elizabeth Lawrence Ryder.[3] This branch of the family belonged to the Church of Ireland and were successful butter merchants, a profession into which Henry Lawrence junior also entered.[4] However, it is for his work in the daily newspaper industry, rather than dairy, that Tivy is best-known.

Tivy was highly active in civic life. He served as a justice of the peace, and was a trustee of the Cork Savings Bank, Skiddy's Charity, and St Stephen's Hospital, as well as a council member of the Cork Historical and Archaeological Society. A Cork Corporation seat in the North-East Ward became vacant in 1879, arising from Robert Day's elevation to alderman. Tivy, standing as a Conservative, won the election and served until his resignation in 1885.[5] He was later a trustee of Cork Butter Market as one of the Corporation's nominees.[6] Tivy was also a committee member for the Cork Industrial Exhibitions of 1883, 1902, and 1903, serving on the executive committee in 1902.[7] He proclaimed that 'the greatest wonders of the age would be seen in Cork next year' and 'There was nothing that the ingenuity of man could devise that would not be included in the attractions that the Exhibition Committee would be able to supply'.[8] Prior to the opening of the exhibition, Tivy wrote to *The Times* of London seeking to highlight the participation of all sections of society in its design and execution, at a time when 'So much is heard in Great Britain of any political disturbances which occur in Ireland and so little, by comparison, of the many peaceful social and industrial movements in this country'.[9] While the letter outlines his unionist credentials, it is also clear that Tivy saw his native city as central to his imperial world view.

[3] Ryder family records (CCCA, U116/B/4, p. ii).

[4] Richard J. Hodges, *Cork and County Cork in the Twentieth Century* (Brighton, 1911), p. 292, contemporary biography of Henry Lawrence Tivy.

[5] *Cork Examiner*, 23 Dec. 1879; 10 Apr. 1880; 17 Nov. 1881; 4 Sep. 1883; *Cork Constitution*, 11 Dec. 1885; *Guy's Directory* (1884), p. 111. Tivy was also known for delivering cakes to the city's orphanages during winter and was affiliated to the Cork Society of the Prevention of Cruelty to Animals. See *Cork Weekly News*, 21 Nov. 1914 and *Cork Examiner*, 18 Jan. 1887.

[6] *Guy's Directory* (1893), p. 30; *Guy's Directory* (1903), p. 140; *Cork Constitution*, 9 Apr. 1892; 23 Mar. 1895.

[7] Cork Industrial Exhibition, 1902, *The Official Catalogue*, Guy and Co., Cork, pp. 22–3, 27: www.corkpastandpresent.ie/history/corktradeexhibitions/uploadexhibition/croppedpdfs/1902_catalogue.pdf (accessed 9 Sep. 2017); Hodges, *Cork and County Cork in the Twentieth Century*, p. 292.

[8] *Irish Times*, 26 Aug. 1901.

[9] Henry Lawrence Tivy letter to *The Times*, 3 May 1902, quoted in Daniel Breen and Tom Spalding, *The Cork International Exhibition, 1902–1903: A Snapshot of Edwardian Cork* (Sallins, 2014), pp. 11–12.

During the 1890s, the *Cork Constitution* did not publish on Sundays. The leisure time available allowed for the foundation of a cricket club, and later a rugby club, by the staff in 1892.[10] Initially drawing its players exclusively from the newspaper's employees, the club opened up its membership in the 1895/6 season. Success came quickly: six years after its formation Cork Constitution Rugby Football Club had four players represent Munster and one make it on to the Irish team.[11] The team was bankrolled by Tivy, who also served as the club's first president. Several players enlisted during the Great War, among them former club captain Harry Magrath, who was killed at the Somme.[12] The Tivys were also members of the Cork County Club, which was described as an 'exclusive institution in the heart of the City of Cork. It is the Carlton Club of Munster'.[13] At a meeting of the Cork Land League in 1880, P.J. Lordan described H.L. Tivy as 'a member of the Town Council, an extensive butter trader, and a gentleman who, he believed, held an advanced position in the society of Freemasons'.[14] Tivy had joined the Cork No. 8 Lodge in 1873, while the *Irish Times*'s obituary of his son Henry Francis claimed that he, Henry Francis Tivy, was a member of the Masonic Order and of the Friendly Brothers of St Patrick.[15] They do not, however, appear to have been particularly active members and were not listed as Freemasons in the IRA's Cork No. 1 Brigade area summary of Freemasons, despite the inclusion of associates like Lord Bandon.[16]

Tivy acted as joint secretary of the reception committee on the visit of the prince and princess of Wales in 1885, as well as assisting in organising the

---

[10] Edmund Van Esbeck, *100 Years of Cork Constitution Football Club* (Cork, 1991), pp. 16–17. See also Donal O'Sullivan, *Sport in Cork: A History* (Dublin, 2010), p. 114.

[11] Paul Rouse, 'Sporting and Cultural Life in Cork in the Early 20th Century', 1911 Census website, National Archives of Ireland: http://census.nationalarchives.ie/ (accessed 1 Jun. 2018).

[12] O'Sullivan, *Sport in Cork*, p. 122; Van Esbeck, *100 Years of Cork Constitution Football Club*, p. 72.

[13] *Sydney Morning Herald*, 20 Jul. 1920.

[14] *Cork Examiner*, 5 Jul. 1880, p. 4.

[15] The Grand Lodge of Freemasons of Ireland, Dublin, Freemasons of Ireland Membership Registers, vol. 1: ancestry.co.uk (accessed 16 Oct. 2018); *Irish Times*, 13 Oct. 1960.

[16] 'Lists of Freemasons in Munster Area' (NLI, MS 31,200, Florrie O'Donoghue papers). In the roll, which lists Henry Lawrence Tivy as a member of the Masonic Order, the 'Observation' section is left blank, whereas the resignations or deaths of other members are recorded. It is noted, for example, that a merchant named Herbert Forrest resigned from the organisation in 1928 and passed away in 1943. H.L. Tivy died in 1929. See The Grand Lodge of Freemasons of Ireland, Dublin, Freemasons of Ireland Membership Registers, vol. 1.

reception of the King Edward and Queen Alexandria in 1903.[17] The Diamond Jubilee of Queen Victoria was widely celebrated in 1897, when 'Union Jacks flew from the principal buildings [in Dublin], including the Bank of Ireland, Trinity College and Guinness's Brewery'.[18] In Cork, Tivy displayed a 'non-party flag representing her Majesty', which he claims resulted in his home being 'completely smashed' and his life 'repeatedly threatened'.[19]

Tivy was later lampooned as 'Miley', the editor of the *Ballybawn Blazer*, in Susanne Day's satirical novel *The Amazing Philanthropists*. As well as mirroring Tivy physically, the editor of Ballybawn's unionist newspaper shares Tivy's opposition to the suffrage movement. Miley, discussing the suffragettes, states that 'shocking immorality among women is becoming a marked feature of the movement'; 'they are freaks, degenerates, "unsexed females", utterly unworthy of the confidence and respect of any decent community. The presence of even one upon a public Board would be an unmixed calamity'.[20] Indeed, comments such as 'Contrary to common belief, militant Suffragettes retain some feminine vanity' were not uncommon in Tivy's papers, with columns and articles in the *Cork Weekly News* also criticising drinking amongst separation women.[21] Lester Martin, the novel's protagonist, also claims that Miley yearned for a knighthood. Tivy may well have shared this ambition, given the references to knighthoods awarded to Belfast newspaper proprietors made by his son Henry Francis Tivy in his Irish Grants Committee application (discussed below). Susanne R. Day had family connections with Tivy: her father, the noted antiquarian Robert Day, proposed his membership of the Royal Society of Antiquaries of Ireland in 1891, and Susanne R. Day served on a public committee with Mrs Eleanor Florence Tivy in 1911.[22]

The Amazing Philanthropists may not have been Tivy's only literary appearance of note. I believe the character 'Dick Tivy', who appears in the Hades episode of *Ulysses*, is based on H.L. Tivy, rather than Richard Tivy of Summerhill in Cork city, secretary of Murphy's brewery and antique enthusiast, as has been suggested elsewhere.[23] In 1911, there were just 29 Tivys

[17] Hodges, *Cork and County Cork in the Twentieth Century*, p. 292.
[18] Jack White, *Minority Report: The Protestant Community in the Irish Republic* (Dublin, 1975), p. 53.
[19] H.L. Tivy to Nathan, 10 Apr. 1916 (Oxford, Bodleian Library, Weston Library Special Collections, MS Nathan 478, fos 214–15).
[20] Susanne R. Day, *The Amazing Philanthropists: Being Extracts from the Letters of Lester Martin, P.L.G.* (London, 1916), pp. 18–19.
[21] *Cork Weekly News*, 3 Jan. 1914; 12 Feb. 1916.
[22] *The Journal of the Royal Society of Antiquaries of Ireland*, 5th series, 1/8 (1891), p. 633; *Cork Examiner*, 28 Nov. 1911.
[23] James Joyce, *Ulysses* (Penguin Books edn, London, 2000), pp. 128–9; Vivien Igoe, *The Real People of Joyce's* Ulysses*: A Biographical Guide* (Dublin, 2016), p. 291; John

in the country, of whom Henry Lawrence was the most prominent. Henry Lawrence, who was born within a year of Joyce's Cork-resident father (though there is no evidence they were personally acquainted),[24] was closely associated with the game of rugby, while Cork Park served as one of the first homes of rugby in the city. In Joyce's novel, 'Dick Tivy' appears at the park during the Cork Races (John Stanislaus Joyce was a sporting enthusiast).[25] Dick Tivy is described as having 'nothing between his head and heaven', which may be a quip at the expense of the bald H.L. Tivy. As noted by Vivien Igoe, 'When portraying the people in *Ulysses*, Joyce manipulates and abuses some of them. He treats some with contempt, some satirically, others in a disrespectful fashion, and others with affection'.[26] Tivy falls into the realm of satire. In 1882, as a member of Cork Corporation, Tivy had opposed the naming of the new bridge across the south channel of the River Lee as the 'Parnell Bridge'.[27] He was later threatened with legal action by Katharine O'Shea in 1891 unless 'absolutely false and libellous' comments made in the *Cork Constitution* were retracted.[28] Given Joyce's admiration for Parnell, he may have wished to satirise Tivy, who played a managerial role with the Dublin *Daily Express* in 1902, around the time Joyce began supplying literary reviews to the paper.[29] The *Express* is referred to as a 'rag' in Joyce's short story 'The Dead'.[30] Lord Ardilaun, owner of the *Daily Express* at this time, is said in *Ulysses* to 'change his shirt four times a day … Skin breeds lice or vermin'.[31] Comparatively, Tivy appears

Wyse Jackson and Peter Costello, *John Stanislaus Joyce: The Voluminous Life and Genius of James Joyce's Father* (London, 1997), p. 54; *Cork Examiner*, 9 Jul. 1928. Jackson and Costello argue that one of Richard Tivy's relations, William J. Tivy, studied at what was then Queen's College Cork at the same time as John Stanislaus Joyce.

[24] Jackson and Costello, *John Stanislaus Joyce*, pp. 24–30, 45–66.

[25] Jackson and Costello, *John Stanislaus Joyce*, pp. 47, 55, 63.

[26] Igoe, *The Real People of Joyce's* Ulysses, p. 6.

[27] *Cork Examiner*, 2 Aug. 1882. The bridge was nevertheless named Parnell Bridge and opened in November 1882. This bridge was replaced in 1971, but still carries the name Parnell.

[28] Letter from Katherine O'Shea to Henry Lawrence Tivy, dated 15 Apr. 1891 (Cork Public Museum [CPM], L1960:342, E.B. Tivy papers).

[29] Agreement between Lord Ardilaun and H.L. Tivy, 28 Jan. 1902 (TCD, MS 5217, Misc. Box 21). Tivy's contract was for three years; there is no evidence that he stayed on longer than this before purchasing the paper in 1915. For Joyce supplying reviews, see Richard Ellmann, *James Joyce* (New York, 1959), pp. 112, 116, 131, 144.

[30] James Joyce, 'The Dead', in *Dubliners* (Oxford University Press edn., Oxford, 2008), p. 148. Ellmann acknowledges that Joyce was probably teased by nationalist contemporaries for writing for the 'pro-English' *Express*. See Ellmann, *James Joyce*, pp. 255–6.

[31] Joyce, *Ulysses*, p. 97.

to have got off lightly. Tivy's connection to the *Daily Express* was reinforced when he purchased both that paper and the *Evening Mail* in 1915, both being edited by the conservative Henry Doig.[32] By this stage, Tivy's business and newspaper holdings were extensive. Having succeeded in the butter trade, he diversified into newspapers and wholesaling. From the 1880s onwards, Tivy developed the wholesaling newspaper and periodical business, News & Co., which enjoyed a monopoly in West Cork for a number of years.[33]

Tivy's concerns were his newspapers. R.B. McDowell notes that the *Cork Constitution* was 'circulated amongst the nobility, the gentry, landed proprietors and mercantile classes, [and] forcefully advocated the unionist cause in the south'.[34] The *Cork Constitution*'s office stationery contained a map that graphically laid out the *Constitution*'s area of circulation, claiming that it covered the province of Munster in its entirety, moving north of Limerick city into Clare, without penetrating the province of Connacht. It moved across the midlands and east, taking in Offaly, Laois, Kilkenny, Carlow, and Kildare, as far east as Rosslare, but bypassing much of Wexford, Wicklow, and South Dublin.[35] The available evidence relating to circulation is fragmentary and is hindered by the tendency of papers to exaggerate their circulation. For example, the *West Cork People*, a local paper produced in Clonakilty but printed by News & Co. speculatively claimed to have a circulation of 200,000. I estimate the *Constitution*'s circulation at less than 11,428 copies sold per day, based on the available data.[36] While it is doubtful that the paper enjoyed as substantial a circulation as it claimed, with his purchase of the Dublin *Daily Express* and the *Evening Mail* in 1915, Tivy would enter the competitive Dublin market.

In Limerick, the *Constitution* competed with the *Limerick Chronicle*, Munster's second largest loyalist paper. Appearing three times a week, as opposed to the daily *Constitution*, the *Chronicle* often adopted an apolitical approach to the leading issues of the day, or an unwillingness directly to engage with heated ones. While reporting on the surrender of the anti-Treaty garrison in the Four Courts in Dublin during the summer of 1922, for instance, the *Limerick Chronicle* editorialised about the forthcoming debate in the House

---

[32] *Irish Times*, 11 Apr. 1931, obituary of Mr Henry Stuart Doig; Douglas Gageby, *The Last Secretary General: Seán Lester and the League of Nations* (Dublin, 1999), p. 12; Patrick Maume, 'The *Dublin Evening Mail* and Pro-landlord Conservatism in the Age of Gladstone and Parnell', *Irish Historical Studies*, 37/148 (2011), p. 565.

[33] L.M. Cullen, *Eason & Son: A History* (Dublin, 1989), pp. 71, 319, 352–3, 396.

[34] McDowell, *Crisis and Decline*, p. 34.

[35] John Topping of the *Cork Constitution* to Lord Decies, Press Censor, 28 Dec. 1916 (NAI, Censorship Records [White], No. 3).

[36] See Alan McCarthy, 'Press, Politics and Revolution: Newspapers and Journalism in Cork City and County, 1910–1923', PhD thesis, University College Cork, 2018, Appendix B (pp. 280–1).

of Commons concerning the Canadian cattle embargo.[37] This contrasted with the pugnacious editorials of the *Constitution*, which one-time assistant press censor R.H. Shaw viewed as the voice 'of the Southern Unionist Die-Hards'.[38]

War and Politics

Tivy aligned himself with the 'no surrender' faction of southern Irish unionism and remained a vociferous opponent of any form of self-government for Ireland.[39] In 1887, he was listed as attending a meeting in the South Mall Assembly Rooms for individuals eager 'to show their interest in the Unionist cause' and, according to the *Skibbereen Eagle*, to give 'two English Tory members of parliament the opportunity of giving vent to their hatred of the Nationalist and Home Rule movement in this country'.[40] In 1900, Tivy wrote to Arthur Balfour urging the formation of a volunteer force, owing to disloyalty in the south and west of Ireland. Balfour disagreed with this proposal, believing the extent of disloyalty to be exaggerated.[41] Others found Tivy's views alarmist. Commenting on Tivy's statements concerning the visit of a Canadian regiment to Cork in 1917, one member of the military stationed at Victoria Barracks wrote to press censor Lord Decies stating that 'I don't know what you think of his views as therein expressed, but my humble opinion is that the only place for such "rot" is in the fire', before continuing that Tivy 'is always looking around every corner and at the back of everything for trouble'.[42] Tivy's advice, indeed, was not always warmly received. In March 1916, Sir Matthew Nathan wrote to General Lovick Friend, stating that Tivy 'has fairly sound judgement though it is warped by strong political bias'.[43]

Tivy's papers, naturally, devoted much coverage to the Great War. Tivy's son George served with the Royal Garrison Artillery, while another son,

---

[37] *Limerick Chronicle*, 1 Jul. 1922, p. 2. This aspect of the *Chronicle*'s reporting is examined in Siobhán Jones, 'Southern Irish Unionism', PhD thesis, University College Cork, 2005, p. 251.

[38] R.H. Shaw to W.G.S. Adams, 26 Mar. 1918 (UK Parliamentary Archives, LG/F/65/4/12). It should be noted that Shaw saw the influence of southern Unionists as being largely negligible.

[39] John Borgonovo, *The Dynamics of War and Revolution: Cork City, 1916–1918* (Cork, 2013), p. 16.

[40] *Skibbereen Eagle*, 19 Nov. 1887.

[41] Arthur Balfour to H.L. Tivy, 5 Feb. 1900 (CPM, L1960:337, Tivy papers).

[42] Letter received by Lord Decies, 25 Jan. 1917 (NAI, PC 7033/722/13/3).

[43] Nathan to Friend, 30 Mar. 1916 (Bodleian Library, MS Nathan 478, fo. 206). Also cited in Charles Townshend, *Easter 1916: The Irish Rebellion* (London, 2006), pp. 145–6.

Robert, was an airman. Their older brother Cecil, a physician, served with the Field Ambulance and Royal Army Medical Corps, and their sister Eleanor Brianne was a nurse with the Territorial Force.[44] It was later reported that one of the brothers, probably George, had been seriously wounded at Ypres.[45] In keeping with wartime trends concerning the organisation of auxiliary committees formed by middle- and upper-class women, Eleanor Florence Tivy and her daughter Eleanor Brianne were involved in the Cork Emergency Committee, which organised volunteers for nursing and medical aid.[46]

Another marked feature of Tivy's newspapers was their willingness to highlight, and criticise, advanced nationalist politics. While under-secretary for Ireland Sir Matthew Nathan resented this tendency, arguing that Tivy was merely serving to advertise the republican cause, Tivy himself maintained that 'nothing kills so much in Ireland as ridicule'.[47] Reflecting on the sitting of the First Dáil in January 1919, for example, the *Cork Constitution* reported that 'a feature of the proceedings was that they were in the main conducted in Irish, though probably three-parts of the ticket-holders in the hall, and very probably a number of Sinn Fein leaders on the platform, knew as little of the language as they do of Sanskrit'.[48]

In 1915, Tivy warned under-secretary Nathan that 'under no circumstances should the authorities permit a public funeral of O'Donovan Rossa in either Dublin or Cork at the present time as much mischief must result from such a demonstration'.[49] Tivy entered into a fairly regular correspondence with Nathan, offering his opinion on issues affecting Ireland. While Tivy could never be accused of being reluctant to share his opinions in the pages of his newspapers (even adopting noms de plume), his correspondence with Nathan provides an insight into his thinking.[50] During the summer of 1915, for example, he assured the under-secretary that 'any pro-German feeling here is confined

---

[44] Captain George Lucius William Tivy service record (TNA, WO 339/29547); Robert Edward Forrest Tivy service record (TNA, AIR 79/1379/153638); Medal card of Cecil Brian Forsayed Tivy (TNA, WO 372/20/42503); Eleanor Tivy nursing service record (TNA, WO 399/15073).

[45] *Sunday Independent*, 30 Jun. 1929; *Cork Examiner*, 15 Aug. 1917.

[46] Catriona Clear, 'Fewer Ladies, More Women', in John Horne (ed.), *Our War: Ireland and the Great War* (Dublin, 2008), p. 163; Donal Ó Drisceoil and Diarmuid Ó Drisceoil, *Beamish & Crawford: The History of an Irish Brewery* (Cork, 2015), p. 254; *Cork Examiner*, 12 Aug. 1914. See also Chapter 6.

[47] H.L. Tivy to Nathan, 29 Mar. 1916, p. 2 (Bodleian Library, MS Nathan 478, fo. 204). See MS Nathan 478, fos 199, 200, 203, 211, 212, 213, 214, 215 for general discussion and debate.

[48] *Cork Constitution*, 22 Jan. 1919.

[49] H.L. Tivy to Nathan, 10 Jul. 1916 (Bodleian Library, MS Nathan 461, fo. 211).

[50] See *Cork Constitution*, 2 Jan. 1919 and Borgonovo, *Dynamics of War and Revolution*, p. 110 for Tivy's adoption of pseudonyms.

to a very limited number', before claiming 'if the Irish government now saw fit to deal purposefully and even severely with enemy sympathizers it will be found that such a policy will be generally most popular among those who limit their policy to being opposed to British rule … severe steps should be taken to deal with all who are suspected of sympathy with the enemy'.[51]

Unsurprisingly, Tivy reacted to the Easter Rising with indignation.[52] The *Cork Constitution* and *Weekly News* had the most vitriolic reaction to the Rising among the Cork papers, dismissing the insurgents as 'wreckers' and the Proclamation of the Irish Republic as 'arrant nonsense'. The premises of the Dublin *Daily Express* and its sister paper the *Evening Mail*, only recently purchased by Tivy, were occupied by the rebels.[53] In the aftermath of the Rising, Tivy discouraged his employee Seán Lester from associating 'among these Blythes, Connollys and Becks and Hobsons. Some of these, I believe, are now in a sphere of high temperature [Lester's biographer Douglas Gageby presumed this was a reference to hell] and considering what was done to the office, I hope some of the rest will follow them'.[54] (Unknown to Tivy, Lester, later the last secretary general of the League of Nations, was an active republican.) Tivy had earlier bemoaned the fact that Ireland had been excluded from the Compulsory Service bill 'as the Sinn Feiners would have made excellent soldiers'. He continued that 'this would have been the best thing for the future of the country'.[55] It is tempting to view this claim in a 'cannon fodder' context; that by conscripting Irish Volunteers they would be slaughtered at the Front, thereby removing them as a domestic problem. It is doubtful, however, that Tivy would have possessed such a reductive view of the Great War given the service of his own children. It is possible that Tivy's comments were sincere, that the Irish Volunteers would have made good soldiers, but in so arguing Tivy was applying a negative stereotype of Irishmen as a martial race, undermining the intellectual and ideological commitment of the Volunteers to the cause of separatism.[56] Nathan noted that during their meeting Tivy 'talked about English people not understanding Ireland'.

---

[51] H.L. Tivy to Nathan, 1 Jun. 1915, pp. 1–2 (Bodleian Library, MS Nathan 461, fo. 209).

[52] H.L. Tivy to Nathan, 29 Mar. 1916 (Bodleian Library, MS Nathan 478, fo. 205).

[53] Patrick Maume, 'Maunsell, James Poole', in James McGuire and James Quinn (eds), *Dictionary of Irish Biography* (Cambridge, 2014): http://dib.cambridge.org/viewReadPage.do?articleId=a9561; Property Losses (Ireland) Committee, 1916, claim of James Francis Walshe (NAI, PLIC/1/5644).

[54] Gageby, *The Last Secretary General*, pp. 8–9.

[55] Interview with Lord Midleton and Mr Tivy, 18 Jan. 1916 (Bodleian Library, MS Nathan 478).

[56] For more on the 'fighting Irish' trope, see Keith Jeffery, *Ireland and the Great War* (Cambridge, 2000), pp. 14, 42–3.

Frustrated by the tendency to view all Irishmen and women as one after the uprising, Tivy lamented that 'They [Dublin Castle] were inclined to class me as a Sinn Féiner whereas the fact is that I should be glad to do my bit in kicking the carcass of every Sinn Féiner and other rebel in Ireland into the Liffey'.[57]

Advanced nationalists in turn had little time for Tivy and his papers. On the subject of the withdrawal of educational grants to Ireland, the future Sinn Féin TD Liam de Róiste recorded that 'What is perhaps most remarkable is that, by the very necessity of the case, the most bigoted pro-English Irishman – even the editor of the *Cork Constitution* itself – is forced to think and speak of Ireland as a national entity separate from England in this matter'.[58] Tivy did regularly emphasise that the constituent parts of the United Kingdom were not homogeneous, if not in the way that nationalists did. Whilst supporting the Empire, he frequently highlighted issues specifically affecting Ireland. In 1903, for example, he used a speech to the Press Association to suggest that an Irish representative should be appointed to the organisation's committee or consultative board.[59]

In March 1918, as the Irish Convention drew to a close, Tivy wrote to Sir Edward Carson to reassure him of his papers' opposition to the coercion of Ulster and support for his position. Referencing hostility by southern Unionists towards Ulster Unionists, Tivy stated that 'although I have no doubt such a feeling prevails among some it is far from being extensively held by Southern Unionists and their Press'.[60] Tivy believed that 'a Parliament in College Green would do nothing to cure the evils in Ireland', and throughout this period his papers adopted an inflexible pro-Union position.[61] In 1918, the *Constitution* and *Daily Express* promoted the 'Call to Unionists' campaign, which attempted to obstruct the passage of Home Rule. In a similar manner, the *Daily Express* and *Evening Mail* acknowledged in the run-up to the 1918 General Election that the Irish Party could expect to be routed: 'The Nationalist Party cannot be surprised. It has lived so long on catch-words on the empty formula of Home Rule – though what Home Rule was intended to do nobody was ever told'. Even less palatable was Sinn Féin, 'with its policy of sulk and abstention from Parliament, with its crazy dream of an Irish Republic'.[62] Encouraging voters to elect Dublin Unionist candidates, the *Express* warned its readers

---

[57] Gageby, *The Last Secretary General*, pp. 10–11.
[58] De Róliste diaries, Dec. 1915–Apr. 1916, pp. 55–6 (Cork City and County Archives [CCCA], U271/A/19).
[59] Report of Press Association AGM, 1903, quoted in James T. O'Donnell, 'International News Supply in Ireland, c.1899–1949', PhD thesis, NUI Galway, 2014, p. 47.
[60] H.L. Tivy to Edward Carson, 5 Mar. 1918 (PRONI, D1507/A/26/54).
[61] Interview with Lord Midleton and Mr Tivy (Bodleian Library, MS Nathan 478).
[62] *Daily Express*, 14 Dec. 1918.

that a vote for Sinn Féin 'may well bring about another rebellion'.[63] Not even the repeated endorsement of republican candidates by southern electors would compel Tivy to modify his editorial line: shortly after Sinn Féin had augmented their general election victory in 1918 with a strong showing in the 1920 municipal elections, the *Constitution* insisted that 'any tampering with the Legislative Union must bring in its train far worse evils than are now to be contended with'.[64]

The Revolutionary Years

During the revolutionary years the Tivy newspapers' attacks on Sinn Féin and reports on the behaviour of their supporters were criticised by the British authorities who viewed them as counterproductive. Following a confrontation between soldiers and recently released internees in Ballincollig in late 1916, the *Constitution* was censured for magnifying what the authorities considered to be 'a most trivial' affair. The military found Tivy to be wholly repentant and potentially in breach of Section 27 of the Defence of the Realm Act. Having been warned over its appearance in the *Constitution*, the article was reproduced in the *Cork Weekly News*, whether through editorial error or otherwise. Nevertheless, Tivy made a fine impression on the press censor, Lord Decies, who believed the matter should be dropped, noting that Tivy appeared 'anxious to assist us and distressed at having caused any trouble'.[65] The *Constitution* was censured once more in December 1916 for, in the authorities' estimation, exaggerating a report of a disturbance at the Palace Theatre during a performance of the play *An Irish Lead*, written by alleged clairvoyant Mrs Eleanor Standish Barry.[66] The police account maintained that the demonstration which took place was of a religious, as opposed to political, nature, and that 'The *Cork Constitution* reporter is out of touch with facts and appears to have lost his head absolutely in his report'.[67] Protests had been organised by priests owing to the play's depiction of a character's decision to join a convent stemming from romantic frustration rather than religious vocation, but the protests nevertheless appeared to have a republican flavour,

[63] *Daily Express*, 14 Dec. 1918.
[64] *Cork Constitution*, 22 Jan. 1920.
[65] Publication of seditious articles in the *Cork Constitution, Cork Examiner, Cork Free Press, Cork Weekly News, Midland Reporter,* and *Southern Star* (TNA, WO 35/69/6). See also Lord Decies to Henry Duke, 12 Jan. 1917 (TNA, WO 35/69/6).
[66] *Cork Examiner*, 2 Dec. 1916 and *Evening Echo*, 18 Dec. 1979.
[67] RIC County Inspector's Monthly Confidential Report, Cork East Riding, 11 Dec. 1916 (NAI, Censorship Records [White], Nos. 1–60, 3/722/13/3).

complete with ballad-singing and refusing to stand for 'God Save the King'
at the performance's conclusion.[68]

Whilst staying on the right side of censorship regulations thereafter, the
Constitution continued to criticise Sinn Féin, stating that 'To all law-abiding
people, and to all those who desire to see the Union maintained, there is
something of a menace in the attitude of the Party'.[69] The *Constitution* did
concede that 'The men controlling the Sinn Féin movement do not lack
courage. Imprisonment does not frighten them, and they are willing to face
death itself for the sake of their ideals ... These are very serious and grave
words for the law-abiding and the loyal'.[70] Such pronouncements frustrated
the authorities, who saw such statements as hardly 'conducive to good
government'.[71] Tivy had held this attitude for a number of years, ignoring
earlier requests from Sir Matthew Nathan to refrain from reporting on
republicans.[72] Tivy's contempt for Sinn Féin clouded his judgement, resulting
in the *Constitution* inadvertently giving free publicity to the republican
movement. He failed to appreciate that many did not consider the movement's
aims and objectives to be as absurd as he did.

With little clear evidence of widespread unionism among the southern or
Cork electorate, how did the Tivy press imagine Home Rule or independence
would be prevented? The *Express* and the *Mail* hoped for the return of coalition
government in 1918, declaring that 'Great Britain cannot consent to have a
hostile and independent country on her flank'. It appears that they imagined
that the coalition government would never allow Sinn Féin to take control.[73]
However, Sinn Féin's enormous victory in 1918 would make some form of Irish
self-government inevitable in the eyes of nationalists. In the aftermath of the
victory, elated republicans attempted to blow up the Boer War memorial on
Connaught Avenue, which Tivy helped build, damaging it in the process. The
following year, attempts were made to topple the monument over the cliff
upon which it stands.[74] The memorial is one of the last remaining loyalist
monuments in the city.

The *Constitution* survived the War of Independence largely unscathed.
Both the *Skibbereen Eagle*, which had earlier supported the conciliatory
nationalist All-for-Ireland League, and the Redmondite *Cork Examiner* had
their presses wrecked by the IRA. Tivy probably should have counted himself

---

[68] Borgonovo, *The Dynamics of War and Revolution*, pp. 120–2.

[69] *Cork Constitution*, 4 Jan. 1919.

[70] *Cork Constitution*, 16 Jan. 1919.

[71] RIC County Inspector's Monthly Confidential Report, Cork East Riding, Oct. 1920
(TNA, CO 904/113).

[72] H.L. Tivy to Nathan, 29 Mar. 1916 (Bodleian Library, MS Nathan 478, fo. 204).

[73] *Daily Express*, 16 Dec. 1918.

[74] *Cork Constitution*, 2 Jan. 1919; Borgonovo, *Dynamics of War and Revolution*, p. 110.

lucky: the *Constitution* advocated the use of official reprisals as a deterrent to the IRA.[75] Tivy was, however, ordered to leave the country by republicans, an order which he ignored.[76] In November 1920, he received a letter telling him to 'prepare for – (DEATH) for you will shortly meet the end'. The letter stated that he was an enemy 'to Ireland & its people' and that his 'foul carcass' would 'go down unwept, unhonoured & unsung'. The threat made reference to Tivy as a 'planter', as well as an 'alien', despite his family's deep roots in Cork.[77] The RIC County Inspector for Cork's East Riding attributed this intimidation to Tivy's description 'of the murder of Mr Alan Bell [a resident magistrate involved in intelligence work] as a "Brutal Deed by Human Brutes"'.[78]

The *Daily Express* shut its doors ten days before the declaration of a Truce that brought a halt to the fighting between the IRA and Crown forces. It was only at the last possible moment that the *Express* softened its Unionist stance: weeks before its closure the paper argued that 'any road that might lead to peace would be well worth exploring'.[79] With the declaration of the Truce on 11 July 1921, Tivy and the *Constitution* found themselves supporting the Anglo-Irish Treaty, particularly after the outbreak of civil war. The *Constitution* advocated the sternest measures against republicans who refused to support the Treaty: 'If the judgement of the electors is to be flouted and the will of the people is to be turned down, there must be an end of democratic government and the substitution thereafter of autocratic rule'.[80] Belatedly, Tivy and the *Cork Constitution* came to see the inevitability of Irish self-government and hoped that unionists would play a key role in it. The *Constitution* welcomed speeches such as that of the Lord Chancellor of England, Lord Birkenhead, in which he stated: 'There could be no better future for Southern Ireland, and for Ireland as a whole than that Unionists of Southern Ireland should be willing to contribute their experience and strength to the Provisional Government'.[81] Having previously refused to countenance any parliament in Dublin, the hardline unionist Tivy and his paper finally adopted a more pragmatic position.

Tivy's opposition to the Civil War reflected the war weariness of the commercial class, which was mirrored by both the nationalist and unionist

---

[75] McDowell, *Crisis and Decline*, pp. 101–2; *Cork Constitution*, 25 Nov. 1920.

[76] Ian Kenneally, *The Paper Wall: Newspapers and Propaganda in Ireland, 1919–21* (Cork, 2008), pp. 66–7. See also John Borgonovo, *Spies, Informers and the 'Anti-Sinn Féin Society'* (Dublin, 2007), p. 93.

[77] Death threat sent to H.L. Tivy, 24 Nov. 1920, p. 2 (CPM, L1960: 344).

[78] RIC County Inspector's Monthly Confidential Report, Cork East Riding, Mar. 1920 (TNA, CO 904/148). For the killing of Bell, see T. Ryle Dwyer, *Michael Collins: The Man Who Won the War* (Cork, 2009), pp. 149–51.

[79] *Daily Express*, 24 May 1921.

[80] *Cork Constitution*, 2 Jan. 1922.

[81] *Cork Weekly News*, 22 Jul. 1922.

press, with newspapers such as the unionist *Limerick Chronicle* and nationalist journals like the *Cork Examiner, Freeman's Journal,* and *Irish Independent* all supporting the Treaty.[82] During the Civil War, the offices of both the *Cork Examiner* and Tivy's *Cork Constitution* were occupied by anti-Treatyite censors following the rise of the so-called 'Munster Republic', when those opposed to the Treaty found themselves in control of much of the south of Ireland. The censorship imposed by the anti-Treatyites was as swift as it was rigid, with references to 'Irregulars' being replaced with references to 'Republicans' over the course of a single weekend.[83] In her diaries, the Anglo-Irish writer Edith Somerville claimed on several occasions that the *Cork Constitution* at this time was 'bossed' and censored by 'the egregious Mary McSweeney [*sic*]'.[84] Although MacSwiney's alleged ascendancy over the *Constitution* is not referred to by her biographer, republican censorship of the paper was denounced at the Irish Labour and Trade Union Congress.[85] Rather than operate as an anti-Treaty mouthpiece, Tivy ceased publication in July. Weeks later, following the amphibious landing of Free State troops in Cork, anti-Treatyites evacuated the city. In a 'scorched earth' policy of sorts, they attacked and destroyed the offices of the *Examiner* and now-vacant *Constitution*, ensuring that they could not resume their written attacks on the anti-Treaty movement. These raids were commented upon adversely by Tivy's other paper, the *Evening Mail*, which reported that 'the Irregulars are behaving in Cork in the face of defeat, with the same indifference to the public welfare that has characterized their actions in other parts of the country from which they have been driven'.[86] Tivy's new-found flexibility was evident in an impassioned final editorial before shutting the doors of the *Constitution*. In it, he had outlined his hope for 'some formula under which Irishmen of every class can dwell together in unity'.[87]

[82] See, for example, *Limerick Chronicle*, 27 Jul. 1922.

[83] See the *Cork Constitution*, 1 Jul., 3 Jul. 1922. For more on Tivy, the *Constitution*, and the Civil War, see Alan McCarthy, 'The Story Behind the Storytellers: Cork Newspapermen during the Irish Revolutionary Period', in Ian Kenneally and James T. O'Donnell, *The Irish Regional Press: Revival, Revolution and Republic* (Dublin, 2018), pp. 86–8.

[84] Diaries of Edith Somerville, 7 Jul., 10 Jul., and 13 Jul. 1922 (Queen's University Belfast Special Collections and Archives, MS17/874/1).

[85] Charlotte H. Fallon, *Soul of Fire: A Biography of Mary MacSwiney* (Cork and Dublin, 1986), pp. 75–112; de Róiste diaries, 21 Jul. 1922 (CCCA, U271/A/45); *Report of the Twenty-Eighth Annual Meeting of the Irish Labour and Trade Union Congress*, pp. 110–14.

[86] *Evening Mail*, 11 Aug. 1922.

[87] *Cork Constitution*, 22 Jul. 1922.

Post-Revolution

In the aftermath of the Civil War, the Tivy family sought to take advantage of the various compensation schemes that emerged from 1923. The Irish Free State Damage to Property (Compensation) Act 1923 provided compensation to people and property injured between 21 January 1919 and 11 July 1921. This initiative was later expanded to include the post-Truce period, up to the end of the Civil War, in collaboration with the British Wood-Renton Commission. The Tivys also applied to the second Irish Grants Committee, funded by the British Treasury, which focused on redress for southern Irish loyalists for losses sustained between 11 July 1921 and 12 May 1923 owing to allegiance to the United Kingdom.[88] The Tivy family were extremely disappointed by the Free State's award of £15,000 under the Criminal Injuries Act, which was later reduced to £7,500 in light of the reduction of funds necessitated by the introduction of the Damage to Property Act.[89] Of this, £2,000 was paid in cash and the remainder in 'compensation' stock, which recipients claimed was not worth very much. The *Constitution* originally requested £23,000 from the county court, with £15,000 being decreed for damage to machinery. The paper's claim for £8,000 for disruption to circulation was dismissed on the grounds that by closing the paper himself (despite the risk to his own life and that of his sons) Tivy was responsible for disrupting his own paper's circulation.[90] Eventually, the British government-funded Irish Grants Committee awarded the Tivys what amounted to a year's salary to George and Henry Francis, £150 and £221 respectively. Henry Lawrence Tivy was given £800, double his annual salary. This was still far less than they had hoped to receive.[91] Henry Francis

---

[88] The initial scheme had been under-funded and over-subscribed. See Niamh Brennan, 'A Political Minefield: Southern Loyalists, the Irish Grants Committee and the British Government, 1922–31', *Irish Historical Studies*, 30/119 (1997), pp. 410–12, 415–16, 419.

[89] Henry Francis Tivy claim on behalf of the *Cork Constitution* (TNA, CO 762/8/3). The *Constitution*'s application was submitted via the Southern Irish Loyalists Relief Association, a London-based lobby group. The application claimed they accepted what they considered to be an insufficient advance owing to pressure from creditors and the sense from the committee that they could 'take it or leave it'.

[90] Henry Francis Tivy claim on behalf of the *Cork Constitution* (TNA, CO 762/8/3).

[91] Henry Francis Tivy claim (TNA, CO 762/145/8), G.L.W. Tivy claim (TNA, CO 762/145/10), and Henry Lawrence Tivy claim (TNA, CO 762/145/9). The family also held extensive shares in the paper. Henry Francis had £700 in ordinary shares, while George had £500. Henry Lawrence held £4,240 in ordinary shares and £2,525 in preference shares. In today's terms these salaries would have a relative income value of approximately £47,100, £69,390, and £125,600. Calculated using www.measuringworth.com/calculators/ppoweruk/ (accessed 17 Feb. 2019).

handled the Tivy family applications due to his father's feeble condition, 'a result of the mental and physical upset caused by the destruction of his property'. Frustrated by the committee's seemingly endless deliberation, Henry Francis complained bitterly to committee secretary Major Reid Jamieson:

> The proprietors of the nationalist newspaper in Cork have made large fortunes while those of the loyalist paper are out of business and begging for help! In Belfast – where loyalty has always been highly profitable – the proprietors of two newspapers have in recent years been rewarded with knighthoods for their services to the Crown which have incidentally brought them much treasure. In Cork the unhappy newspaper owner who risked (and lost) everything in an unequal struggle for the same principles received neither gratitude nor encouragement.[92]

Pronouncements such as these were not untypical in these applications owing to a reluctance within the British Treasury to contribute further funding to an increasingly expensive scheme, which encouraged applicants to exaggerate their claims to ensure they received a sizeable sum.[93] Henry Francis, for example, stated that he and his father were entirely dependent on his 'precarious' earnings as managing director of the Dublin *Evening Mail*, conveniently overlooking the existence of the family wholesale business, as the financial position of applicants was taken into consideration when awarding compensation.[94] Henry Francis wrote that his father 'is in a very feeble state of health, and the family are adverse to disturbing his mind by introducing the subject unless they have something definite and favourable to tell him'.[95] The family, despite their travails, remained wealthy; H.L. Tivy would eventually bequeath £23,000 in his will (over £1,300,000 in modern currency).[96] This may be attributable to the rapid growth of the family wholesale newsagent's business during and after the Civil War. This business was eventually sold to Eason's in 1958.[97] The family seemed determined to re-establish the *Cork Constitution*, with the help of new shareholders. Prior to the outbreak of the Civil War in May 1922, Henry Francis Tivy wrote to Walter Hume Long, former chief secretary of Ireland, to 'venture to ask your advice now upon

---

[92] Henry Francis Tivy to Major Reid Jamieson, 25 Jan. 1927 (TNA, CO 762/8/4).

[93] See Brennan, 'A Political Minefield', pp. 410–12, 415–16, 419. See also Brian Hughes, *Defying the IRA? Intimidation, Coercion, and Communities during the Irish Revolution* (Liverpool, 2016), p. 101.

[94] Henry Francis Tivy claim (TNA, CO 762/145/8); Brennan, 'A Political Minefield', pp. 416–17.

[95] Henry Francis Tivy claim (TNA, CO 762/145/8).

[96] Will of Henry Lawrence Tivy (NAI, CS/HC/PO/4/82/8776).

[97] Cullen, *Eason & Son*, pp. 354, 374.

a matter of great importance as regards this journal and consequently to the loyalists of the South of Ireland whose interests have been upheld in it since the year 1822'. Tivy was seeking investors to the paper. He succeeded in procuring £500 from Sir George Younger and sought others willing to 'do their bit'.[98] While this investment drive would indicate falling sales, perhaps due to demobilisation of the British military in Cork along with a declining Protestant population,[99] the audited accounts of the newspaper provided to the Irish Grants Committee indicate a healthy turnover, with an average net profit of £1,935 in the three years preceding its closure, an improvement on the average £1,600 to £1,800 that the firm enjoyed in the 15 years prior to the Great War.[100]

However, failure to receive compensation speedily prevented the family from re-establishing their flagship newspaper. H.F. Tivy wrote that 'It is giving me great anxiety that the claim of the *Cork Constitution* company for compensation is going on so long and the position there is made worse by every day's delay. The chance of restarting and renewing the employment which we gave before the outrage will be entirely destroyed if we are delayed much longer in getting going'. He concluded by stating that 'Our position with a daily dwindling goodwill is a very cruel and unjust one'.[101] In January 1924, a year and a half after the raid, they noted: 'We have been placed in a most cruel position and our loss immeasurably increased, by the long delay which has already occurred in restoring us to a business earning condition'.[102] The month previously, they resolved that 'we must wind up the concern as best we can, and dismiss the nucleus staff we have been retaining at heavy expense'.[103] Henry Francis even feared that 'strings are being pulled (perhaps by friends of another paper)' to leave the matter unsettled.[104] In April 1924, Margaret Collins-O'Driscoll TD interceded on the part of the *Cork Constitution* to arrange a meeting between H.F. Tivy and Minister for Finance Ernest Blythe. Writing to Blythe, Collins-O'Driscoll stated that Tivy's 'firm has been always, even though they were pro-Britishers in the past, very good employers of labour and

---

[98] Henry F. Tivy to Lord Long, 15 May 1922 and Henry F. Tivy to Lord Long, 3 Jun. 1922 (Wiltshire and Swindon History Centre, Chippenham, Walter Long Hume papers, 947/377).

[99] See Chapter 3.

[100] H.F. Tivy claim (TNA, CO 762/8/3). For Cork Protestant decline, see Andy Bielenberg, 'Exodus: The Emigration of Southern Irish Protestants during the Irish War of Independence and the Civil War', *Past & Present*, 218 (2013), pp. 199–233. See also Chapter 3.

[101] H.F. Tivy to Ministry of Finance, 30 Jan. 1924 (NAI, FIN/COMP/2/27/71).

[102] H.F. Tivy, 23 Jan. 1924 (NAI, FIN/COMP/2/27/71).

[103] H.F. Tivy to Ministry of Finance, 4 Dec. 1923 (NAI, FIN/COMP/2/27/71).

[104] H.F. Tivy to Mr Driscoll, 25 Jun. 1924 (NAI, FIN/COMP/2/27/71).

it is to the detriment of labour in Cork that their claim is not settled'.[105] The *Constitution* had over 50 employees, working as reporters, linotype operators, clerks, and delivery drivers.[106] The paper certainly appears multi-denominational; it was owned and operated by Church of Ireland members in the Tivy family and William Ludgate, while Catholic journalists like D.D. Sheehan and Michael McSwiney had worked for the paper. W.H. Pyne, one of its leading linotype operators, was a Baptist.[107] This show of goodwill by Collins-O'Driscoll demonstrates the good faith in which Cumann na nGaedheal sought to act with regard to southern loyalists. However, the *Cork Constitution* would not make a return. It continued to print short, one-page registration issues containing titbits of international news before being wound up completely in 1924. Another major Tivy press asset was also lost during this period. The *Daily Express* argued in May 1921 that the successful implementation of a northern parliament would rule out the creation of a republic in the south.[108] The Tivys closed the paper on 1 July 1921, with a representative from the *Express* informing Basil Clarke a fortnight before its closure that it had been struggling to attract advertising support.[109] It was the loss of a noticeable southern loyalist voice.

Henry Lawrence Tivy died in 1929. In its obituary, the *Irish Times* noted that the destruction of his paper was 'a shock from which he never quite recovered'.[110] A motion of sympathy passed by Cork Harbour Board stated that 'during the past few days a gentleman had passed away, who had not been before the gaze of the public for some few years but, who took, for many years, a very prominent part in the public life of the city and neighbourhood, and in fact of the whole of Ireland'.[111] In fact, in 1924, Tivy served as vice-president of the Incorporated Church of Ireland Cork Young Men's Association, and he was re-elected president of Cork Constitution Rugby Football Club in October 1922, suggesting that he did not *completely* withdraw from public life.[112] It is noteworthy that membership of the Young Men's Association increased between 1923 and 1924, perhaps indicating a

---

[105] Margaret Collins-O'Driscoll to Ernest Blythe, 10 Apr. 1924 (NAI, FIN/COMP/2/27/71).

[106] *Cork Examiner*, 3 Jan. 1889; 15 Feb. 1907.

[107] 1911 census return, Michael McSwiney, Mashanaglass, and 1911 census return, William Henry Pyne: census.nationalarchives.ie (accessed 10 May 2018); *Cork Examiner*, 21 Sep. 1945; *Cork Examiner*, 2 May 1922.

[108] *Daily Express*, 24 May 1921.

[109] *Evening Mail* representative to Basil Clarke, 15 Jun. 1921 (TNA, CO 904/168/2).

[110] *Irish Times*, 6 Jul. 1929.

[111] *Cork Examiner*, 4 Jul. 1929.

[112] Minutes of Cork Constitution RFC AGM, 30 Sep. 1922 (CCCA, SP/CC/5). Furthermore, Van Esbeck writes that despite his patronage of the rugby club

certain degree of ring-fencing within the Protestant community during a period of high migration.[113]

As indicated by the extensive burnings of copies of newspapers throughout the revolutionary period, newspapers as material objects were clearly an important political signifier. Consequently, the disappearance of the *Cork Constitution* from Cork's streets and trams may have exacerbated a sense of isolation within the southern loyalist community. With the closure of the *Constitution* and *Express*, the Tivy family seems to have been content to focus on the *Evening Mail* and a growing wholesale newsagent's business. It may be useful to consider the potential direction the *Constitution* could have taken had it returned to print. With regard to the closure of a number of unionist newspapers, Andy Bielenberg tells us that 'While Southern unionism had become politically redundant, the fall in readership through population loss and revolutionary interference had also taken its toll. Protestant voices had certainly become less exclusive and more muted under the new regime'.[114] It is possible that the *Cork Constitution* could have survived and found a place in the new state; it was external factors that ultimately forced its closure. Had the family received sufficient and timely compensation for the damage done to the *Constitution*, the re-established newspaper may have advanced a conservative viewpoint and supported the Cumann na nGaedheal government. The newspaper enterprise, rather than opposing the new state, might well have adapted, in the same way as another ex-unionist paper, the *Irish Times*. Ian d'Alton states that 'This economically significant minority had a vital interest in how the new state approached taxation, business, education, the professions and the public service', and Tivy was no exception.[115]

As the Irish Free State had a Protestant population of over 200,000 into the 1920s, it is not inconceivable that the *Constitution* could have provided a viable alternative to the *Examiner*, which was often heavy on facts but light on opinion, for thousands of ex-unionists still living in the region.[116] Similarly, the paper could have potentially served as a southern counterpoint to the *Irish Times*. In Dublin, the *Evening Mail* continued, with the Tivy association with that paper ultimately lasting almost 60 years. Henry Francis remained in financial control until 1960, although editorially the paper moved away

---

Tivy did not play an active role 'in the running of the club'. See Edmund Van Esbeck, *125 Years of Cork Constitution Football Club* (Cork, 2017), p. 9.

[113] *Cork Examiner*, 9 Oct. 1924.

[114] Andy Bielenberg, 'Southern Irish Protestant Experiences of the Irish Revolution', in John Crowley, Donal Ó Drisceoil, Mike Murphy (eds), and John Borgonovo (associate ed.), *Atlas of the Irish Revolution* (Cork, 2017), p. 772.

[115] Ian d'Alton, 'A Protestant Paper for a Protestant People: The *Irish Times* and the Southern Irish Minority', *Irish Communications Review*, 12/1 (2010), p. 66.

[116] *Saorstát Éireann: Census of Population 1926*, vol. 3 (1929), Table 1A.

from loyalism towards, as Patrick Maume records, 'a Dublin-centred social-and-advertising paper with little comment on public affairs'.[117] The sale of the *Evening Mail* to the *Irish Times* in 1960 for £220,000 marked an interesting venture into the evening newspaper market by the latter. Mark O'Brien highlights how, with the *Evening Mail*'s circulation in seemingly perpetual decline, a point exacerbated by the arrival of the *Evening Press*,

> the board went ahead with the purchase of the paper from Henry Tivy, a move that was viewed by some as religious solidarity rather than commercial sense ... As one executive remembered, 'It was more, I think at the time, a decision made by Tivy's friends who were directors of the *Irish Times* ... I got the impression it wasn't a commercial decision at all'.

Unfortunately, the commercial decline of the *Evening Mail* passed the point of no return, and the paper folded two years after the sale. Mark O'Brien writes: 'As one reporter remembered, "the resultant drain on the company's finances dragged down their Sunday paper, the *Sunday Review*, and went close to destroying the *Irish Times* itself"'.[118] The *Evening Mail* ceased publication in 1962, with Henry Francis having died a year earlier.

Conclusion

Long after his death Henry Lawrence's children maintained links with their pre-revolutionary way of life. George Tivy, for example, remained a member of the Cork County Club up to his death in 1960.[119] H.L. Tivy also left his mark on his home place; the *Cork Examiner*'s obituary observed that 'Mr Tivy was looked upon as a broad-minded, tolerant citizen, who had the welfare of Cork sincerely at heart'.[120] Over the course of his life, Tivy made the lengthy political journey from conservative unionist to Free State sympathiser, ultimately suffering at the hands of both anti-Treaty censors and frugal compensation schemes. In the end, like many other loyalists, Tivy was forced to seek terms with the new state. In this regard his family's 'fall' mirrored the declining influence of the Protestant minority in general – the

---

[117] Maume, *'Dublin Evening Mail'*, pp. 551–2, 565.

[118] Mark O'Brien, *The Irish Times: A History* (Dublin, 2008), p. 161. Although not referring to the role of H.F. Tivy, Terence Brown similarly observes that the purchase of the *Evening Mail* was a risky venture as it struggled to compete with the *Evening Press* and *Evening Herald*. See Terence Brown, *The Irish Times: 150 Years of Influence* (London and New York, 2015), p. 234.

[119] *Irish Independent*, 7 Feb. 1961.

[120] *Cork Examiner*, 1 Sep. 1929.

Tivys were exceptional in that they were highly influential through their newspaper holdings, were wealthy, well-educated, and well-connected, but their reduced influence brought about by the regime change combined with a lack of marriages, which contributed to ongoing Protestant population decline, fits in to an extent with the picture formed of the southern loyalist experience more broadly.[121] Indeed, a lack of offspring amongst Henry Lawrence's sons meant the name died out in the 1960s. It was recorded in the obituary of Henry Francis that:

> He stated that he particularly desired and requested that no monument or memorial of any kind whatever be set up for him at any time 'as I consider that a man's own work should be his memorial, and if it has not been of a kind to cause him to be remembered he is better forgotten in a world which is already overburdened with memorials of unimportant people'.[122]

While his family's name may have slipped for a time from public consciousness, they nevertheless left an indelible mark on the civic, economic, philanthropic, sporting, and journalistic life of their native city.

---

[121] See, for example, McDowell, *Crisis and Decline*, pp. 163–7, 177; Bielenberg, 'Exodus', pp. 206–7, 224–6, 230–2; Tim Wilson, 'Ghost Provinces, Mislaid Minorities: The Experiences of Southern Ireland and Prussian Poland Compared, 1918–23', *Irish Studies in International Affairs*, 13 (2002), pp. 68–70, 78, 86.

[122] *Cork Examiner*, 13 May 1961.

CHAPTER X

A Beleaguered Community? Waterford Loyalists during the Revolution, 1912–1924

Pat McCarthy

During a debate on the Home Rule bill on 24 February 1914, Andrew Bonar Law, leader of the Conservative party, rose to speak, taking the growing tension in Ireland as his theme. He focused on one incident:

> Evidence reaches me every day, and I am sure it comes with even greater certainty to the Government, that in the rest of Ireland a feeling of unrest is growing up, and which is becoming daily more serious. An indication of it was given to me to-day by an hon. Friend of the action of constituents of the hon. Gentleman who leads the Nationalist party. There was to be a service of prayer of peace. Anywhere, except in Ireland, one would have thought that was harmless, but by those constituents of the hon. Member it was regarded as an offence, and steps were taken to mark those who were there, and to indicate them.[1]

A strongly nationalist newspaper, the *Waterford News*, had sent a reporter who stood outside the Protestant cathedral noting the names of those who attended a prayer service called by Dr Henry Stewart O'Hara, the local Church of Ireland bishop, to ask for divine intercession that 'the coming calamity of Home Rule be averted'. That list was printed in the next edition of the paper and caused grave disquiet within the local loyalist community.[2] The fact that the incident referred to happened in Waterford city, in the constituency of John Redmond, leader of the IPP, was hugely embarrassing to Redmond and to the Liberal government. It also highlighted that the divisions caused by the Home Rule proposal extended beyond the nine counties of Ulster. This essay describes the impact of the revolutionary period, *c.*1912–24, on the loyalist community of Waterford.

Like other counties in the south of Ireland, Waterford had a small but influential loyalist community, about 5 per cent of the population in 1911.

---

1 Hansard, HC, vol. 58 col. 1706 (24 Feb. 1914).
2 *Waterford News*, 20 Feb. 1914; Rosamond Jacob diaries, Feb. 1914 (NLI, MS 32,582).

Predominantly Protestant, it had major social and economic influence locally. It dominated the commercial and professional life of the city, and throughout the county the big houses and their demesnes demonstrated their wealth and power. Led by outspoken leaders like Dr Henry Stewart O'Hara (Church of Ireland bishop of Waterford, Lismore, Cashel and Emly since 1900), Sir William Goff Davis-Goff, the Duke of Devonshire, and Sir John Keane, the loyalist community in Waterford reacted strongly, as described below, to the introduction of the home rule bill in 1912.

A native of Derry, O'Hara resided in Waterford. Staunchly unionist and at times outspokenly anti-Catholic, he drew much criticism for one widely reported sermon. Preaching in Coleraine in 1902, shortly after his election as bishop, he described his new position: 'at present I am placed in a part of the country where our people are very poor, a part overshadowed by a dark cloud of ignorance and superstition, a part made miserable by wicked and violent agitation, and I know how our little flocks in their Protestant churches have to struggle for mere existence'.[3] His words caused considerable disquiet, especially in Waterford. Both Waterford Corporation and the Board of Guardians convened special meetings to condemn the remarks. Robert Dobbyn, a local Church of Ireland solicitor, noted in his diary how 'the old respectable Protestants are very indignant as they and the RCs are always good friends'.[4] By 1913, conscious that his church was 'but a feeble minority', O'Hara tended to be more guarded in his public utterances: 'all we can do in this part of Ireland is to put ourselves in God's hands and seek his guidance and help'.[5] He tended to his widely dispersed flock assiduously and R.B. McDowell credits him with 'fusing to an extraordinary degree fiery enthusiasm for his church with a shrewd grasp of practical detail'.[6]

The Protestant and loyalist community in the city dominated the professions and trade and included a small cohort of wealthy businessmen who lived in substantial residences, mainly on the Dunmore Road. Families such as the Jacobs, who were architects and solicitors, the Goffs, who had shipping, railway, and construction interests, and the Strangmans, who were brewers and bacon-curers, were the leaders of this community. Their comfortable and leisurely lifestyle has been captured evocatively in the unpublished diaries of Rosamond Jacob and Emily Ussher and in Annabel Davis-Goff's memoir *Walled Gardens*.[7] Sir William Goff, a major employer of labour through his

---

[3] *Munster Express* and *Waterford News*, 4, 11 May 1902.
[4] Robert Dobbyn diaries, May 1902 (Waterford City Library).
[5] Henry Stuart O'Hara, 'Address to synod of Waterford and Lismore', 27 Jun. 1913, *Church of Ireland Gazette*, 2 Jul. 1913.
[6] R.B. McDowell, *The Church of Ireland, 1869–1969* (London, 1975), p. 73.
[7] Rosamond Jacob diaries (NLI, MS 32,582); Emily Ussher, 'True Story of a

various enterprises, was the acknowledged leader and spokesman of this elite. He also served as south-east provincial grand master of the Freemasons and was master of the local lodge, the Royal Shamrock Masonic Lodge, No. 32.[8]

The Protestant community was not a unionist monolith. Rosamond and Tom Jacob, Quakers, had joined the Gaelic League and later Sinn Féin, but their nationalism was frowned upon within her family and the wider Quaker community.[9] In rural areas, the landlords and aristocracy in their castles and country houses were clustered along the valleys of the Suir, the Bride, and the Blackwater. Although the widening of franchise, disestablishment of the Church of Ireland, and land purchase had greatly reduced their power, their status and wealth were largely undiminished. Sir John Keane of Cappoquin House was the most visible and active of this class, often speaking publicly on farming issues.[10] His membership of Waterford County Council gave him a platform from which to air his views and to represent the interests of his class.[11] Keane's own views on Home Rule had evolved over the years. An ardent unionist in his youth, by 1912 he was confiding to his diary that 'I do not like Home Rule but see the complete failure of the union'.[12] A year later he wrote to the *Irish Times*: 'I am a strong believer in Home Rule'.[13] Politically he aligned himself with the All-for-Ireland League of William O'Brien.[14] He and the Usshers of Cappagh House were in a small minority within their peers. Committed to maintaining the Union, the large landowners viewed themselves as having most to lose in the event of revolutionary change. Most of them supported Victor Cavendish, the 9th Duke of Devonshire, occasional resident of Lismore Castle and owner of 27,483 acres in County Waterford, who was virulently opposed to any form of Irish nationalism. He led the opposition to the Home Rule bill in the House of Lords and campaigned vigorously

Revolution' (TCD, MS 9269); Annabel Davis-Goff, *Walled Gardens: Scenes from an Anglo-Irish Childhood* (London, 1991), pp. 14–20.

8   Thomas Fewer, *Waterford People: A Biographical Dictionary of Waterford* (Waterford, 1998), pp. 60–1.

9   Leann Lane, *Rosamond Jacob: Third Person Singular* (Dublin, 2010), pp. 31–2.

10 Fewer, *Waterford People*, p. 79.

11 Major H.C. Villiers-Stuart of Dromana had been elected to the first council in 1898. On his death, his son Captain Gerard Villiers-Stuart had been co-opted in his place. Sir John Keane was elected in 1911. Both men represented the unionist viewpoint on the council. Brian McNally and Maurice McHugh, *Chomhairle Chontae Phortláirge, 1899–1999* (Lismore, 1999), pp. 95–7.

12 Glascott J.R.M. Symes, *Sir John Keane and Cappoquin House in Time of War and Revolution* (Dublin, 2016), pp. 23–4.

13 *Irish Times*, 15 Feb. 1913.

14 Patrick Maume, 'Keane, Sir John', in James McGuire and James Quinn (eds), *Dictionary of Irish Biography* (Cambridge, 2009): http://dib.cambridge.org/viewReadPage.do?articleId=a4400.

outside parliament. There were two branches of the Irish Unionist Alliance in the county, West and East. Devonshire was president of the West Waterford branch; the Marquis of Waterford normally chaired the East Waterford branch. The 7th marquis died in 1911 and his son and heir was only eleven years old. Sir William Goff assumed the role in his place.

Local newspapers were extremely important in forming and reflecting local opinion. The *Waterford Standard* was the voice of the Protestant and commercial community. Robert Whalley, its owner and editor, took a strong unionist line politically and campaigned against high business rates and other taxes. The national weekly *Church of Ireland Gazette* also reflected the concerns of the Protestant community in its editorials, diocesan reports, and correspondence.

On 11 April 1912, Prime Minister H.H. Asquith introduced the third Home Rule bill to the House of Commons.[15] While Conservative and Unionist members shouted and jeered, John Redmond sat quietly reflecting on his moment of triumph. With support from both the Liberals and the Labour Party, and with the Lords' veto abolished, the passage of the bill could only be delayed for two years. The occasion was celebrated in nationalist circles throughout Ireland, but for the unionist community it generated fear and anger. With the support of Andrew Bonar Law, unionists prepared to resist the measure by all means possible both inside and outside parliament. The debate over Home Rule dominated politics in Ireland and in Britain for the next two years. Arising from the unique bond between Redmond and the nationalists of Waterford city and county,[16] his constituents demonstrated unwavering loyalty and support at every opportunity. However, the small unionist community in Waterford city and county opposed the bill and awaited its enactment with apprehension.

In the immediate aftermath of the introduction of the bill, Redmond was inundated with messages of congratulations from nationalist groups at home and abroad.[17] Waterford City Corporation, the County Council, and the district councils all moved congratulatory motions. The Corporation met in special session on 25 April to do so and also agreed that 'the mayor, high sheriff and members of the corporation would attend in state on Mr. Redmond to present the motion to him'.[18] Local branches of the United Irish League (UIL) launched collections for the Home Rule Fund, which was to be

---

[15] *Irish Independent*, 12 Apr. 1912.

[16] See Pat McCarthy, *The Redmonds and Waterford: A Political Dynasty 1891–1952* (Dublin, 2018), pp. 19–55.

[17] *Irish Independent*, 15 Apr. 1912; Denis Gwynn, *The Life of John Redmond* (London, 1932), p. 202; Dermot Meleady, *John Redmond the National Leader* (Dublin, 2013), p. 215.

[18] *Munster Express*, 27 Mar. 1912.

used to counter popular support for unionism in Britain.[19] Neither the local nor the national press carried significant analysis of the bill's contents, which gave only limited powers to the proposed Irish parliament.[20] While the Irish parliament would have jurisdiction over internal affairs, all matters pertaining to defence, foreign policy, and, initially, control of the RIC, and, most crucially, control over revenue, were to be reserved to Westminster.[21] However, the majority of nationalists accepted Redmond's assurance that this was 'a great and historic measure'.[22] The limitations on the powers of the proposed executive, which were a concern to advanced nationalists, did not mollify unionist opposition.[23] Local newspaper coverage in Waterford was cautiously optimistic. The *Munster Express* confidently predicted 'Bill sure to pass' and 'Unionists and the home rule bill – a hopeless battle'.[24] The *Waterford News* carried interviews with prominent local citizens including the mayor and the Catholic bishop and summed up their reactions: 'Mr. Redmond's acceptance of the government's measure reassures local nationalists and on his promise of acceptance they have pinned their faith'.[25] In his speech to the Commons on 11 April 1912 Redmond assured his listeners that this measure would satisfy nationalist demands and that it would be 'the death knell of separatist sentiment in Ireland'.[26] For the next two years, Irish newspapers, both local and national, reported the proceedings in parliament with each stage of the process being celebrated as a victory. From an Irish point of view, Redmond dominated the parliamentary proceedings although his leadership and tactics have been subject to recent analysis and criticism.[27] Delegates from Waterford featured prominently at meetings to support Redmond. At the 'Great National Convention' organised by the UIL at the Mansion House in Dublin on 30 April 1912, Waterford was represented by mayor Michael Kirwan, chairman of the county council, Patrick O'Gorman of Lismore, and a large number of

[19] Gwynn, *Life of John Redmond*, p. 202; Daniel M. Jackson, *Popular Opposition to Irish Home Rule in Edwardian Britain* (Liverpool, 2009), pp. 146–7.
[20] F.S.L. Lyons, 'The Developing Crisis, 1907–14', in W.E. Vaughan (ed.), *A New History of Ireland*, vol. 6: *Ireland Under the Union, II (1870–1921)* (Oxford, 1996), pp. 129–31; Alvin Jackson, *Home Rule: An Irish History, 1800–2000* (London, 2003), pp. 109–11.
[21] Lyons, 'The Developing Crisis, 1907–14', pp. 131–2.
[22] *Irish Independent*, 1 Apr. 1912.
[23] Jackson, *Home Rule*, pp. 110–11.
[24] *Munster Express*, 20 Apr. 1912.
[25] *Waterford News*, 12 Apr. 1912.
[26] *Irish Independent*, 12 Apr. 1912.
[27] Jackson, *Home Rule*, pp. 106–41; Paul Bew, *Ireland the Politics of Enmity, 1789–2006* (Oxford, 2007), pp. 367–71; Paul Bew, *John Redmond* (Dundalk, 1996), pp. 35–7; Cornelius O'Leary and Patrick Maume, *Controversial Issues in Anglo-Irish Relations, 1910–1921* (Dublin, 2004), pp. 9–45.

delegates including priests.[28] The Waterford corporation representatives took advantage of the convention to present their address to Redmond and a cheque for £100, the first instalment of their contribution to the Home Rule Fund.[29] Neither Redmond nor any other local representative gave any reassurance to the local unionist community. Nationalist triumphalism reigned locally as it did in the rest of nationalist Ireland.

If the reaction of nationalists to the prospect of home rule was euphoric, that of their unionist fellow citizens was a mixture of trepidation and determination to resist. Both the *Waterford Standard* and the *Church of Ireland Gazette* reflected their concerns. The main local unionist spokesmen, Goff and O'Hara, attended the special general synod of the Church of Ireland on 16 April 1912 and a meeting of Munster unionists in Cork on 20 April.[30] The special general synod was probably the most important event in defining the Church of Ireland's position towards Home Rule and it endorsed a series of motions which committed the church to opposing any Home Rule bill.[31] At the meeting in Cork over 2,000 unionists were addressed by the Duke of Devonshire and Viscount Midleton, both of whom warned of the threat to the liberties and prosperity of the Protestant community under Home Rule.[32] In Waterford, Goff spoke repeatedly about the fiscal consequences of home rule, which, he claimed, would result in increased taxation, reduced trade and an end to prosperity.[33] This economic theme was also taken up by O'Hara. On 29 June 1912, he warned the diocesan synod of Waterford and Lismore that Home Rule would lead inexorably to separation: 'Under settled government or anarchy, a monarch or a republic, a separate Ireland must be a very poor Ireland and a very weak Ireland'.[34] Inspired by the success of the Cork meeting, Goff decided to organise a similar event in Waterford. However, the mayor, Michael Kirwan, a UIL stalwart, refused him use of the City Hall, stating that he 'would be glad to give it for any purpose except that of holding an anti-home rule demonstration'.[35] The meeting went ahead instead in the grounds of the Goff mansion, Glenville, on 13 June 1912. There what a police report described as 'a large and representative crowd' heard Sir William speak

---

[28] *Munster Express*, 3 May 1912.
[29] *Waterford News*, 3 May 1912.
[30] *Waterford Standard*, 24 Apr. 1912.
[31] Andrew Scholes, *The Church of Ireland and the Third Home Rule Bill* (Dublin, 2010), pp. 32–6.
[32] *Waterford Standard*, 24 Apr. 1912; *Church of Ireland Gazette*, 24 Apr. 1912; R.B. McDowell, *Crisis and Decline: The Fate of the Southern Unionists* (Dublin, 1997), p. 46.
[33] *Waterford Standard*, 5 Jun. 1912.
[34] *Church of Ireland Gazette*, 5 Jul. 1912.
[35] *Waterford Standard*, 5 Jun. 1912.

at length on the economic woes that would inevitably follow Home Rule.[36] He also suggested that the mayor's refusal of the use of City Hall was a foretaste of discrimination to come.[37] The *Waterford News* tried to cast scorn on the meeting, claiming that it was attended by fewer than 300 people of whom over 200 were women, that the majority were from the 'furthest reaches of the county', and that 'the muster of citizens of this city did not pass a round dozen'.[38] The list of prominent attendees published in the *Waterford Standard* suggests that the RIC were more accurate in their assessment of the crowd.[39]

The Solemn League and Covenant was signed on Ulster Day, 28 September 1912, as a popular protest against Home Rule. Four days later Bishop O'Hara presided over a special prayer service in Christchurch Cathedral, Waterford, convened ostensibly to give Ulstermen resident in the city and county an opportunity to sign the covenant.[40] Of the thirty-seven men who signed, most, but not all, were from Ulster. Four were Waterford born. Eighteen women signed the Declaration (the equivalent document for women).[41] Many others declared that they would be happy to sign but in some cases were precluded by their employment – for example, William Dobbin, governor of Waterford prison.[42] No similar ceremony was held in the surrounding counties of Wexford, Kilkenny, Tipperary, or Cork. The Glenville meeting and the signing of the covenant were the highpoints of unionist resistance to Home Rule in Waterford. No other public meetings were held though Robert Whalley and the *Waterford Standard* continued to track the legislative passage of the Home Rule bill and to record the utterances of Goff and O'Hara. Unionist women were seemingly content to express their opposition by signing the Declaration and no branch of the Women's Unionist Alliance was formed in Waterford. By mid-1914, O'Hara had decided that 'it was best for him to say as little as possible on political matters' and informed the diocesan synod that 'all they could do in this part of Ireland was to put themselves in God's hands and to turn to Him for deliverance'.[43]

As the Home Rule bill was completing its final passage through the Commons during the early months of 1914, nationalist Ireland celebrated each stage as a triumph. In January, Redmond visited Waterford for a major

---

[36] RIC County Inspector's Monthly Confidential Report, Waterford, Jun. 1912 (TNA, CO 904/86).

[37] *Waterford Standard*, 5, 15 Jun. 1912.

[38] *Waterford News*, 14 Jun. 1912.

[39] *Waterford Standard*, 17 Jun. 1912.

[40] *Waterford Standard*, 5 Oct. 1912.

[41] Ulster Covenant online: www.nidirect.gov.uk/services/search-ulster-covenant.

[42] *Waterford Standard*, 5 Oct. 1912.

[43] *Church of Ireland Gazette*, 3 Jul. 1914.

rally.[44] An estimated 50,000 people thronged the city streets as he drove to Ballybricken, where a banner proudly proclaimed: 'historic Ballybricken pledges allegiance to Redmond'. He told the assembled crowd that this was 'the most remarkable nationalist demonstration ever held in Munster'. A succession of speakers paid tribute to him and thanked him 'for leading our oppressed people from political slavery to legislative freedom'. Redmond concluded the proceedings with a ringing declaration: 'we have fought and we have won. Lift up your hearts. Ireland's long travail is at an end. You are to witness the rebirth of Irish freedom, prosperity and happiness'.[45] The meeting received widespread coverage in the national press. One headline in the *Irish Independent* referred to 'The eve of triumph'.[46] By contrast, the editorial in the unionist *Irish Times* suggested that the meeting illustrated 'Redmond's failure as a statesman' as his speech was 'devoted to an enthusiastic hailing of the triumph of home rule rather than confronting the political reality of Ulster resistance'.[47] Three weeks later, the Waterford city Protestant community attended a service in Christchurch Cathedral to pray for guidance in their hour of danger.[48] Rosamond Jacob noted that a reporter from the *Waterford News* had been sent to record the names of those present.[49] This 'marking of those opposed to home rule' was the occasion referred to in the House of Commons by Bonar Law.[50] This in turn prompted Waterford Corporation to meet in special session and declare that 'the people of Waterford have always respected the religious opinions of their Protestant fellow citizens with whom they have always lived in amity'.[51] To Emily Ussher, of Cappagh House near Dungarvan, the political atmosphere was 'electric', and among her friends, gunrunning and the prospect of Home Rule were the sole topics of conversation. She noted a rumour that a unit of the Ulster Volunteer Force (UVF) was being organised in west Waterford for armed resistance to any home rule government.[52] Similar rumours may have circulated in other southern counties but only one unit was actually formed outside Ulster, in Dublin.[53] The Usshers were a prominent landowning family known to be liberal in their politics and pro Home-Rule, and were gradually excluded from all meetings

[44] Gwynn, *Life of John Redmond*, p. 249.
[45] *Munster Express*, 31 Jan. 1914; RIC County Inspector's Monthly Confidential Report, Waterford, Jan. 1914 (TNA, CO 904/92).
[46] *Irish Independent*, 26 Jan. 1914.
[47] *Irish Times*, 27 Jan. 1914.
[48] *Waterford Standard*, 14 Feb. 1914.
[49] Jacob diaries, 1914 (NLI, MS 32,582).
[50] Hansard, HC, vol. 58, cols 1691–727 (24 Feb. 1914).
[51] Waterford Corporation Minutes, 1 Mar. 1914 (Waterford County Archives).
[52] Emily Ussher, 'True Story of a Revolution' (TCD, MS 9269).
[53] Quincy Dougan, 'Dublin's Loyal Volunteers', *History Ireland*, 22 (2014), pp. 36–8.

of their landed neighbours.[54] The appointment of Sir George Richardson, a retired Indian army lieutenant-general, as commander of the UVF gave rise to a degree of unrest in Lismore where Richardson normally resided with his brother in law, Colonel Charles Gordon. The RIC felt it necessary to provide security at his house.[55] That Redmond failed to address the concerns of his unionist constituents who had voted for him as a Parnellite in the turbulent elections of 1891, 1892, and 1895, was a missed opportunity to set forth his vision of an inclusive Ireland within the British Empire. Their assistance in his electoral battles against Michael Davitt and David Sheehy during the height of the Parnell divorce crisis had been crucial according to Davitt. Now they were ignored.[56]

The British declaration of war on 4 August 1914 and John Redmond's support for it had a unifying effect throughout Ireland and especially in Waterford city. Support for Redmond's policy crossed all classes and political views. Many loyalists with military experience but too old for active duty offered their services to the local Irish Volunteers.[57] Sir John Keane and Sir William Goff wrote to the *Waterford Standard* commending Redmond and urging support for the Volunteers.[58] Others pledged practical help. Gerald Purcell Fitzgerald, a prominent local Catholic conservative, wrote to the *Munster Express* volunteering his services to the Volunteers as inspector-general.[59] Colonel Charles Gordon of Lismore made a similar offer to Maurice Moore. Gordon, a retired Indian army officer, had been contacted by the War Office for remount duty in Ireland but, as he explained in his letter, 'If an old soldier may say so without egoism, I think I could help Ireland better in this crisis in an appointment similar to the one I am applying for'.[60] Gordon's offer was not accepted and he later became commanding officer of the Belfast district of the UVF.[61] The RIC County Inspector for Waterford claimed that 'the Irish National Volunteers can be depended upon to a man to fight any foreign foe and the unionists here are of the same opinion'.[62] At least outside of Ulster it seemed that an Irish equivalent of *l'union sacrée* had been formed,

---

54 Dougan, 'Dublin's Loyal Volunteers', p. 3.
55 RIC County Inspector's Monthly Confidential Report, Waterford, Mar. 1914 (TNA, CO 904/93).
56 McCarthy, *Redmonds and Waterford*, pp. 24–6.
57 McCarthy, *Redmonds and Waterford*, pp. 69–80.
58 *Waterford Standard*, 8, 15 Aug. 1914.
59 *Munster Express*, 8 Aug. 1914.
60 Col. J.C.T. Gordon to Maurice Moore, 4 Aug. 1914 (NLI, MS 10,551).
61 *Waterford Standard*, 23 Dec. 1914.
62 RIC County Inspector's Monthly Confidential Report, Waterford, Aug. 1914 (TNA, CO 904/94).

as Protestant and Catholic, unionist and nationalist rallied behind Redmond and his support for the government.[63]

As might be expected, the unionist community of city and county responded to the call to arms. Men of all ages and all classes rejoined their regiments or volunteered for the first time. At least 52 of them paid the ultimate sacrifice.[64] Colonel Robert Carew of Ballinamona was 56 when he died in hospital in Alexandria in 1917 from a disease contracted while on active service with the Leinster Regiment in Salonika. Rupert Bell, son of a shopkeeper, was only 24 when he was killed in France in 1916. Major Hugh Dawnay, serving with the 2nd Life Guards, was among the first Waterford men to die, killed in action in France on 6 November 1914. Reverend Maurice Day, dean of Christchurch Cathedral, lost both of his sons, Maurice and John. Maurice was killed in action on 3 November 1914 in East Africa. John served with Major William Redmond in the 6th Royal Irish Regiment. Both men were killed at Messines in 1917. John had been just 18 when he volunteered at the outbreak of the war. The death of Redmond, brother of John Redmond and MP for East Clare, provoked widespread expressions of sympathy by public bodies in Waterford. The Catholic cathedral was crowded for a requiem mass for him. The death of John Day, a few weeks later, was virtually unnoticed except within his own small community. Others died at sea, reflecting the long tradition of naval service in Waterford city and the coastal towns and villages: Able Seaman Albert Randall, Church of Ireland, was among those killed at the Battle of Jutland.

Soon after the outbreak of the war, various cross-community committees, often led by prominent loyalist ladies such as the Marchioness of Waterford, Lady Eleanor Keane, and the Duchess of Devonshire, were set up in Waterford city and county, as happened throughout Great Britain and Ireland, to provide comforts for the troops.[65] On 2 September, the *Waterford Standard* reported that wealthy citizens of the city had provided a fully equipped ambulance to be named 'The Waterford car' for use at the front.[66] Six months later, three similar vehicles were provided by a committee under the patronage of the Duke of Devonshire and the Marchioness of Waterford. There were also regular public

---

[63] Patrick Maume, *The Long Gestation: Irish Nationalist Life, 1891–1918* (Dublin, 1999), pp. 147–51; Catriona Pennell, *A Kingdom United: Popular Responses to the Outbreak of the First World War in Britain and Ireland* (Oxford, 2012), pp. 194–7.

[64] Tom Burnell, *The Waterford War Dead* (Dublin, 2010).

[65] Eileen Reilly, 'Women and Voluntary War Work', in Adrian Gregory and Senia Pašeta (eds), *Ireland and the Great War, 'A War to Unite Us All'?* (Manchester, 2002), pp. 49–72; Pennell, *A Kingdom United*, pp. 72–6, 168–71; Melanie O'Sullivan and Kevin McCarthy, *Cappoquin: A Walk Through History* (Cappoquin, undated), p. 292.

[66] *Waterford Standard*, 2 Sep. 1914. See also Chapter 6.

appeals for clothing, cigarettes and other comforts for the troops. Among the officers and men of the Royal Irish Regiment captured at the battle of Le Pilly (17–20 October 1914) were a large number of Waterford men.[67] Their plight as prisoners of war soon came to the attention of their friends and relatives and they too were assisted by Waterford relief committees.[68] In March 1915, a flag day was held throughout the city and the county to raise funds for them. When Private J. Casey from Waterford city, a badly wounded prisoner, was exchanged home in August 1915, he wrote to the *Waterford News* claiming that the prisoners were living solely on the contents of the relief parcels they received from home.[69] This had an immediate and positive impact on collections. In November 1914, preparations began for the reception of Belgian refugees. Numerous public appeals for funds and clothing were made and elicited a generous response. In February 1915, three Belgian families arrived in Waterford and these were accommodated in Tramore, Portlaw, and in the city.[70] Membership of the various fund-raising committees comprised a cross-section of Waterford society, usually including Protestant and Catholic clergy, members of the landed gentry, businessmen, and local politicians, supporters of Redmond. In December 1917, tragedy struck when the two locally based small steamships, the *Coningbeg* and the *Formby*, were sunk within days of each other with the loss of 83 lives, 69 of them from the city. On 21 December, a committee was formed to raise funds for the relief of the families of those who had been lost. The committee was jointly chaired by the two bishops of Waterford, Dr O'Hara and Dr Hackett, and had prominent members from both communities in its membership. Within weeks the committee had raised the considerable sum of £7,979.[71]

While men of military age were at the front and their womenfolk supported them in every way possible, O'Hara and Whalley and his *Waterford Standard* kept a watchful eye on political developments at home. When Sir Edward Carson was included in Asquith's coalition government in May 1915, the *Standard* proclaimed in a headline: 'Home Rule is Dead'.[72] Waterford did not play any part in the 1916 Rising and all of the local elected bodies, dominated by supporters of Redmond, roundly condemned it. O'Hara echoed these sentiments: 'we have again great cause to thank God for a very great

[67] Stannus Geoghegan, *The Campaigns and History of the Royal Irish Regiment*, vol. 2: *From 1900 to 1922* (London, 1927), pp. 25–8.

[68] *Waterford Standard*, 20, 24 Mar. 1915; *Munster Express*, 27 Mar. 1915.

[69] *Waterford News*, 17 Sep. 1915.

[70] *Waterford Standard*, 19 Jan. 1914.

[71] Richard McElwee, *The Last Voyages of the Waterford Steamers* (Waterford, 1992), pp. 132–6.

[72] *Waterford Standard*, 29 May 1915.

deliverance',[73] while the *Standard* headlined its coverage: 'Collapse of the ill-starred republic'.[74] In the aftermath of the Easter Rising, Asquith sent Lloyd George to Ireland to broker a settlement. Both Redmond and Carson expended a great deal of political capital and agreement appeared near until the talks collapsed on the intransigence of the leaders of the southern unionists who refused to countenance Home Rule in any form.[75] The *Standard* greeted this with glee: 'The gratitude of the country and of the empire is due to the statesmanship of our unionist leaders'.[76] A year later, as the Irish Convention met, it warned its readers: 'Let us keep a watchful eye on this convention lest anything come of it'.[77] The guns might roar along the Western Front but the unionists of Waterford remained mindful of their own potential fate.

In 1919, the men returned to a radically changed Ireland. Some form of Home Rule and the exclusion of the six counties of north-east Ulster was inevitable. Abandoned by their fellow loyalists in Ulster and their allies in the Conservative party in Britain, the southern loyalists faced an uncertain future. In Waterford, their leadership had changed. In 1916, the Duke of Devonshire had been appointed Governor General of Canada. Sir William Goff died in November 1917 leaving no male heir. Dr O'Hara resigned his episcopal see early in 1919 and retired to Coleraine.[78] He was replaced by Dr Robert Miller, a native of Limerick, a man more measured in his public utterances. He would later be praised for his tact 'at a most critical time in the history of the church and country'.[79] The most remarkable change was in the *Waterford Standard*, so long the voice of Waterford unionism. In August 1916, Whalley, suffering from ill health, hired a new reporter – David Boyd. Boyd was from Belfast, a Presbyterian and from a staunchly unionist background. Shortly after he began his career in journalism, he was sworn into the Irish Republican Brotherhood (IRB) by Ernest Blythe. Like many IRB men he worked discreetly in the background to build and influence the Irish Volunteers. At Easter 1916, he intended to join the Belfast Irish Volunteers on their march west to link up with the Volunteers holding 'the line of the Shannon'. When that was cancelled as a result of Eóin MacNeill's countermanding order he spent Easter week in Belfast. Shortly afterwards he left Dublin and joined the *Standard*. Over the following years Whalley came to

---

[73] *Church of Ireland Gazette*, 1 Jul. 1916.

[74] *Waterford Standard*, 6 May 1916.

[75] Ronan Fanning, *Fatal Path: British Government and Irish Revolution, 1910–1922* (London, 2013), pp. 145–7; Patrick Buckland, *Irish Unionism I: The Anglo-Irish and the New Ireland, 1885–1922* (Dublin, 1972), p. 82.

[76] *Waterford Standard*, 12 Jul. 1916.

[77] *Waterford Standard*, 14 Jul. 1917.

[78] *Waterford Standard*, 22 Feb. 1919.

[79] *Irish Times*, 16 Mar. 1931; *Waterford Standard*, 21 Mar. 1931.

rely on him more and more. He was appointed editor in 1920 and bought the paper on the death of Whalley in May 1921. As a closet Fenian, owning and editing the voice of Waterford unionism, Boyd was uniquely placed to influence the local loyalist community, especially during the truce and after the signing of the Anglo-Irish Treaty (see below).

Sir John Keane, who had served with the Royal Field Artillery in France throughout the war, devoted himself to farming and other business interests on his return.[80] The cause of southern unionism was not helped by a split in their ranks.[81] By 1919, the Irish Unionist Alliance, dominated by Ulster representatives, was bitterly divided over partition. The leading members of the southern unionists, seeing themselves as abandoned by their Ulster brethren, formed a separate organisation, the Unionist Anti-Partition League, led by Lord Midleton. While the new body attracted many of the leading lights in southern unionism, such as the Earl of Donoughmore, the Earl of Iveagh, and Sir John Arnott, the ordinary members stayed loyal to the Irish Unionist Alliance, clinging to the hope that their northern brethren would not abandon them. From 1919 onwards, Waterford Unionists were represented on the Irish Unionist Alliance (IUA) Council by Commander Richard Carew, RN, a Church of Ireland landowner, and by John Craig Ferguson, a Belfast-born chartered accountant and Methodist.[82] The *Irish Times* published long lists of the notables who resigned from the IUA to follow Lord Midleton.[83] There was no Waterford representative among them though the surrounding counties of Cork, Tipperary, and Kilkenny were well represented.

Throughout the War of Independence local unionists kept a low profile.[84] There is no evidence of any sectarian targeting by the IRA in Waterford between 1919 and 1921. The IRA was organised into two brigades: East Waterford (No. 1) and West Waterford (No. 2). The East Waterford Brigade was small in numbers, poorly led and very conscious that Sinn Féin had lost in the Waterford City constituency in the 1918 election. Apart from occasional raids for arms the IRA there did not affect the local community. The West Waterford IRA were far more active, killing individual policemen and staging well-prepared and successful ambushes, but there is no evidence here either of any targeting of members of the local loyalist community. When the Usshers sheltered the family of a RIC sergeant after Cappagh barracks was

[80] Maume, 'Keane, Sir John', *Dictionary of Irish Biography*; O'Sullivan and McCarthy, *Cappoquin*, pp. 298, 310.
[81] Buckland, *Irish Unionism I*, pp. 186–94.
[82] IUA, *Thirtieth Annual Report, 1919–20* (Dublin, 1920), p. 20.
[83] *Irish Times*, 25, 31 Jan., 13 Feb. 1919.
[84] For an account of the War of Independence in Waterford, including details of the incidents mentioned below, see Pat McCarthy, *The Irish Revolution 1912–23: Waterford* (Dublin, 2015), pp. 61–87.

destroyed, they received an anonymous letter warning them that their house would be burned unless they evicted the policeman's family. Two nights later a party of IRA arrived at the house, under orders, they said, to protect the house from 'gangster elements' operating in the name of the IRA. One ex-serviceman was killed, William Moran of Dungarvan, aged 65. His killing was not officially sanctioned by the local IRA. Arms levies were collected in the West Waterford Brigade area but not systematically. On 23 June 1921, IRA Volunteers called at Dromana House, home of Sir Gerard Villiers-Stuart, and collected £100. At the same time other loyalist landowners, including Sir John Keane, were not approached for funds.[85] One civilian of loyalist background was killed – Wilfrid Hyde Marmion, son of the Lismore justice of the peace – but not by the IRA. He died on 28 January 1921 when he was fired on by an RIC patrol near Lismore after failing to stop when challenged. Two men claimed compensation for damage to property to the Irish Grants Committee, Claude Anson of Ballysaggartmore, a Church of Ireland landowner and justice of the peace, and Thomas Bride, a demobilised soldier living in a house on the Devonshire estate where he was employed as a labourer (his religion has not been established). Anson's house was raided in June 1921; Bride's on 21 September 1920. The motive for either, whether a result of their loyalism, opportunistic theft, revenge, or a search for arms is not specified.[86]

The Truce in July 1921 was universally welcomed but brought great uncertainty to the loyalist community. With the RIC and the British army virtually confined to barracks, law and order was in the hands of the republican police. The IRA focused much of their attention on training and revenue raising. The cost of maintaining the republican police, training camps, and men on full-time duty put an immense strain on the meagre resources of the Waterford Brigade. The arms levy which had been collected in the west of the county was now extended to the east and to the city, with amounts of up to £150 being claimed from businesses and individuals, many of them loyalists.[87] Edwin Jacob, secretary to the Chamber of Commerce, wrote to Cathal Brugha, Minister for Defence and TD for Waterford, seeking clarification on the status of the levy, whether contributions were expected to be voluntary or not. The IRA's chief liaison officer replied on behalf of the minister that all collections and levies were on a voluntary basis only. Jacob was delighted to publish the reply in the local newspapers.[88] Any solace that the citizens of Waterford may have derived from this correspondence was quickly lost when a notice

---

[85] Sir John Keane diary, 10 Jun. 1921, quoted in Symes, *Sir John Keane*, p. 29.
[86] Details of the two raids are taken from the Irish Grants Committee database compiled by Prof. Liam Kennedy, Queen's University Belfast.
[87] *Waterford Standard*, 21, 28 Oct. 1921.
[88] *Waterford Standard*, 21 Oct. 1921.

appeared in the local press stating that the levy had been authorised, that all were expected to contribute, and that the proceeds would be used to put 'the Brigade in a state of efficiency'.[89] To many the distinction between a compulsory levy and a voluntary contribution collected by armed men was academic. The houses of two Church of Ireland farmers, Benjamin Schofield and Robert Wheelock, were looted and damaged when they refused to pay the IRA levy. The money continued to be collected and the imposition of this levy may have contributed to growing ill-feeling towards the IRA, which resulted in a lack of support for the republican side in the Civil War.

The Anglo-Irish Treaty of December 1921 was welcomed by the Waterford loyalist community, in particular the inclusion of an oath of allegiance and Ireland's continued membership of the Empire. The *Waterford Standard* spoke for many when it declared: 'We have much to offer the new state. Let us give it in full measure'. Bishop Robert Miller took his first opportunity to endorse the settlement, highlighting the importance of the oath and the Empire.[90] After the treaty was ratified, Boyd wrote a strong editorial:

> Success to the Irish Free State. Unionism is dead and buried and we see little chance of a happy resurrection! Southern conservatives have ardently longed for a peaceful settlement in Ireland. The constitution of the Irish Free State makes it possible for them to work for the advancement of the New Ireland. We will render loyal service to the Irish Free State. Southern loyalists have sacrificed what is to them just as great an ideal as the republicans.[91]

That was the last time that Boyd referred to 'southern loyalists' or 'unionists'. From then on he always called his community 'the conservatives'. He concluded on a more sombre note: 'we are not optimistic as to the immediate establishment of law and order'. His forebodings were realised over the next twelve months as the loyalist community in Waterford suffered its greatest trial. Sir John Keane's observation on the treaty was prescient: 'this morning [came] the announcement of peace whatever that means. I am relieved but do not rejoice. They will find that peace is harder than war'.[92]

The period between the approval of the Treaty by the Dáil in January 1922 and the end of the Civil War in May 1923 saw much violence in the city and county, a significant part of which was targeted at members of the loyalist

---

[89] *Waterford News*, 28 Oct. 1921; Charles Townshend, *The Republic: The Fight for Irish Independence, 1918–1923* (London, 2013), pp. 322–3.

[90] *Waterford Standard*, 10 Dec. 1921.

[91] *Waterford Standard*, 11 Jan. 1922.

[92] Symes, *Sir John Keane*, p. 29.

community. Most of this was opportunistic, as advantage was taken of the absence of the forces of law and order. Boycotts, visits by masked, armed men, and anonymous threatening letters were used. The IRA condemned such actions but were apparently powerless to halt them. Although there is no evidence of a systematic campaign against loyalists and Protestants in Waterford city and county there were instances of opportunistic violence.[93] Ex-RIC members returning to their homes after demobilisation were an obvious – and easy – target. When ex-Sergeant Patrick Golden, who had been in charge of the barracks in Kilmanahan, County Tipperary, returned to his home in Waterford in April his house was surrounded by armed men and he was advised to leave the country. He did so the next day.[94] Ex-Head Constable Gleeson from Tallow and ex-Sergeant Coogan from the city had similar experiences.[95] In his compensation claim to the Irish Grants Committee, Coogan claimed that 'all the disbanded RIC had left the city having received notices to quit the country'.[96] When James O'Donoghue, an RIC constable who had served in Tyrone, returned home to Cappoquin after he had been demobilised he was peremptorily ordered out of the town at gunpoint by republicans. His brother Vincent, engineering officer with the Cork No. 1 Brigade and himself strongly against the Treaty, was appalled. For him it was 'just one of the many acts of bullying and brutal tyranny indulged in at that time by petty local Republican "warriors" to show their arrogant authority and self-importance'.[97] For other loyalists the force applied was economic. The files of the Irish Grants Committee contain ample evidence of the pressures exerted on individuals because of their alleged loyalty and service to the British government.[98] Hugh Jones, a solicitor in Waterford city, had served as the Crown solicitor for Wexford during the War of Independence. He claimed that from February 1922 his business was boycotted and that it did not return to normal until 1925.[99] William Roe, a Methodist shopkeeper in Lismore, was forced to leave the country after repeated threatening letters that warned him 'to clear out or we will riddle you with bullets when you least expect it'.[100] Benjamin Schofield, a farmer, claimed he was ordered to leave at gunpoint for refusing to pay the IRA levy. A cycle merchant, William Cordner and his

---

[93] Gemma Clark, *Everyday Violence in the Irish Civil War* (Cambridge, 2014), pp. 149–51.
[94] Patrick Golden claim (TNA, CO 762/80/4).
[95] Timothy Gleeson claim (TNA, CO 762/66/14).
[96] James Coogan claim (TNA, CO 762/80/3).
[97] BMH WS 1,741 (Michael V. O'Donoghue).
[98] Niamh Brennan, 'A Political Minefield: The Irish Grants Committee and the British Government, 1922–31', *Irish Historical Studies*, 30/119 (1997), pp. 406–19.
[99] Hugh Jones claim (TNA, CO 762/77/11).
[100] William Roe claim (TNA, CO 762/108/11).

family, fled the country when their premises were occupied and the stock stolen.[101] In all, 36 loyalists in the city and county claimed compensation for losses suffered on account of their allegiance to the British government during this period.[102] Of those whose religion can be ascertained, 19 were Protestant and 12 Catholic (of whom 5 were ex-RIC).

When two city residents were ordered to leave at gunpoint, the local IRA battalion condemned the action and warned the perpetrators of 'stern measures' should they be apprehended. The two men were Thomas Firth, a Presbyterian and employee of the Waterford Harbour Commissioners, and John Ferguson, an accountant.[103] Although both men had been born in Belfast, neither had signed the Ulster Covenant in Waterford in 1912 though resident in the city at that time. Ferguson was treasurer of the East Waterford branch of the IUA. Both men left Waterford immediately amid emotional scenes at the quayside. At the same time, the IRA supplied an armed guard for the home of Mrs Whalley when her house was threatened.[104] Boyd repeatedly reported and condemned these events in the pages of the *Waterford Standard*: 'we condemn totally the expulsion of former members of the Constabulary'; 'The Defenceless Southern Minority. Things are happening which are not appearing in the press of Southern Ireland ... We ask only for fair play and elementary justice':

> Two citizens have been ordered to leave their native land [Firth and Ferguson] within 24 hours and they departed, forlorn examples of injustice ... One reassuring feature of this local episode was the prompt measures taken by the IRA in Waterford not only to denounce those orders as bogus [but] to offer the fullest protection to the unfortunate victims.[105]

On 12 May, Dr Miller, along with Archbishop of Dublin Dr John Gregg and Sir William Goulding, formed a three-man delegation nominated by the general synod of the Church of Ireland, which met Michael Collins. They asked 'to be informed if they were to be permitted to live in Ireland or if it was desired that they should leave the country'.[106] Collins could only offer them verbal reassurance about their place in the new Ireland; he was in no position to offer them meaningful protection. In her study of Waterford, Tipperary, and

---

[101] William Cordner (TNA, CO 762/139/3).
[102] Irish Grants Committee, Files and Minutes (TNA CO/762).
[103] *Waterford Standard*, 6 May 1922.
[104] *Waterford Standard*, 6 May 1922.
[105] *Waterford Standard*, 19, 29 Apr., 6 May 1922.
[106] *Irish Times*, 10, 13 May 1922.

Limerick, Gemma Clark has shown how a threatening, sectarian atmosphere pervaded the small isolated Protestant communities in these counties, affecting all members, not only those who were directly threatened.[107] Her analysis of arson attacks shows that they were far less frequent in Waterford (20) than in Limerick (108) and Tipperary (164), though this would have been of little consolation to the victims in Waterford.[108] Many unionists in the south felt that they had been thrown to the wolves, a feeling expressed by R.J. Uniacke Fitzgerald of East Cork in a letter to Austin Chamberlain expressing his heartbreak 'at the duplicity, mendacity and cowardice of our former friends' who had 'now handed them over to their enemies'.[109]

By June 1922, Waterford city and county, like many other parts of the country, had degenerated into a state of anarchy and uncertainty. Commandeering of goods, and bank robberies by republicans as well as opportunistic violence against loyalists, left people feeling helpless, with no recognised force of law and order to turn to. Most must have welcomed the news that on 28 June government forces had finally moved against the republican forces who were occupying the Four Courts in Dublin. After the surrender in Dublin, the republican forces proclaimed a 'Munster Republic' and their intention of defending it on a line running from Waterford to Limerick. In reality they had not the men, the weaponry, nor the military expertise to do so. A three-day siege of Waterford city ended on 21 July with the withdrawal of the republican forces.[110] They commandeered four big houses, three of which were the homes of noted loyalists – Mount Congreve (Sir William Congreve), Curraghmore (Lord Waterford), and Whitfield Manor (Major Dawnay) – and formed a loose cordon about five miles from the city. Prudently, the owners were in England where they and others such as Devonshire remained until after the end of the Civil War. After a few weeks, National Army troops resumed their advance and the republicans withdrew without having done much damage to the houses except, in at least one instance, to the contents of the wine cellar. Lismore Castle, home of the Duke of Devonshire, was the last stronghold to be evacuated by the republicans. An attempt to set fire to the building failed, foiled by the arrival of National Army troops. By the end of August, all the main towns in the county were in the hands of the government but there now followed a period of vicious guerrilla warfare as the republicans reverted to the tactics which had been so successful in the War of Independence.

---

[107] Clark, *Everyday Violence*, pp. 202–3.
[108] Clark, *Everyday Violence*, pp. 62–3.
[109] Buckland, *Irish Unionism I*, pp. 276–7.
[110] For details of the Civil War in Waterford, see McCarthy, *The Irish Revolution 1912–23: Waterford*, pp. 105–26.

During this period, September 1922 to January 1923, apart from frequent attacks on National Army troops there was much 'everyday violence', some of it carried out by members of the IRA. In one attempted robbery, Charles Boyce, son of a shop owner and member of the Church of Ireland, was killed when members of the IRA tried to steal binoculars from his pawn shop. By the end of January 1923 the tide had turned decisively against the republicans. In February they started a campaign of burning the houses of prominent government supporters.[111] The first to be burnt was the mansion of Sir John Keane who had just been appointed to the new Free State Senate.[112] The same night two other residences, those of Miss Caroline Fairholme[113] and Mr Arthur Hunt, were also burned.[114] Caroline Fairholme was firmly of the view that her well-known loyalism during the War of Independence was the reason she was singled out.[115] Three nights later the country house of the Poer O'Shea family at Gardenmorris was destroyed.[116] In the words of Emily Ussher, each of these burnings left behind 'a little island of unemployment, poverty and despair'.[117] They also further alienated the people from the republicans. Terence Dooley contends that a significant number of the 300 'Big Houses' burned during the period 1920 to 1923 can be put down to local agitators who simply wanted to expel local landlords and redistribute their lands.[118] There is no evidence of any agrarian motivation in the Waterford burnings. In February to April 1923, 7 big houses were burned in Waterford. This compares to the surrounding counties: 29 in Tipperary, 19 in Cork, 11 in Wexford, and 5 in Kilkenny.[119]

With the return of peace in 1923, the loyalist community faced new challenges. Their numbers had declined dramatically as many fled the country. Reflecting on the departure of some of her landed neighbours, Emily Ussher believed that 'every empty house has left the country less able to pay its way and stands desolate in its own little pool of unemployment'.[120] Those who remained found that everything around them had changed. Some retreated

---

[111] Terence Dooley, *The Decline of the Big House in Ireland: A Study of Irish Landed Families, 1860–1960* (Dublin, 2001), pp. 187–92.

[112] *Munster Express*, 2 Mar. 1923; Cork Command reports, Mar. 1923 (MAI, W/ Ops/04); Damage to Property Act claims (NAI, OPW/1/18/1); Sir John Keane Compensation claim (TNA CO 762/82/11); Symes, *Sir John Keane*, pp. 41–7.

[113] *Munster Express*, 2 Mar. 1923; Damage to Property Act claims (NAI, OPW/1/18/1); C. Fairholme claim (TNA, CO762/94/3).

[114] *Munster Express*, 2 Mar. 1923; Damage to Property Act claims (NAI OPW/1/18/1).

[115] C. Fairholme claim (TNA, CO 762/94/3).

[116] *Munster Express*, 9 Mar. 1923; Damage to Property Act claim (NAI, OPW/1/18/2).

[117] Ussher, 'True Story of a Revolution' (TCD, MS 9269).

[118] Dooley, *Decline of the Big House*, p. 191.

[119] Dooley, *Decline of the Big House*, p. 287.

[120] Ussher, 'True Story of a Revolution' (TCD, MS 9269).

into a world of lost memories but many others, led locally by Sir John Keane, played an active part in the economic, political, and social development of the new state, their country. When the Treaty was signed, Richard Dawson, London representative of the IUA, admitted of the southern unionists that 'to retain their means of living they have to support a government which they hate'.[121] Most of them did so.

The loyalist community in Waterford, and in the Irish Free State generally, suffered major population loss in the period between the censuses of 1911 and 1926. In the 26 counties as a whole, the non-Catholic population declined by 33 per cent compared with a decline of just over 2 per cent for Catholics.[122] After allowing for the withdrawal of British army personnel and Great War deaths within the minority community nationally, Andy Bielenberg has estimated that about 20 per cent of the non-Catholic population left for economic or voluntary reasons.[123] In Waterford the figures are 40 per cent of the total non-Catholic population and 28 per cent after allowing for the factors above. These figures are similar to those for the surrounding counties of Wexford, Kilkenny, Tipperary, and Cork.[124] A sense of apprehension about the transition to national independence in 1922 and the anarchy that characterised that transition contributed to this exodus, as did the emerging Gaelic, Catholic, and nationalist ethos of the new state. The sentiment of C.P. Crane, a Tipperary resident magistrate, was echoed by many: 'I had been brought up under the union jack and had no desire to live under any other emblem'.[125] Those that remained seem to have adapted quickly to the changed circumstances. As Annabel Davis-Goff put it, 'there was no immediate or dramatic reason for them to emigrate. They were no longer English, and many thought themselves as Irish'.[126] All of the big houses that were destroyed during the Civil War in Waterford were rebuilt, in contrast with other parts of the country where the stark ruins became a feature of the landscape. Some embraced the opportunities presented by the new state. In his editorial welcoming the Treaty, David Boyd had appealed to the unionist community: 'There is much that we can contribute to the building up of the new Ireland. We will give it in full

---

[121] Donnacha Ó Beacháin, 'The Dog that Didn't Bark: Southern Unionism in Pre- and Post-Revolutionary Ireland', *History Ireland*, 23/4 (2015), pp. 44–7.

[122] Andy Bielenberg, 'Exodus: The Emigration of Southern Irish Protestants during the Irish War of Independence and the Civil War', *Past & Present*, 218 (2013), p. 21.

[123] Bielenberg, 'Exodus', p. 223 (Table 6). For alternative figures on the Protestant decline, see Chapter 3.

[124] Bielenberg, 'Exodus', p. 205 (Table 3).

[125] C.P. Crane, *Memories of a Resident Magistrate* (Edinburgh, 1938), p. 223.

[126] Davis-Goff, *Walled Gardens*, p. 37.

measure'.[127] For others, life continued as before. In the words of Brian Inglis: 'The Unionists closed their depleted ranks; as soon as they found that the new Irish government could be trusted not to expropriate their land, debase the currency, or to make general legislative mayhem, they settled down to ignore its existence'.[128]

---

[127] *Waterford Standard*, 10 Dec. 1921.
[128] Inglis, *West Briton* (London, 1962), p. 15.

CHAPTER XI

Loyalists in a Garrison County:
Kildare, 1912–1923

Seamus Cullen

Loyalists in County Kildare constituted a significant and influential community throughout the revolutionary period from *c*.1912 to 1923. Despite this, their experiences have largely been forgotten. Although loyalists are identified as mainly belonging to the Protestant religious tradition, in Kildare a significant minority were Catholic. The 1911 census indicated that the county had a population of 66,627, with Protestants comprising 18 per cent.[1] Given that the vast majority of Protestants in the county and a small number of Catholics were loyalists, it is more than likely that the unionist population in Kildare exceeded 18 per cent. Kildare loyalists were somewhat unique in contrast to those from elsewhere owing to the garrison status of the county. Almost 10 per cent of the population of Kildare were members of the British army, who were stationed in four major establishments at Naas, Newbridge, Kildare town, and the Curragh camp, the largest military encampment in the country.[2] In addition to the military, army dependants constituted sizeable numbers. Some 7,650 individuals, or 11.5 per cent of the population, were persons born in Britain.[3] This figure is largely made up of army personnel with their wives and children, but it also includes British-born traders and their dependants. The army garrisons, which were located in the centre of the county, provided a certain level of security to the loyalists in Kildare during the first nine years of the Irish Revolution.

In Kildare, loyalists enjoyed a social life connected with the army. They attended and participated in all the major army public activities, including ceremonial events, entertainment, and dances, and, in particular, army sports. In some instances, army sporting events, such as the final

---

[1] *Census of Ireland, 1911. Area, Houses, and Population: Also the Ages, Civil or Conjugal Condition, Occupations, Birthplaces, Religion, and Education of the People. Province of Leinster* [Cd. 6049], HC 1912–13, pp. vii, 75.

[2] *Census of Ireland, 1911. County Kildare*, p. 49.

[3] *Census of Ireland, 1911. County Kildare*, p. 71.

game of the Squadron Football League in February 1918, attracted in excess of 5,000 spectators.[4] Loyalists dominated local equestrian events such as the Punchestown and Curragh race meetings. Fox-hunting with the Kildare Hunt Club was almost entirely comprised of loyalists. Army officers and local loyalists mixed freely, and intermarriage between officers and ladies from influential families was common. In 1919, Evelyn Synnott, daughter of Nicholas Synnott of Kill, chairman of the Bank of Ireland, married Lieutenant Lockhart St Clair, an officer of the 21st Lancers.[5] An earlier marriage included Cecelia, daughter of George Wray of Monasterevin, who married Lieutenant Henry Wilson (who as Field Martial Sir Henry Wilson served as chief of the imperial general staff from 1918 to February 1922).[6]

While the two Kildare constituencies each returned one nationalist MP to the House of Commons in 1910, unionists were also represented in Westminster, with three peers, Lord Mayo, Lord Cloncurry, and Lord Drogheda eligible to sit in the Lords. In practice, only Lord Mayo was active politically and he emerged as the political leader of Kildare Unionism in its opposition to Home Rule.[7] The Duke of Leinster was the leading peer in the county, but during the revolutionary period he was confined to an institution because of mental instability. The Leinster estate at Carton House was run by his uncle, Lord Frederick FitzGerald, who was one of three unionists regularly elected to Kildare County Council for the Maynooth area.[8] The two remaining Unionist councillors, Major William Dease from Celbridge and Ambrose More O'Ferrall from Carbury, were both Catholic.[9] Unionists also enjoyed strong representation on various district councils and boards of guardians in the county.

The Home Rule crisis began in 1912, but tensions in Kildare between unionism and nationalism, which had not been a serious issue since the nineteenth century Land War, surfaced in the first decade of the twentieth century. In 1908, Lord Frederick FitzGerald, on behalf of his nephew, the Duke of Leinster, donated £300 to the Irish Unionist Alliance (IUA). When this news

---

[4] Con Costello, *A Most Delightful Station: The British Army on the Curragh of Kildare Ireland, 1855–1922* (Cork, 1999), p. 303.

[5] *Leinster Leader*, 3 May 1919.

[6] *Cork Examiner*, 21 Oct. 1861; Keith Jeffery, *Field Marshal Sir Henry Wilson: A Political Soldier* (Oxford, 2006), p. 15.

[7] Patrick Maume, 'Bourke, Dermot Robert Wyndham – 7th earl of Mayo', in James McGuire and James Quinn (eds), *Dictionary of Irish Biography* (Cambridge, 2009): http://dib.cambridge.org/viewReadPage.do?articleId=a0811.

[8] Terence Dooley, *The Decline and Fall of the Dukes of Leinster, 1872–1948: Love, War, Debt and Madness* (Dublin, 2014), pp. 117–21.

[9] Thomas Nelson, *Through Peace and War: Kildare County Council in the Years of Revolution, 1899–1926* (Maynooth, 2015), pp. 330–1.

leaked it caused dismay in Maynooth, and, following a meeting, arrangements for celebrations in the town for the Duke on his coming of age were cancelled.[10] Lord Frederick, as an elected Unionist county councillor, subsequently adopted a low political profile and did not participate in anti-Home Rule activity.

Kildare unionists were determined to organise resistance to Home Rule in their county. Clerical domination and the severance of links with Britain and the Empire were just two of their concerns regarding a Home Rule parliament. There was also a sincere fear of forced migration.[11] Tensions over the Home Rule issue began to widen the divisions that existed between the loyalist gentry and former landowner class, and the overwhelmingly nationalist majority. The third Home Rule bill was introduced in the Commons on 11 April 1912, but opposition by Kildare Unionists had commenced three months previously. In January 1912, two branches of the Women's Unionist Association (WUA) had emerged in the county, one representing ladies in the North Kildare constituency and the second centred in the southern constituency. The first meeting organised by the South Kildare branch was held in Barretstown Castle, near Ballymore-Eustace, on 2 February 1912. The president of the branch, Lady Alice Borrowes, wife of Sir Kildare Borrowes, chaired a meeting which included influential ladies such as Lady Albreda Burke, Mrs St Leger Moore, Mrs Olivia Cape, and a number of gentlemen. Lord Mayo and Captain John Cape, a retired army officer and a Catholic unionist, from Killashee House, close to Naas, gave speeches opposing Home Rule.[12] This was followed in February by a well-attended drawing-room meeting of the North Kildare branch of the WUA in Killadoon House, the residence of the Clements family, close to Celbridge. Although unable to attend, Lady Londonderry, president of the Ulster Women's Unionist Council (UWUC) and wife of a former lord lieutenant, sent a letter urging the unionist women of Ireland, and in particular those in Kildare, to oppose Home Rule.[13] At this meeting, a speech by Reverend Lionel Fletcher, the rector of Straffan, led to controversy. Fletcher asked, 'who was to rule Ireland, Pope Pius X or King George V?', and stated that 'if Home Rule is given to Ireland it is putting the country under the rule of a foreign potentate and that foreign potentate was on the aggressive now'.[14] Two weeks later, at a United Irish League (UIL) meeting in Staplestown, a village in west Kildare, a resolution was passed protesting at the remarks. Reverend Fletcher was accused of 'stirring up religious animosity in the country'.[15] This may

[10] *Evening Telegraph*, 31 Mar. 1908.
[11] *Kildare Observer*, 2 Mar. 1912.
[12] *Kildare Observer*, 10 Feb. 1912.
[13] *Kildare Observer*, 2 Mar. 1912.
[14] *Kildare Observer*, 2 Mar. 1912.
[15] Lionel Fletcher claim (TNA, CO 762/134/11); *Kildare Observer*, 16 Mar. 1912.

have influenced Church of Ireland clergymen in the county to refrain from making public statements relating to Home Rule, as Reverend Fletcher and other rectors in Kildare kept a public silence on political matters throughout the revolution.

By the autumn of 1912, practically the entire landed gentry actively supported organised opposition to Home Rule. This was demonstrated by the attendance at an anti-Home Rule meeting arranged by Lord Mayo at his residence on 24 August 1912. This constituted virtually a 'who's who' of Kildare landed gentry and included families such as the Connollys of Castletown House, the Bartons of Straffan House, the Aylmers of Kerdiffstown House, Wogan-Brownes from Keredern, and Baron de Robeck of Gowran Grange. The vast majority of Kildare magistrates and almost the entire membership of the Grand Jury were also in attendance. One notable exception was George Wolfe, a Protestant member of the landed gentry who supported Home Rule. On this occasion, Lord Mayo avoided provocative statements, saying that the purpose of the meeting was to protest against the Home Rule bill and to show solidarity with unionists in other counties.[16]

As the Home Rule bill made its way through the Commons, unionist opposition in Ulster intensified, culminating in the signing of the Solemn League and Covenant and the Women's Declaration on 28 September 1912.[17] At least two women living in Ballysax, Helen and Marie Gordon, signed the Women's Declaration at the Curragh.[18] They were the wife and daughter of Thomas Gisborne Gordon, a prominent horse trainer and former Irish rugby international.[19] The family were originally from Ulster and the two ladies were prominent members of the South Kildare Women's Unionist Association.[20]

The political temperature in Kildare cooled somewhat throughout 1913 but was reignited owing to the Curragh 'incident' of March 1914. At the time, 24,032 soldiers of all ranks were garrisoned in Ireland. Of this number, 5,806, or almost 25 per cent, were stationed in Kildare, with 4,067 in the Curragh camp. In the nine counties of Ulster, British army strength totalled 2,773, which constituted less than half the number stationed in County Kildare.[21] In

---

[16] *Kildare Observer*, 31 Aug. 1912.

[17] Alvin Jackson, *Home Rule: An Irish History, 1800–2000* (London, 2003), p. 118; A.T.Q. Stewart, *The Ulster Crisis: Resistance to Home Rule, 1912–14* (London, 1967), pp. 58–68.

[18] Ulster Covenant online: www.nidirect.gov.uk/services/search-ulster-covenant.

[19] 1911 census returns, T. Gisborne Gordon: www.census.nationalarchives.ie (accessed 16 Dec. 2015). Gordon was a JP and race-horse trainer from Ballysax, the Curragh.

[20] *Kildare Observer*, 10 Feb. 1912.

[21] General monthly return on the regimental strength of the British army for March 1914, pp. 90–7 (TNA, WO 73/96).

the spring of 1914, due to the threat posed by paramilitarism, most seriously in Ulster where membership of the Ulster Volunteer Force (UVF) totalled 84,000, the government decided to redeploy extra military to the northern province. The bulk of army personnel chosen for redeployment were from the Curragh camp. However, army officers in the Curragh and Newbridge, led by Brigadier General Hubert Gough, commander of the 3rd Calvary Brigade, suspecting they would be required to participate in military action to coerce unionists into accepting Home Rule, chose resignation rather than redeployment. Faced with an escalating and unprecedented crisis, the cabinet reversed its position, claiming that the issue had been a misunderstanding. Ronan Fanning described the event as among the most successful of bloodless revolutions, pointing out that 'the mere threat of force, sustained and carefully co-ordinated, sufficed to achieve the unionist revolution'.[22] During the crisis, leading Kildare unionists who were in contact with the army officers in question provided details of the affair to the leadership of the opposition Conservative party. Sir William Goulding, of Millicent House close to Sallins, one of the most prominent industrialists in the country, wrote to Bonar Law, providing him with the exact number of resignations in the Curragh area.[23] Captain Henry Greer, a retired army officer who lived close to the Curragh, was sent to London on behalf of the officers to lay their case before Law and Lord Lansdowne, the Conservative leader in the Lords.[24]

In light of events at the Curragh and the Larne gunrunning incident, a disgruntled nationalist population in County Kildare, who had not previously supported advanced nationalists, began to favour the emerging Irish Volunteers, which increased throughout the county. Within weeks, Volunteer branches emerged in all the towns, villages, and even townlands surrounding the Curragh camp.[25] During the summer of 1914, as the country drifted close to civil war, unionists in Kildare refrained from any public opposition to Home

---

[22] Ronan Fanning, *Fatal Path: British Government and Irish Revolution, 1910–1922* (London, 2013), p. 2.

[23] Sir William Goulding to Bonar Law, 21 Mar. 1914 (Parliamentary Archives, London [PAL], BL 32/1/40). William Goulding, of Millicent, Sallins, Co. Kildare, was chairman of W. and H.M. Goulding Limited, chemical manufacturers, chairman of the Great Southern and Western Railway, and served as high sheriff of Kildare in 1907.

[24] Letter from Lord Derby to Bonar Law recommending he meet Captain Greer, 22 Mar. 1914, Bonar Law papers (PAL, BL 32/1/43). Henry Greer (1855–1934), a native of Co. Tyrone, was appointed director of the Irish National Stud in 1915, and served as a Senator from 1922 to 1928. He received a knighthood in 1925.

[25] RIC County Inspector's Monthly Confidential Reports, Kildare, May 1914 (TNA, CO 904/57).

Rule. They appeared to be silenced due to the sheer numerical strength of the Home Rule movement in the county.

Initially, the outbreak of the Great War in August 1914 cooled the temperature between nationalists and unionists in the county, and for a short time seemed to unite opposing factions. John Redmond's speech in the Commons, in which he proposed that the National Volunteers should join with the Ulster Volunteers and take the place of the army in guarding the country against a German invasion, was well received by both nationalists and unionists in County Kildare. The largely unionist *Kildare Observer* welcomed the proposal, pointing out that 'no Irishman will read the speech without a thrill of pride'.[26] Prominent local unionists, many of them leading figures in the anti-Home Rule campaign, began to offer financial support for the Irish Volunteers. Lord Mayo, for instance, sent a donation of £15 and his near neighbour, Colonel T.J. de Burgh, donated £25.[27]

Improved relations, however, did not last long and tensions surfaced when a local loyalist-led volunteer force was formed in the county. On the initiative of retired colonel Francis Wogan-Browne, one of the leading Catholic unionists in the county, a mounted volunteer corps, drawn from the gentry and farming class, was established in early August 1914. Having first obtained official sanction from Maurice Moore, inspector-general of the Irish Volunteers, Wogan-Browne gained considerable support from fellow retired army officers. However, this new Volunteer Corp was regarded by nationalists as either an anti-Home Rule independent faction of the Irish Volunteers or a Kildare version of the UVF rather than an integral part of the Irish Volunteer movement. The bulk of members who had attended IUA meetings in the county were supporters of Edward Carson and opponents of John Redmond.

On 13 August, some 20 members of the mounted corps, named the 'Kildare Horse', assembled in the square of Naas barracks for its first drill. In addition to Wogan-Browne, three fellow retired army officers – Sir Kildare Borrowes, who had been appointed trainer of the new corps, Captain John Cape, and Colonel St Ledger Moore, a former commander of the South of Ireland yeomanry – were present. However, when a deputation representing the Naas Volunteers, headed by three prominent members, Fr P. Hipwell CC, a local curate, P.J. McCann, a solicitor in the town, and Thomas Langan, secretary of Kildare County Council, approached the new volunteers and invited them to sign the Irish Volunteer enrolment form, they refused, believing it would have implied support for Home Rule.[28] The issue was defused at a meeting of the Kildare County Committee of the Irish Volunteers later that week, when it

---

[26] *Kildare Observer*, 8 Aug. 1914.
[27] *Kildare Observer*, 8 Aug. 1914; *Irish Independent*, 10 Aug. 1914.
[28] *Leinster Leader*, 15 Aug. 1914; *Kildare Observer*, 15 Aug. 1914.

was acknowledged that members of the new corps were not required to sign the form.[29] Although the new volunteer corps is not recorded as having any meaningful subsequent role, they continued in existence, with newspapers reporting training exercises continuing until early November.[30]

The Irish Volunteer movement split into two factions in October over the issue of support and enlistment for the war. The majority, under the leadership of John Redmond, formed the National Volunteers and supported the war effort, while the smaller section under the leadership of Eóin MacNeill, which continued to be known as the Irish Volunteers, opposed the war.[31] Although Lord Mayo had given a measure of support to the Irish Volunteers before the split in August 1914, relations subsequently deteriorated. In January 1915, Mayo, in a speech in the House of Lords, criticised the Irish Volunteers who distributed leaflets at an anti-recruitment demonstration in Dublin the previous month. He alleged that if the Germans came to Ireland the Irish Volunteers would 'most likely run away'.[32] Although his reference related to the Irish Volunteers, who enjoyed little support in Kildare, nationalists in the county denounced the statement arguing that it might be misinterpreted as referring to the National Volunteers. The remarks were denounced by Kildare County Council, Naas Urban District Council, and other boards. Some elected nationalists even called on the government to intern Mayo as the speech could 'be interpreted as impeding recruitment amongst Irishmen'.[33] Mayo's credibility was damaged, and he made no further public comments regarding either section of the Volunteers for the remainder of the war.

The events of Easter week 1916 came as a shock to the loyalist community in Kildare. Many officers in the British army had planned to attend social events with local loyalists over the weekend. On Easter Monday, Eleonore Clements from Killadoon, accompanied by her 11-year-old son Charles, visited Colonel Bertram Portal and his wife in Newbridge, where they were due to attend a military sports event after lunch. But the event was cancelled, as Colonel Portal was called to duty.[34] He was the officer commanding the cavalry reserve in the Curragh and served as the operational commander in Dublin throughout Easter week. Captain Henry de Courcy-Wheeler, a native of Robertstown, is probably the best-known Kildare army officer who participated. He had been prominent in the unionist movement in Kildare prior to enlisting in the army and served during the rising as a senior officer in the staff of the

29 *Leinster Leader*, 22 Aug. 1914.
30 *Kildare Observer*, 7 Nov. 1914.
31 Dermot Meleady, *John Redmond: The National Leader* (Dublin, 1973), pp. 307–9.
32 Hansard, HL, vol. 18, cols 358–60 (8 Jan. 1915); *Irish Times*, 9 Jan. 1915; *Irish Independent*, 9 Jan. 1915; *Leinster Leader*, 16 Jan. 1915.
33 *Leinster Leader*, 16, 23 Jan. 1915.
34 Costello, *A Most Delightful Station*, pp. 295–6.

commander of the British forces in Dublin, General William Lowe. He also had an important role supervising the surrender of many of the rebel leaders.[35] Captain Warmington from Naas, son of a local bank manager, was the highest-ranking native Kildare army officer killed in the Rising.[36]

Prominent Kildare unionist, Sir William Goulding, the chairman of the Great Southern Railway and managing director of Goulding Chemicals, had been marooned at Kingsbridge during Easter Week, and under fire for two days. On 4 May 1916, he wrote to Bonar Law, now secretary of state for the colonies, with concerns about what he believed were false claims in press reports that the Rising had been confined to Dublin. Goulding alleged that:

> In my own County Kildare three fourths of the people were waiting for news of success of the rebels to at once join in, so-called National Volunteers and others. And I have met every train from the country and friends from all parts of the south and west have told me that it was exactly the same in every county.[37]

This was far from accurate. The bulk of the National Volunteers in Kildare, many with relatives serving at the front, were supporters of the war effort. However, the quote is indicative of the fears experienced by loyalists during the rising and Goulding had some genuine cause for concern. Apart from personal financial losses, the Rising had rekindled stories of atrocities from 1798 among Kildare loyalists.[38] An account of events in 1798 published in 1905 in the *Journal of the Kildare Archaeological Society*, which at the time had a largely loyalist readership, described how the rebellion in Kildare 'degenerated into a plundering banditti', in which the rebels 'left the gentlemen and rich farmers neither furniture nor stock of any kind'.[39] Goulding was aware of advanced nationalist activity, which was openly displayed annually at the Wolfe Tone Commemoration at Bodenstown, within half a mile of his residence, Millicent House.[40] Clearly, loyalists in Kildare were worried that National Volunteers who had attended events organised by Thomas Clarke, such as at Bodenstown

[35] Alex Findlater, *Findlaters: The Story of a Dublin Merchant Family, 1774–2001* (Dublin, 2001), pp. 281–2.

[36] *Kildare Observer*, 6 May 1916; Stannus Geoghegan, *The Campaigns and History of the Royal Irish Regiment*, vol. 2: *From 1900 to 1922* (Edinburgh, 1927), p. 159.

[37] Sir William Goulding to Bonar Law, 4 May 1916 (PAL, BL 53/2/5).

[38] Liam Chambers, *Rebellion in Kildare, 1790–1803* (Dublin, 1998), pp. 74, 89; Mario Corrigan, *All that Delirium of the Brave: Kildare in 1798* (Naas, 1997), pp. 84, 91.

[39] Rev. Canon Sherlock, 'Further Notes on the History and Antiquities of the Parish of Clane', *Journal of the Kildare Archaeological Society*, 4/1 (1903–5), p. 43.

[40] C.J. Woods, *Bodenstown Revisited: The Grave of Theobald Wolf Tone, its Monuments and its Pilgrimages* (Dublin, 2018), pp. 81–6.

in June 1915 and the O'Donovan Rossa funeral in Dublin in August 1915, could actively support the cause of the insurgents.[41] The National Volunteers that attended Bodenstown in June 1915 did so largely to commemorate Wolfe Tone, but by early 1916 some had switched their allegiance to the Eóin MacNeill-led Irish Volunteers.

In response to the dramatically altered political climate after the Rising, the government proposed an Irish Convention composed of representative Irishmen from different political parties and spheres of interest to address constitutional issues, including Home Rule. Kildare unionists had a strong voice at the Irish Convention of 1917, with two residents from the county, Lord Mayo, a representative of the Irish peers, and Sir William Goulding, a government nominee, among the membership. The nationalist majority in the county was represented by one nominee: Matthew Minch, chairman of Kildare County Council.[42] Goulding was the most active of the three, strongly supporting the Midleton initiative which proposed a plan involving a Home Rule settlement without partition.[43] Goulding had become well known nationally, as he chaired the Property Losses (Ireland) Committee, set up to adjudicate on compensation for losses incurred as a result of the Rising.[44] It was during this period that differences emerged among Kildare unionists, with some in the leadership such as Mayo and Goulding favouring some concession on the issue of Home Rule in order to avoid partition.

But while this shift in opinion was occurring another crisis emerged. The conscription crisis in April 1918 saw nationalists and loyalists in the county once more pitted on opposite sides. In March 1918, following a German offensive on the Western Front, the government decided to impose conscription to Ireland. Loyalists supported the measure, alleging that a higher percentage of their population had joined the colours and that conscription would address that imbalance. William Kirkpatrick, a Protestant and JP from Celbridge, who was an executive member of the IUA, supported the government's view, suggesting that 'what we should do is fill up the Irish regiments'.[45]

Reaction in County Kildare to conscription was swift; within a week of the news breaking, local councils and boards had passed resolutions protesting against the measure. Although most of the resolutions were

[41] *Leinster Leader*, 26 Jun. 1915; *Kildare Observer*, 26 Jun. 1915.
[42] R.B. McDowell, *The Irish Convention, 1917–18* (London, 1970), pp. 221, 224–5.
[43] McDowell, *The Irish Convention*, p. 151.
[44] For a full account of post-Rising compensation, see Daithí Ó Corráin, '"They Blew up the Best Portion of our City and … it is Their Duty to Replace It": Compensation and Reconstruction in the Aftermath of the Easter Rising', *Irish Historical Studies*, 39/154 (2014), pp. 272–95.
[45] *Leinster Leader*, 20 Apr. 1918.

unanimous, split votes were recorded particularly where the membership included Unionists, who had representation on many of the local authorities in the county. At a meeting of Athy Urban District Council, Thomas Plewman, a local Protestant farmer, stated that as a 'loyalist' he could not vote for the anti-conscription resolution which had been proposed: 'he did not object to English laws, as the Irish people would be better off with them than with Home Rule under German rule'. In the same week there was also a dissenting voice at a meeting of Athy Board of Guardians when a Unionist member, George Gilmore, another Protestant farmer, voted against an anti-conscription resolution.[46] In the north of the county the issue produced a lively debate at a meeting of Celbridge Board of Guardians, where the membership included three Unionists. Kirkpatrick, who chaired the meeting, pointed out that the government could not propose to conscript men up to 50 years of age in England and leave Ireland untouched. John Shackleton of the well-known Quaker milling family regarded the opposition to conscription as a cowardly attitude taken up by the Irish people. A resolution proposed by the nationalist majority on the board pledging support for the anti-conscription measures was carried with three Unionists, including Kirkpatrick and Shackleton, voting against.[47] Although overwhelmingly in the minority on local boards, Unionist members vigorously opposed anti-conscription resolutions and supported the government line. However, some indications suggest that unionist support for the measure was not unanimous.

The anti-conscription pledge was taken by almost the entire nationalist population of the county on Pledge Sunday, 21 April 1918. Although press censorship was strictly enforced, the limited coverage in the local newspapers in Kildare gave accounts of the numbers engaged in the protest. Some unionist opposition to conscription was also evident. At Kill, a well-known Catholic unionist, Nicholas Synnott, addressed the meeting and was among the 3,000 people who took the pledge.[48] In some villages, such as Staplestown, taking of the pledge was carried out over two Sundays to facilitate Protestants. As the pledge was taken after Mass in the local chapel when Protestants from the locality would be attending their own church service, the extra week gave them an opportunity to sign. Reports indicated that a sizeable number of Protestants in the area signed.[49] In the parish of Ballymore-Eustace, two local men assisted the campaign organised by Nelly O'Brien, an anti-conscription activist who was leading a Protestant anti-conscription campaign. In the

---

[46] *Kildare Observer*, 13 Apr. 1918.
[47] *Leinster Leader*, 27 Apr. 1918; *Kildare Observer*, 27 Apr. 1918.
[48] *Freeman's Journal*, 24 Apr. 1918.
[49] *Kildare Observer*, 4 May 1918.

canvass, 20 signatures against conscription were obtained, 2 others expressed themselves in favour, and 5 indicated a neutral stance.[50]

The 1918 general election, which saw Sinn Féin emerge as the principal voice of nationalist Ireland and the government's determination to use partition as a solution to the Irish crisis, caused dismay and tension among Kildare loyalists. This led to a splintering of the unionist movement in the country between southern unionists and Ulster unionists over the proposed partition of Ireland. Southern unionists saw partition as the defeat of their aim to keep a united Ireland within the United Kingdom. Ulster unionists came to see partition as the only way to safeguard Protestant and unionist interests in Ulster. Following a meeting of the IUA in Dublin on 24 January 1919, influential southern Unionists led by Lord Midleton and supported by the two principal Unionist figures from Kildare, Lord Mayo and Sir William Goulding, formed the breakaway Unionist Anti-Partition League (UAPL).[51] Although the *Irish Independent* claimed that every unionist of note in the south had joined the new movement, this was not the case in Kildare.[52] Lord Cloncurry remained as one of the joint vice-presidents of the 'diehard' IUA, with four other leading Unionists from the county – Percy Le Touche, John A. Aylmer, William Tyrrell, and Herbert Warren – members of its executive.[53] Other well-known IUA figures from the county, such as Henry Clements and William Kirkpatrick, opted to join the UAPL.[54]

In the aftermath of the local elections in January and June 1920, which saw republicans increase their representation, unionism in the county continued to fracture, with support drifting to the Irish Dominion League (IDL), a moderate body. This movement, which was founded by Sir Horace Plunkett, favoured dominion status for Ireland within the Empire as a compromise between partition and republicanism.[55] The Irish Peace Conference, organised largely by the IDL in Dublin in August 1920, was attended by a large number of Kildare loyalists. They included the Reverend Lionel Fletcher, George Mansfield, a Catholic and leading member of the landed gentry, William Fennell, an ex-high sheriff, and Henry de Courcy-Wheeler, who was retired.[56] One of the contributors

---

50 *Leinster Leader*, 4 May 1918; Carmel Doyle, 'O'Brien, Ellen Lucy ("Nelly")', in James McGuire and James Quinn (eds), *Dictionary of Irish Biography* (Cambridge, 2009): http://dib.cambridge.org/viewReadPage.do?articleId=a6466.

51 *Sunday Independent*, 26 Jan 1919; *Irish Independent*, 27 Jan 1919; Alvin Jackson, *The Two Unions: Ireland, Scotland, and the Survival of the United Kingdom, 1707–2007* (Oxford, 2012), p. 309; McDowell, *Crisis and Decline*, pp. 65–6.

52 *Irish Independent*, 12 Feb. 1919.

53 *Irish Independent*, 25 Jan. 1919.

54 *Irish Independent*, 29 Jan. 1919.

55 *Irish Independent*, 28 Jun. 1919.

56 *Freeman's Journal*, 25 Aug. 1920.

who spoke at the event was Samuel Wray, a farmer from Prosperous. Making an impassioned plea to other farmers in the country, he sought their co-operation in seeking peace. He stated that as a Protestant he had lived on the most amicable terms with his Catholic neighbours and that amongst those engaged in the Sinn Féin movement he never found the slightest trace of religious bigotry. He wished 'their brethren in the north of Ireland would take cognizance of that fact'. In supporting the aims of the IDL he pointed out 'that he had been a unionist, but for some years he had come to the conclusion that the settlement of the Irish question could only be brought about by giving to Ireland proper self-government and the charge of her own destiny'.[57] Wray received applause for his contribution, but this initiative received virtually no support. Although the new movement appeared to indicate a growing acceptance of self-rule among loyalists in the county, the change of opinion was more than likely a panic response to the inevitability of partition and a fear of isolation and severance from the numerically strong Ulster unionist population.

Support for the aims of the IDL in Kildare was reinforced by magistrates from the south of the county at a meeting held in Athy on 20 September 1920. Twelve justices of the peace, concerned at the state of disorder in the country and particularly the proposed Government of Ireland bill which would enforce partition, passed the following motion (proposed by William Fennell and seconded by Thomas Plewman):

> That we the Justices of the Petty Sessions districts of Athy and Castledermot ... call on the government ... to adopt a measure of the fullest and most comprehensive Colonial Home Rule, believing, as we do, that by this or some similar action alone can an end be put to the present intolerable state of things, and which the proposed Home Rule Bill only tends to intensify, being, as it is, entirely unacceptable to any section of the community.[58]

This was a major concession by previously uncompromising loyalists. Lord Monteagle of Brandon, a leading member of the IDL, introduced a Dominion of Ireland bill in the Lords, which proposed convening an elected constituent assembly. This would determine a form of dominion status with limitations and restrictions such as reserving armed forces and safeguards for Ulster.[59] The proposals, however, obtained little support either in Ireland or Westminster, and the bill was defeated at a second reading on 1 July 1920.[60] Following the

---

[57] *Freeman's Journal*, 25 Aug. 1920.
[58] *Kildare Observer*, 25 Sep. 1920.
[59] Hansard, HL, vol. 40, cols 1120–5 (1 Jul. 1920).
[60] Hansard, HL, vol. 40, col. 1157 (1 Jul. 1920).

defeat, with loyalists in the south hopelessly divided, the unstoppable drift to partition continued.

Throughout the second half of 1920, opposition to the Government of Ireland bill by southern unionists continued unabated, with Kildare unionists prominent at executive level of both the IUA and the UAPL. In the Lords, Lord Mayo stated:

> The partition which the bill would bring about is resented all over Ireland ... Not one word in the bill is accepted in the south of Ireland, and not a single public body had expressed a wish to have the bill. The bill has been imposed upon them, and I would like to ask who would work it in the south and west of Ireland? ... I have never known during my whole life, such a sulky hatred throughout Ireland to British rule as exists today. What is to become of the minor[i]ties in the south and west? These were the men whos[e] sons and daughters gave their lives during the war, and were they to be left to the tender mercies of a Sinn Féin parliament?[61]

The only concessions the southern unionists could win in the Government of Ireland Act was safeguards in a southern Irish senate.[62] The senate was to have a membership of 40 and Kildare Unionists were well represented in the chamber with four from the county accepting nominations: Lord Cloncurry, Lord Mayo, Sir William Goulding, and General Bryan Mahon. Mahon, who was a former general officer commanding of the army in Ireland, resided in Ballymore-Eustace. The senate met only once, with Lord Cloncurry and General Mahon among the 15 that attended.[63]

The violence that was widespread during the War of Independence, particularly in Munster, was not as prevalent in Kildare due to the presence of the military barracks and a reluctance to kill unarmed RIC. Counter-mobility operations by the IRA, however, such as road blocking, caused considerable hardship to the entire local population. Dorothea Findlater, daughter of de Courcy-Wheeler, offered the following description of the inconvenience experienced by local unionists:

> During the troubles when my father was out and about in the Ford, he brought with him a spade and two planks, to get across trenches dug across the road and a saw to cut through branches where trees had been

---

[61] *Irish Times*, 25 Nov. 1920.
[62] McDowell, *Crisis and Decline*, pp. 74–7.
[63] For a full list of senators, see www.ark.ac.uk/elections/h1921.htm (accessed 1 Oct. 2017).

felled. We sometimes had to climb over two or three trees getting from our house in Robertstown to church in Kilmeague two miles away, on Sundays.[64]

The de Courcy-Wheeler family, who were held in high esteem in their locality, were not seriously targeted by local militants. In August 1914, the Robertstown Volunteers publicly assured the Captain of the safety of his family and property while he was absent on military duty.[65] Another loyalist hindered by road blocking at this time was the former RIC County Inspector for Kildare, Kerry Supple, who had a lucky escape following his retirement in January 1921 when his car hit one of the trenches, causing the vehicle to drive off the road. On this occasion he was accompanied by his wife and step-grandson Francis Bacon, the future artist, who was ten years old at the time. Bacon recalls how the party were chased by 'rebel forces across the countryside to safety'.[66] Supple, following his retirement, resided in two residences: Straffan Lodge and Farmleigh near Abbeyleix. The incident probably occurred at the latter residence, which needed to be sandbagged for protection.[67]

The closure of RIC barracks outside the big towns in Kildare throughout early 1920 left loyalists exposed to the possibility of attack by the IRA, who regularly targeted owners of legally held firearms. One significant incident between a Kildare loyalist and the IRA in 1920 occurred at Ballindoolan, a remote area of Kildare half-way between Edenderry and Kinnegad, when William Tyrrell, grand master of Edenderry Orange Lodge and an executive member of the IUA, successfully resisted attempts by the IRA to seize his firearms.[68] The encounter, which was a relatively rare example of resistance of this kind, led to an exchange of shots which wounded one of the attackers.[69] Despite the violent campaign against the RIC at this time, support for the police from local loyalists remained strong, with recruitment continuing on a small scale from Ireland. One of these Irish-born recruits, Albert Carter, a 19-year-old farmer's son from a loyalist background in Kilmeague, joined in

[64] Findlater, *Findlaters*, pp. 295–6.
[65] Letter from Robertstown Volunteers to de Courcy-Wheeler, 10 Aug. 1914 (NLI, MS 5,670, fo. 5892); *Leinster Leader*, 29 Aug. 1914.
[66] Barbara Dawson, *Traces of Time: Francis Bacon*: www.palazzostrozzi.org/allegati/ Barbara_Dawson_121016120054.pdf. (accessed 30 May 2019).
[67] www.hughlane.ie/bacons-life (accessed 30 May 2019); *Kildare Observer*, 12 Nov. 1921.
[68] Compensation (Ireland) Committee, County Kildare, 1919–22 (CO, 905/7/277); *Kildare Observer*, 14 Aug. 1920.
[69] BMH WS 850 (Patrick Colgan).

late 1920 but was shot dead while on patrol duty in the town of Letterkenny on 18 May 1921.[70]

The boycott of the RIC and the army in Kildare, which became widespread from early 1920, greatly impacted on the loyalist community. Prominent loyalists throughout Kildare who were on good terms with the Crown forces were looked upon as potential 'spies'. They became easy targets for retaliation for atrocities committed by the 'Black and Tans' and atrocities committed against the Catholic/nationalist community in the Belfast area.[71] The Belfast boycott, which was initiated in September 1920 in response to the outbreak of sectarian violence in that city, caused substantial inconvenience to loyalists in rural areas of Kildare, with ex-servicemen prominently targeted. In June 1921, Paul Goodwin, a 26-year-old Protestant farmer from South Kildare with a holding of 180 acres, was ordered by the IRA to leave the country for passing information to the authorities. He moved to England for a short time before returning to Ireland and eventually, in a discreet way, returning to his farm.[72] Pim Goodbody, a former army captain who farmed 300 acres in Ballytore, also suffered intimidation. At night he sometimes had to escape through a back window of his house and hide in the fields. He left for London in May 1921 but returned briefly following the Treaty. Eventually he was forced to sell his holding for one-third of its market value.[73] James Bedford was another ex-serviceman who suffered intimidation but he took refuge in the Curragh camp before moving to England.[74]

Following the Truce in July 1921, intimidation of unionists increased. On 15 July, four days into the Truce, Leonard Wilson-Wright, high sheriff of Kildare, received an urgent telegram from London advising him to leave Ireland immediately as his life and that of his cousin, John Granville Wilson of Daramona, County Westmeath (both cousins of Sir Henry Wilson), were in danger.[75] Wilson-Wright lived in Timahoe, an isolated area of west Kildare where the nearest RIC barracks was 12 miles away in Edenderry. He left Ireland, as directed, and spent a number of years outside the country before returning to his property. As a substantial employer in the area with a steward in charge of the operation, the livelihood of many families would be affected

[70] *Donegal Democrat*, 20 May 1921; Richard Abbott, *Police Casualties in Ireland, 1919–1922* (Cork, 2000), p. 243.
[71] For details of the sectarian violence in Belfast, see Kieran Glennon, *From Pogrom to Civil War: Tom Glennon and the Belfast IRA* (Cork, 2013).
[72] Paul Goodwin claim (TNA, CO 762/193/7).
[73] Pim Goodbody claim (TNA, CO 762/85/1).
[74] James Bedford claim (TNA, CO 762/84/8).
[75] L.A.W. Wright claim (TNA, CO 762/117/16).

if his farm were fully boycotted and this may account for the fact that his property was not as severely targeted as that of other unionists.[76]

Following the Treaty, many unionists in Kildare moved quickly to recognise the new Provisional Government while others adopted a more cautious attitude. Lord Mayo was one of the first senior southern loyalists to recognise the new government. He organised a meeting in Dublin on 19 January to endorse and offer support to the government. However, he was opposed by the UAPL, which advised members not to take part in the meeting as the issue was to be discussed at a forthcoming party gathering.[77] Ignoring the warning, Mayo went ahead with the meeting and was supported by a sizeable number of southern loyalists, including a large contingent from Kildare, such as Lord Cloncurry, General Bryan Mahon, Major Edward Connolly, Major William Dease, Bertram Barton, and Algernon Aylmer. Others from the county, such as George Mansfield and Lord Walter FitzGerald from the family of the Duke of Leinster, sent their support. Opening the proceedings, Mayo declared that the Union had gone, and they were no longer unionists, and he urged the gathering to realise that the past was dead. Archbishop Gregg pointed out that it would be a serious mistake for former supporters of the Union to withhold their co-operation from the new constitutionally appointed government.[78] A resolution, proposed by Lord Dunraven, that 'Southern Unionists recognising that a Provisional government has been formed, desire to support our fellow-countrymen in this Government in order that peace may be brought about and the welfare of the community secured' was passed unanimously.[79]

A general meeting of the UAPL, chaired by Lord Midleton, was held two days later. The attendance from Kildare included the Earl of Mayo, Sir William Goulding, Colonel T.J. de Burgh, H.J.B. Clements, and W.T. Kirkpatrick. In view of the altered situation, it was decided to drop the term unionist from the party name and adopt the title 'Constitutional Anti-Partition League' instead. It was also agreed to make every effort to secure co-operation of all classes in establishing stable and constitutional government in the country. The decisions at the two meetings attended by representatives from practically the entire loyalist community in Kildare effectively ended unionist opposition to self-determination and also resulted in a public offer of allegiance to the new government. The more hardline IUA met in Dublin on 26 January, but decided, due to political uncertainty, not to take any definite action.[80]

[76] Interview of John Wilson-Wright by Des O'Leary and Seamus Cullen, Apr. 1993.
[77] *Irish Times*, 17 Jan. 1922.
[78] *Irish Independent*, 20 Jan. 1922.
[79] *Kildare Observer*, 21 Jan. 1922.
[80] *Irish Times*, 28 Jan. 1922.

Mayo was critical of fellow unionists who withheld support for the Provisional Government and who issued inaccurate reports that could affect the security of the southern minority. In May, Field Marshal Henry Wilson criticised Lloyd George, arguing that he was responsible for reducing the 26 counties of the south 'to a welter of chaos and murder'.[81] Mayo publicly refuted the claim, suggesting that Wilson, with his great military knowledge, should deal with the 'bad work' taking place in Belfast.[82] Clearly, Mayo was worried that the ongoing 'pogrom' taking place in Belfast would backfire in the south, with southern Protestants targeted even more severely than before.

Although there is no record of intentional killing of Protestants in Kildare, a number of loyalist deaths can be attributed to intimidation and violence. In August 1920, the farmhouse of Henry Hendy, who lived close to Athy, was raided by the IRA. As a result, Hendy's wife Jane suffered severe trauma, a nervous breakdown, and gave birth prematurely to twins. She died from her illness on 17 June 1922, having been predeceased by both of her twins.[83] Another loyalist, Thomas Glynn, from Moone in South Kildare, a 54-acre farmer, was assaulted in May 1922, receiving kicks to his head when a gang claiming to be members of the IRA broke into his house. He suffered an injury to his brain and died four years later.[84]

The most high-profile incident relating to the death of a Kildare loyalist occurred during the period of the British army evacuation. On 10 February 1922, Lieutenant Jack Wogan-Browne, an army officer attached to Kildare military barracks, was shot dead in a robbery at Kildare. He was from Naas, the son of Colonel Wogan-Browne. The incident occurred close to the army barracks in Kildare when Wogan-Browne, having collected the regimental pay from a local bank, was accosted by two armed men, and while resisting their attempts to grab the money, was shot in the head.[85] Investigations carried out by Sean Kavanagh, the local IRA liaison officer, identified three active IRA members from the Suncroft area on the southern fringes of the Curragh as the likely offenders.[86] The incident jeopardised the process of the withdrawal of the British army, though tensions eased following the arrests of the three suspects. Although the suspects were never brought to trial, the evacuation process continued and was completed by 16 May.[87]

[81] *Irish Times*, 25 Mar. 1922.
[82] *Irish Times*, 25 Mar. 1922.
[83] Henry Hendy claim (TNA, CO 762/1974); detail from the Hendy family gravestone in Timolin churchyard.
[84] Anna Glynn claim (TNA, CO 762/79/16).
[85] Officers service papers, Lt. John Wogan-Browne, 1914–23 (TNA, WO 339/43238).
[86] See 3rd Easter Division Records (MAI, MSPC/RO/560).
[87] Evacuation of the Curragh camp, 1 Apr.–31 May 1922 (TNA, WO 35/182A); Hugh

Loyalists in Kildare, who could previously rely on the security of the British army presence in the county, now had no protection, and intimidation escalated. According to General Macready, 'Protestants and all forms of loyalists are having a devil of a time'.[88] As a result, many with business interests left. Robert Eccles, a veteran of the Boer War and a chemist in Athy, received a threatening letter on 22 May 1922 ordering him to leave Athy within five days. He sold his business in November 1922 and together with his family emigrated to Melbourne.[89] Harry Andree, a photographer in Newbridge, was another who left. In the early months of 1922, he received threatening letters which included a death threat to his son who was in the army. He moved to England the following May.[90] Even unmarried loyalist ladies living alone in isolated farmhouses were not immune from IRA raids. Sarah Giltrap, who lived close to Ballymore Eustace, had six of her best cattle stolen. She believed the animals were driven by anti-Treaty IRA to Kilbride camp and killed to feed occupants of the Four Courts in Dublin.[91]

The constitution of the Irish Free State provided for a senate, which would deliver representation for various vocational interests including unionists. While three TDs representing the constituency of Kildare were elected to the fourth Dáil Éireann, three prominent former Kildare unionists: Lord Mayo, General Bryan Mahon, and Sir Henry Greer of the National Stud were nominated to the Senate.[92] This resulted in Kildare's former unionists obtaining an imbalance of representation in the newly established Oireachtas in comparison with other political parties from the county. Resentment was inevitable. The Civil War was taking place at the time and the anti-Treaty IRA campaign of burning houses of unionist senators resulted in the destruction of Mayo's residence, Palmerstown House, and General Mahon's residence at Mullaboden Lodge.[93] Greer's residence, Curragh Grange House near Newbridge, was not targeted.

Jeudwine, 'History of the 5th Division in Ireland, Nov. 1919–Mar. 1922' (IWM, 72/82/2); *Irish Times*, 15 Feb. 1922.

[88] Macready to Jeudwine, 2 May 1922 (IWM).

[89] Robert Eccles claim (TNA, CO 762/189/3).

[90] Harry Andree claim (TNA, CO 762/59/11).

[91] Sarah Giltrap (TNA, CO 762/147/12). Kilbride camp is situated four miles north-east of Blessington.

[92] Seanad Debates, vol. 1, no. 1, 11 Dec 1922; vol. 1 no. 2, 13 Dec. 1922: http://oireachtasdebates.oireachtas.ie/debates (accessed 1 May 2018); Donal O'Sullivan, *The Irish Free State and its Senate: A Study in Contemporary Politics* (London, 1940), pp. 90–1.

[93] For details of the burning of Palmerstown, see Countess Mayo claim (TNA, CO /762/133/1); *Irish Independent*, 31 Jan. 1923; *Kildare Observer*, 3 Feb. 1923. For Mullaboden, see General Bryan Mahon claim (TNA, CO/762/97/15); *Kildare Observer*, 24 Feb. 1923.

In the post-independence period, Kildare loyalists not only suffered at the hands of anti-Treaty IRA but many also claimed to have suffered unfairly at the hands of the Free State authorities. Charles Bury, from Downings House, Prosperous, is a typical example. His estate consisted of 624 acres. In early 1922, it was occupied by anti-Treaty IRA, stables and farm implements were destroyed by fire, and he received threatening letters. He was fired on while attempting to prevent his cattle being driven from his land. According to Bury's Irish Grants Committee claim, the land at this time 'was used as a commonage, meadow letting in 1922 was boycotted and only one third was let which realised half of its value'. Bury, in poor financial circumstances, was forced to move to Dublin while his daughters emigrated to London. In early 1923, he claimed between 40 and 50 Republicans were in the house at one time and he was required to enter the dwelling by way of a republican sentry.[94] One of the motives for targeting Bury seemed to be a desire to obtain his land. Following his death in 1924, the land was acquired by the Irish Land Commission, at a deflated price, for distribution among smallholders in the area.[95] But, in this case, blatant favouritism was undertaken by the new government as Bury's house and 100 acres was allocated to a retired National Army officer.[96]

Altogether, more than 40 loyalists from Kildare who claimed to have suffered violence and intimidation at the hands of the anti-Treaty IRA, or those claiming to be republicans, sought compensation from the British government.[97] While this figure includes those who actually applied for relief, it does not include the total figure, as some had already successfully obtained compensation from Kildare County Council, while others simply did not claim at all. In some areas of the county, mainly areas close to Dublin, loyalists were relatively safe, but in particular regions such as South Kildare and West Kildare, intimidation was widespread. The following comment and description of lawlessness in his area was given by Reverend L.M. Hewson, who lived at Ballinafagh, close to Prosperous in west Kildare:

> Altogether both the English Government and the Free State Government
> have shown a totally incapable ability to keep that particular corner quiet:
> any decent law-abiding man or woman be he member of the Church of
> Ireland or Roman Catholic: in politics 'Loyalist' (whatever that means)

94 Esmee Lascelles and Doreen Buchanan claim (TNA, CO 762/199/5).
95 Dáil Debates 11 Mar. 1925, vol. 10, no. 11: http://oireachtasdebates.oireachtas.ie/ debates (accessed 1 May 2018).
96 Andrew Rynne, *The Vasectomy Doctor: A Memoir* (Cork, 2005), p. 24.
97 According to the Irish Grants Committee files, a total of 48 with Co. Kildare addresses claimed compensation; however, a small number of the claimants had lived outside the county at the time of their distress.

or 'Republican' or 'Free State' got it in the neck unless they kept their gun handy and used it.[98]

Although anti-Treaty-IRA were responsible for much of the disturbance, some of the violence and theft had come from an element merely claiming to be republican.

Intimidation of loyalists in Kildare, mainly in the Athy area, continued throughout the 1920s. Henry Large was the owner of Castlerheban and 230 acres near Athy. In 1922, he let the house to Captain Henry Hosie, who was boycotted; the dwelling was burned down on 20 February 1924. The following November, Henry Large, the freeholder of the property, was driven out of his house in Tullow and moved into a converted outhouse adjacent to the burnt-out house at Castlerheban. However, the outhouse remained his residence throughout the late 1920s as he was unable to rent a house in the Athy area due to continued boycotting.[99]

Despite the difficulties experienced by some loyalists in County Kildare, they were not subjected to the same levels of violence as those in other counties. According to the Irish Grants Committee files, the northern and central regions of Kildare were more peaceful than the southern section of the county, where considerable violence was used. The county was to some extent a safe haven for those forced to flee from more troubled counties, and several loyalist families from these areas moved to Kildare in the 1920s. Henry Sampey, a substantial landowner, who was boycotted and driven from his native Roscommon, for example, moved to the Ballymore Eustace area.[100] Alexander Cornelius, who had provided accommodation for British troops on his farm in County Laois and as a result was boycotted, relocated 30 miles to a farm close to the Curragh where the family lived, without interference.[101]

In the 15-year period following 1911, the population of the county declined by 13 per cent. While a slight decline of the Catholic population was recorded, the Protestant population fell by 70 per cent, far greater than in any other county in the Irish Free State.[102] Of the total Protestant population of 11,900 in 1911, 5,000 were serving members of the British army, with permanent resident Protestants numbering 6,900. By 1926, the latter category numbered 3,600, which represents a decline of 52 per cent from 1911.[103] Although the evacuation of the British army accounted for most of the exodus, other factors, such as

---

[98] Cecil Johnston claim (TNA, CO 762/193/21).
[99] Henry Large claim (CO 762/139/2); Henry Hosie claim (CO 762/153/4).
[100] Henry Sampey claim (TNA, CO 762/189/2).
[101] Emmie Cornelius claim (TNA, CO 762/198/7).
[102] *Saorstát Éireann: Census of Population, 1926*, vol. 3, Table 8b.
[103] *Saorstát Éireann: Census of population, 1926*, vol. 3, Table 9.

intimidation during the latter stages of the Irish Revolution, economic reasons, and a preference not to live in the Free State contributed to the decline.[104]

The decline continued in the decades following independence, with the former landed gentry among the hardest hit.[105] A number of factors such as local government rates and high running costs contributed, but the principal factor was the introduction of the 1923 Land Act, which forced many to sell up as the new state accelerated the process of land reform.[106] Leonard Wilson-Wright fared better than most, as his residence, Coolcarrigan House, although occupied for a time by anti-Treaty IRA, escaped destruction. One reason was that his estate was a working farm providing local employment.[107] Eventually, he returned home to manage his extensive farming interests.

Until 1922, loyalists in Kildare enjoyed the security experienced by no other county outside Ulster owing to the presence of British army garrisons who were considered integral members of their community. Steadfastly anti-Home Rule, this community resisted concessions to nationalist aspirations. Developments such as Easter Week 1916 and the conscription crisis caused deep concern but did not produce any conciliatory movement. However, the government's decision to implement Home Rule based on partition caused panic throughout unionism in Kildare, resulting in many adopting a more compromising view. Fears expressed in 1920 by their principal spokesman Lord Mayo, of being left 'to the mercies of a Sinn Féin parliament', came to fruition. Concessions to former unionists in the constitution of the Irish Free State did not compensate for the previous privileges they enjoyed, but, despite the violence, intimidation, and trauma of the early 1920s, the community in Kildare survived, and while depleted in numbers would prosper when the country returned to peaceful conditions.

---

[104] For more on this, see Chapter 3.

[105] Terence Dooley, *The Decline of the Big House in Ireland: A Study of Irish Landed Families, 1860–1960* (Dublin, 2001), pp. 171–97; Bielenberg, 'Exodus', p. 206.

[106] See Terence Dooley, *The Land for the People: The Land Question in Independent Ireland* (Dublin, 2004).

[107] Interview with John Wilson-Wright.

IV

Lost Counties?
Loyalism at the Border

CHAPTER XII

'Cast Out!': Cavan and Monaghan Loyalists and Partition, 1916–1923

Daniel Purcell

With the benefit of nearly a century of hindsight, it is tempting to view the partition of Ireland as falling along reasonably obvious lines. While there were, and still are, significant areas of Catholic majority in the north, all those counties that were included in Northern Ireland had either majority Protestant populations or Protestant populations large enough that the religious difference came to only a few thousand people. Discussions of alternative lines of partition have generally focused on the potential for a smaller northern state and not a larger one. However, the original territorial claim of Ulster Unionism, as laid out in the 1912 Ulster Covenant, was for nine counties. The eventual six-county settlement represented not so much a last-minute land grab as a renunciation of previous claims to even greater territory.

The loyalists of counties Cavan, Monaghan, and Donegal considered themselves Ulstermen just the same as could be found anywhere else in the province. They had enthusiastically signed the Covenant and were equally eligible to join the Ulster Volunteers and other unionist organisations. Mere months before the final partition of Ireland, the *Northern Standard* was confidently reassuring its readers that any future settlement would inevitably fall along nine county lines.[1] However, as the future political settlement would suggest, this commitment to the Ulster loyalist cause was not uncontested. Cavan, Monaghan, and Donegal were notably different from the other Ulster counties. The 1911 census revealed four distinct tiers of 'Protestantness' in Ulster. The most Protestant areas were Antrim (80 per cent Protestant), Belfast Borough (76 per cent), and Down (68 per cent). Then came the narrow Protestant majorities of Armagh (55 per cent) and Londonderry (58 per cent). This was followed by the narrow minorities of Fermanagh (44 per cent), Tyrone (45 per cent), and Londonderry Borough (44 per cent). Monaghan (25

---

[1] *Northern Standard*, 20 Mar. 1920.

per cent), Donegal (21 per cent), and Cavan (19 per cent) were strikingly less Protestant than anywhere else in Ulster.[2]

They also existed on the fringes of what could be culturally considered Ulster. If Clones in Monaghan, near the Fermanagh border and with a Protestant population of 37 per cent in 1911, was 'of Ulster', this was less certain of Carrickmacross, just three miles from Meath and 20 per cent Protestant.[3] Despite the confidence of the *Standard* in 1920, deviations from a nine-county settlement had been proposed before. Most seriously in 1916, Lloyd George had already offered Edward Carson a final settlement on a six-county basis.[4] Three-county loyalists therefore existed in a strange, ambiguous position prior to partition.[5] This study will add to those examinations by looking at the crisis of identity suffered by the Protestants of Cavan and Monaghan, and how they adapted to it. Not entirely either 'Ulster' or 'southern' loyalists, they awkwardly straddled both worlds and raise pertinent questions about the 'naturalness' of the partition split as well as where the borders of an Ulster identity can be said to end. Few other groups were as immediately resistant to the idea of a six-county Northern Ireland. When the Ulster Unionist Council accepted the principle of six county partition on 19 May 1920, it provoked shock and genuine despair in three-county loyalists. Michael Knight, the Monaghan Unionist leader, declared it a 'betrayal by those who professed to be our friends'.[6] The aim of this chapter is to examine this loyalist community in

---

[2] *Census of Ireland, 1911. General Report, with Tables and Appendix* [Cd. 6663], HC 1913, p. 211. Protestant in this case is defined as 'non-Catholic', as, barring a small Jewish community in Belfast, this definition captures the Protestant community accurately.

[3] Figures taken from *Census of Ireland, 1911*, p. 211. Clones defined as Clones and Clones Rural District Electoral Divisions (DEDs), Carrickmacross defined as Carrickmacross Urban and Carrickmacross Rural DEDs.

[4] Francis Costello, 'Lloyd George and Ireland, 1919–1921: An Uncertain Policy', *Canadian Journal of Irish Studies*, 14/1 (1988), pp. 5–16.

[5] Terence Dooley has a range of material published particularly on Monaghan of which the most important are: Terence Dooley, *The Decline of Unionist Politics in Monaghan, 1911–1923* (Maynooth, 1988); Terence Dooley, 'From the Belfast Boycott to the Boundary Commission: Fears and Hopes in County Monaghan, 1920–26', *Clogher Record*, 15/1 (1994); Terence Dooley, 'The Organisation of Unionist Opposition to Home Rule in Counties Monaghan, Cavan and Donegal, 1885–1914', *Clogher Record*, 16/1 (1997); Terence Dooley, *The Plight of Monaghan Protestants, 1912–1926* (Dublin, 2000). See also Tim Wilson, 'The Strange Death of Loyalist Monaghan', in Senia Pašeta (ed.), *Uncertain Futures: Essays about the Irish Past for Roy Foster* (Oxford, 2016). For Cavan, see Brian Hughes, 'Loyalists and Loyalism in a Southern Irish Community, 1921–1922', *Historical Journal*, 59/4 (2016) and Sandra Carolan, 'Cavan Protestants in an Age of Upheaval, 1919–22', MA thesis, NUI Maynooth, 2002.

[6] Patrick Buckland, *Irish Unionism II: Ulster Unionism and the Origins of Northern Ireland, 1886–1922* (Dublin, 1973), p. 119.

two of these counties: Cavan and Monaghan. It will show how they defended their claim to membership of loyal Ulster and how they resisted the growing support for a six-county solution. In doing so, it will demonstrate some of the ambiguities within early Ulster loyalism itself and describe a unique, largely forgotten crisis that took place during the Irish Revolution.

Donegal is not included in this investigation primarily for reasons of expediency.[7] Cavan and Monaghan work well together, representing a reasonably cohesive unit. Cavan and Monaghan were neighbours with a similar religious make-up and strong cross-county links. They were home to an Ulster Protestant movement existing on the fringes of its homeland and outside of the numerical majority that its adherents enjoyed elsewhere and which bolstered their sense of identity. For Cavan and Monaghan Protestants, it was more difficult to belong to the Ulster loyalist tradition than for the rest of the province. The internal denominational make-up of Protestantism in Cavan and Monaghan did not vary hugely, although Monaghan did contain a larger Presbyterian community. Cavan Protestants were 61 per cent Anglican, 35 per cent Presbyterian, and 4 per cent Methodist. Additionally, there were smaller collections of other denominations, such as the Plymouth Brethren and non-aligned Christians. Monaghan Protestants meanwhile were 50 per cent Anglican, 46 per cent Presbyterian, and 4 per cent Methodist. Population in Cavan was focused in the east of the county away from its border with Fermanagh and close to its border with Leinster. The primary towns were Cavan in the centre of the county, Ballyjamesduff and Virginia in the south-east, Bailieborough in the east, and Cootehill in the north. Belturbet and Ballyconnell were the most significant settlements on the Fermanagh border. The Protestant population in the county clustered in those towns and along the Monaghan border. Monaghan was less urban than Cavan, with Monaghan, Clones, Carrickmacross, and Castleblayney dominant. Population clustered in a band from Monaghan town to Castleblayney and around Clones on the Fermanagh border. The Protestant population was more strongly localised in the north of the county and particularly around Clones.[8]

'Ulsterism' in Cavan and Monaghan

The position of Cavan and Monaghan in historical Ulster is not contestable. However, their position in a cultural Ulster zone (and therefore the placing of its loyalist community under the aegis of Ulster Unionism) was more problematic.

---

[7] For the experiences of a Donegal loyalist, see Chapter 14.

[8] Data extracted from *Census of Ireland, 1911*.

The Fermanagh-based *Impartial Reporter*, for example, dismissively referred to Cavan as 'not in the ancient Ulster, it was in Connaught'.[9] The key reason for the discrepancy between Ulster as a geographic unit and Ulster as a cultural symbol is the association of cultural Ulster with Protestantism. In this context Cavan and Monaghan's markedly larger Catholic populations and their contested Ulster status make sense, as does the relative readiness of the leaders of Ulster Unionism to support a partition settlement that excluded them.

The extent of 'Ulster' as a cultural term is problematic. It was defined by its divergent historical experience following the plantations, its distinct geographical features, and the institutions and organisations that took its name. However, the most significant element that defined Ulster Protestantism, and by extension Ulster itself, was religion. As Marcus Heslinga said, the Irish border was fundamentally a 'spiritual divide'.[10] This shared religion also reinforced a shared history, something evidenced by Edward Carson's repeated errors in referring to the six counties that would become Northern Ireland as the 'plantation counties'.[11] While religious make-up was not the only determinant of Ulster status in the political context of the Third Home Rule crisis, it became increasingly dominant. The British government, nationalist and unionist politicians, and the three-county delegates to the Ulster Unionist Council (UUC) were confident in using those 1911 religious returns to base claims for inclusion in Northern Ireland or the Irish Free State.[12] This is further complicated by the obvious benefits that buying into a broader Ulster tradition would bring loyalists in Cavan and Monaghan, and the desire of Ulster Unionist leaders to maximise the size of their movement, particularly in its early phases. Amid the growing likelihood of some form of Home Rule for Ireland in the early twentieth century, an all-Ireland approach to resistance looked increasingly impracticable. As Irish loyalism splintered, Ulster Unionism was the safer horse to back. This section will, therefore, analyse the 'Ulsterism' that was expressed in the two counties, the view of Cavan and Monaghan loyalism in the rest of Ulster, and propose a number of tests to measure the depth of the community's commitment to an Ulster loyalist identity.

The complications of Cavan and Monaghan's claim to a place in Ulster were recognised by many six-county loyalists. Fermanagh loyalists were particularly

---

[9] *Impartial Reporter*, 9 Dec. 1920.
[10] Marcus Heslinga, *The Irish Border as a Cultural Divide* (Belfast, 1971), p. 78.
[11] Carson to Bonar-Law, 20 Sep. 1913 (TNA, BL/33/5/57).
[12] See, for example, *Ulster and Home Rule: No Partition of Ulster*, the anti-partition pamphlet published by unionists of Monaghan, Cavan, and Donegal, Apr. 1920 (PRONI D1545/8). Visualisations of the 1911 census' religious figures were also contained in the Boundary Commission (TNA, CAB/61/14) and the North Eastern Boundary Bureau (NAI, NEBB/1/5/3).

preoccupied with characterising the limits of the Ulster character due to their own sense of precariousness over their future position in Northern Ireland. W.C. Trimble, when discussing the electoral map of Fermanagh, claimed that South Fermanagh would have returned a Unionist MP in all previous elections were it not for the western areas of the county bordering Cavan and Leitrim. These areas were unnatural as they 'formerly belonged to the province of Connaught'.[13] Similarly, the border town of Roslea, which had an active IRA unit, was declared to belong 'more to Monaghan than Fermanagh'.[14]

While Cavan and Monaghan may have been distinct from the other Ulster counties, they were equally distinct from their neighbours in Connacht or Leinster. Protestant population levels in Monaghan (25 per cent) had something in common with County Dublin (29 per cent) or Wicklow (21 per cent) (whose numbers included British military and administrative personnel), but nothing with Cork (3 per cent) or Mayo (1 per cent). On a provincial level this difference was most clearly pronounced in Ulster's Protestant population (56 per cent), far greater than in Leinster (15 per cent), Munster (6 per cent), or Connacht (4 per cent).[15] Additionally, the simple fact that Cavan and Monaghan Protestants were in historical Ulster meant that they were able to sign the Ulster Covenant. They were host to Ulster Clubs, Orange lodges, and Ulster Volunteers which bolstered an Ulster identity.[16] Public rhetoric emphasised this strong Ulster character. Protestant election candidates organised under the Ulster Unionist banner, such as Michael Knight in North Monaghan in 1918. Despite running against the odds, Knight's speeches aimed to give the impression that North Monaghan especially was a thriving outpost of Ulster loyalism: '[the] unionists in this part of Ulster have a fine opportunity ... of being represented for the first time truly in the Imperial Parliament'.[17] In his speech opening his 1918 campaign he declared his purpose in running: 'in order that the unionists might have an opportunity of recording their votes for the Union ... and of showing that there is in Co. Monaghan a strong united and determined body of unionists'.[18] In a private letter to Hugh de Fellenberg Montgomery following partition, Lord Farnham sadly noted that 'we in Cavan were prouder of being Ulstermen than anyone in the whole Province'.[19]

13 *Impartial Reporter*, 9 Dec. 1920.
14 *Impartial Reporter*, 27 Jul. 1922.
15 *Census of Ireland, 1911*, p. 211. All religious percentages are rounded to the nearest whole number.
16 David Fitzpatrick, *Descendancy: Irish Protestant Histories Since 1795* (Cambridge, 2014), p. 243.
17 *Northern Standard*, 14 Dec. 1918.
18 *Impartial Reporter*, 12 Dec. 1918.
19 Farnham to Montgomery, 13 Mar. 1920 (PRONI, D627/435/10). For more on Farnham in this period, see Chapter 13.

Cavan and Monaghan loyalists expressed pride in the achievements of the province as a whole. During the War of Independence, the *Northern Standard* noted with satisfaction the 'almost complete immunity of the greater part of Ulster from the dreadful crimes that blackened the rest of Ireland'.[20] Belfast in particular was a source of admiration. In speeches such as that of a Major Robert McClean to the Monaghan Unionist Club in 1918, the virtues of the city's industry and infrastructure were taken as matters of great pride.[21] The ties between Cavan and Monaghan Protestants and Belfast led many to attempt to break the Belfast Boycott.[22] Protestants in Newbliss, County Monaghan in August 1920 organised a convoy of 50 Ulster Volunteers to escort bread vans from Belfast to the town. The same escorts were planned in Clones and Drum, although they were foiled, as the bread vans were attacked before they reached their escort.[23]

Moving beyond such subjective expressions of an Ulster identity, however, we are left with the question of whether we can measure the depth of an Ulster identity present in the two counties. To do this, we must look at the level at which the community actively engaged with organisations associated with the Ulster movement: Unionist Clubs, the Ulster Volunteer Force (UVF), and the British army.

Signed primarily on Ulster Day, 28 September 1912, the Ulster Covenant was an oath binding its signatories to oppose any attempt to coerce Ulster into Home Rule. Implicitly this extended to open violent resistance. We should be careful with assigning a particular depth of fervour to any signatory of the Covenant. In Cavan, the RIC County Inspector noted that in the majority of cases the Covenant was probably signed more as a statement of political preference than as a commitment to military resistance.[24]

David Fitzpatrick has tabulated the contribution of Cavan and Monaghan to the Ulster Covenant and its women's equivalent, the Women's Declaration. He calculated that 71 per cent of the eligible Protestant Cavan men and 65 per cent of the women signed. For Monaghan, these figures were 83 per cent for men and 80 per cent for women.[25] Not only was there significant divergence between Cavan and Monaghan in terms of commitment to the Covenant, but Monaghan was among the most subscribed counties in the province, while Cavan languished at the bottom of the table – its men only

---

[20] *Northern Standard*, 10 Apr. 1920.
[21] *Irish Times*, 13 Mar. 1918.
[22] Terence Dooley, 'Fears and Hopes in County Monaghan', pp. 91–2.
[23] *Northern Standard*, 28 Aug. 1920.
[24] RIC County Inspector's Monthly Confidential Report, Cavan, Sep. 1912 (TNA, CO 904/88).
[25] Fitzpatrick, *Descendancy*, p. 243.

underperformed by those in Antrim and its women by those in Belfast.[26] Antrim and Belfast, however, had far larger Protestant populations to begin with and saw far higher total turnout than did Cavan.[27] Cavan in particular experienced an upsurge in interest in the Unionist Clubs at the time of the Home Rule crisis. In November 1912, Cavan had 12 Unionist Clubs with 1,425 members. By comparison, Monaghan's membership in November 1912 was 20 per cent. For both counties, these numbers were comparable with Antrim (20 per cent) and Down (23 per cent) and both were far ahead of their more northerly neighbour Fermanagh (15 per cent).[28]

Membership of the UVF in these counties was particularly strong when compared with the rest of the province; 56 per cent of adult male Protestants in Cavan were recorded as being a member of the UVF in 1914 while in Monaghan this figure was 34 per cent. In the strongly Protestant Ulster areas of Antrim, Down, and Belfast Borough this figure was only 25 per cent. Indeed, Cavan's rate of membership was higher than anywhere else in Ulster. In spite of Monaghan's larger Protestant population, the Cavan UVF boasted a membership of 3,451, while Monaghan could only muster 2,188.[29] Cavan also fared better in the number of arms held for the UVF. In November 1913, the Monaghan UVF's 1,650 members had to share 385 arms between them, roughly one gun between every four volunteers. Cavan, meanwhile, held 1,691 weapons between 3,041 men. By March 1914, Cavan boasted 2,676 arms, including a quarter of all Martini-Enfield rifles held in Ulster. Overall it held roughly 10 per cent of all arms in Ulster in the period just before the Larne gunrunning in a county with just 2 per cent of all Protestants in Ulster. Monaghan, meanwhile, only increased its cache to 561, a fifth of what was held by Cavan.[30] This echoes Tim Wilson's observations about the tendency of such frontier areas, homogeneous 'areas of "disloyalty"', to experience higher levels of tension and military activity.[31] However, it is worth noting that such high levels of arms did not translate into more significant violence in the War of Independence, and Cavan's revolution was far quieter than that of

---

[26] Fitzpatrick, *Descendancy*, p. 243.

[27] Ulster Covenant online: www.nidirect.gov.uk/services/search-ulster-covenant.

[28] All data taken from Breandán Mac Giolla Choille, *Chief Secretary's Office, Dublin Castle Intelligence Notes, 1913–1916* (Dublin, 1966), pp. 19–20. Expression of data as a percentage of adult male population taken from Fitzpatrick, *Descendancy*, p. 244.

[29] Mac Giolla Choille, *Intelligence Notes*, p. 37; also in Fitzpatrick, *Descendancy*, p. 244.

[30] Mac Giolla Choille, *Intelligence Notes*, p. 33–4.

[31] Tim Wilson, *Frontiers of Violence: Conflict and Identity in Ulster and Upper Silesia, 1918–1922* (Oxford, 2010), pp. 172, 189, 190–201.

Monaghan.[32] Despite this greater commitment, Cavan's more isolated Protestant population was reflected in how their commitment to the Ulster Volunteers was framed in very different terms from elsewhere. Aware of their isolated position in the county and fearful of hostility that could be engendered by the actions of the more bellicose Belfast Volunteers, Colonel Oliver Nugent, the Commanding Officer of the UVF in Cavan, renamed the organisation the Cavan Volunteer Force in 1913 and played down any military associations.[33]

Great War recruiting was another area in which Ulster loyalists had distinguished themselves from the rest of the country. The rate of recruitment in Ulster roughly matched that in Britain and was far ahead of recruitment in any other Irish province.[34] Initial recruitment in Cavan and Monaghan was high, with Monaghan singled out in September 1914 as having seen a particularly large proportion of its Ulster Volunteers leave.[35]

On the outbreak of war, between 15 December 1914 and 15 December 1915, Cavan had an extremely high ratio of Protestant recruits to Protestant males with non-agricultural occupations, of 105 per thousand. This was the second highest ratio in Ulster, only behind Antrim and Belfast (110 per thousand). Nationally, it tied with its neighbour Longford and fell short of Carlow (146 per thousand), both counties with substantially smaller Protestant populations. The ratio for Monaghan was much lower (65 per thousand), which correlates closely to the disparity in UVF membership.[36] As early as December 1914, the County Inspector noted that even this limited initial enthusiasm had waned and now there was nobody coming forward.[37] A recruiting meeting in Rockcorry, County Monaghan, in January 1915, despite attracting 140 members of the UVF, failed to yield a single recruit. By October 1916, only 738 recruits had come forward in Monaghan from an estimated eligible population of 2,234.[38] This is attributable partially to the Great War increasing agricultural prices and the profitability of staying home to sell one's labour, but also due

---

[32] Robert Lynch, *The Northern IRA and the Early Years of Partition 1920–1922* (Dublin, 2006), p. 58. While this quietness was primarily due to poor IRA organisation in the county it is noteworthy that we do not see the equivalent of the Protestant town guards that existed in Monaghan: *Northern Standard*, 24 Sep. 1920 [in Drum] and 'Treasury correspondence discussing Trade Boycott in Monaghan' (PRONI, FIN18/1/103) [in Rockcorry].

[33] Booklet entitled 'C.V.F. Scheme, Copy No. VI' (PRONI, MIC/57119).

[34] Charles Townsend, *Easter 1916: The Irish Rebellion* (Dublin, 2005), p. 65.

[35] RIC County Inspector's Monthly Confidential Report, Monaghan, Sep. 1914 (TNA, CO 904/94).

[36] Figures provided and reproduced with permission of Prof. David Fitzpatrick.

[37] RIC County Inspector's Monthly Confidential Report, Monaghan, Dec. 1914 (TNA, CO 904/95).

[38] Terence Dooley, 'County Monaghan, 1914–1918: Recruitment, the Rise of Sinn Féin and the Partition Crisis', *Clogher Record*, 16/2 (1998), p. 146.

to a certain lack of enthusiasm.[39] Ironically, this lack of enthusiasm was best summarised by the nationalist chair of Monaghan County Council, Thomas Toal, who declared 'the Protestant and Orange farmers in this part of the country were just as much opposed to this as they were. They had done their part in cropping the land and were they prepared now to sacrifice all that now to go out to Flanders and lose their lives'. This echoes what future TD Kevin O'Shiel had noted while canvassing in the county, where he was surprised to see how much support their anti-compulsion speeches were given by 'typical young Protestant farmers'.[40] Geoffrey Coulter, the Protestant future deputy editor of *An Phoblacht*, had also capitalised on this reluctance by founding the Protestant Anti-Conscription Association, which focused on Dublin and the border counties.[41]

Even though the Great War itself did not see a significant level of enthusiasm among the Protestant community in Cavan and Monaghan, it still formed an important part of its self-image. Loyalist papers like the *Northern Standard* thrilled at the exploits of local men abroad and printed tales of the heroism and sacrifice of those killed, often with an accompanying biography.[42] The Cavan loyalist paper, the *Irish Post and Weekly Telegraph*, took the step of abandoning advertisements on its front page and instead ran with various photographs of the war. Additionally, both papers carried frequent reports of pro-war recruiting events, generally entirely Protestant and held in Protestant halls.[43] The concept of the Great War as Ulster's war was as prevalent in Cavan and Monaghan as elsewhere. In August 1917, the *Northern Standard* published an editorial praising the 'glory' won by Ulster soldiers for Ulster as a whole: 'The splendid record of Ulster's share in the war has been added to by the part which her sons took in the fourth battle of Ypres on Thursday of last week ... Ulster has done splendidly in this conflict but has not yet done all of which she is capable'. At least in part, this was made in a favourable comparison with the other three provinces: 'We do not wish to draw distinctions, yet we cannot but regret that in comparisons with the Northern Province the rest of Ireland has done so little'.[44] The *Irish Post* led their articles detailing the exploits of the Ulsterman fighting in France with the headline 'Hats off to the Ulster Division'.[45] The counties' own records as regards recruiting was ignored.

[39] Dooley, 'County Monaghan, 1914–1918', p. 147.
[40] BMH WS 1770 (Kevin O'Shiel).
[41] Geoffrey Coulter Interview (Cardinal Ó Fiaich Memorial Library, 01-LOK IV_A_84A).
[42] As an example, see *Northern Standard*, 1 Jan. 1916.
[43] *Irish Post and Weekly Telegraph*, 15 Jul. 1916.
[44] *Northern Standard*, 25 Aug. 1917.
[45] *Irish Post and Weekly Telegraph*, 6 Apr. 1920.

The issue of conscription became a way of distinguishing the Protestant community from their Catholic neighbours. *Northern Standard* editorials called for the inclusion of Ireland or at least Ulster in the scheme. Michael Knight (1869–1960), a Clones solicitor and the most prominent Monaghan loyalist of the period, contributed to a meeting of Monaghan County Council in 1918 outlining his own support for the matter along lines that were typical in the county: 'On every principle of justice and equity I support the application of conscription to Ireland, holding as I do that we are vitally concerned in the result of the war as any other part of the United Kingdom'.[46] In the same month, the Presbytery of Monaghan met and unanimously passed a motion supporting conscription and decrying the 'contemptible spirit' of those members of the Church who had yet to join up. This rhetoric combined the traditional call for equality and fairness with the other nations of the Empire, but also brought in the more uniquely 'Ulster' call when saying, 'we sincerely hope that Ulster will not say "we have done our part" but will rather say "we are willing for any sacrifice that is necessary to safeguard our shores from the invasion of the German horde"'.[47] These sentiments were echoed by the Presbyterian Synod of Monaghan and Armagh a month later.[48] The District Orange Lodges around the two counties also expressed their own support for a county-wide introduction of conscription.[49]

As the Great War progressed and Irish politics became radicalised in the years following the Easter Rising, Monaghan and Cavan Protestants were able to overcome their inglorious recruiting record and buy into the greater Ulster war tradition by simply forming a contrast with the Catholic/nationalist community. The announcement of the armistice in Monaghan in 1918 was greeted by exclusively Protestant cheers.[50] Elizabeth Adams remembered in her compensation application going to ring the bells of the Local Anglican Church to celebrate. This act, she insisted, marked her out in the community as 'Protestant and loyalist'.[51] In Cavan, the celebrations were strongly coded as Protestant. Fireworks were let off near Lord Farnham's estate, a special service was held in Kilmore Anglican cathedral, and a sports day was organised outside Cavan town with the local rector William Askins handing out the prizes. In Ballyconnell, revellers marched from the Anglican parochial hall to the rectory, while in Redhills a band holding Union flags formed at the Protestant hall and marched through the village.[52]

---

[46] *Northern Standard*, 20 Apr. 1918.
[47] *Irish Post and Weekly Telegraph*, 20 Apr. 1918.
[48] *Belfast Newsletter*, 1 May 1918.
[49] *Irish Post and Weekly Telegraph*, 11 May 1918.
[50] *Northern Standard*, 17 Nov. 1918.
[51] Elizabeth Adams claim (TNA, CO 762/137/9).
[52] *Irish Post and Weekly Telegraph*, 25 Jul. 1918.

Partition in Cavan and Monaghan

Cavan and Monaghan loyalists still understood the precariousness of their position. In the case of a partition settlement that broke the integrity of Ulster, Cavan and Monaghan were the two most likely casualties. It is difficult to determine how likely partition was thought to be by Monaghan and Cavan Protestants before 1916. The concept of partition as a solution to the Home Rule crisis underwent a number of redefinitions before coming to the form that established the division of the six and 26 county states. In June 1912, in the midst of the crisis over the third Home Rule bill, Thomas Agar-Robartes, a Liberal MP, first seriously suggested partition to Sir Edward Carson. He proposed a four-county Ulster state, comprising the most Protestant counties: Antrim, Down, Armagh, and Derry. At this time, the proposal was rejected out of hand by Unionist and Nationalist politicians, although the only reservation Carson expressed was an unwillingness to jettison Fermanagh and Tyrone. Cavan, Monaghan, and Donegal were not considered.[53] The Covenant itself, with its enthusiastic uptake in the three counties, served as a direct rebuke to this reduced Ulsterism.[54] This point was made by Carson in an address to loyalists in August 1913 at Newbliss, County Monaghan.[55]

When partition was next proposed it was in the House of Lords in January 1913 as an amendment to the third Home Rule bill and pertained to Ulster as a whole.[56] However, Carson's thinking was not so clear-cut as he suggested. In private correspondence with Andrew Bonar Law, he had already expressed a willingness to compromise on the final settlement: 'A difficulty arises as to defining Ulster and my own view is that the whole of Ulster should be excluded but the minimum would be the six plantation counties'.[57] Jackson has noted that it was around this time that Carson moved away from using Ulster exclusion as a wrecking tactic for the third Home Rule bill and towards viewing it as a legitimate solution to the Ulster crisis.[58] In this context, it is most sensible to view Carson's characterisation of nine- and six-county settlements as representing what he saw as an ideal settlement and an acceptable one.

---

[53] Kieran J. Rankin, 'The Search for Statutory Ulster', *History Ireland*, 17/3 (2009), p. 29.

[54] Ronan Fanning, *Fatal Path: British Government and Irish Revolution, 1910–1922* (London, 2013), p. 71.

[55] *Northern Standard*, 9 Aug. 1913.

[56] Fanning, *Fatal Path*, p. 74.

[57] Carson to Bonar-Law, 20 Sep. 1913 (TNA, BL/33/5/57). As noted above, Carson was incorrect in referring to the six counties of Northern Ireland as 'plantation counties'.

[58] Alvin Jackson, *Home Rule: An Irish History, 1800–2000* (London, 2003), p. 124.

Despite Carson's private views, Terence Dooley has highlighted that the first time Monaghan loyalists really had to engage with their potential abandonment was in March 1914 when Prime Minster H.H. Asquith took his proposals for Ulster exclusion public. In both 1913 and 1914, in the context of rising Nationalist and Unionist militancy over the prospect of the third Home Rule bill, the British government undertook a series of negotiations with both groups to try and reach a peaceful resolution to the crisis. While Fanning has correctly characterised the growing popularity of calls for a solution that included the exclusion of Ulster, the actual form of the Ulster excluded was not engaged with in depth.[59] By March 1914, Asquith had settled on a solution in which Ulster would be excluded from a Home Rule settlement for six years and in which any Ulster county could vote themselves out of Home Rule.[60] Monaghan, Cavan, and Donegal, with their heavy Catholic majorities, would have been effectively abandoned under this policy, with the future of Tyrone and Fermanagh more ambiguous. Frederick Crawford, the prominent Ulster Unionist who was to gain notoriety as the main driver behind the Larne gunrunning, wrote to Carson from Hamburg and noted that such a proposal would 'place the Protestants of Cavan, Donegal, Fermanagh, and Monaghan in a position to say we deserted them'.[61] The proposal was denounced by the *Northern Standard* on 4 March 1914 as 'of such contemptuous merit as to not deserve discussion' but it did establish the potential of an alternative six-county framework for Ulster.[62]

Although they were initially receptive, this proposal was ultimately resisted by Carson and the Ulster Unionist Council.[63] However, Carson's misgivings were based more on the temporary nature of the exclusion than on the county-by-county plebiscite element. Carson famously dismissed temporary exclusion as a 'stay of execution'.[64] In this crisis, the Ulster Covenant became an important article of faith among the loyalist population in Cavan and Monaghan: they saw it as representing an undertaking to continue negotiations only on an Ulster-wide basis. In July 1914, Carson travelled to the Buckingham Palace conference, a reopening of negotiations between the government, Unionists, and Nationalists following their breakdown in March. He received a telegram from Monaghan loyalists saying, 'Fellow covenanters in Monaghan expect you to stand firm better fight than break Covenant'.[65]

---

[59] Fanning, *Fatal Path*, pp. 76–90.
[60] Fanning, *Fatal Path*, pp. 100–6.
[61] Crawford to Carson, 13 Mar. 1914 (PRONI, D1700/5/17/1/11).
[62] Dooley, 'County Monaghan, 1914–1918', p. 55.
[63] Buckland, *Irish Unionism II*, pp. 96–7.
[64] Fanning, *Fatal Path*, p. 105.
[65] Dooley, 'County Monaghan, 1914–1918', p. 55.

Following the outbreak of war these questions were placed on hold until 1916 when Asquith, wishing to resolve the tensions of the Easter Rising but preoccupied with the war effort, asked Lloyd George to 'take up Ireland' and attempt to work a solution.[66] Lloyd George's focus in these negotiations was to push a settlement down the path of least resistance and he therefore attempted to avoid the controversial issue of including Cavan, Monaghan, or Donegal in a northern state.[67] He put forward a solution in which Home Rule would be granted to southern Ireland while a six-county Ulster would continue to be administered directly from Westminster. In the context of an ongoing war, three-county delegates to the Ulster Unionist Council voted with their six-county counterparts to accept this settlement on 12 June 1916.[68] Although the scheme quickly collapsed when it emerged that the Nationalists had believed that this partition was temporary, all loyalist sources spoke of it as permanent and the Protestants of the three counties internalised this as the acceptance of a permanent sundering from their homeland.[69]

Unlike the partition which would occur four years later, this was seen not as a betrayal by the six-county loyalists but rather as a patriotic decision taken by three-county loyalists for the benefit of others. This particular portrayal of the events of 1916 served a political purpose as it provided hard evidence of the willingness of three-county loyalists to make the ultimate sacrifice for the benefit of Ulster. Counterintuitively, this was primarily used to attack the same six-county proposal four years later. It was argued that the wartime circumstances that drove that decision had passed and the reward of three-county loyalists was that they would never be asked to make such a sacrifice again. Commenting on the advent of partition in 1920, the *Northern Standard* declared:

> It was on the same lines as the action taken in 1916, when the Unionists of the three counties listened to an appeal said to come from the Government, and reluctantly agreed to make a great sacrifice for 'the sake of the Empire' – a sacrifice which they were afterwards assured would 'never again' be asked from them.[70]

The anti-partition pamphlet published in 1920 by the representatives to the UUC from Cavan, Monaghan, and Donegal characterised this incident in

---

[66] Fanning, *Fatal Path*, p. 144.

[67] Fanning, *Fatal Path*, p. 146.

[68] Resolution on six-county partition passed unanimously by UUC, 12 Jun. 1916 (PRONI, D627/435).

[69] Buckland, *Irish Unionism II*, pp. 106–7.

[70] *Northern Standard*, 20 Mar. 1920.

similarly heroic terms. In a time of 'great national emergency' the three counties placed themselves in 'the hands of the other six counties' but never 'abandoned the Covenant'.[71] Michael Knight, speaking at an election rally in 1918, also asserted that the three counties should never again be forced to make such a decision. This was an assertion he would repeat in private correspondence.[72] Carson had praised this decision as 'the greatest piece of lasting evidence of their devoted, unselfish loyalty to the king, constitution and empire' that he had seen in his career.[73]

This was an oversimplification on the part of all concerned. The delegates of 1916 never consulted with their home constituents and instead reached a consensus amongst themselves based on a political deal that had already passed. Their official statement at the time offered no heroic stoicism but rather protested against the government's proposals, especially while so many three-county covenanters were fighting a war for the same government. They did not accept the decision but 'abided by it'.[74] It also ignored the attempts of Major Somerset Saunderson, one of the Cavan delegates, to have the decision revoked after he learned Lloyd George's proposals had never even been before the Cabinet.[75] The Church of Ireland Archbishop of Armagh John Crozier – himself a 'Cavan Covenanter' – protested to Carson that it represented a 'flagrant breach of faith and honour'.[76] Nevertheless, this was a useful fiction that allowed three-county loyalists to stake a legitimate claim to inclusion in the Northern state.

This event was important for establishing to the UUC that there were circumstances in which the three counties could be jettisoned, as well as making that a reality to three-county loyalists. The failure of Lloyd George's scheme led to some celebration in Cavan and Monaghan. By the end of 1918, the *Northern Standard* was in a bullish mood and reasonably confident regarding any partition of Ulster: 'Monaghan is not going to tamely submit to be governed by a Dublin Parliament and when the time comes will let it be understood that our county is still a part of Ulster'.[77] At a speech to the Cavan Twelfth in 1917, the head of the Cavan Orange Lodge, Travers Blackley, declared the Covenant proven inviolable by events and ironically advised Cavan Protestants to prepare themselves for 'frontier duty'.[78]

---

[71] *Ulster and Home Rule: No Partition of Ulster,* Apr. 1920; *Northern Standard,* 4 Oct. 1919.

[72] Knight to Montgomery, 22 Nov. 1918 (PRONI, D627/435/2).

[73] *Northern Standard,* 14 Dec. 1918.

[74] *Northern Standard,* 19 Jun. 1920.

[75] Saunderson to Martin, 10 Jul. 1916 in *Northern Standard,* 22 Jul. 1916; Saunderson to Unionist Delegates of Monaghan, 13 Jul. 1916 (PRONI, D1507/A/18/13).

[76] Crozier to Carson, 26 Jun. 1916 (PRONI, D1507/A/17/26).

[77] *Northern Standard,* 30 Nov. 1918.

[78] *Irish Post and Weekly Telegraph,* 21 Jul. 1917.

However, the incident had planted seeds of distrust in the minds of the three-county loyalists. Michael Knight, speaking to the Monaghan Grand Orange Lodge in 1917, hoped that 'we not again be asked to sacrifice ourselves in that way'.[79] Speaking at a loyalist meeting in Drum in 1920, James Madden declared his wish never again to see the three counties 'place themselves into the hands of the six counties'.[80] In the years between 1916 and 1920, events such as 'Covenant Day', the anniversary of the signing of the Covenant, were marked in Cavan and Monaghan by religious services. The *Northern Standard* covered these events quite heavily: 'very little has been said about "the three counties" during the past week, but it is enough for us to know that the Ulster Unionists stand where they did five or six years ago – a thoroughly united party'.[81] The *Irish Post* published a series by Herbert Moore Pim on different covenants throughout history, casting them in a heroic light and ending on the refrain: 'we know what we mean and we mean what we say'.[82]

This mistrust of six-county loyalists did not seem to extend to Carson himself, who was still held in high esteem in the loyalist press. His good intentions to the three counties were never in doubt. In this way, at least Cavan and Monaghan were in line with the rest of Ulster. As was noted by George Peel as early as 1914, Carson's own popularity 'might have been envied by kings'.[83] A letter of September 1919 from Mary Murray-Ker of Newbliss House to the *Northern Standard* noted with pleasure Carson's speech to the UUC in which he praised the self-sacrifice of the three-county loyalist. Murray-Ker and the *Standard*'s editor took this as evidence of Carson's commitment to the inclusion of the three counties in Ulster: 'there is no uncertain sound there!'[84] The *Standard* enthusiastically endorsed Carson's statement as a 'great speech' and drew laboured attention to every round of applause it coaxed from the audience. Of course, as shown earlier, even by 1913 Carson had accepted the likelihood of a six-county settlement and his effusiveness here may have been a reaction to the trouble caused to him in 1916 by Somerset Saunderson's concerted opposition to the Lloyd George six-county settlement.[85]

Importantly, the crisis also established the three- and six-county dichotomy that had become well established by the time James Madden spoke. A meeting

---

[79] *Irish Post and Weekly Telegraph*, 26 May 1917.
[80] *Northern Standard*, 26 Jul. 1920.
[81] *Northern Standard*, 4 Oct. 1918.
[82] *Irish Post and Weekly Telegraph*, 7 Sep. 1918.
[83] George Peel, *The Reign of Sir Edward Carson* (London, 1914), p. 3. For a detailed discussion of the hero worship that was accorded to Carson, see Andre Gailey, 'King Carson: An Essay on the Invention of Leadership', *Irish Historical Studies*, 30/117 (1996), pp. 66–87.
[84] *Northern Standard*, 13 Sep. 1919.
[85] Geoffrey Lewis, *Carson: The Man Who Divided Ireland* (London, 2005), pp. 189–90.

of the Royal Black Chapter in Clones in 1917 welcomed members from Cavan, Monaghan, and Donegal and declared their cause under the collective 'three-county' name. They did so in traditional Ulster terms, focusing on the sacrifice of their sons and brothers in the war and on the need for Ulster Protestantism to stand together as it had against James II.[86] A similar meeting was held that day in Cootehill in Cavan and a similar resolution passed.[87] The first Twelfth since the war began, held in 1918, was marked by numerous assemblies organised on this same three county basis.[88]

In March 1920, the Government of Ireland bill, which legislated for two parliaments, one to cover a six-county Northern Ireland and the other for a 26-county Southern Ireland, was accepted by the Ulster Unionist Council. The response to the UUC's decision from Cavan and Monaghan was outrage. The *Northern Standard* ran an editorial entitled 'Cast Out!'[89] For many in the three counties their loyalty to the Crown had brought great suffering, which now appeared pointless: 'we have committed no crime. We have been loyal to the flag when loyalty to the flag meant boycott, outrage and insult for us'.[90] At a Twelfth assembly in Clones, Robert Burns, rector of Drum, stated: 'in this country it does not pay to be loyal ... one would almost think that we would get far more consideration from the British Government if we plotted again the King and murdered His Majesty's forces from behind stone walls and hedges'.[91]

At a general meeting of the three-county delegates to the UUC in Clones, delegates to the Council unanimously agreed to resign.[92] However, it was also agreed to call for a special meeting of the UUC to try and reverse the decision and 'try and save a split never to be healed'.[93] This meeting was requested by submitting a written protest, signed by 100 members of the council from every county in Ulster, citing Rule 3 of the council's constitution and forcing a special meeting on 27 May to reconsider the issue. The statement requesting this meeting called on their six-county brethren not to abandon them: 'the Ulster people have stood together for many generations and that confidence and reliance in each other has been the chief cause of their success and prosperity'.[94]

---

[86] *Northern Standard*, 26 Aug. 1916.
[87] *Northern Standard*, 26 Aug. 1916.
[88] *Northern Standard*, 15 Jul. 1918.
[89] *Northern Standard*, 13 Mar. 1920.
[90] *Northern Standard*, 18 Nov. 1921.
[91] *Northern Standard*, 15 Jul. 1921.
[92] Correspondence with the UUC secretary including letters of resignation, May 1920 (PRONI, D1327/18/29–30).
[93] Ricardo to Montgomery, 8 Apr. 1920 (PRONI, D627/435/10).
[94] Buckland, *Irish Unionism II*, pp. 120–1; *Northern Standard*, 24 Apr. 1920.

Once again, the issue of the Covenant and what it had actually committed its signatories to became central. Resistance to partition had focused heavily on the Covenant, employing a stricter and stricter definition of what the Covenant stood for, just as more six-county Unionists were attempting to define it more loosely.[95] A pamphlet sent by three-county Protestants to the Ulster Unionist Council opened with the text of the Covenant as an attempt to sway other delegates' minds. The document had been typeset with the word 'nine' in the title printed upper case, so it read: 'The Solemn Covenant entered into between the Unionists of the NINE Counties of Ulster'.[96] A meeting of the County Cavan Unionist Association passed a motion protesting 'most emphatically against the breach of the Covenant caused by ... the Ulster Council on March 10 in deserting their fellow Covenanters'.[97] Similar motions were passed by Donegal and Monaghan and then collectively at a meeting in Clones in March 1920. The idea of the violation of the Covenant had currency even outside of Cavan and Monaghan. Irish Parliamentary Party MP T.P. O'Connor teased James Craig in the House of Commons on 29 March 1920: 'the Covenanters of Donegal and Cavan and Monaghan are given up to the Papists and Nationalists'.[98]

This approach was effective against many loyalists outside of the three counties. General A. Ricardo of Sion Mills in Tyrone resigned from the UUC on 10 March 1920 declaring himself 'too stupid to appreciate the arguments ... that the Covenant is but a pledge among friends'.[99] Frederick Crawford felt sufficiently threatened by these moves that he wrote and circulated his own pamphlet defending his actions: 'if I had voted for the nine counties I would have been going against both the spirit and the letter of the Covenant'. He went on to compare six-county Ulster to a lifeboat escaping a sinking ship in which Cavan, Monaghan, and Donegal were drowning passengers who, were they to escape to the boat, would overburden and sink it.[100]

In the lead up to this meeting, a pamphlet was produced by the delegates to the UUC from the three counties. The pamphlet argued, fairly reasonably, that the same demographic and political facts were true of the three counties in 1920 as they had been when the census was taken in 1911 and when the Covenant was signed in 1912. Abandoning the counties now in the face of such little change was to invalidate the word of Ulster Unionism. The decision

[95] Correspondence with the UUC secretary including letters of resignation, Apr. 1920 (PRONI, D1327/18/28).

[96] *Ulster and Home Rule: No Partition of Ulster*, Apr. 1920.

[97] *Irish Post and Weekly Telegraph*, 13 Mar. 1920.

[98] Hansard, HC, vol. 127, col. 968 (29 Mar. 1920).

[99] Ricardo to Montgomery, 8 Apr. 1920 (PRONI: D627/435/10).

[100] Frederick Crawford, *Why I Voted for the Six Counties* (Belfast, 1920 (PRONI, D1700/5/16)).

of the UUC was criticised as rushed, as delegates had lacked time to consult with their local associations, and ill-informed, as it had been incorrectly stated by some delegates (notably Thomas Moles, MP for Belfast Ormeau) that Sinn Féin would hold a majority across nine counties.[101] The perfidy of the six-county delegates was denounced. Suggestions that the Covenant had been only a temporary commitment were dismissed as 'idiotic' and 'childish'. The impracticality of a state with the borders and size of Northern Ireland was criticised as was its political uniformity: 'it would appear to be unwise that the Northern Parliament should have too great a Unionist majority, just as it is to be deplored that the Southern Parliament should have (and will have) too great a Nationalist majority'.[102] The key argument was to dismiss the idea that the three counties should be excluded because of their Nationalist majority:

> That is true. But so does Derry City, Fermanagh County, Tyrone County, South Armagh, South Down and the Falls Division of Belfast. Yet no one proposes to exclude them. The truth is that it is impossible to fix upon any exclusively Unionist area. There are more Unionists in the Southern area than there are Nationalists in the three Counties and no provision whatever is made for them. In their case we are told minorities must suffer, but that doctrine seems to be ignored when the minority is a Nationalist one.[103]

Unfortunately for three-county loyalists, the UUC again affirmed their commitment to a six-county state.[104] While three-county loyalists were assured the decision had only been taken after 'much heart-searching', presumably this was of little solace.[105]

The three-county loyalist press criticised the dishonesty of the six-county delegates: 'it is clearly obvious that to attain the full measure of selfish safety for themselves they are prepared to jeopardise the safety of their Southern

---

[101] Moles's position was never clearly defined and certainly flew in the face of the previous election results. It was based on the idea that the Protestant working class of Belfast, under the sway of labour interests, could not be relied upon to vote for the Unionist Party, which put their majority at risk.

[102] *Ulster and Home Rule: No Partition of Ulster*, Apr. 1920.

[103] *Ulster and Home Rule: No Partition of Ulster*, Apr. 1920. Note: this calculation seems correct when tested with data from the 1911 census, using the rough method of equating Catholics to nationalists and Protestants to unionists. Cavan, Monaghan, and Donegal contained 260,655 Catholics while the 'southern area' (taken as the 26 counties that became the Irish Free State) contained 327,179 unionists, although by the 1926 census this was reduced to only 220,723.

[104] Buckland, *Irish Unionism II*, p. 120.

[105] *Northern Standard*, 22 May 1920.

friends'.[106] Lord Farnham had been so incensed by the acceptance of partition that he even rebuked the initial attempts by three-county delegates to overturn the decision, stating angrily that he was 'done with them for all time'.[107] In a speech to the House of Lords on 1 December 1920, the Earl of Clanwilliam noted that six-county loyalists had earned 'the hostility, and perhaps the hatred, of those who live in the three counties' for reasons which were 'more selfish than anything else'.[108] Sir James Strong of Tynan Abbey noted that 'the impression left is that the three counties have been thrown to the wolves with very little compunction'.[109] On 23 December 1920, the Government of Ireland Act became law, partitioning Ireland into north and south. On 24 May 1921, the first elections were held in the new northern territory and in June of the same year the Northern Irish parliament sat for the first time. From the perspective of the loyalists of Cavan and Monaghan, the same traitorous delegates who had voted for partition were now running the new state.

As R.B. McDowell has described, for all this anger, adaptation (and perhaps resignation) followed resistance almost as rapidly.[110] For some this manifested itself in a willingness to co-operate with the Irish Free State, once established. Others invested hope in the ability of the Boundary Commission to rescue them from southern domination.[111] At the combined Cavan-Monaghan Twelfth held at Drum in 1920, Thomas Clements DL of Rathkenny offered a resigned vision of their place in Ireland. He assured the audience that: 'for ourselves and our property I honestly think there is no special danger' before contenting himself to note that the worst-case scenario would not come to pass: Sinn Féin were 'not Communists'. He urged the Protestant community to commit themselves to the new Irish state and, above all else, to the protection of the Protestant schools in the counties which he feared would be the real victims of any new regime.[112] Judge Samuel Browne KC opened the Clones Quarter Sessions of February 1922 with a pledge of allegiance to the new Irish government.[113] So rapidly did resistance break down that by early 1922 the *Northern Standard* was referring to its audience as 'ex-unionists' and urging them to take an active role:

> [they] will play an important part in deciding the contest in this country … the fate of Ireland is in the balance … we are concerned

[106] *Northern Standard*, 19 Jun. 1920; *Irish Post and Weekly Telegraph*, 20 Jul. 1918.
[107] Ricardo to Montgomery, 8 Apr. 1920 (PRONI, D627/435/10).
[108] Hansard, HL vol. 42, col. 808 (1 Dec. 1920).
[109] Strong to Montgomery, 12 Mar. 1920 (PRONI, D627/435/10).
[110] McDowell, *Crisis and Decline*, pp. 109–10.
[111] *Northern Standard*, 11 Feb. 1922.
[112] *Irish Post and Weekly Telegraph*, 17 Jul. 1920.
[113] *Northern Standard*, 3 Feb. 1922.

solely and absolutely for the fate of the plain people ... the ex-unionist
voters therefore must decide which candidates are more likely to bring
peace and prosperity.[114]

In a speech to the 155 Monaghan Lodge in November 1921, the chairman of
the lodge, Dr J. Campbell Hall, counselled his brethren to show 'restraint,
defence, not defiance and appealed to Orangemen and loyalists to do nothing
without consulting their leaders'. The same meeting saw a speech by William
Coote, MP for Tyrone and Fermanagh, in which he framed the terms of
accommodation with the new Irish state in a very traditional loyalist manner:
'loyalists must take things like trusty Britons, make the best of them. They
had to keep a stiff upper lip and hammer away'.[115]

This adaptation was echoed by the *Northern Standard*, which noted the
passing of the new Government of Ireland Bill through the Parliament with a
jaded eye but also commented on the attitude required in Cavan, Monaghan,
and Donegal: 'The Unionists of Monaghan and the other excluded counties
must ... look at the Bill from the point of view of the Southern Unionists
and the Irish Unionist Alliance, instead of from the old (or correct) Ulster
standpoint'.[116] As Lord Farnham had noted at the mass resignation of three-
county delegates to the UUC: 'how can we remain members of a body that
have plainly told us that they don't want us and that we are an incumbrance
to them?'[117] By July 1921, this position was even more advanced with the paper
now viewing the 'Six Counties' as a wholly distinct entity and speaking on
behalf of 'Unionists of the twenty-six counties' and 'Southern Unionists'. The
paper accepted that this group did 'not belong to the Six Counties' and would
have to continue on their own course.[118] This is reflected too in the greater
interest the loyalist papers started devoting to the affairs of the IUA, lending
criticism and analysis.[119]

This new southern perspective was facilitated by the growing discontent
with the 'traitors' who now led Northern Ireland. In a speech near Clones,
Michael Knight, grand master of the Monaghan Orange Lodge, declared the
'six-county "Unionists" had accomplished their desire. They had sat tight in
order to make for themselves places of trust and emolument'.[120] We do not
know if the quotation marks around Unionist in this quotation were added
by the editor of the *Northern Standard* or contextually implied, or both. The

---

[114] *Northern Standard*, 9 Jun. 1922.
[115] *Northern Standard*, 18 Nov. 1921.
[116] *Northern Standard*, 19 Jun. 1920.
[117] Farnham to Montgomery, 13 Apr. 1920 (PRONI, D627/435/10).
[118] *Northern Standard*, 15 Jul. 1921.
[119] *Northern Standard*, 25 Feb. 1921; *Northern Standard*, 7 Oct. 1921.
[120] *Northern Standard*, 15 Jul. 1921.

claims of the UUC that a nine-county Ulster state could not guarantee a Unionist majority were also disparaged. The comfortable Unionist majority attained in the first Northern Irish elections seemed to confirm in the eyes of three-county loyalists that this argument had simply been a pretence by those in the North to shore up their own position.[121] By May 1921, the *Northern Standard* was of the opinion that the true issue with the Government of Ireland Act was partition itself and not the establishment of a home government. 'If the Six Counties were to be induced or forced, to give up the idea of a separate parliament and agree to a central Assembly in Dublin, we would probably have a peace'.[122] In April of the same year, the paper complained about the expense of setting up two such parliaments and advised that costs would be reduced should one Parliament be established in Dublin.[123]

While Ian d'Alton has described the manner in which southern Protestants kept their heads down and largely associated amongst themselves following partition as a 'parallel state', this was not exactly the case in Cavan and Monaghan with their larger and more assertive communities.[124] Michael Knight demonstrated his own 'comfortable adjustment' to the Free State by being elected in 1936 as President of the Incorporated Law Society.[125] While Cavan Protestants had lacked a presence on local councils since the early 1900s in Monaghan, Protestants (referred to from 1921 onwards as 'ex-unionists' by Thomas Toal, chair of Monaghan County Council) such as Colonel James Madden and William Martin remained active in local government.[126] They played a crucial role in supporting Toal in maintaining the chair of Monaghan County Council after 1934 in the face of opposition from Fianna Fáil. This is significant as Toal had been the leader of Sinn Féin in the Council before partition and had been viewed by local Unionists as one of their most influential, though respected, adversaries.

This adaptation did not mean the complete abandonment of loyalism as an element of their political identity, and Madden, in particular, continued to put forward a 'Protestant' perspective in debates. Despite owing his political survival to the support of the Protestant councillors, Thomas Toal refused outright to hear a motion proposed by Colonel Madden congratulating the king and queen on their jubilee. Madden's proposal was justified by Ireland's status as a dominion. Even over a decade after its establishment, the Free

---

121 *Northern Standard*, 15 Jul. 1921; *Northern Standard*, 14 May 1921.
122 *Northern Standard*, 13 May 1921.
123 *Northern Standard*, 8 Jun. 1921
124 Ian d'Alton, '"No Country"? Protestant "Belongings" in Independent Ireland, 1922–49', in Ian d'Alton and Ida Milne (eds), *Protestant and Irish: The Minority's Search for a Place in Independent Ireland* (Cork, 2019), pp. 19–33.
125 Fitzpatrick *Descendancy*, p. 56.
126 Diary of Thomas Toal (Monaghan County Museum).

State meant different things to Protestant and Catholic.[127] The adaptation and persistence of the Protestant political identity can be seen in the foundation of the Monaghan Protestant Association (originally the Monaghan Protestant Defence Association) and Cavan Progressive Association, which aimed to select and support Protestant candidates for local and general elections in the new state.[128] In the next two decades, Cavan and Monaghan would both return TDs who ran as explicitly 'Ulster Protestant' candidates: Alexander Haslett in 1927 and 1933 in Monaghan and John James Cole in Cavan in 1923 and 1927.[129]

However, this assimilation was not as simple as shifting from an 'Ulster' to a 'southern' perspective and the ambiguities of their position before partition persisted after it. As the counties shifted into a 'southern' perspective they moved to associate amongst each other. They shared a unique position not fully understood now as either 'north' or 'south'. Canon Given of Dartrey gloomily conceded that they could no longer consider themselves to be in Ulster but rather 'they were the buffers between the North and South'.[130] In the words of William Martin, of Lodge 155 in Monaghan, 'we are rather in a state of suspended animation: we are neither the one thing nor the other'.[131] Traditional cross-Ulster events such as the Twelfth moved towards a three-county basis with the Twelfth of 1920 and the Clones Twelfth of 1921 organised on a three-county basis.[132] In November 1921, the Cavan, Donegal and Monaghan Loyalist Association was established to 'safeguard the interests of the 70,000 loyalists in the three counties'.[133]

Conclusion

Even had we not such strong evidence of loyalist organisation in Cavan and Monaghan pre-1920, nor the accounts of a separate and distinct Protestant community in those counties, the strength of the loyalist response to the establishment of the Northern state would convince us of the sincerity of their Ulster loyalism. The rallies, resolutions, and speeches of the community in the months following the decision of the UUC to accept partition are rife

---

[127] Diary of Thomas Toal (Monaghan County Museum).

[128] Liam Weeks, *Independents in Irish Party Democracy* (Manchester, 2017), p. 36.

[129] Weeks, *Independents in Irish Democracy*, p. 36.

[130] *Northern Standard*, 22 Jul. 1921.

[131] *Northern Standard*, 18 Nov. 1921.

[132] *Irish Post and Weekly Telegraph*, 17 Jul. 1920; *Northern Standard*, 17 Jul. 1920; *Northern Standard*, 5 Aug. 1921.

[133] *Northern Standard*, 4 Nov. 1921. Note: The 70,000 figure is a rough estimate of the total Protestant population of Cavan, Monaghan, and Donegal in the 1911 census.

with acid tones and wounded feelings. A poor recruiting record is offset by enthusiasm for the UVF and Ulster Clubs. An early appeal of the Ulster movement, particularly in South Monaghan and West Cavan, was not in its intrinsic ancestral call but in the connection it offered to a broader, more vibrant movement. However, by the time of our examination it was pointless to try and isolate individual motives for what had become a commonly felt, cross-border commitment which had bound its members together through their shared struggles and sacrifices. The sincerity of their connection to Ulster and the pain it caused when broken were key features in the Cavan and Monaghan Protestant experience not just of the war but of the twentieth century.

The rapid adaptation of the community to their new circumstances is striking and is the most important complicating factor in this analysis. However, the intensity of emotions around the decision to accept partition in 1920 and the strength of the sense of 'betrayal' is fundamental to understanding the speed of this adaptation. Even as the community shifted into a 'southern' mindset they continued to look north with envy and bitterness. This is further evidenced by the tenacity of a 'three-county' loyalist identity, which expressed itself through the continuation of Twelfth celebrations, the persistence of Orange lodges, and the running of 'Ulster Protestant' political candidates. While the community quickly accepted their new reality, they could not fully leave their old one behind.

CHAPTER XIII

Adaptive Coexistence?
Lord Farnham (1879–1957) and Southern
Loyalism in Pre- and Post-Independence Ireland

Jonathan Cherry

Lot 53, 'A collection; including four coronet shields; flags; etc.', was by no means the most conspicuous lot on display at the residual clearance auction at Farnham House, County Cavan in January 2002.[1] However, the flags, a few tattered and faded Union flags, and four wooden shields that had hung on the entrance gates to Farnham House to celebrate the coronation of George V in 1911, were symbolic remnants of the Maxwell family's loyalty to the Crown.[2] From 1700 onwards, the landowning elite – of which the Maxwell family were part – dominated Ireland economically, socially, and politically. With ownership of the country's most important commodity, this numerically small group enjoyed the attendant rights, privileges, and status that landownership conferred. This elite maintained and cultivated strong connections with their counterparts in Britain. Often, the sons of Irish landlords were educated in British public schools, with many going on to careers in the military and politics. Familial connections with Britain were maintained through marriage and property interests, while a shared adherence, in the main, to Protestantism cemented these bonds. From this common heritage, a cultural identity of 'Britishness', which had at its core loyalty to Britain and its monarch, developed among Irish landlords.

From the late nineteenth century onwards, and with a greater intensity during the early decades of the twentieth century, the position enjoyed by Irish landlords was challenged on a number of fronts. Extensive land reform

---

[1] Hamilton Osborne King Fine Art, 'Catalogue of Residual House Clearance Auction at Farnham House, Co. Cavan, 27 Jan. 2002'. Copy in possession of author.

[2] An image of the lot is contained in Jack Johnston, 'Farnham End of an Era', *The Spark: Journal of the Border Counties History Collective*, 16 (2003), pp. 27–8 (at p. 28). The original use of the shields and flags is captured in a photograph published in Brendan Scott, *Farnham Images from the Maxwell Estate, Co. Cavan* (Dublin, 2010), p. 56.

weakened their socio-economic status.[3] Their political connection with Britain was also shaken and overshadowed by the impending introduction of Home Rule, which, while threatening their way of life, simultaneously provided landlords and other loyalists an opportunity to demonstrate and display their loyalty. But by 1920 the partition of Ireland was a reality and, despite their protests, southern unionists would ultimately find themselves separated from the majority of their fellow unionists. As a minority group in the Irish Free State of the 1920s, Protestant landlords and Protestants more generally faced a range of decisions, challenges, and trials in this 'new' Ireland. This chapter traces the career and experiences of one such southern unionist, Arthur Kenlis Maxwell, Lord Farnham, in pre- and post-independent Ireland. Farnham was a familiar figure in the upper ranks of Ulster Unionism until 1920. However, from around 1916 onwards, as the prospective nature of partition emerged, Farnham became one of the main spokespersons for southern unionists, particularly those in Cavan, Donegal, and Monaghan, in giving voice to their grievances at being abandoned by their fellow Ulster unionists.

Arthur Kenlis Maxwell, 11th Baron Farnham (1879–1957) was born in London in 1879. He was the second son of Somerset Henry Maxwell, a small landowner in south Cavan who had made a military career, and was heir apparent to his childless uncle James Pierce Maxwell, the ninth Baron Farnham.[4] In November 1880, Somerset Maxwell came to national attention as one of the leaders of the men who travelled to save the harvest of Captain Boycott at Lough Mask, County Mayo after his own labourers had refused to do so.[5] Arthur was educated at Harrow and Sandhurst. The tragic death of his eldest brother in 1896 meant Arthur became heir apparent, and in 1900, aged 21, he succeeded his father as Lord Farnham and to the 24,000 acre estate in Cavan, with annual rents of £11,500.[6] On returning from service in the Boer War, he married Aileen Selina Coote, of Bearforest, Mallow, County Cork, after which they established themselves at Farnham House. While military service, leadership of the Orange Order in Cavan, and involvement in the running of the Church of Ireland illustrate – in part – Lord Farnham's cultural identity as a unionist, it was his involvement with Ulster Unionism at both a local and provincial level, and his determination that Cavan, Monaghan, and

---

[3] Terence Dooley, *The Decline of the Big House in Ireland: A Study of Irish Landed Families, 1860–1960* (Dublin, 2001).

[4] *Burke's Genealogical and Heraldic History of the Peerage, Baronetage & Knightage* [*Burke's Peerage*] (London, 1959), p. 840.

[5] Joyce Marlow, *Captain Boycott and the Irish* (London, 1973); Charles Arthur Boycott, *Boycott: The Life Behind the Word* (London, 1997).

[6] Jonathan Cherry, 'The Maxwell Family of Farnham: An Introduction', *Breifne*, 42 (2006), pp. 125–47 (at p. 142).

Donegal would remain part of unionist Ulster, which was Lord Farnham's greatest expression of loyalism before 1922.

Lord Farnham and Politics Pre-1922

With Home Rule the dominant political challenge facing Unionism, the formation of the Ulster Unionist Council in 1905 co-ordinated political resistance in the northern province.[7] As their de facto leader, Lord Farnham was one of the leading delegates representing County Cavan unionists in this new body. Following his election in 1908 as a Conservative representative peer for Ireland, he became an important voice for Ulster Unionism in the House of Lords.[8] The introduction of the third Home Rule bill in April 1912 was a major concern for Unionists, as some form of Home Rule, at least in the south of Ireland, became inevitable.[9] A mass mobilisation of Unionist opposition was organised for 'Ulster Day', Saturday, 28 September 1912, in which a covenant and declaration were signed by men and women respectively, expressing their determination to resist the imposition of Home Rule by all means. Surprisingly, given Lord Farnham's status, he did not organise any of the signing ceremonies in Cavan, but did sign the Covenant in Cavan town.[10] His wife, however, was one of the principal organisers of the signing of the Women's Declaration in the town's Protestant Hall.[11] Farnham's fears of Home Rule are evident from his speeches as deputy grand master of the Orange Order in County Cavan at the annual 12 July celebrations.[12] Addressing the Orangemen who had assembled on his demesne in July 1913, Farnham assured them that Home Rule would be resisted, warning that its introduction would bring civil war.[13] The following July, at Belturbet, County Cavan, Farnham stated that 'They were members of the Protestant United Kingdom', asking, 'would they allow

---

[7] Graham Walker, *A History of the Ulster Unionist Party: Protest, Pragmatism and Pessimism* (Manchester, 2004).

[8] *Burke's Peerage*, p. 841.

[9] Alvin Jackson, *Home Rule: An Irish History, 1800–2000* (London, 2003), pp. 108–16.

[10] For Lord Farnham's signature to the Ulster Covenant, see Ulster Covenant online: https://apps.proni.gov.uk/ulstercovenant/image.aspx?image=M0014200010 (accessed 30 Jul. 2018).

[11] For more on the role played by women from Ulster's country houses in Ulster Day, see Jonathan Cherry and Arlene Crampsie, 'Declaring Loyalty to the Union: The Women of Ulster's Country Houses and the Organization of Ulster Day', in Terence Dooley, Maeve O'Riordan, and Christopher Ridgway (eds), *Women and the Country House in Ireland and Britain* (Dublin, 2018), pp. 76–94.

[12] Jack Johnston, 'The Orange Order in County Cavan, 1798–2014', in Jonathan Cherry and Brendan Scott (eds), *Cavan History and Society* (Dublin, 2014), p. 377.

[13] *Irish Times*, 14 Jul. 1913.

themselves to be driven out and handed over to the domination of a Catholic parliament?'[14] His remarks demonstrate the essence of loyalism to Cavan's unionists: a shared Protestant religion and heritage, coupled with fealty to the Crown and Empire.

In 1911, 14.2 per cent of County Cavan's population were members of the Church of Ireland.[15] The network of Church of Ireland parishes with their associated church buildings and rectories scattered across the county was significant in unifying the majority of Cavan's Protestants before 1922. It was for many a key component of their cultural identity as loyal Ulster Protestants, proud of their birthright and loyalty to the monarch. Such a tendency was illustrated by the resolution passed at the Kilmore diocesan synod in October 1914, which declared:

> That this synod protests against the placing of the Home Rule Bill upon the statute book at a time of deep national disquietude ... But in spite of this deplorable breach of faith we shall exert ourselves to the utmost in the future as hitherto to support our gallant soldiers and sailors in their conflict for the freedom of Europe and the integrity of the Empire, resolving at the same time to maintain our birth right as free citizens, subject only to the King and the Imperial Parliament.[16]

When the Ulster Volunteer Force (UVF) was formed in January 1913, the commanding officers of each of the three battalions in County Cavan, Lord Farnham, Captain Somerset Saunderson, and Captain Mervyn Pratt, and the regimental commander Major Oliver Nugent – all members of the county landowning class – drew upon prior military experience.[17] The primary purpose in forming the UVF was, as Timothy Bowman has noted, to 'maintain Unionist discipline and unity' at a time of heightened tensions, as they prepared to oppose the introduction of Home Rule.[18] In June 1913, the

---

[14] *The Anglo-Celt*, 18 Jul. 1914.

[15] The other Protestant denominations were Presbyterians at 3.1 per cent, Methodists at 0.9 per cent, and all other non-Roman Catholic denominations at 0.35 per cent. Details taken from Table XXIX, 'Religious Profession and Sexes of the Inhabitants in each Parish in the County of Antrim in 1911', in *Census of Ireland, 1911. Area, Houses, and Population: Also the Ages, Civil or Conjugal Condition, Occupations, Birthplaces, Religion, and Education of the People. Province of Ulster* [Cd. 6051], HC 1912–13.

[16] Minute book of the Diocesan Synod, 1914 (Representative Church Body Library, D3/4/1).

[17] Timothy Bowman, *Carson's Army: The Ulster Volunteer Force, 1910–22* (Manchester, 2007), p. 57.

[18] Bowman, *Carson's Army*, p. 205.

Irish Times reported that a consignment of 500 rifles and bayonets addressed to Lord Farnham had been intercepted at Dublin port.[19] The gunrunning operation was overseen by Fred Crawford, who identified Lord Farnham as one of his fellow 'hawks'.[20] The consignment intended for Farnham had been sent by the front firm, 'John Ferguson and Co. London', set up to conceal the identity of those shipping arms to the UVF.[21] Undeterred, the Cavan UVF continued to drill and train and in March 1914 a week-long instruction and training camp was held at Farnham. The Dublin *Daily Express* subsequently carried a series of photographs entitled 'Lord Farnham teaches the Orangemen of Cavan how to shoot'.[22] As one of the more militant unionist leaders in Cavan, an attempt was made on Farnham's life in December 1913. He was saved by the windscreen on his open topped car, which bore the brunt of a wire stretched across the road aiming to decapitate him.[23] Farnham's capabilities as a military organiser would be celebrated by Arthur Barton, the former Church of Ireland archbishop of Dublin, following his death in 1957. Barton noted how:

> A bugle sounded in Ulster. Hearing again the call of duty and to difficult leadership, he responded, not lightly, but fully realising the seriousness of his task. Few, perhaps, realise how fortunate it was that the leadership of local battalions of Ulster Volunteers was in the hands of such men as Lord Farnham. Not only, his high principles, but his military training enabled him to exercise a discipline which may well have saved districts from chaos and bloodshed.[24]

Indeed, Sir Shane Leslie, writing in the late 1960s, also noted that his father Sir John Leslie and Lord Farnham 'took command of the Monaghan and Cavan regiments chiefly to keep hot heads in order'.[25] In adopting this role,

---

[19] *Irish Times*, 9 Jun. 1913.

[20] The term hawk is used here in describing those who were happy to use military force. For more on this, see Bowman, *Carson's Army*, pp. 138–9.

[21] Timothy Bowman, 'Irish Paramilitarism and Gun Cultures, 1910–1921', in Karen Jones, Giacomo Macola, and David Welch (eds), *A Cultural History of Firearms in the Age of Empire* (London, 2013), p. 274.

[22] *Daily Express*, 14 Mar. 1914.

[23] Eileen Reilly, 'Cavan in the Era of the Great War 1914–1918', in Raymond Gillespie (ed.), *Cavan: Essays on the History of an Irish County* (Dublin, 1995), p. 181.

[24] *Irish Times*, 14 Feb. 1957. The See House at Kilmore where Barton as bishop of Kilmore, Elphin and Ardagh between 1930 and 1939 resided was located within a mile of Lord Farnham's home Farnham House.

[25] Quoted in Bowman, *Carson's Army*, p. 48.

Farnham and other Ulster landlords reflected what Tim Wilson has referred to as the spirit of 'patriotism as paternalism'.[26]

The outbreak of war in summer 1914 put a brake on the introduction of Home Rule and prevented the outbreak of conflict between north and south.[27] Like many loyalists, Farnham, then aged 35, went to war. He initially took control of the depot of the yeomanry unit of the North Irish Horse in Londonderry before his appointment in September 1915 as aide-de-camp to Major General Oliver Nugent, a fellow Cavan man, the commander of the 36th Ulster Division in France.[28] However, political changes were afoot at home. On 12 June 1916, a meeting of Unionists was convened to respond to Lloyd George's proposed Home Rule settlement which envisaged self-government for Ireland with the exception of the six Ulster counties of Antrim, Armagh, Down, Tyrone, Fermanagh, and Londonderry. Lord Farnham, as the most prominent Unionist from the three excluded Ulster counties, in an emotional speech, 'with breaking voice', thanked Edward Carson 'for the clearness, and the fairness, and the manliness with which he has put the deplorable situation that has arisen before us, and for his manly advice as leader'.[29] Following his speech, Farnham read a resolution from the delegates of what were to become the three 'lost' counties. While it protested against any settlement that excluded them from Ulster, it also expressed willingness to agree to the proposal for the greater good of Ulster Unionism. It was, as Ronald McNeill wrote, 'the saddest hour the Ulster Unionist Council ever spent. Men not prone to emotion shed tears'.[30]

Farnham returned to the war but was captured in March 1918 and spent the remainder of the conflict as a prisoner of war at Karlsruhe in Germany. On his return to Cavan in late 1918 he was greeted at the train station in Cavan town by a number of the county's unionists, who presented him with an illuminated address:

> We are proud to remember the distinguished services that you have rendered to your King and country worthily upholding the record of your noble family. As our leader in the county of Cavan we recall

---

[26] Tim Wilson, 'The Strange Death of Loyalist Monaghan, 1912–1921', in Senia Pašeta (ed.), *Uncertain Futures: Essays about the Irish Past for Roy Foster* (Oxford, 2016), p. 180.

[27] Jackson, *Home Rule*, pp. 142–74.

[28] Nicholas Perry (ed.), *Major General Oliver Nugent and the Ulster Division* (Stroud, 2007). For detail on Farnham's full service and experience during the Great War, see www.northirishhorse.com.au/NIH/Images/People/Full%20pictures/Lord%20Farnham.htm (accessed 21 Aug. 2018).

[29] Ronald McNeill, *Ulster's Stand for Union* (London, 1922), p. 249.

[30] McNeill, *Ulster's Stand for Union*, p. 249.

with gratitude your untiring exertions and conspicuous ability in the furtherance of the great issue we have so much at heart – the maintenance of the Legislative Union of Great Britain and Ireland – and we are happy to have you amongst us once again in these critical times to direct our counsels and to champion our cause.[31]

In 1919, Farnham was appointed chairman of the fractured IUA, following the resignation of Lord Midleton. Under Midleton's chairmanship, the IUA had argued that the partition of Ireland should be avoided at all costs, the union maintained, and some form of Home Rule negotiated for the whole island. However, this position was totally unacceptable to many IUA grassroots members and diehard Ulster Unionists, who rejected any form of Home Rule and ultimately forced Midleton's resignation.[32] By early 1920, the Government of Ireland bill was prepared proposing the division of Ireland into Northern Ireland, comprised of six Ulster counties, and Southern Ireland. Although the idea of abandoning counties Donegal, Monaghan, and Cavan had been mooted in 1916, the reality alarmed the diehard unionists from these counties, who, as Patrick Buckland has noted, 'clung to the belief that the exclusion of nine counties of Ulster would wreck home rule'.[33] At a meeting of the Ulster Unionist Council in March 1920, Farnham proposed an amendment to the bill suggesting that the council should seek the inclusion of all nine counties.[34] The growth of Sinn Féin and their demands for a republic had left Farnham and unionists from the three counties uneasy and fearful of a future separated economically from Belfast and politically from their fellow six-county unionists. Farnham's amendment was defeated and the fate of southern unionists sealed. Six-county unionists feared that by including the predominantly Catholic counties of Cavan, Monaghan, and Donegal (where just under 38 per cent of the entire Catholic population of the nine counties resided), the Protestant majority could not be maintained.[35] Their position was

---

[31] Illuminated address to Arthur Kenlis, Lord Farnham, Dec. 1918 (Cavan County Museum, 2005-562).

[32] Patrick Buckland, *Irish Unionism I: The Anglo-Irish and the New Ireland, 1885–1922* (Dublin, 1972), p. 180; R.B. McDowell, *Crisis and Decline: The Fate of the Southern Unionists* (Dublin, 1997), pp. 63–6.

[33] Buckland, *Irish Unionism I*, p. 198.

[34] Bridget Hourican, 'Maxwell, Somerset Henry 10th Baron Farnham', in James McGuire and James Quinn (eds), *Dictionary of Irish Biography* (Cambridge, 2009): http://dib.cambridge.org/viewReadPage.do?articleId=a5533.

[35] The number of Protestants in Ulster in 1911 was comprised of 366,773 Protestant Episcopalians, 421,410 Presbyterians, 48,816 Methodists, and 53,881 of all other denominations. See Table XXIX, 'Religious Profession and Sexes of the Inhabitants

summarised in the pamphlet *Why I Voted for the Six Counties* by Frederick
Hugh Crawford, published in April 1920:

> There are 890,880 Protestants in the whole of the nine counties of Ulster.
> There are 70,510 Protestants and 260,655 Roman Catholics in the three
> counties. I cannot believe the Protestants in the three counties are willing
> to swamp 820,370 Protestants merely for the satisfaction of knowing they
> are all going down to disaster in the same boat.[36]

Enclosing his pamphlet in a letter to Farnham, Crawford wrote:

> Will you read it carefully over and while doing so 'think impersonally'.
> You know that there is no personal sacrifice including my own life that I
> would not make to save you people from being left out, if it were possible
> to do so and safeguard Ulster as a whole for the Protestant Faith and
> against being put under a Dublin Parliament.[37]

In protest, Farnham and other southern unionists highlighted their sense
of abandonment by their fellow Ulster Unionists. Their collective heritage
of resistance and opposition to Home Rule, most recently manifested in the
signing of the Ulster Covenant, had been betrayed. Farnham's last attempt to
arrest the fate of southern unionists occurred during the winter of 1920 as
the Government of Ireland bill was being debated.[38] Addressing the House
of Lords as 'an unrepentant Unionist' and as chairman of the IUA, Farnham
declared: 'I am not and those I represent are not prepared to support any
Bill which interferes with the broad principle of the maintenance of the
Union'. He detailed the sacrifices that had been made for king and Empire
by 'those loyal men and women who through several generations have been
the outposts of British civilisation in Ireland, who have upheld the honour
of their King and country and fought for the welfare of the British Empire.
Through times of great danger and difficulty they have always remained
loyal'.[39]

    Summing up the sense of betrayal and fear felt by many southern unionists,
Farnham stated:

---

    in each Parish in the County of Antrim in 1911', in *Census of Ireland, 1911.*
    Province of Ulster.
[36] F.H. Crawford, *Why I Voted for the Six Counties* (Apr. 1920) (PRONI, D/3975/E/10).
[37] F.H. Crawford to Lord Farnham, 27 Apr. 1920 (PRONI, D/3975/E/10).
[38] Hansard, HL, vol. 42, cols 1–1310 (19 Oct.–8 Dec. 1920).
[39] Hansard, HL, vol. 42, cols 629–30 (25 Nov. 1920).

It is now proposed to hand over these loyal people to the allies of the great enemy against whom their sons and brothers fought and died. I cannot believe that either the Government or the British people can realise the enormity or baseness of this great betrayal, or can fully realise the conditions under which the loyalists would be forced to live.[40]

He also highlighted the potential loss of identity resulting from the breaking up of Ulster and noted that he and his fellow unionists from the three border counties would:

no longer have the right which was won for us and handed down to us by our ancestors of belonging to the great Imperial Province of Ulster ... I assure you there is nothing that we in the three counties feel more than that we may no longer be entitled to our proud title of Ulstermen. In fact, already we are no longer regarded as Ulstermen.[41]

Farnham noted with resignation, and 'a real personal grief', his severance from his former political allies. He would no longer 'be able to be one of the most devoted helpers of our great leader, Sir Edward Carson'. But, he concluded, 'the question between us is one of conscience, and when consciences differ so utterly as to what is right there is no further room for argument'.[42] The lack of appreciation for the plight of southern loyalists was also highlighted: 'For our loyalty throughout ... we are now told that we are to be handed over ... to be governed by those very enemies of the Crown against whom we have been striving for so long'. He noted that 'If this Bill passes it will only serve to prove to the Empire one thing – that loyalty no longer pays; that loyalty can no longer claim or expect any reward'; it would 'shake the whole Empire to its very foundations'.[43] In concluding his plea to the Lords to reject the bill, Farnham asked them 'to save us once again from this great betrayal'.[44]

During the debate that followed Farnham was almost the lone opponent of the bill. He was dismissed by the foreign secretary, Earl Curzon, who remarked:

I admit that everyone is not converted. Nothing will convert my noble friend Lord Willoughby de Broke. He still remains a magnificent relic of the old guard, but the backwoods in which my noble friend ranged at the head of a formidable band some years ago are now relatively deserted, and

[40] Hansard, HL, vol. 42, cols 631 (25 Nov. 1920).
[41] Hansard, HL, vol. 42, col. 636 (25 Nov. 1920).
[42] Hansard, HL, vol. 42, col. 637 (25 Nov. 1920).
[43] Hansard, HL, vol. 42, col. 632 (25 Nov. 1920).
[44] Hansard, HL, vol. 42, col. 638 (25 Nov. 1920).

his picturesque figure is seen stalking, consoled only by Lord Farnham, amid the scenes that were once those of his adventures and triumphs.[45]

With the Government of Ireland bill passed, the new state of Northern Ireland was established in May 1921, without Cavan, Monaghan, and Donegal. Politically, Farnham and his fellow southern unionists had been severed from the majority of their unionist peers, becoming a minority grouping in the Irish Free State established in December 1922.

Farnham in Exile, c.1920–1926

The Farnhams departed from Ireland during the early 'Troubles', although an exact date has proven difficult to ascertain.[46] Heightened tension appears to have resulted in the Maxwells spending a good deal of 1920 and 1921 away from Cavan, with Lord Farnham returning only intermittently. He and his wife spent part of March and April 1921 golfing on the French Riviera.[47] In September of that year the family were photographed attending the Romsey Agricultural and Horse Show in Hampshire,[48] and by year's end it was reported that they had been 'spending the Autumn months in New Forest, Hampshire'.[49] *The Tatler*, in September 1922, devoted an entire page entitled 'Lord and Lady Farnham at "Sutherland" Hampshire' to a series of four pictures of Lord and Lady Farnham, their three children, Somerset, Marjory, and Verena Maxwell and their aunt Stella Maxwell, in various groupings. The ambience which the photographs transmit is one of contentment and ease, attested to by the relaxed poses of the teenage Maxwell children dressed in their tennis whites, alongside the smiles of their parents and aunt. A short description of the family's circumstances noted that 'Lord Farnham's family seat is at Farnham,

---

[45] Hansard, HL, vol. 42, col. 667 (25 Nov. 1920). Lord Willoughby de Broke was a diehard unionist peer who sat in the House of Lords between 1906 and 1923. In March 1913, he founded the 'British League for the Support of Ulster and the Union' to fight if Home Rule was introduced. For more, see Mark Pottle, 'Verney, Richard Greville, nineteenth Baron Willoughby de Broke (1869–1923), politician and fox-hunter', in *Oxford Dictionary of National Biography* (Oxford, 2008): https://doi.org/10.1093/ref:odnb/47172 (accessed 23 Nov. 2018).

[46] In a short biography of Lord Farnham composed in 1983 by his daughter, the Hon. Verena Milbank, she noted that the family had spent seven years away from Farnham during the 1920s. If this is the case, it may be suggested that they left in 1919 (Cavan County Library and Archives Service [CCLAS], P025/018).

[47] *The Tatler*, 16 Mar., 6 Apr. 1921.

[48] *The Bystander*, 21 Sep. 1921.

[49] *Irish Society and Social Review*, 19 Nov. 1921.

co. Cavan, but in the present state of affairs, when country-houses are the favourite bonfire with the "Shinners" he has temporarily removed himself and his family to less warlike Hampshire, and has taken "Sutherland," a beautiful place in Lymington'.[50] Indeed, while the Farnhams posed for *The Tatler*, Arley Cottage and Fortland, two houses on the shores of Lough Sheelin, County Cavan, which belonged to Lord Farnham's cousin, Captain Richard Maxwell, were looted to such an extent that 'there was nothing left but remnants of the four walls'.[51] The destruction and burning of the 'Big House' was a deep blow to any landed family and for many it marked the end of their connection with Ireland. These ancestral homes, accumulations of past generations, tastes, and ideas, were central to a family's sense of identity, belonging, and connectedness to a particular place. But while several other big houses in Cavan were targeted, Farnham House was spared.[52]

In exile, Lord Farnham gained employment as a private secretary to Sir Glynn Hamilton West, chairman of numerous English-based steel and coal companies. Between 1923 and 1924, Farnham undertook several business tours of Germany, selling pig iron and coal on behalf of two of West's companies, Armstrong Whitworth and Co. (based at Elswick, Manchester) and Pearson and Knowles Coal and Iron Company (based at Warrington).[53] He remained West's private secretary until 1926.[54] Despite their changed circumstances, for the Farnhams, family life in England appeared quite comfortable. His son and heir Somerset, a keen cricketer, became head boy at Harrow in 1923.[55] He, alongside his sisters and parents, also had the opportunity to indulge a passion for tennis, attending and competing in numerous tournaments around London between 1922 and 1925.[56] Lord Farnham, however, was determined to return to live in Cavan. This desire is best portrayed by his protracted battle with the Irish Land Commission over the amount of demesne land which they took through compulsory acquisition under the 1923 Land Act.[57]

[50] *The Tatler*, 20 Sep. 1922; *Irish Times*, 27 Sep. 1922.

[51] *Irish Times*, 5 Feb. 1924.

[52] Jonathan Cherry, 'The Structure, Legacy and Demise of Landlordism in County Cavan, *c.*1870–*c.*1970', in Cherry and Scott, *Cavan History and Society*, pp. 471–4.

[53] Two small outgoing letter books of correspondence between Lord Farnham and Sir G.H. West, regarding Farnham's business trip to Germany for Armstrong Whitworth & Co. (PRONI: D/3975/E/11/1–2); folder of correspondence relating to business in Germany (PRONI: D/3975/E/12/1); folders of correspondence relating to Pearson and Knowles Iron and Steel Company and Partington Steel and Iron Co. (NLI, MSS 41,159–MS 41,164).

[54] M.Cochrane to Lord Farnham, 22 Jun. 1926 (PRONI, D/3975/E/13/1).

[55] *The Bystander*, 3 Oct. 1923.

[56] See, for example, *The Tatler*, 6 Sep. 1922; 25 Jun. 1924; 24 Jun., 14 Oct. 1925.

[57] Irish Land Commission, Records Branch, Farnham Estate S.655, Box 12601.

The Maxwell family connection with Farnham stretched back to 1664, and the lure of the family home set amidst Cavan's drumlins had secured Lord Farnham's affection and appears to have superseded any fears he may have had about residing in a 'new' Ireland. He convinced the Land Commission that he was going to return and managed to retain a large agricultural holding centred on Farnham House which he could farm intensively.[58] Lord Farnham's ability to reconcile his training of the UVF at Farnham in 1914 and his decision to return there a decade later reflects his own resilience and temperament, and what R.B. McDowell referred to as the 'self-confidence bred by generations of governing' found among southern unionists.[59]

Return to Farnham, 1926

By June 1926, Lord Farnham had returned to Cavan.[60] By year's end the *Irish Times* reported that Farnham and his daughters had hunted with the Meath Hounds, suggesting a return to some normality.[61] It is not known what Farnham's thoughts, fears, concerns, or hopes were on returning to this 'new' Ireland.[62] Sir Oliver Nugent, in a letter to his daughter prior to his own return home in late 1920, would write:

> I wonder what it will be like at home. I do not expect the people will be allowed to show any civility and I think everything is likely to be very unpleasant but I do not think they will shoot at us when we appear out of doors. I hope they won't. It would be such a nuisance having to go out for a walk crawling on one's tummy.[63]

While several of the county's prominent landed families, such as the Burrowes of Stradone and the Saundersons of Castle Saunderson, were forced from Cavan between 1920 and 1922 owing to attacks on their homes, over 70 per cent – or 24 out of 34 – big houses identified from a 1906 survey of the county remained intact and inhabited by their original owners in the decade after 1922.[64] The

---

[58] *Iris Oifigiúil*, 5 Nov. 1926.

[59] R.B. McDowell, *The Irish Convention, 1917–18* (London, 1970), p. 127.

[60] *Irish Times*, 4 Jun. 1926.

[61] *Irish Times*, 29 Dec. 1926.

[62] For an insight and perspective on unionists who remained in Ireland, see McDowell, *Crisis and Decline*, pp. 163–96.

[63] Nicholas Perry, 'Oliver Nugent, the Gentry and the Great War', in Cherry and Scott, *Cavan History and Society*, p. 497.

[64] Cherry, 'The Structure, Legacy and Demise of Landlordism', in Cherry and Scott, *Cavan History and Society*, pp. 471–6.

bitterness and strife that had characterised the period in other Irish counties was less evident in Cavan. Writing about the visibility of minorities, Ian d'Alton has noted that 'Too small a minority, and the majority is indifferent; too large a minority, and the majority is reluctant to take on its rivals'.[65] Perhaps in the case of Cavan the sizeable and visible Protestant population might just have been 'too large a minority', as individuals such as Nugent and Farnham integrated back into life in Cavan and the Free State in a relatively easy manner.[66]

Writing in 1983 about her father, Lord Farnham, Verena Milbank remarked that 'Political problems drove him from his home', but he 'returned to Farnham to the Gardeners Cottage to try and set up house again and to put the place in order once more. This he did in no small way and once again became the pillar of all he stood for, the Guardian of all who were beholden to him'. She noted that 'not only was he a great character but one who amongst other things was the biggest enthusiast of all time ... through immeasurable vicissitudes both politically and family tragedies he retained all that he believed in'.[67] Lord Farnham's own personal characteristics and temperament were of paramount importance in easing his return to Cavan. Other factors which played a role in bringing about his successful return included his family's prior residency and investment in the property at Farnham and in Cavan town; the fact that his ancestral family home had survived the period; his maintenance of a viable holding of land; the continuing existence of a network of landowning families with whom he could socialise; his relatively young age at 47 years old; and the fact that he had developed strong relationships across the community before 1922.

One way in which these relationships had been developed was through Farnham's passion and promotion of a range of sports. As his daughter noted, Farnham had 'a tremendous love of sport and everything that could give pleasure to all and sundry'.[68] A passion for tennis and golf brought him into contact with a wide and diverse range of people in Cavan from different social and political backgrounds. In 1920, he had leased the property known as Arnmore, at Drumelis, on the outskirts of Cavan town, to County Cavan Golf Club, of which he was a member. In addition, he gave land for the construction of tennis courts behind the Protestant hall on Farnham Street in Cavan town. The interest and patronage that Farnham had shown had secured for him an extensive personal network across the political spectrum

[65] Ian d'Alton '"A Vestigial Population"? Perspectives on Southern Irish Protestants in the Twentieth Century', *Éire-Ireland*, 44/3&4 (2009), pp. 9–42 (at p. 28).
[66] Perry, 'Oliver Nugent', in Cherry and Scott, *Cavan History and Society*, pp. 497–8.
[67] Milbank, biography of Farnham, 20 Sep. 1983 (CCLAS, P025/018).
[68] Milbank, biography of Farnham (CCLAS, P025/018).

which he could rely upon on his return. Golf, which was to prove attractive to both the town's Protestant and Catholic professional classes, facilitated Farnham in meeting those outside his traditional social circle, while lawn tennis, which had a largely upper- and middle-class Protestant following in Ireland, cemented Farnham's connections with his co-religionists. The tennis club at Cavan where Lord Farnham was one of the main patrons was seen as amongst the more 'exclusive' county clubs in the country at the time.[69] His activities there were captured by poet John Betjeman in a letter from September 1930:

> the other day we went to the Cavan Tennis Tournament. It was all organised by Lord Farnham who did the umpiring, carried a bucket of sand to the place the competitors serve and arranged that a subscriptions dance should take place at his house. His house is called Farnham and, as he has had to sell most of his furniture, it is a little bare but the acetylene gas makes a brave show'.[70]

While Farnham resided permanently in Ireland until his death in 1957, none of his children did so. Both daughters married Englishmen and settled in England. His son, and heir to the Farnham title, Somerset, after a career as a London stockbroker, became Conservative MP for King's Lynn in Norfolk in 1935. He died from injuries received at the battle of El Alamein in December 1942.[71] Lord Farnham's brother Denis Maxwell became a vice-admiral in the Royal Navy and was aide-de-camp to George VI.[72] The continuation of these familial ties with the British armed services after independence helped maintain the Farnham family's affection for and interest in Britain during the 1930s and 1940s.[73]

How then, in the changed Ireland in which they found themselves, were individuals such as Lord Farnham able to display and demonstrate their continued loyalty?[74] While Farnham spent the last 30 years of his life in an Ireland which transitioned from Free State to Republic, he continued to display

---

[69] Tom Higgins, *The History of Irish Tennis* (Sligo, 2006); Robert J. Lake, *A Social History of Tennis in Britain* (Abingdon, 2015).

[70] John Betjeman to Patrick Balfour, 13 Sep. 1930, in Candida Lycett Green (ed.), *John Betjeman, Letters*, vol. 1: *1926–1951* (London, 1994), p. 69.

[71] *Burke's Peerage*, p. 841.

[72] *Burke's Peerage*, p. 841.

[73] For more on the continuing connections between Irish families and the British military after independence, see Steven O'Connor, *Irish Officers in the British Forces, 1922–45* (Basingstoke, 2014).

[74] For more on the Protestant population generally during this time, see d'Alton '"A Vestigial Population"?', pp. 9–42.

and express traditional loyalism through declarations of fealty to the monarch, and as guardian and advocate of Protestant values and religion, especially in the Church of Ireland. Simultaneously, as seen in the next section, he was able to carve out a respected role amongst his fellow Cavan men and women, both Protestant and Catholic.

Support of the Protestant Interest

Lord Farnham's absence from Cavan during the early 1920s meant that the county's sizeable Protestant population looked to others for political representation. The dispersed nature of the county's Protestants left them unrepresented by Unionist councillors at local elections during the early years of the twentieth century. However, in the new four-seater constituency of Cavan in 1923, the County Down-born Presbyterian, John James Cole, was elected an Independent TD. Cole, a pharmacist by training, had established a pharmacy in Cavan town in the early 1900s. His marriage in October 1909 to Jeannie Jones, the heiress of a relatively large estate centred on Nahillah Park, Cloverhill, was to prove significant in cementing his connections in the county. He was elected between 1923 and 1944, although he would contest each election up to 1957.[75] Essentially, Lord Farnham's position as spokesman for Cavan Protestants had been taken by Cole.

In 1926, the Protestant Parliamentary Committee for Cavan was established by Cole and other loyalists in the county, including solicitors, large farmers, and Church of Ireland clergy, most of whom were members of the Orange Order. Its purpose was to organise the mobilisation of the Protestant vote in Cavan.[76] In addition to this committee, Cole also had the support of the county Orange Order. Cole had become grand master of Cavan's Orangemen in 1937 having served as deputy master from 1934. The Orange Order in the county comprised eight district lodges by 1934, providing a useful network for campaigning.[77] Farnham did not take a role in the Protestant Parliamentary Committee for Cavan, which in some way reflects the gradual decline in relevance of the landed class in Irish society, even within Protestantism. Indeed, Farnham's connection with the Orange Order appears to have fizzled out as he left the post of deputy grand master of the Order in Cavan

---

[75] Pauric J. Dempsey, 'Cole, John James', in James McGuire and James Quinn (eds), *Dictionary of Irish Biography* (Cambridge, 2009): http://dib.cambridge.org/viewReadPage.do?articleId=a1826.

[76] Minute book of the Protestant Parliamentary Committee for Cavan. In possession of Mr John Cole, Nahillah, Cloverhill, Co. Cavan.

[77] Johnston, 'The Orange Order in County Cavan', pp. 376–7.

in 1927.[78] The following year he became master of the Masonic Provincial Grand Lodge of Meath.[79] The Masonic Order provided individuals like Farnham greater opportunities and connections amongst middle and higher social classes across the island, and indeed internationally, when compared with the more localised Orange Order which traditionally had attracted the bulk of its membership from lower socio-economic classes. Farnham's only formal foray into politics in the Free State was his nomination for election in the triennial elections to the Senate in November 1928.[80] He failed to be elected.[81] In June of the following year he was again nominated to fill the seat made vacant by the resignation of the marquess of Lansdowne; he was again unsuccessful.[82] Farnham's willingness to contest senate elections indicates his readiness to continue his political life in the Free State. However, while unable to represent Protestants in formal politics, Farnham was, by more subtle means, able to champion their interests and values in the new Ireland.

The unaltered structures and organisation of the Church of Ireland after 1922 provided a familiar space within which Lord Farnham, on his return, could become involved again in the management, advancement, and defence of the church, as a cornerstone institution linking southern Protestants. At Easter 1927, he was appointed churchwarden at St Fethlimidh's Cathedral, Kilmore, which lay a short distance from his home and was where his family traditionally worshipped.[83] His deep involvement with the Church of Ireland is best illustrated by detailing his activities in one particular year – 1936. At the Kilmore diocesan synod of that year he was appointed or elected a diocesan trustee; a delegate to the General Synod; a member of the diocesan council; and a member of the board of patronage, the board of religious education, and the board of missions.[84] In this year he was also appointed president of the Hibernian Church Missionary Society.[85] At a national level, Farnham's membership of both the Representative Church Body – which oversaw the management of church property and finance – and the General Synod, where 'his clear and emphatic speeches made a deep impression and at times, were

[78] Johnston, 'The Orange Order in County Cavan', p. 377.
[79] See www.meath.org/ (accessed 3 Aug. 2018).
[80] *Irish Times*, 3 Nov. 1928.
[81] Seanad Éireann Debate, Wednesday, 7 Nov. 1928: www.oireachtas.ie/en/debates/ debate/dail/1928-11-07/34/ (accessed 31 Jul. 2018).
[82] Seanad Éireann Debate, Thursday, 29 Jun. 1929: www.oireachtas.ie/en/debates/ debate/seanad/1929-06-20/3/ (accessed 31 Jul. 2018) and *Irish Times*, 29 Jun. 1929.
[83] John Charles Combe, *St. Fethlimidh's Cathedral, Kilmore: A Short History* (published privately, no date, *c*.1992).
[84] *Church of Ireland Gazette*, 17 Jul. 1936.
[85] *Church of Ireland Gazette*, 22 Feb. 1957.

the deciding influence in debates on burning issues',[86] illustrate his determination to safeguard interests of the Church of Ireland.

In these days of warm ecumenical relations between the Church of Ireland and the Roman Catholic Church, it is hard to comprehend the tense relationship that existed from the 1920s to the 1960s. The provision of healthcare and education within an ethos that catered for the Protestant minority in Ireland was a particularly sensitive topic.[87] From 1902, Farnham was patron of the County Cavan Protestant Orphan Society, which organised and financially supported the care of orphans in Protestant homes.[88] He also acted as a governor of Cavan Royal School, the sole provider of secondary education under Protestant patronage in the county.[89] In 1934, Farnham was appointed president of the board of management of the Adelaide Hospital, Dublin, a position he retained until death.[90] While other hospitals reaped the benefits of funding from the Irish Hospital Sweepstakes from the 1930s onwards, the Adelaide, with its strong Protestant ethos, refused to take this funding, fearing that their independence in decision making would be weakened.[91] The hospital finances were therefore generated primarily through fundraising and donations, with Farnham chairing the hospital 'through many anxious years, when the problems of finances would have daunted a less courageous spirit'.[92]

Cavan, Coronations, and Cattle

As owner of over 2,800 acres – which included extensive lakes and woodlands – Lord Farnham was still the most significant landowner in Cavan in the 1930s.[93] He adjusted to life quickly once back in familiar surroundings. Barton

[86] *Irish Times*, 14 Feb. 1957.
[87] Alan Megahey, *The Irish Protestant Churches in the Twentieth Century* (London, 2000), pp. 108–20; Daithi Ó Corráin, *Rendering to God and Caesar: The Churches and the Two States in Ireland, 1949–73* (Manchester, 2008), pp. 93–4; d'Alton '"A Vestigial Population"?', p. 34.
[88] *Fifty-sixth Report of the County of Cavan Protestant Orphan Society, being the report for the year ending 31st December 1902*. Copy in possession of author.
[89] *Church of Ireland Gazette*, 22 Feb. 1957.
[90] *Irish Times*, 15 May 1934.
[91] David Mitchell, *A 'Peculiar' Place: The Adelaide Hospital, Dublin, 1838–1989* (Dublin, 1989), pp. 202–4; Robbie Roulston, 'The Church of Ireland and the Irish State, 1950–1972: Education, Healthcare and Moral Welfare', PhD thesis (University College Dublin, 2013).
[92] *Irish Times*, 14 Feb. 1957.
[93] Statement of ownership, Farnham Estate 1931 (Records Branch of the Irish Land Commission, Farnham Estate, S.655 and S.3286).

noted how he threw himself 'with his accustomed energy, into the work of his estate in Cavan, a wholetime task ... He not only gave it personal supervision but could be found hard at work with his men in the harvest field or driving a tractor'.[94]

Despite Lord Farnham's readjustment to everyday life in the new Ireland of the late 1920s, certain aspects of his cultural identity as a loyalist remained intact. One such characteristic was the long-held fealty to the monarchy. The most symbolic demonstration of this loyalty was offered in person. The Farnhams' attendance at the coronation of George VI in May 1937 illustrates their continuing allegiance and loyalty to the monarch.[95] The Farnhams were not alone in their wish to maintain their connection with the Crown; Protestants in southern Ireland generally remained loyal to the monarchy.[96] At the Kilmore Diocesan Synod in July 1937, a resolution stating 'That this synod at its first meeting since their majesties coronation, begs respectfully to His Majesty King George VI and Queen Elizabeth its dutiful homage and service, and express[es] the hope that God will give them a long, prosperous and peaceful reign' was passed 'with acclamation and by the singing of God Save the King'[97] and reflected the continued loyalty of Cavan Protestants to the monarch.

The singing of 'God Save the King' was one of the more public expressions of loyalty[98] and was a feature of some gatherings at Farnham during the 1930s, as attested to by Frank Pakenham, Lord Longford:

> Every year there was a tennis dance at Farnham Castle ... Every year Lord Farnham, who was a loyal Britisher, insisted on 'God Save the King' being played. It was during the 1930s. Of course, a number of local nationalists would walk out and therefore there was always a question of whether the dance would take place ... think of him having 'God Save the King' played 15 years after the signing of the treaty. That was the only place in Ireland where it was played and his memory should be happily preserved.[99]

---

94 *Irish Times*, 14 Feb. 1957.
95 *Supplement to the London Gazette*, 10 Nov. 1937, cols 7062, 7070.
96 d'Alton '"A Vestigial Population"?', p. 38.
97 Minute book of the Diocesan Synod 1937 (Representative Church Body Library, D3/4/1).
98 McDowell, *Crisis and Decline*, p. 170.
99 Hansard, HL, vol. 565, col. 1097 (5 Jul. 1995). Of course, Lord Longford was in error when he suggested that Farnham was the only place in Ireland where 'God Save the King' was sung during the 1930s. For example, it was sung at the Remembrance Sunday ceremony in St Patrick's Cathedral, in Dublin, in November 1932. See *Irish Times*, 7 Nov. 1932.

While this insight illustrates that Farnham socialised with those who shared differing political values – most probably upwardly mobile Catholic middle classes in Cavan – and is indicative of his engagement and integration to some extent at a local level, he simultaneously maintained connections with a socially exclusive set drawn from remaining landed families. *The Tatler* and *The Tatler and Bystander* magazines give a flavour of the social circles in which the Farnhams moved from the 1930s through to the 1950s. In January 1934, they were at Lord Headfort's shoot in Kells, County Meath,[100] while in May of that year Lord Farnham was photographed dressed in white tie with Lady Powerscourt at a charity ball in Dublin.[101] In March 1949, the Farnhams were photographed at the wedding of John Brooke, son of Northern Ireland's Prime Minister Sir Basil Brooke,[102] while in 1950 they attended a coming-out ball given by Mr and Mrs Gerald E. Tenison for their daughter Hilaria, at Loughbawn, their family home in County Monaghan.[103] The Farnhams' longstanding connection with the Wingfield family at Powerscourt in County Wicklow was also maintained and in 1952 they were amongst the guests at the coming-out ball for the Hon. Grania Wingfield.[104]

Lord Farnham's loyalism remained intact through to the coronation of Elizabeth II in 1953. Although entitled to sit in the House of Lords, Farnham appears to have made no speeches there after his contribution to the debate on the Government of Ireland bill in 1920. However, in October 1952, Hansard records Lord Farnham taking an oath of allegiance to the new queen.[105] In a letter to his grandson and heir, Barry Owen Somerset Maxwell, in February 1953, Farnham bemoaned the fact that he and Lady Farnham had failed in the ballot to gain a seat in Westminster Abbey for the coronation in June of that year and that they would have to be content with a seat in the stand which had been constructed outside of the Abbey to cater for the overflow of peers.[106]

Farnham's desire to be in London for the coronation highlights his continued loyalty to the Crown. Indeed, the family's connection with the

---

[100] *The Tatler*, 17 Jan. 1934.

[101] *The Tatler*, 2 May 1934.

[102] *The Tatler and Bystander*, 23 Mar. 1949.

[103] *The Tatler and Bystander*, 23 Aug. 1950.

[104] *The Tatler and Bystander*, 20 Aug. 1952.

[105] Hansard, HL, vol. 178, col. 1063 (29 Oct. 1952). Email communication with David White, Somerset Herald, College of Arms, London, 2 Aug. 2018, who writes: 'The taking of the oath by Lord Farnham on 29 Oct. 1952 would have been when he took his seat in the Lords for the first time in the new reign'.

[106] Lord Farnham to Barry Owen Somerset Maxwell, 11 Feb. 1953 (CCLAS, 0260). Email communication with David White, Somerset Herald, College of Arms, London, 2 Aug. 2018.

Crown was reaffirmed when their son-in-law Sir Mark Milbank became master of the household in 1954.[107] While Farnham's display of loyalty in 1953 was in a relatively private capacity, more public displays of affection for the new queen were shown in Cavan at Cloverhill – about six miles north of Farnham. Here the local landowner Major John Purdon invited the people of the surrounding parishes to his house for an afternoon tea and sports, where each child was given a souvenir coronation cup and saucer. The day of celebrations ended with the lighting of bonfires on top of several of the drumlins.[108] Such events illustrated that loyalty amongst some of Cavan's Protestants – like that of many of their co-religionists around Ireland – lasted well beyond the declaration of a Republic in 1948.[109]

While Farnham's attendance at the 1953 coronation may be read as a manifestation of his loyalist heritage and identity, another event in late 1953 illustrates how he negotiated a careful balance in terms of the wider community in Cavan: a presentation to him by the County Cavan Agricultural Society to mark his Golden Wedding Anniversary. The Farnhams had maintained their connection with the Society since its foundation in 1899, and Lord Farnham was a most enthusiastic supporter of its annual shows, exhibiting horses, livestock, and farm and garden produce. The presentation illustrated how agriculture and its improvement in County Cavan had transcended political and religious barriers. John Frederick O'Hanlon, the proprietor and editor of the local nationalist newspaper *The Anglo-Celt*, read the address:

> Speaking as the senior surviving founder of the Cavan Agricultural Society ... [O'Hanlon] would say that any honour that the society could pay to Lord Farnham at any time, and more especially on this unique occasion, was certainly well deserved. He did not see eye to eye with Lord Farnham on many things, but ... it was his honest opinion that all of these qualities were concentrated in their guest of honour. Those of them who had been at Cavan Show in years past would have seen Lord Farnham ... oozing enthusiasm and seeing that everything was done right.[110]

These were significant remarks from the veteran nationalist O'Hanlon, who had contested East Cavan for the Irish Parliamentary Party in the by-election of 1918 against Arthur Griffith of Sinn Féin. During the 1910s and 1920s, he

---

[107] *London Gazette*, 4 Apr. 1967.
[108] Jonathan Cherry, *Cloverhill: A Church of Ireland Parish in County Cavan, c.1720–2010* (Dublin, 2010), p. 69.
[109] d'Alton, '"A Vestigial Population"?', p. 40.
[110] *The Anglo-Celt*, 26 Dec. 1953.

had written scathing editorials concerning Farnham, critiquing his record as a landlord as well as his politics. In response to O'Hanlon's speech, Lord Farnham stated 'that he and Lady Farnham particularly appreciated the fact that this presentation came from the Show Society, for that Society was most representative of the people of all classes and politics in the town and country. They were proud, indeed, to receive the congratulations of all of them'.[111] Lord Farnham told the assembled crowd that the plaque (comprised of silver gilt medallions depicting a bull's head and a sheaf of wheat in relief, with some Celtic designs and scrolls mounted on wood) 'would always be kept in their home to remind them and not only them, but those who were to come after them, of the very strong ties that bound the Maxwells to Cavan and the county of Cavan'.[112]

This was not empty public rhetoric, but a genuine reflection of his true feelings at being honoured in this manner as he neared the end of his life. In correspondence with his grandson and heir, he stated, 'it was a very representative gathering of all classes and creeds and politics so it was really a gift worth receiving'.[113] Lord Farnham may have felt that this presentation put to rest any animosity against him from his fellow countrymen. In many ways, this event marked the culmination of Farnham's successful negotiation of life and his efforts toward adaptive coexistence in Ireland after 1922 – and his balancing of wider community relations, despite his continued loyalism, by the latter years of his life.

Conclusion

This chapter has traced the career of one high-profile southern unionist and his experiences of life in Ireland both before and after independence. As leader of Cavan unionists and as spokesman for unionists in the other 'lost' counties of Donegal and Monaghan, Lord Farnham's protests against their severance from their fellow unionists were in vain. Leaving Ireland during the early 'Troubles' that marked the formation of the new state, Farnham spent a number of years in England during which time tensions and the risk of hostility in Ireland lessened somewhat. Lord Farnham returned to his ancestral home in the late 1920s and embraced the familiar – his land and farming, the network of landed families that remained across the country,

---

[111] *The Anglo-Celt*, 26 Dec. 1953.

[112] A presentation plaque inscribed 'To Lord & Lady Farnham on the occasion of their Golden Wedding 1903–1953 from the members of the County Cavan Agricultural Society' (Cavan County Museum, 2005-621); *The Anglo-Celt*, 26 Dec. 1953.

[113] Lord Farnham to Barry Owen Somerset Maxwell, 24 Nov. 1953 (CCLAS, 0260).

the Church of Ireland, the Adelaide Hospital, the Masonic Order, other charitable causes, and of course his favoured pastimes of golf and tennis – carving out a meaningful life for himself. Lord Farnham's experience of negotiating his way through life in the Free State and Republic provides an insight into how landed southern loyalists attempted to foster an approach of adaptive coexistence in response to changed circumstances. Ultimately, while attempts to assimilate into the new Ireland were a key feature of Farnham's experience, it was impossible for him and other loyalists ever fully to accept the dominant political and cultural values of nationalism and Catholicism. Long held allegiances, affections, and connections that formed the core of Lord Farnham's 'Britishness', and his loyalist cultural identity, could not be severed in response to Ireland's changing political status.

CHAPTER XIV

Defying the Partition of Ulster: Colonel John George Vaughan Hart and the Unionist Experience of the Irish Revolution in East Donegal, c.1919–1944

Katherine Magee

In 1928, Colonel John George Vaughan Hart, a wealthy Church of Ireland landowner, moved his family from their ancestral home in Kilderry, County Donegal, to Ballynagard, County Londonderry.[1] Geographically, the properties were only several miles apart. However, it was, crucially, on the other side of the Londonderry/Donegal border. The contrast between the two homes was stark and Ballynagard would not provide the same comfort that the family had become accustomed to. Writing in 1924, several years before the move, Hart had complained about the quality of the land at Ballynagard, stating there was 'no comparison between this place [Kilderry] and Ballynagard'.[2] Despite this he felt the move was necessary. Ultimately, as an Irish unionist, Hart felt alienated by the separation of Donegal from the newly created state of Northern Ireland.

Hart offers an example of the ways in which loyalists in the 'south' felt about and experienced revolution. With Hart's family history encompassing a long tradition of unionism, his opinions are those of an East Donegal unionist and Hart's homeland of East Donegal was largely populated with others like him. The 1911 census records show that at that time there were 1,919 Catholics and 3,230 non-Catholics in East Donegal.[3] Not all Protestants were unionists and vice versa, but Hart offers an insight into other unionists' perspectives during this time. For instance, he was prominent in the Donegal Protestant Registration Association (DPRA) and was instrumental in voicing their concerns

---

[1] 'Introduction: Hart papers': www.nidirect.gov.uk/sites/default/files/publications/hart-d3077.pdf (accessed 2 Feb. 2017).

[2] Colonel John George Vaughan Hart [hereafter referred to as Hart] to Mr Orr, 8 Mar. 1924 (PRONI, D/3077/J/35).

[3] R.A. Boger, Map of North East Ireland, 'Religious Composition 1911 Census Map', in *Report of the Irish Boundary Commission 1925* (Shannon, 1969).

regarding East Donegal to the Boundary Commission between 1924 and 1925. Hart, therefore, played an important role in articulating the views of fellow southern unionists. The DPRA made statements to the commission claiming that on political, religious, and economic grounds the majority in specific areas wished to remain in the United Kingdom.[4] The Boundary Commission would conclude that these areas should be transferred to Northern Ireland, although ultimately the border was not changed. Prior to this, Hart found himself isolated from much of the rest of Ulster and in a jurisdiction he was not comfortable with. He was an Ulster unionist who now found himself living as a 'southern' unionist. In this way, exploring Hart's experience of the Irish Revolution tells us not only about his character but something about how other Ulster unionists and loyalists felt during this period.

The main historical source for reconstructing Hart's Story is his carbon copy letter books. These are preserved in the Public Record Office of Northern Ireland (PRONI) and cover the period 1919 to 1944. The collection was deposited in PRONI by Francis (Frank) Hart, the Colonel's son, after he sold the Ballynagard home in 1980. In total, 70 letter books survive.[5] In this correspondence we see a man who articulates fears concerning the possibility of a divided country, the role he played in assisting the DPRA in making submissions to the Boundary Commission, and eventually his decision to leave Donegal for Londonderry. In 1937, it was revealed that the Protestant population of Ireland across the 26 counties had dropped by 106,000 (32 per cent) in 15 years.[6] By exploring Hart's letters we can get an insight into some of the reasons for this decline.

The Fear of the Unknown: Life before and after Partition

From the eighteenth century, along with other Protestant families, the Harts became prominent landowners in Inishowen.[7] By the mid-nineteenth century, the family owned 6,598 acres in Donegal and 434 acres in Londonderry.[8] As

---

[4] DPRA submissions to the Boundary Commission (TNA, CAB/61/51 and CAB/61/53).

[5] The larger Hart collection includes material from the early nineteenth century to the 1940s and can be viewed in PRONI under the reference D3077.

[6] *Derry Standard*, 29 Oct. 1937

[7] David Dickson, 'Derry's Backyard: The Barony of Inishowen, 1650–1800', in William Nolan, Liam Ronayne, and Mairead Dunlevy (eds), *Donegal: History & Society* (Dublin, 1995), p. 417.

[8] U.H. Hussey de Burgh, *The Landowners of Ireland: An Alphabetical List of the Owners of Estates of 500 Acres or £500 Valuation and Upwards in Ireland* (Dublin, 1878), p. 208.

well as land, the family owned several large properties, including Kilderry House, Ballynagard House, and Doe Castle.[9] Kilderry House had been home to the Hart family since the mid-seventeenth century, and they built their own Church of Ireland chapel there, later handing it over to the church in the nineteenth century. It would later be claimed that 'Major Hart [J.G.V. Hart's great grandfather] used to drive the people into church with his gold headed cane, determined to fill his church'.[10]

J.G.V. Hart was born on 30 May 1879 to William Edward Hart and Bessie Louisa Allman. He grew up in Kilderry, County Donegal, and was educated at Sedbergh, Yorkshire. He followed his family's tradition of military service, receiving a commission in 1899 for the British West Indies Regiment.[11] On 23 July 1917, Hart married Katherine Georgina May Garstin (known as May) from Raphoe, County Donegal in a ceremony at Rathgar, County Dublin.[12] The couple had six children: Marian, born 18 May 1920; Catherine, born 24 August 1921 (died as an infant from fever in 1924); George, born 10 February 1923; Tristram born 2 January 1925; Francis born 17 June 1928; and Richard, born 18 April 1930.[13] The children's birth dates are important as a reminder that Hart was a family man and, against the political backdrop, his personal life continued with an ever-growing family.

The Hart family had a long association with Protestant and Unionist politics. For example, J.G.V'.s ancestor, Lieutenant-General Hart, Governor of Londonderry and Culmore from 1820 to 1832, voted against Catholic relief in 1821.[14] The family's support for Unionism is also evidenced by their signing of the Ulster Covenant in 1912, though Hart himself was on service in Upper Gambia at the time and therefore did not sign.[15] When Hart returned home in 1919 after over 20 years of service, he found Muff a very different place. He soon felt alienated and abandoned by six-county Ulster Unionists and

[9] De Burgh, *Landowners of Ireland*, p. 5.

[10] H.T. Hart, *The Family History of Hart of Donegal* (London, 1907), p. 55.

[11] Hart, *Family History*, p. 55.

[12] 'Copy of confirmation of arms to descendants of Lt. Gen. George Vaughan Hart, M.P., and to his great grandson, Lt. Col. John George Vaughan Hart, son of William Edward Hart, all of Kilderry', 1 Aug. 1924 (NLI, MS 111c, fo. 50).

[13] 'Copy of confirmation of arms'; Sean Beattie, 'History of Donegal', Male descendants of George Vaughan Hart of Doe Castle, 21 May 2017: https://history-ofdonegal.com/2017/05/21/hart-of-muff-county-donegal/ (accessed 2 Jun. 2017).

[14] 'HART, George Vaughan (1752–1832), of Kilderry House, co. Donegal', in D.R. Fisher (ed.), *The History of Parliament: The House of Commons, 1820–1832*: www.historyofparliamentonline.org/volume/1820-1832/member/hart-george-1752-1832 (accessed 9 Oct. 2016).

[15] See results for Hart in Ulster Covenant online: www.nidirect.gov.uk/services/search-ulster-covenant.

was concerned by the political direction of the country: 'We ... understand that it is not really religion ... in which we are interested ... It is all very well for people to bleat about "coming out under one's true colours" and [so on], but if one were to become a ... Buddhist tomorrow, it would not alter one's political convictions & principles'.[16]

The period after the end of the Great War was one of dramatic change and instability, with the rise of Sinn Féin in 1918 and the outbreak of the War of Independence in 1919. For unionists, this period was gruelling. In 1919, Hart, who in the early 1900s had served in Upper Gambia and West Africa as a member of the Fourth Battalion of the British West Indies Regiment, returned home on leave after his father's sudden death.[17] He never returned to his post, partly due to the unrest which had broken out in Ireland.[18] Writing in July 1920, he explained to a regimental colleague that 'I should have liked much to rejoin after my leave but there is much work to attend to here & the state of the country does not encourage one to push off & leave ones family to the tender attention of Sinn Féin & Co'.[19] Hart was particularly concerned about the rise of Sinn Féin, which in 1917 had declared for an Irish Republic. That year in Donegal they had '34 clubs and 1,634 members, all of whom had been "very active" in propaganda work'.[20] The party swept the polls in the 1918 General Election, winning 73 of a possible 105 seats.[21] Graham Walker states that 'the outcome of the 1918 election saw a batch of Unionists, 23 out of 26 from Ulster, face the overnight Leviathan of the rise of Sinn Féin'.[22] The symbolism of Hugh O'Doherty's election as the first Catholic mayor of Derry was another worrying development for local unionists.[23]

Hart first mentioned the political situation in his letters as early as October 1919, when referring to the nuisance of strikes which were caused by riots in Derry. Writing to the Dublin booksellers Hodges Figgis, he stated that 'last week I rec[eived] no Literary Supplement to the Times ... probably due to

---

[16] Hart to Captain Scott, 19 Feb. 1925 (PRONI, D3077/J/44).
[17] 'Introduction: Hart Papers': www.nidirect.gov.uk/sites/default/files/publications/ hart-d3077.pdf (accessed 2 Feb. 2017).
[18] Hart to the Palman Institute, 20 Sep. 1920 (PRONI, D3077/J/6).
[19] Hart to A.M. Furber, 9 Jul. 1920 (PRONI, D3077/J/4).
[20] Benjamin Grob-Fitzgibbon, *Turning Points of the Irish Revolution: The British Government, Intelligence, and the Cost of Indifference, 1912–1921* (Basingstoke, 2007), p. 129.
[21] The Irish Election of 1918: www.ark.ac.uk/elections/h1918.htm (accessed 18 Mar. 2017).
[22] Graham Walker, *A History of the Ulster Unionist Party: Protest, Pragmatism and Pessimism* (Manchester, 2004), p. 44.
[23] Ronan Gallagher, *Violence and Nationalist Politics in Derry City, 1920–1923* (Dublin, 2003), p. 20.

strikes'.[24] The political situation would occupy more and more of Hart's time in the weeks and months to come. By July 1920, he was able to state in a letter to his cousin Harry that 'things are moderately quiet now, & will remain so as long as sufficient troops remain in Derry'.[25] Hart, however, seemed certain that peace would not last. Writing in August 1921, he stated that 'this district has been one of the most peaceful in Ireland – not that that's saying much ... but how long that will last, one can't say'.[26]

As the violence in Derry intensified during the summer, so too did Hart's anger. Reflecting in a letter to a relative in Canada, Hart observed:

> You'll have seen about the little war we've been having here: people talk about it as 'midsummer madness' & so on, but there really was very little madness about it. You'll understand the palaver perfectly, but put shortly it amounts to this: The Unionists in Derry have seen the whole of the other three provinces terrorized by Sinn Fein: S.F. now thinks it time they began to force themselves on Ulster: the natural result is a clash.[27]

Hart was particularly concerned with unrest in Muff, his own locality. When inviting old army friend Arthur Miles Furber to visit he included a wry comment on Sinn Féin, as he often did, proposing that Furber and his family come and have a peaceful holiday unless 'Sinn Fein are more busy here than they are at present'.[28] Hart's lighter comments, however, only serve to conceal his real concerns regarding Sinn Féin. He stated in the same letter that Sinn Féin had raided every house in Muff for arms except his own, because 'they know quite well that if one wanted to hide arms here, they could not be found in one night's search, for the buildings cover at least 2 acres of ground & most are in such bad repair (except for main house) that there would be lots of hiding places'.[29]

Kilderry was ultimately not raided and it appears that his initial fears of unrest in 1919 had subsided by spring 1921, around which time we see evidence that he believed the political situation was not as fraught in Derry as it was elsewhere. Hart's changing views are illustrated by his opinion on the 1921 House of Commons elections, which he noted 'went off very peacefully & successfully: I've never seen so well-tempered an election as that in Derry before'.[30] The election took place as a result of the Government of Ireland

[24] Hart to Hodges Figgis, 6 Oct. 1919 (PRONI, D3077/J/1).
[25] Hart to Harry, 2 Jul. 1920 (PRONI, D3077/J/4).
[26] Hart to Mr Thompson, 29 Aug. 1921 (PRONI, D3077/J/19).
[27] Hart to George, 2 Jul. 1920 (PRONI, D3077/J/4).
[28] Hart to Mr Furber, 22 Sep. 1920 (PRONI, D3077/J/7).
[29] Hart to Mr Furber, 22 Sep. 1920 (PRONI, D3077/J/7).
[30] Hart to Mr Orr, 29 May 1921 (PRONI, D3077/J/16).

Act 1920, which stated that both the north and south of Ireland would have a self-governing parliament. Two elections were due to be held on 24 May 1921, one to establish the House of Commons of Southern Ireland and another for the House of Commons of Northern Ireland (although no polling took place in the south). In County Londonderry, five candidates were elected to the northern parliament: three Unionists, one Nationalist, and one Sinn Féin.[31] Unionists won a majority in the six north-eastern counties that made up Northern Ireland (excluding Donegal), with 40 seats, while the Nationalists gained 6 seats.[32] Hart and those he surrounded himself with would have found the result in the north very agreeable.

Hart was, though, affected by some practical annoyances during the revolutionary period. Peter Leary has demonstrated that after partition people in border counties had to grow accustomed to the practical issues raised by the new border.[33] Leary gives an example of residents in Pettigo, County Donegal, who received water from the north but paid their rates for the service to Donegal County Council, and how 'for those who lived in close quarters with the border, otherwise mundane activities such as shopping, visiting family, or travelling to a place of worship were complicated by custom restrictions'.[34] Hart also experienced some of these difficulties, as is discussed below.

The postal system was a persistent nuisance for Hart. He first mentions this in early October 1919. He stated to a friend that 'I rec[eived] your letter this morning in our mail-bag. You will see by the envelope that it is p[ost] m[arked] 6 A.M. 2 Oct. & should therefore, have come out on the 2nd'.[35] In a letter addressed to his brother in September 1920, he wrote: 'please address letters as above. We have our own mail bag which is made up in Derry: but letters addressed "Muff, Co. Donegal," or even "Muff, Derry" come loose & are not always delivered without delay'.[36] Hart chose not to have his mail collected in Donegal, which would have been the norm. Instead, he had his letters sorted into a private mailbag in Derry and made arrangements for the bag to come direct to the house twice a day. To accommodate this he had his letters addressed as 'N[ea]r. Londonderry' instead of County Donegal.[37] But the arrangement led to much confusion among those less familiar with

---

[31] The Northern Ireland House of Commons, 1921–1972, Election Results: www.ark.ac.uk/elections/hnihoc.htm (accessed 17 Mar. 2017).

[32] Nicholas Whyte, 'Dail Elections since 1918': www.ark.ac.uk/elections/gdala.htm (accessed 28 Jan. 2017).

[33] Peter Leary, *Unapproved Routes: Histories of the Irish Border, 1922–1972* (Oxford, 2016).

[34] Leary, *Unapproved Routes*, pp. 14–15.

[35] Hart to Mr Harvey, 3 Oct. 1919 (PRONI, D3077/J/1).

[36] Hart to Harry, 14 Sep. 1920 (PRONI, D3077/J/6).

[37] See Hart's letter to Mr M'Cay, 4 Oct. 1919 as an example (PRONI, D3077/J/1).

the family or the area, as they mistook his address for County Londonderry. Hart's name was, though, recognisable locally, as his family were prominent landowners. There is, therefore, a possibility that he believed someone may have wanted to open his mail. In a letter to his solicitor in 1921, he stated: 'Will you please have your letters sealed. The last ... arrived opened – I should say steamed ... & then heavily gummed up. This is not due to local authority, as all my letters come made up in locked bag from G.P.O. in Derry'.[38] Hart's postal arrangements may have been facilitated by an old military friend. Writing to a former soldier in his division, he stated: 'I don't know if I told you that old Todd (the D.P.S. at Tarrants & Marseilles, you remember) is now the postmaster in Derry. We had him out to lunch here some time back'.[39] Relationships such as this were important; indeed, it is evident throughout his writing that fellow unionists and loyalists looked out for each other and formed close social groups.[40]

Despite the Hart family's strong connections to the area, as early as 1920 he contemplated the possibility of a move. When his aunt died in April 1919, Hart inherited Woodville, an estate on the Waterside of Derry in the village of Eglinton.[41] Hart rented the house to a Mr Macrory on a short-term basis. Macrory had stated his desire to buy the house, but Hart was reluctant to sell, writing: 'I do not know how the present political situation is going to turn out, but in the view of the above [regarding his expenditure] one might find it necessary to later sell Woodville ... or to go there ourselves (in the case of [the current political situation] ... turning out badly).'[42] Hart clarified that due to inheriting his father's estates, as well as those of his aunts, he was spending a lot of money and the political situation had caused him to consider a move to Londonderry.[43] He did not actually move until 1928, however, and it was the Boundary Commission that prolonged his stay in Kilderry by a number of years as Hart awaited its final result.

---

[38] Hart to Mr Orr, 3 May 1921 (PRONI, D3077/J/16).

[39] Hart to 'My dear Colonel', 3 Jan. 1920 (PRONI, D3077/J/12).

[40] See Hart to Norman, 1 Mar. 1924, for an example of how such relationships helped (PRONI, D/3077/J/35). In this letter Hart is writing about having a friend in customer control who allows him to bring his car, which was bought in Northern Ireland, to the Irish Free State without the usual taxes.

[41] Hart to Palman, 5 Oct. 1920 (PRONI, D3077/J/8).

[42] Hart to Mr Macrory, 16 Aug. 1920 (PRONI, D3077/J/5).

[43] Hart to Mr Macrory, 16 Aug. 1920 (PRONI, D3077/J/5).

The Boundary Commission Years, 1924–1925

After his return from his military post in 1919, Hart had turned his hand to farming. In 1924, he found it necessary to employ a land steward; however, this proved difficult, as many Protestants were not keen to live in the Irish Free State. Hart advertised the post in the *Belfast News-Letter* in July 1924, and when one potential steward responded with queries on local schools, Hart replied that 'there is a school within a mile of the house with C[hurch] of I[reland] teacher, quite good & well reported on'.[44] In a letter to another respondent he made a further attempt to sell the area: 'The house is in the Free State but protestant population is in majority & locality has always been quiet. Please state denomination – Both Protestant churches are within a mile of Muff – C[hurch] of I[reland] a few hundred yards'.[45] In another letter Hart asked the same question but elaborated on why the question of denomination was important, stating: 'this makes little difference to me personally, but I have to consider offers – & also whether you belong to any organization or societies, & if so which'.[46] Some fears or suspicions must have played some part in his concern about membership of organisations or societies, and Hart's suggestion that the answer made little difference to himself may have been a little untruthful. Writing in January 1920, Hart had explained to his cousin Harry that following the death of his aunt, Josephine Hart, it had been decided to let one of her employees, Maggie Lynch, go. He explained that 'she seems to have been unhinged ever since they were ordered to do the 40 hours "special adoration – lot of gas" ... all these political stunts seem to have upset her ... since the adoration especially she's been impossible'.[47] Here Hart was drawing attention to Maggie Lynch's religious affiliation, the Catholic Church having called members to partake in a 40-hour devotional prayer time, mainly focused on the Holy Eucharist.[48] This suggests that Hart was letting Lynch go on religious grounds and this is confirmed further on: 'we are getting a Protestant instead so perhaps it's just as well'.[49] At the very least, this gives the impression that Hart preferred to engage with those who were of the same religious affiliation as himself and that, like many Protestants, he had a tendency to prefer Protestant indoor servants.[50]

---

[44] Hart to Mr J. Alton, 22 Jan. 1925 (PRONI, D3077/J/43).

[45] Letter from Hart, 25 Jul. 1924 (PRONI, D3077/J/38).

[46] Hart to Mr John Martin, 5 Sep. 1924 (PRONI, D3077/J/39).

[47] Hart to Harry, 9 Sep. 1920 (PRONI, D3077/J/6).

[48] See www.catholiceducation.org/en/culture/catholic-contributions/40-hours-with-jesus-christ.html (accessed 20 Jan. 2017).

[49] Hart to Harry, 9 Sep. 1920 (PRONI, D3077/J/6).

[50] For a summary of the history of anti-Catholicism in Northern Ireland, see John D. Brewer and Gareth I. Higgins, *Anti-Catholicism in Northern Ireland, 1600–1998: The Mote and the Beam* (London, 1998).

Hart remained unable to appoint a suitable land steward by June 1925. He was also keen in this period to ensure Unionist representation at a local level. Writing to his wife in June 1925, he stated that 'you'll have to try & come over to vote for the C[ounty] C[ouncil] elections on the 23rd. ... They're very keen to get Rankin & Black on to help [so] every vote is needed'.[51] Hart was hoping that, for one thing, new councillors would be able to lower the cost of rates in the south. John Black and Thomas Boyd Rankin, both farmers, ran for seats on Tirconaill (Donegal) County Council for the Buncrana area in that year's local elections.[52] Black was successful, but his election ultimately did nothing to convince Hart to stay in the Irish Free State.[53]

The family's intention to move from Kilderry had been hinted at as early as 1920, but any decision was postponed once the formation of the Boundary Commission was announced in late 1924. Hart had always suggested that the reason for the move would be purely political, but evidence from his letters hints that finance may also have played a part. In a letter dated February 1924 to Mr Colhoun, Hart expressed his grievances, noting: 'I should have liked to send more [money], but you'll understand that Free State landlords, are not a good mark[et] at present – few rents & heavy expenses!'[54] Hart's issues with the postal system continued as well. He was reluctant to let anything go to Lifford, County Donegal, for customs and therefore gave an alternative address to use if sending anything bigger than a letter. For example, Hart wrote to a Mr Young in May 1924, regarding a book that had been borrowed: 'may I request that, when you have finished with it, you will please return it to me ... [at] "c/o Messers. J.G.M. Harvey & Son, Land Agents, Northern Bank, Londonderry." This is important as it would otherwise go to Lifford for examination'.[55] Hart wrote to Mr Young again in June 1924, stating: 'Please do not think there is any hurry about the book ... I am only writing because it has not yet reached Messrs Harvey's office: so I presume you have not yet sent it? It is only to satisfy myself that it has not gone astray, or to Lifford, that I am asking about it'.[56] Hart appears to have been apprehensive about anything going to Lifford and therefore sought to avoid this. This may have been because, if a parcel were to go to Lifford, it would have been checked and possible custom taxes would have to be paid. Hart appeared to want as few dealings as possible with the Free State administration, and their handling of his post was no exception.

[51] Hart to May, 16 Jun. 1925 (PRONI, D3077/J/42).
[52] *Donegal News*, 13 Jun. 1925.
[53] *Donegal Democrat*, 10 Jul. 1925.
[54] Hart to Mr Colhoun, 14 Feb. 1924 (PRONI, D3077/J/34).
[55] Hart to Mr Young, 30 May 1924 (PRONI, D3077/J/37).
[56] Hart to Mr Young, 24 Jun. 1924 (PRONI, D3077/J/37).

Hart's main concern during this period remained the Boundary Commission. The years 1924 to 1925 were an important time for border loyalists such as Hart, as Article 12 of the Anglo-Irish Treaty of 1921 was finally implemented on 11 December 1924 when the Boundary Commission held their first meeting. The agreement provided for the establishment of 'a Commission consisting of three persons [to] determine in accordance with the wishes of the inhabitants, so far as may be compatible with economic and geographic conditions, the boundaries between Northern Ireland and the rest of Ireland'.[57] This was a tri-party committee formed with one representative each from the Irish Free State, Northern Ireland, and Britain. The committee first met in late 1924, by which time Eóin MacNeill had been selected as commissioner for the Irish Free State, Mr Justice Richard Feetham was appointed by the British government to be chairman, while Joseph Fisher was the Northern Irish representative.[58] The gap between the signing of the Anglo-Irish Treaty in 1921, which provided for the commission, and the commission's eventual establishment in 1924, was partly due to the unwillingness of Northern Ireland to appoint a commissioner. Fisher was eventually selected by Westminster to represent Northern Ireland as the Belfast government refused to do so themselves.[59] This unwillingness to co-operate would no doubt have increased the sense of abandonment already felt by Donegal loyalists. Fisher did, however, agree with James Craig that the volume of East Donegal loyalists 'severed from Northern Ireland' was concerning. Fisher also went so far as telling Craig in a personal letter that 'Ulster can never be complete without Donegal'.[60]

Around 1924, Hart began addressing correspondence to 'dear Mr Scott', of Birdstown House, Burnfoot, County Donegal.[61] Captain John Scott was chairman of the DPRA, a land agent, and had lived in Donegal for 20 years.[62] As will be seen, Hart and Scott appear to have had conflicting views about how best to approach the Boundary Commission negotiations.[63] Hart tried to persuade Scott to see the situation as a political issue, not a religious one: he believed that if they explained their aim as being that of seeking decent governance and having nothing to do with religion he could try to convince

---

[57] Articles of Agreement for a Treaty between Great Britain and Ireland, signed 6 Dec. 1921, available at: www.difp.ie/viewdoc.asp?DocID=214 (3 Mar. 2017).

[58] Euan O'Halpin, 'Politics and the State, 1922–1932', in J.R. Hill (ed.), *A New History of Ireland*, vol. 7: *Ireland, 1921–1984* (Oxford, 2003), p. 106.

[59] O'Halpin, 'Politics and the State', p. 106.

[60] Paul Murray, *The Irish Boundary Commission and its Origins, 1886–1925* (Dublin, 2011), pp. 231–2.

[61] Hart to Captain Scott, 2 Jul. 1924 (PRONI, D3077/J/38).

[62] Captain J Scott's submission to the Boundary Commission, 25 May 1925 (TNA, CAB 61/53).

[63] Hart to Captain Scott, 19 Feb. 1925 (PRONI, D3077/J/44).

nationalists to join the DPRA.[64] He appears genuine concerning this, although in truth religion and politics were always connected. This is underlined by the DPRA's name change from the Donegal Unionist Association to the Donegal Protestant Registration Association. But while they had some different ideas about how to operate, Hart and Scott were united by their shared interest in seeing that certain areas of East Donegal be brought under the jurisdiction of Northern Ireland.

We can learn more about the practical workings of the DPRA from Hart's letters. For instance, the association conducted a survey to collect information on the feelings of the residents of Muff. Hart's correspondence highlights the difficulties of doing so, stating in March 1925 that 'there is so much fear of retaliation & interference with those who come forward to give evidence. If there were none of this, I believe we should get plenty [of evidence] even from people of different ideas from our own – they're all so "fed up" with customs duties & so on'.[65] Here Hart suggests – whether it was really true or not – that the political situation was worsening and, were it not for fear, nationalists would side with him over the boundary dispute. Hart also noted of one potential new member that 'he was supposed to be a Home Ruler before ... but now we have H.R. he's all for decent governing as much as the rest of us'.[66] There were clearly debates within the DRPA about who they should target for support, and how widely to spread their net, as seen in a letter Hart sent Scott in February 1924:

> I'm afraid I'm not yet converted by what was said the other day; one can't help thinking that as times have changed the ideas of many may have also. Many former Home Rulers must now feel that they have as much to gain by good, & as much to lose by bad, as we have ourselves, but could hardly be expected to come in under the name of Protestants: while if our own people can't see sense without bringing religion into the question, the Lord may help them, but I doubt it.[67]

Hart was also concerned with making a practical and transparent case to the Boundary Commission. We see this in a letter to Scott in October 1924 when he suggested they should 'do what we do as openly as possible ... If we try to keep everything to ourselves, it comes out just the same, & in the way of gossip, with much added (such as the suggestion of becoming Republicans etc.)

[64] Hart to 'Colonel', 1 Mar. 1925 (PRONI, D3077/J/44).
[65] Hart to 'Colonel', 1 Mar. 1925 (PRONI, D3077/J/44).
[66] Hart to Captain Scott, 11 Feb. 1924 (PRONI, D/3077/J/33).
[67] Hart to Captain Scott, 11 Feb. 1924 (PRONI, D/3077/J/33).

this is far worse than to have people know exactly what we are doing'.[68] Hart preferred the truth be known about what he was doing than for opponents to suggest they were planning a unionist rebellion.

After conducting surveys, the association seemed satisfied that there was a strong case to be made in support of the claim that small areas around Muff (Hart's home was situated on the outskirts of the village) and Culmore be brought under the Belfast parliament. Scott, however, seemed to suggest that the association try to argue for the transfer of as much land as possible, instead of sticking to the original plan of suggesting small areas around the Derry/Donegal border for transfer. Writing to Scott in March 1925, Hart stated:

> I'm afraid I could not be a part of doing as suggested ... I quite agree with the idea of trying to get what we can, but, tho' it is obvious that for the portion mentioned we have an extremely good claim, & not for other parts – or at least, not so good ... we cannot (at least in my opinion) let them think we are asking for Derry II, as has been publicly stated, & then ask for, or offer to accept, only a small portion of it, without letting everyone know about it. I quite see that it would advantage a large number of people besides our-selves, but if the case is good, then let everyone concerned know about it. The other idea is too much of a 'political waggle' for me – who am most certainly no politician.[69]

Hart's belief that attempting to secure the entirety of Derry II (district electoral divisions that covered land in Donegal and Londonderry) was unrealistic is revealing. Instead, Hart's research suggested they should make modest but achievable demands instead of asking for more in the hope of getting enough.

Paul Murray, in *The Irish Boundary Commission and its Origins*, draws attention to other east Donegal Protestant committees that were set up at this time to make claims to the Boundary Commission in support of areas in East Donegal being transferred into Northern Ireland.[70] For example, the Raphoe Presbytery Committee represented over 900 Presbyterian families, and instead of taking the same approach as the DPRA, made claims to the Boundary Commission that East Donegal should be transferred to the North because Protestants owned a majority of the land in that area and therefore paid a larger portion of the rates.[71] This is another reminder that border unionists took different approaches when making their statements to the commission and that even though the DPRA and the Raphoe Presbytery Committee

---

[68] Hart to Captain Scott, 18 Oct. 1924 (PRONI, D3077/J/40) [emphasis in original].
[69] Hart to Scott, 9 Mar. 1925 (PRONI, D3077/J/44).
[70] Murray, *The Irish Boundary Commission*, p. 218.
[71] Murray, *The Irish Boundary Commission*, p. 166.

wanted the same outcome they made their case in different ways. Moreover, the Raphoe Presbytery Committee only represented the smaller Presbyterian community whereas Hart wanted the DPRA to appeal to all who wished for what he believed was 'stable governance'.

In summary, the official Boundary Commission report stated:

> The Donegal Protestant Registration Association claimed that the Unionist inhabitants of Tirconaill desired that it should be included in Northern Ireland, and that the economic difficulties occasioned by the boundary would therefore be removed.
>
> The Association further claimed that in certain areas adjoining the boundary the majority of the inhabitants, including almost all the farmers and landowners, were Unionists, and that in other neighbouring areas the majority of the landowners and farmers were Unionists. The areas specially claimed in the neighbourhood of Londonderry, were former Rural Districts of Londonderry No. 2 and Strabane No. 2, with small additional areas adjoining them.[72]

The commission ultimately recommended that small areas of Donegal, including Muff and Saint Johnson, should be transferred into Northern Ireland.[73] This in itself was a significant accomplishment on the part of the DPRA. The commission's findings were, however, leaked to the *Morning Post* in November 1925 and the political fallout, particularly around the loss of Irish Free State territory, meant the final report was hastily suppressed and the border remained as it was. No doubt Hart was deeply pained at seeing how they had succeeded in convincing the commission of their case, only for defeat to be snatched from the jaws of victory. Hart died in 1946 and never saw the full report, which was not released until 1969.

Moving house in this particular period was not Hart's primary focus. Yet it was still something he considered as a last resort if the Boundary Commission did not return results in his favour. As noted above, Hart did not wish to sell his late aunt's home in Woodville, believing he may need to reside there himself at some stage. Hart's tenant, Mr Macrory, eventually left Woodville in June 1924.[74] This resulted in Hart having to explain the situation to other potential tenants:

> You will have understood that the thing [not wishing to sell the house] is mixed up with present politics, at the moment the outlook does not

---

[72] *Report of the Irish Boundary Commission* (1925), p. 82 (TNA, CAB/61/161).
[73] Boger, Map of North East Ireland, 'Religious Composition 1911 Census Map'.
[74] Hart to Miss Gilliland, 12 Jun. 1924 (PRONI, D3077/J/37).

seem to be improving. Under certain circumstances I might wish to take my family to Woodville hurriedly. So far as one can see, the possibility does not appear to be getting any more remote, & one would therefore wish to be in a position to take over the house with the smallest of delay, & to be able to go into it.[75]

Hart explained the situation further in another letter dated September 1925, in which he confirmed the financial implications of staying in the south:

There is little thought of hereabouts except this Boundary business. We are just on it, & the district is, in the majority, unionist: so you may believe that it will affect us considerably how it is decided. If there's a decision that we shall have to remain in the F[ree] S[tate] I think we shall sooner or later have to clear out – sounds a bit Irish, but you'll understand. The whole of this country is likely to be swept by the Republicans, because the F.S. supporters are so 'fed up' with taxes & customs & so on that they will, almost certainly abstain from voting. If that happens, it won't be pleasant for those of our ideas who remain; nor will they be likely to be allowed to remain long.[76]

In some of his earlier letters, Hart was not hopeful that the Boundary Commission would return any result in his favour; however, he did appear somewhat more optimistic after his submissions to the Boundary Commission had been made. In July 1925, he wrote: 'we have not yet made up our minds to leave here: also we believe that – apart from political "waggles" – we should have a very fair chance of coming into N.I'.[77]

For Hart, the Boundary Commission was a last chance. When it became clear that the border would remain as it was, he made plans to move. It appears, though, that Hart was in a minority. As David Fitzpatrick noted, no southern county between 1911 and 1926 managed to retain more than four-fifths of their Protestant population but in the 'three lost counties of Ulster' the decline was relatively small because they had stronger communities.[78] Ultimately, Hart's reaction to the suppression of the Boundary Commission was one of bitterness and anger. Writing in December 1925, he stated that all hope was now lost and that 'no further adjustments will affect this district, because by the time anything of this kind comes forward again (if it ever does) the exodus which

---

[75] Hart to Miss Gilliland, 12 Jun. 1924 (PRONI, D3077/J/37).
[76] Hart to Mrs Chichester, 4 Sep. 1925 (PRONI, D3077/39).
[77] Hart to Mr Malseed, 2 Jul. 1925 (PRONI, D3077/J/42).
[78] David Fitzpatrick *Descendancy: Irish Protestant Histories since 1795* (Cambridge, 2014), p. 165.

is now taking place among Protestants, will have so much depleted ... that instead of having, as at present, a considerable majority of the population, they will be in the minority'.[79] He wrote:

> We knew we had good arguments & data which must impress any B.C. – as it evidently did. We believed that if there were any alterations we would be certain to be in it. Now that there is practically no hope of that, we have made up our mind that it is a case of 'Muhammad going to the Mountain.' We have accordingly advised Mrs McCorkell that we shall require Ballynagard as soon as her lease expires in Jan 1927.[80]

Despite his best efforts, the suppression of the Boundary Commission's report and the solidification of the border left Hart facing life under an independent Irish government when his allegiance lay with Britain. By the end of 1925, Hart accepted the reality of having to move from County Donegal to County Londonderry. Having only ever been a 'worst-case scenario' solution, this is what Hart now faced.

On 'Home' Soil, 1925–1946

In 1927, Hart moved to Ballynagard. Hart had been heavily involved in politics up until the end of 1925, but when the Boundary Commission closed their investigation, he focused his efforts on the move. In August 1927, he wrote to Mrs McNeill (the teacher in charge at his niece and nephew's school in England), stating that 'Mrs McCorkel (the tenant at Ballynagard) has at last left & we have been able to go through the house at last: The result is that I find a lot more requires doing than we had expected: it is most annoying because, owing to recent occurrences, we ought to get our things in as soon as possible'.[81] It is unclear what exactly Hart meant when he referred to 'recent occurrences' but he was obviously keen to move quickly, suggesting the situation had not improved for him.[82] Writing to his uncle Ernie about the forthcoming departure, Hart stated:

> We hope before many more months to have moved to Ballynagard – There was a lot of dry rot, which I hope we have now completely eradicated, besides painting all new & old wood with preservatives.

---

[79] Hart to Harry, 10 Dec. 1925 (PRONI, D3077/J/47).
[80] Hart to Harry, 10 Dec. 1925 (PRONI, D3077/J/47).
[81] Hart to Mrs McNeill, 14 Aug. 1927 (PRONI, D3077/J/50).
[82] Hart to Mrs McNeill, 14 Aug. 1927 (PRONI, D3077/J/50), p. 2.

Fortunately there was none in the roof. We have used our own timber, which had been blown down over a year ago, & are putting in (our own) oak in the floors, stairs ... I need hardly tell you I shall regret leaving here very much: but most of all in having done a lot of repairs to make the house habitable, as well as others to the farm buildings re-stocking the farm & so on. The only thing that pleases all of us is the pleasure we shall have in being quit of the Free State: for leaving that we have no regrets.[83]

During Hart's preparation for departure the postal system served yet again as an illustrative example of his grievances with the new arrangements. Writing to the postmaster on 30 March 1927, he stated:

I have the honour to request that letters reaching Londonderry post office, addressed as above may either be:
Retained till called for, in box No. 6. In the G.P.O. or
Redirected to the Northern Counties Club, Bishop St.
I would point out that the above has been the address used here for at least 100 years   as can be proved by letters here during that period – & that it is in this way that letters are ordinarily directed.[84]

Hart's comments about the family's close connection to the area are of interest. Hart would have been angered that his family, who had addressed their post as 'near Londonderry' for over one hundred years, would now be forced to change, perhaps due to a new local postmaster.[85] Hart's postage was now delayed as it was no longer collected by a private mailbag, as can be seen in a letter which he sent to a friend on 25 April 1927: 'Dear Kelly, your letter reached me a few days ago, much delayed owing to the new postal arrangements (taken over from 1 April by the Free State)'.[86] Hart may have been using the postal system as one way to show that the Free State government was incompetent and inadequate; therefore, rather than a mundane issue for Hart, it was potentially one practical way for him to highlight the ineffectiveness of the new state. If similar delays had arisen in Northern Ireland, he may not have caused such fuss.

From Hart's letter books it is evident that the Irish Revolution affected him in more ways than one. The letters offer insights into the life of a unionist who found himself living on what he saw as the wrong side of a new border. One

[83] Hart to Ernie, 30 Mar. 1928 (PRONI, D3077/J/51).
[84] Hart to 'Postmaster', 30 Mar. 1927 (PRONI, D3077/J/50).
[85] Hart to Kelly, 25 Apr. 1927 (PRONI, D3077/J/50).
[86] Hart to Kelly, 25 Apr. 1927 (PRONI, D3077/J/50).

may have expected to find Hart more involved with political issues following his move to Ballynagard, but from 1926 onwards he cut his ties with politics entirely. Hart's lack of political involvement after 1925 therefore suggests that he had simply accepted his fate and was ready to move on. Although Hart was never directly affected by the violence of the Revolution, he experienced its effects in other ways. The raids in Muff and the issues raised by the customs border all made Hart aware of the change that was occurring in Ireland at that time. It must not be forgotten, however, that Hart was in an advantageous position, in that he owned property elsewhere. The annoyance of moving which he mentions was nothing compared with the hindrance faced by others crossing the border. Although the home in Ballynagard was not as grand, it was still his – nor was it very far away. Hart also remained connected to Donegal, despite often sounding as though he wanted to rid himself entirely of the Free State. The family continued to attend Muff Church of Ireland, for instance. Most of Hart's land was sold via the Land Commission; however, he owned the Kilderry house and estate until 1944, selling it when the Second World War interfered with his timber business (selling scotch fir to Harland and Wolff was deemed a breach of Ireland's neutrality). Evidently a stubborn man, Hart was outraged at this and thus sold the property for less than it was worth, not wishing to sell locally or consider any other alternative.[87]

Conclusion

This research highlights the Irish Revolution from the perspective of a unionist landowner and is not representative of the entire East Donegal loyalist community. Further research is required into this community as a whole, though few have left as significant a set of sources as Hart has. Historian Peter Hart, in *The I.R.A. at War*, argued that unionists in Cavan, Donegal, and Monaghan experienced the revolution differently from other southern loyalists because they were closer to the border. For example, in Connaught, Leinster, and Munster no loyalist party or private army was formed and unionists from these areas did not join organisations such as the Ulster Volunteer Force or the Ulster Special Constabulary. In Cavan, Donegal, and Monaghan, however, thousands joined such organisations.[88] Peter Leary states that Cavan, Donegal, and Monaghan all had strong Protestant populations and this resulted in a cross-border population shift, with Protestants moving from the Irish Free State to Northern Ireland and Catholics from Northern Ireland to the south.

[87] PRONI, 'Introduction: Hart papers': www.nidirect.gov.uk/sites/default/files/publications/hart-d3077.pdf (accessed 2 Feb. 2017).

[88] Peter Hart, *The I.R.A. at War 1916–1923* (Oxford, 2003), pp. 224–8.

This, however, O'Leary argues, was not as common as might be assumed and certainly not a 'dramatic, wholesale "unmixing of peoples" triggered by partitions on the Continent and beyond'.[89] Unlike Colonel Hart, not everyone who was involved in making submissions to the Boundary Commission regarding the transfer of land decided to move when their hopes were not fulfilled. Rather, after partition, many in border counties grew accustomed to crossing the border when necessary.

Hart's experience illustrates the interactions between the political and the quotidian. While Hart moved for ostensibly political reasons, this was combined with other more practical issues, such as the postal service, which was both a source of everyday irritation and one way in which Hart could perceive that the new Free State government was fragile and inept. Hart's letters give the depiction of a serious and shrewd unionist whose decision-making could also often be influenced by pride. Above all else, Hart's correspondence highlights that experiences of the Irish Revolution were not homogeneous and could be deeply personal.

---

[89] Leary, *Unapproved Routes*, p. 12.

Afterword: Layers of Loyalty

Brian Hughes and Conor Morrissey

In the preceding chapters, we have heard a wide variety of southern loyalist voices, from the worlds of politics, business, farming, policing, charities, the churches, the military, the gentry, the civil service, and more. However, a single book will never do justice to the full range and complexity of Irish loyalism. This brief afterword highlights some of the issues raised in this volume concerning the nature of loyalism across the island. In particular, we will assess two of the traditional categories of analysis for Irish loyalism: first, the geographic north–south division, and, secondly, the Protestant–Catholic division. Following this, we reflect on some themes and topics which require further research and suggest that the study of Irish loyalism would benefit from adopting transnational or comparative approaches.

The case has been clearly made in this volume for separate study of 'southern' loyalists. Contributors have highlighted many of the ways in which southern experiences differed from those of their (six-county) Ulster brethren between 1912 and 1949. The differences are stark. In his 1978 *Queen's Rebels*, David W. Miller developed the concept of 'conditional loyalty' to explain Ulster loyalists' relationship with the British state.[1] Miller's argument has been critiqued by several authorities, who point out, inter alia, that almost all forms of loyalty are conditional.[2] However, we simply do not see a similar conditionality to southern loyalty. Indeed, for figures such as H.L. Tivy, discussed by Alan McCarthy in Chapter 9, or Lord Mayo, discussed by Seamus Cullen in Chapter 11, conditional loyalty would have been laughable. Southerners lacked the proletarian class, highly developed Orangeism, or

---

[1] David W. Miller, *Queen's Rebels: Ulster Loyalism in Historical Perspective* (Dublin and New York, 1978).

[2] See Feargal Cochrane, *Unionist Politics and the Politics of Unionism since the Anglo-Irish Agreement* (Cork, 1997), pp. 71ff.; Patrick Mitchel, *Evangelicalism and National Identity in Ulster, 1921–1998* (Oxford, 2003), pp. 37–9. But cf. John Whyte, *Interpreting Northern Ireland* (Oxford, 1990), pp. 128–9.

distinct Presbyterian tradition that allowed northerners, when the Union appeared imperilled, to reimagine themselves as a smaller and more cohesive community. In the years before war broke out in Europe, James Craig could suggest that rule by the Kaiser would be preferable to living under Home Rule.[3] The entirely different structural basis on which southern loyalism rested would allow for no such rhetoric. With no ability to take matters into their own hands, most southern loyalists could do little more than hope for the best. This, in turn, would see many southerners adopt a distinct imperial orientation, away from Ireland, and towards the Empire and Dominions.

Irish loyalism, northern and southern, has always been closely associated with Protestantism and it is therefore no surprise that Protestant loyalists dominate in this book. As a distinct minority (or a minority within a minority), the Catholic loyalist was always 'different', to some extent or other, and therefore likely to occupy a unique – if not totally separate – space. Like Protestants, Catholic unionists and loyalists had mixed experiences during the struggle for independence. The 'occasional Catholic', for instance, was included among the burnings of big houses and mansions between 1920 and 1923.[4] But they led separate lives in many respects. As Frank Barry points out in Chapter 4, the Catholic and Protestant business elites rarely socialised together. The war effort between 1914 and 1918 may have provided opportunities for ecumenical co-operation in a shared cause, but, as Fionnuala Walsh demonstrates in Chapter 6, this was difficult to sustain. War relief work on the home front was dominated by the Protestant churches and Protestant women's organisations.

This prompts our first suggestion for further research: the place of Catholic loyalists in the Irish Free State, including those who did not wear Crown uniform.[5] The lives of the Catholic gentry and other elites in the nineteenth century have been well documented by Ciaran O'Neill, while others have studied individual Catholic loyalists in Victorian Ireland.[6] Little, however, has

---

[3] Geoffrey Lewis, *Carson: The Man Who Divided Ireland* (London, 2005), p. 111.

[4] James S. Donnelly, Jr, 'Big House Burnings in County Cork during the Irish Revolution, 1920–21', *Éire-Ireland* 47/3&4, pp. 141, 179 n. 166.

[5] See the Introduction for discussion and references to existing work on the experiences of Catholic ex-policemen and ex-servicemen.

[6] Ciaran O'Neill, 'Power, Wealth and Catholic Identity in Ireland, 1850–1900', in O. Rafferty (ed.), *Irish Catholic Identities* (Manchester, 2013); Ciaran O'Neill, *Catholics of Consequence: Transnational Education, Social Mobility and the Irish Catholic Elite, 1850–1900* (Oxford, 2014). See also Fergus Campbell, *The Irish Establishment, 1879–1914* (Oxford, 2009); Richard A. Keogh, '"From Education, From Duty, and From Principle": Irish Catholic Loyalty, 1829–1874', *British Catholic History*, 33/3 (2017), pp. 421–50; Richard A. Keogh, '"Nothing is so bad for the Irish as Ireland alone": William Keogh and Catholic Loyalty', *Irish Historical*

been written about the 'afterlives' of Catholic loyalty in the twentieth century. In some cases, sons had moved away from the politics of their fathers. While William Monsell, 1st Baron Emly (d.1894), had been a liberal unionist and firm opponent of Home Rule, his son and heir Gaston was a 'strong Conservative' in his youth but 'in later years he showed much sympathy with the more popular Nationalist movement'.[7] It might be suggested that Catholic unionists and loyalists endured a less turbulent transition to the new order in a state made up of over 90 per cent of their co-religionists and 'subjectively virtually 100 per cent homogeneous'.[8] When he died in 1941, the *Irish Times* described how Valentine Charles Browne, Earl of Kenmare, a Catholic former member of the IUA, had lived 'a quiet, retired life in Killarney for many years, where he was well known in the countryside'. Kenmare had continued a long family tradition of promoting 'not only their tenants, but the whole community' in development, sporting, and cultural pursuits.[9] But at the same time, Catholic loyalists were excluded from the often congenial 'Protestant Free State' described by Ian d'Alton.[10]

Seán William Gannon's chapter in this book complicates any easy assumptions about Catholic loyalists in independent Ireland. For middle-class Catholics like Henry Blackall, Martin Mahoney, or Edward Lumley, a career in the Empire was preferable to life in the new state. Such decisions were rarely made on one factor alone but these Catholic loyalists were just as likely to share a sense of loss at the wrecking of the Union as their Protestant colleagues. Although not all of them were loyalists, the Catholic Irish-born policemen of the disbanded RIC faced similar choices and, in some cases at least, similar feelings.[11] Likewise, as Loughlin Sweeney has recently shown, the foundation of the Irish Free State saw the fracture of the social order for the Irish officer class in the British army, including the 'temporary gentleman' of the Great War. Again, while some suffered threat or violence, and others

---

Studies, 38/150 (2012), pp. 230–48; Matthew Potter, *William Monsell of Tervoe, 1812–1894: Catholic Unionist, Anglo-Irishman* (Dublin, 2009).

[7] Matthew Potter, 'Monsell, William 1st Baron Emly of Tervoe', in James McGuire and James Quinn (eds), *Dictionary of Irish Biography* (Cambridge, 2009): http://dib.cambridge.org/viewReadPage.do?articleId=a5889; *Irish Times*, 26 Nov. 1932.

[8] J.J. Lee, *Ireland, 1912–85: Politics and Society* (Oxford, 1989), p. 77.

[9] *Irish Times*, 22 Nov. 1941.

[10] Ian d'Alton, 'The "Protestant Free State" and the Church of Ireland's Patrician Celebrations, 1932', in Jacqueline Hill and Mary Ann Lyons (eds), *Representing Irish Religious Histories: Historiography, Ideology and Practice* (London, 2016).

[11] Seán William Gannon, 'Very Cruel Cases': The Post-Truce Campaign against the Royal Irish Constabulary in County Limerick, *Old Limerick Journal*, 51 (2016), pp. 15–25.

opted to continue their careers elsewhere in the Empire, many remained rooted where they were.[12]

Those Catholic ex-policemen and ex-servicemen who stayed could occasionally suffer as a result of their past careers. In 1936, a Fianna Fáil member of Ballybay Town Commissioners 'strongly objected to, and protested against' a town clerkship being given to 'a man who served in the R.I.C. during the troubles'.[13] A month later, 'ill-feeling' connected to the appointment of a teacher in County Limerick, which resulted in the burning of the school, was attributed to her father's service as a sergeant in the RIC.[14] As Sir Henry Arthur Wynne, a former chief crown solicitor of Ireland then exiled in England, had put it in 1931: 'it must not be forgotten that Irishmen have very long memories in matters of this kind'.[15] At the same time, we must not forget the less well documented, but not uncommon, examples of successful integration, and quiet, uncontroversial existence. The individuals described in this book lived, for the most part, in disorderly times, and their reactions are frequently difficult to organise into neat categories of analysis.

Such categories can be further challenged by adopting a more transnational approach. The essays in this book are centred largely within the 26 'southern' counties, but southern Irish loyalism travelled across boundaries too. Though less likely to feature in the significant literature on Irish migration, Irish loyalists inevitably formed part of the diaspora, settling in the USA, Canada, the dominions, and the colonies. In his contribution to this volume, Seán William Gannon highlights the scattering of Irish imperial servants, but more remains to be uncovered about the movement of Irish loyalists and unionists, and their ideas.[16] Some of the distinctive varieties of loyalism across the Empire have already been discussed in Allan Blackstock and Frank O'Gorman's collection *Loyalism and the Formation of the British World*. They argue that this loyalism was often conditional, based on the maintenance of Protestant ascendancy, and could be virulently anti-Catholic.[17] The Orange Order in Britain and the 'British World' has also been the subject of significant

---

[12] Loughlin Sweeney, *Irish Military Elites: Nation and Empire, 1870–1925* (Cham, 2019), pp. 237–54.

[13] *Irish Times*, 4 Jun. 1936.

[14] *Irish Times*, 11 Jul. 1936.

[15] Minute, Henry Arthur Wynne, 11 Jun. 1931 (TNA: HO 144/22600).

[16] For an examination of some of these themes in a specifically Ulster unionist context, see Lindsey Flewelling, *Two Irelands beyond the Sea: Ulster Unionism and America, 1880–1920* (Liverpool, 2018).

[17] Allan Blackstock and Frank O'Gorman (eds), *Loyalism and the Formation of the British World, 1775–1914* (Woodbridge, 2014); David Fitzpatrick, 'Review Article: We Are All Transnationalists Now', *Irish Historical Studies*, 41/159 (2017), pp. 125–7.

scholarly study.[18] There are, however, opportunities to look beyond the Ulster and Protestant loyalist identities associated with much of this work. As Niamh Gallagher has recently demonstrated in the context of the Great War, Irish imperial settlers 'were intimately connected to Ireland. They were often staunch Irish nationalists ... but they were also deeply concerned about the British Empire, mixing their allegiances to Ireland and Empire in their support for the imperial war effort'. This loyalty was often devoted to their dominion of settlement, allowing them to see themselves as 'co-owners of the British Empire'. It was, therefore, not always easily broken, even by something like the Easter Rising.[19] Further work on patterns of southern loyalist migration, their networks, correspondence, and engagement with the press would be enlightening.

Other questions may be comparative in nature. How do the experiences of southern Irish loyalists compare with the American loyalists who ended up on the wrong side of the American Revolution, for instance? Maya Jasanoff's study of those who fled across the Empire offers a potentially valuable guide for research that combines the transnational and the comparative in an Irish context.[20] One might also take as a model Tim Wilson's innovative *Frontiers of Violence*, which compared conflict over self-determination in Ulster and Upper Silesia during the post-Great War period.[21] How, for example, did the experiences of the southern Irish gentry compare with the Baltic German nobility in the nineteenth and early twentieth centuries, or with Russian landowners after the Bolshevik Revolution? How did southern Protestants more generally compare with German communities scattered throughout central and eastern Europe? Irish Catholic loyalism suggests comparisons (and contrasts) with group dynamics in Hungary, Austria, and the present-day Czech Republic, among other places. It would be useful to know more about the use of religious language in Irish loyalism in the *longue durée*, or to

---

[18] See, for example, David A. Wilson (ed.), *The Orange Order in Canada* (Dublin, 2007); Eric P. Kauffman, 'The Orange Order in Scotland since 1860: A Social Analysis', in Martin J. Mitchell (ed.), *New Perspectives on the Irish in Scotland* (Edinburgh, 2008); Kyle Hughes and Donald MacRaild, 'Anti-Catholicism and Orange Loyalism in Nineteenth-Century Britain', in O'Gorman and Blackstock, *Loyalism and the Formation of the British World*; Diane Hall, 'Defending the Faith: Orangeism and Ulster Protestant Identities in Colonial New South Wales', *Journal of Religious History*, 38/2 (2014), pp. 207–23; D.A.J. MacPherson, *Women and the Orange Order: Female Activism, Diaspora and Empire in the British World, 1850–1940* (Manchester, 2016).

[19] Niamh Gallagher, *Ireland and the Great War* (London, 2019), chap. 5.

[20] Maya Jasanoff, *Liberty's Exiles: American Loyalists in the Revolutionary World* (New York, 2011).

[21] T.K. Wilson, *Frontiers of Violence: Conflict and Identity in Ulster and Upper Silesia, 1918–1922* (Oxford, 2010).

compare the language used by Catholic loyalists at the end of the eighteenth century and their descendants in the late nineteenth and early twentieth centuries.

These, however, are all questions for another book. Our hope is that this volume will encourage further discussion and spark further research into the complex questions of allegiance and identity in the history of this island.

Index